KU-522-008

EIGHTEENTH CENTURY
ESSAYS ON SHAKESPEARE

EIGHTEENTH CENTURY ESSAYS ON SHAKESPEARE

EDITED BY

D. NICHOL SMITH

822.33/SMI

SECOND EDITION

OXFORD
AT THE CLARENDON PRESS
1963

Oxford University Press, Amen House, London E.C.4

GLASGOW NEW YORK TORONTO MELBOURNE WELLINGTON
BOMBAY CALCUTTA MADRAS KARACHI LAHORE DACCA
CAPE TOWN SALISBURY NAIROBI IBADAN ACCRA
KUALA LUMPUR HONG KONG

© *Oxford University Press 1963*

HERTFORDSHIRE
COUNTY LIBRARY
822/SHA
2348439

FIRST EDITION (PUBLISHED BY JAMES MACLEHOSE
AND SONS, GLASGOW) 1903
SECOND (REVISED) EDITION 1963

B63 15681

PRINTED IN GREAT BRITAIN
AT THE UNIVERSITY PRESS, OXFORD
BY VIVIAN RIDLER
PRINTER TO THE UNIVERSITY

PREFACE TO THE FIRST EDITION

THE purpose of this book is to give an account of Shakespeare's reputation during the eighteenth century, and to suggest that there are grounds for reconsidering the common opinion that the century did not give him his due. The nine Essays or Prefaces here reprinted may claim to represent the chief phases of Shakespearian study from the days of Dryden to those of Coleridge. It is one of the evils following in the train of the romantic revival that the judgements of the older school have been discredited or forgotten. The present volume shows that the eighteenth century knew many things which the nineteenth has rediscovered for itself.

It is at least eighty years since most of these essays were reprinted. Rowe's *Account of Shakespeare* is given in its original and complete form for the first time, it is believed, since 1714; what was printed in the early Variorum editions, and previously in almost every edition since 1725, was Pope's version of Rowe's *Account*. Dennis's Essay has not appeared since the author republished it in 1721. In all cases the texts have been collated with the originals; and the more important changes in the editions published in the lifetime of the author are indicated in the Introduction or Notes.

The Introduction has been planned to show the main lines in the development of Shakespeare's reputation, and to prove that the new criticism, which is said to begin with Coleridge, takes its rise as early as the third quarter of the eighteenth century. On the question of Theobald's qualifications as an editor, it would appear that we must subscribe to the deliberate verdict of Johnson. We require strong evidence before we may disregard contemporary opinion, and in Theobald's case there is abundant evidence to confirm Johnson's view. Johnson's own edition, on the other hand, has not received justice during the last century.

It is a pleasure to the Editor to record his obligations to Professor Raleigh, Mr. Gregory Smith, and Mr. J. H. Lobban.

Edinburgh, October 1903

NOTE ON THE SECOND EDITION

AT the time of his death in January 1962 Professor David Nichol Smith was preparing for the press a new edition of the work which he had published nearly sixty years ago. He had completed the revision of the text and had done much to the notes: in particular, he had completely rewritten the commentary on Johnson. What notes have been added by other hands had for the most part been shown to him and had met with his approval: our task has been little more than that of seeing them through the press. In the Introduction he had altered little, and it is printed as he left it. If here and there it seems now to be out of date—as when he observed that 'the majority of those who chance to speak of Johnson's Preface pronounce it a discreditable performance'—the reason is the change in critical opinion which may be ascribed in great part to this book and to the *Six Essays on Johnson*, 1910, of his friend and colleague Sir Walter Raleigh.

HERBERT DAVIS
F. P. WILSON

Oxford, February 1962

CONTENTS

INTRODUCTION

Shakespearian Criticism in the Eighteenth Century

THE early nineteenth century was too readily convinced by Coleridge and Hazlitt that they were the first to recognize and to explain the greatness of Shakespeare. If amends have recently been made to the literary ideals of Pope and Johnson, the reaction has not yet extended to Shakespearian criticism. Are we not still inclined to hold the verdicts of Hume and Chesterfield as representative of eighteenth-century opinion, and to find proof of a lack of appreciation in the editorial travesties of the playhouse? To this century, as much as to the nineteenth, Shakespeare was the glory of English letters. So Pope and Johnson had stated in unequivocal language, which should not have been forgotten. 'He is not so much an imitator as an instrument of Nature', said Pope, 'and 'tis not so just to say that he speaks from her as that she speaks through him'; and Johnson declared that 'the stream of time, which is continually washing the dissoluble fabrics of other poets, passes without injury by the adamant of Shakespeare'. But Pope and Johnson had ventured to point out, in the honesty of their criticism, that Shakespeare was not free from faults; and it was this which the nineteenth century chose to remark. Johnson's Preface in particular was remembered only to be despised. It is not rash to say that at the present time the majority of those who chance to speak of it pronounce it a discreditable performance.

This false attitude to the eighteenth century had its nemesis in the belief that we were awakened by foreigners to the greatness of Shakespeare. Even one so eminently sane as Hazlitt lent support to this opinion. 'We will confess', says the Preface to the *Characters of Shakespeare's Plays*, 'that some little jealousy of the character of the national understanding was not without its share in producing the following undertaking, for we were piqued that it should be reserved for a foreign critic to give reasons for the faith which we English have in Shakespeare'; and the whole Preface resolves itself, however reluctantly, into praise of Schlegel and censure of Johnson. When a thorough Englishman writes thus, it is not surprising that Germany should have claimed to be the first to give Shakespeare his true place. The heresy has been exposed; but even the slightest investigation of eighteenth-century opinion, or the mere recollection of what Dryden had said, should have prevented its rise. Though Hazlitt took upon himself the defence of the national intelligence, he incorporated in his Preface a long passage from Schlegel, because, in his opinion, no English critic had shown like enthusiasm or philosophical acuteness. We cannot regret the delusion if we owe to it the *Characters of Shakespeare's Plays*, but his patriotic task would have been easier, and might even have appeared unnecessary, had he known that many of Schlegel's acute and enthusiastic observations had been anticipated at home.

Even those who are willing to give the eighteenth century its due have not recognized how it appreciated Shakespeare. At no time in this century was he not popular. The author of *Esmond* tells us that Shakespeare was quite out of fashion until Steele brought him back into the mode.[1] Theatrical records would alone be sufficient to show that the ascription of this honour to Steele is an injustice to his contemporaries. In the year that the *Tatler* was begun, Rowe brought out his edition of the 'best of our poets'; and a reissue was called for five years later. It is said by Johnson[2] that Pope's edition drew the public attention to Shakespeare's works, which, though often mentioned, had been little read. Henceforward there was certainly an increase in the number of critical investigations, but if Shakespeare had been little read, how are we to explain the coffee-house discussions of which we seem to catch echoes in the periodical literature? The

---

[1] *Esmond*, ii. 10. Thackeray was probably recalling a passage in the eighth *Tatler*.   [2] In the *Life of Pope*.

allusions in the *Spectator*, or the essays in the *Censor*, must have
been addressed to a public which knew him. Dennis, who 'read
him over and over and still remained unsatiated', tells how he
was accused, by blind admirers of the poet, of lack of veneration,
because he had ventured to criticize, and how he had appealed
from a private discussion to the judgement of the public. 'Above
all I am pleased', says the *Guardian*, 'in observing that the
Tragedies of Shakespeare, which in my youthful days have so
frequently filled my eyes with tears, hold their rank still, and
are the great support of our theatre.'¹ Theobald could say that
'this author is grown so universal a book that there are very few
studies or collections of books, though small, amongst which it
does not hold a place'; and he could add that 'there is scarce a
poet that our English tongue boasts of who is more the subject of
the Ladies' reading'.² It would be difficult to explain away these
statements. The critical interest in Shakespeare occasioned by
Pope's edition may have increased the knowledge of him, but
he had been regularly cited, long before Pope's day, as England's
representative genius. To argue that he had ever been out of
favour we must rely on later statements, and they are presum-
ably less trustworthy than those which are contemporary.
Lyttelton remarked that a veneration for Shakespeare seems to
be a part of the national religion, and the only part in which
even men of sense are fanatics;³ and Gibbon spoke of the 'idolatry
for the gigantic genius of Shakespeare, which is inculcated from
our infancy as the first duty of an Englishman'.⁴ The present
volume will show how the eighteenth century could almost lose
itself in panegyric of Shakespeare. The evidence is so overwhelm-
ing that it is hard to understand how the century's respect for
Shakespeare was ever doubted. When Tom Jones took Partridge
to the gallery of Drury Lane, the play was *Hamlet*. The fashionable topics on which Mr. Thornhill's friends from town would

---

¹ *Guardian*, No. 37 (23 April 1713). The paper was written by John Hughes
(1677–1720), who had assisted Rowe in his edition of Shakespeare (see Reed's
Variorum edition, 1803, ii, p. 149).   ² Introduction to *Shakespeare Restored*.
³ *Dialogues of the Dead*, xiv, Boileau and Pope.
⁴ *Memoirs*, ed. Birkbeck Hill, 1900, p. 105.

talk, to the embarrassment of the Primroses and the Flam-
boroughs, were 'pictures, taste, Shakespeare, and the musical
glasses'. The greatest poet of the century played a leading
part in erecting the statue in the Poets' Corner. And it was an
eighteenth-century actor who instituted the Stratford cele-
brations.

During the entire century Shakespeare dominated the stage.
He was more to the actor then, and more familiar to the theatre-
goer, than he is now. It is true that from Betterton's days to
Garrick's, and later, his plays were commonly acted from
mangled versions. But these versions were of two distinct types.
The one respected the rules of the classical drama, the other indulged the licence of pantomime. The one was the labour of the
pedant theorist, the other was rather the improvization of the
theatre manager. And if the former were truly representative of
the taste of the century, as has sometimes been implied, it has to
be explained how they were not so popular as the latter. 'Our
taste has gone back a whole century', says the strolling player
in the *Vicar of Wakefield*,[1] 'Fletcher, Ben Jonson, and all the plays
of Shakespeare are the only things that go down.' The whole
passage is a satire on Garrick[2] and a gibe at Drury Lane: 'The
public go only to be amused, and find themselves happy when
they can enjoy a pantomime under the sanction of Jonson's or
Shakespeare's name.' But, whatever was done with Shakespeare's
plays, they were the very life of the theatre. When we remember
also the number of editions which were published, and the con-
troversies to which they gave rise, as well as the fact that the
two literary dictators were among his editors, we are prompted
to ask, What century has felt the influence of Shakespeare more
than the eighteenth?

The century's interest in Shakespeare shows itself in four main
phases. The first deals with his neglect of the so-called rules of

---

[1] Chap. xviii. That the passage is animated by pique and that amusing jealousy
which Goldsmith showed on unexpected occasions is evident from the *Present
State of Polite Learning*, ch. xi.

[2] Cf. Theophilus Cibber's attack on Garrick's adaptations in his *Two Dis-
sertations on the Theatres*, 1756.

the drama; the second determines what was the extent of his
learning; the third considers the treatment of his text; and the
fourth, more purely aesthetic, shows his value as a delineator of
character. The following remarks take these questions in order;
and a concluding section gives an account of the individual
essays here reprinted. Though the phases are closely connected
and overlap to some extent, the order in which they are here
treated accords in the main with their chronological sequence.

I

Dryden is the father of Shakespearian criticism. Though he
disguised his veneration at times, he expressed his true faith
when he wrote, deliberately, the fervent estimate in the *Essay of
Dramatic Poesy*. Johnson saw that Pope had expanded it, and his
own experience made him say that the editors and admirers of
Shakespeare, in all their emulation of reverence, had not done
much more than diffuse and paraphrase this 'epitome of excellence'. But concurrently on to Johnson's time we can trace the
influence of Thomas Rymer, who, in his *Short View of Tragedy*,
had championed the classical drama, and had gone as far in abuse
as his greater contemporary had gone in praise. The authority
which each exerted is well illustrated by Rowe's *Account of
Shakespeare*. Rowe is of the party of Dryden, but he cannot re-
frain from replying to Rymer, though he has resolved to enter
into no critical controversy. He says he will not inquire into the
justness of Rymer's remarks, and yet he replies to him in two
passages. That these were silently omitted by Pope when he
included the *Account of Shakespeare* in his own edition in 1725
does not mean that Rymer was already being forgotten. We
know from other sources that Pope rated his abilities very
highly. But the condensed form in which the *Account* was
regularly reprinted does not convey so plainly as the original the
influence of the rival schools at the beginning of the eighteenth
century. In addition to the passages on Rymer, Pope omitted
several valuable allusions to Dryden. The influence of Dryden,
however, is plain enough. He seems to have been ever present to

Rowe, suggesting ideas to be accepted or refuted. Rowe must have been indebted to the conversation of Dryden as well as to the researches of Betterton.

Rowe's own dramatic work is an interesting comment on the critical portions of his *Account of Shakespeare*. When he professes to have taken Shakespeare as his model,[1] his discipleship is best seen in his versification, which shows that his editorial work had taught him the trick of an occasional line contrary to the normal rules of blank verse. Notwithstanding a brave prologue, he was not able to shake himself free from the rules, which tightened their grip on English tragedy till they choked it. His regard for Shakespeare did not give him courage for the addition of a comic element or an underplot. He must obey the 'hampering critics', though his avowed model had ignored them. Accordingly, in his more deliberate prose criticism we find, amid his veneration of Shakespeare, his regard for the rules of the classical drama. The faults of Shakespeare, we read, were not so much his own as those of his time, for 'tragi-comedy was the common mistake of that age', and there was as yet no definite knowledge of how a play should be constructed.

The burden of Rowe's criticism is that 'strength and nature made amends for art'. The line might serve as the text of many of the early appreciations of Shakespeare. Though the critics all resented Rymer's treatment of the poet, some of them stood by his doctrines. They might appease this resentment by protesting against his manners or refuting his plea for a dramatic chorus; but on the whole they recognized the claims of the classical models. The more the dramatic fervour failed, the more the professed critics counselled observance of the rules. In 1702 Farquhar

[1] See the Prologue to *Jane Shore*:

> In such an age, immortal Shakespeare wrote,
> By no quaint rules, nor hampering critics taught;
> With rough majestic force he mov'd the heart,
> And strength and nature made amends for art.
> Our humble author does his steps pursue,
> He owns he had the mighty bard in view;
> And in these scenes has made it more his care
> To rouse the passions than to charm the ear.

had pleaded for the freedom of the English stage in his *Discourse upon Comedy*, but his arguments were unavailing. The duller men found it easier to support the rigid doctrines, which had been fully expounded by the French critics. The seventh or supplementary volume of Rowe's edition of Shakespeare was introduced by Charles Gildon's *Essay on the Art, Rise, and Progress of the Stage in Greece, Rome, and England*, which, as the title shows, was a laboured exposition of the classical doctrines. Gildon had begun as an enemy of Rymer. In 1694 he had published *Some Reflections on Mr. Rymer's Short View of Tragedy and an Attempt at a Vindication of Shakespeare*. Therein he had spoken of 'noble irregularity', and censured the 'graver pedants' of the age. By 1710 he is a grave pedant himself. In 1694 he had said that Rymer had scarce produced one criticism that was not borrowed from the French writers; in 1710 the remark is now applicable to its author. Gildon's further descent as a critic is evident eight years later in his *Complete Art of Poetry*. He is now a slave to the French doctrine of the rules. He confesses himself the less ready to pardon the 'monstrous absurdities' of Shakespeare, as one or two plays, such as the *Tempest*, are 'very near a regularity'. Yet he acknowledges that Shakespeare abounds in beauties, and he makes some reparation by including a long list of his finer passages. Gildon was a man whose ideas took their colour from his surroundings. In the days of his acquaintanceship with Dryden he appreciated Shakespeare more heartily than when he was left to the friendship of Dennis or the favours of the Duke of Buckinghamshire. His *Art of Poetry* is a dishonest compilation, which owes what value it has to the sprinkling of contemporary allusions. It even incorporates, without any acknowledgement, long passages from Sidney's *Apologie*. We should be tempted to believe that Gildon merely put his name to a hack-work collection, were it not that there is a gradual deterioration in his criticism.

John Dennis also replied to Rymer's *Short View*, and was classed afterwards as one of Rymer's disciples. In his *Impartial Critick* (1693) he endeavoured to show that the methods of the ancient Greek tragedy were not all suitable to the modern English theatre. To introduce a chorus, as Rymer had recommended, or to expel love from the stage, would, he argued, only ruin the English drama. But his belief in the classical rules made him turn the *Merry Wives* into the *Comical Gallant*. As he found in the original three actions, each independent of the other, he had set himself to make the whole 'depend on one common centre'. In the Dedication to the letters *On the Genius and Writings of Shakespeare* we read that Aristotle, 'who may be call'd the Legislator of Parnassus, wrote the laws of tragedy so exactly and so truly in reason and nature that succeeding criticks have writ justly and reasonably upon that art no farther than they have adhered to their great master's notions'. But at the very beginning of the letters themselves he says that 'Shakespeare was one of the greatest geniuses that the world e'er saw'. Notwithstanding his pronounced classical taste, his sense of the greatness of Shakespeare is as strong as Rowe's, and much stronger than Gildon's. His writings prove him a man of competent scholarship, who had thought out his literary doctrines for himself, and could admire beauty in other than classical garb. The result is that at many points his opinions are at marked variance with those of Rymer, for whom, however, he had much respect. Rymer, for instance, had said that Shakespeare's genius lay in comedy, but the main contention of Dennis's letters is that he had an unequalled gift for tragedy. As a critic Dennis is greatly superior to Rymer and his disciples. The ancients guided his taste without blinding him to modern excellence.

Even Lewis Theobald, whom some would consider Shakespeare's greatest friend in this century, believed in the rules. He complied with the taste of the town when he wrote pantomimes, but he was a sterner man when he posed as a critic. He would then speak of the 'general absurdities of Shakespeare', and the 'errors' in the structure of his plays. He passed this criticism both in his edition of Shakespeare and in the early articles in the *Censor* on *King Lear*, which are also of considerable historical interest as being the first essays devoted exclusively to an examination of a single Shakespearian play. His complacent belief in the rules prompted him to correct *Richard II*. 'The many scattered beauties which I have long admired', he says naïvely in the Preface, 'induced me to think they would have stronger charms if they were interwoven in a regular Fable.' No less confident is a note on *Love's Labour's Lost*: 'Besides the exact regularity of the rules of art, which the author has happened to preserve in some few of his pieces, this is demonstration, I think, that though he has more frequently transgressed the unity of Time by cramming years into the compass of a play, yet he knew the absurdity of so doing, and was not unacquainted with the rule to the contrary.'[1] Theobald was a critic of the same type as Gildon. Each had profound respect for what he took to be the accredited doctrines. If on certain points Theobald's ideas were liable to change, the explanation is that he was amenable to the opinions of others. We do not find in Theobald's criticism the courage of originality.

There is little about the rules in Pope's Preface. That Pope respected them cannot be doubted, else he would not have spoken so well of Rymer, and in the critical notes added to his Homer we should not hear so much of Le Bossu's treatise on the Epic.[2] But Pope was a discreet man, who knew when to be silent. He regarded it as a misfortune that Shakespeare was not so circumstanced as to be able to write on the model of the ancients, but, unlike the pedant theorists, he refused to judge Shakespeare by the rules of a foreign drama. Much the same is to be said of

[1] The note has reference to Biron's remark, towards the end of the last scene, that a 'twelvemonth and a day' is 'too long for a play' (ed. 1733, ii, p. 181). In Lounsbury's *Shakespeare as a Dramatic Artist*, 1901—which I regret I did not see before the present Introduction was in type—it is urged as 'demonstration' of Theobald's *sagacity* that he had the insight to see that Shakespeare's disregard of the unities was owing not to ignorance but to intention. Theobald's note, however, has a suspicious similarity to what Gildon had said in his *Art of Poetry*, 1718, i, p. 99. It is, says Gildon, 'plain from his [Shakespeare's] own words he saw the *absurdities* of his own conduct. And I must confess that when I find that . . . he himself has written one or two plays very near a *regularity*, I am the less apt to pardon his errors that seem of choice, as agreeable to his lazyness and easie gain.'
[2] Cf. the *Dunciad*, i. 69–72, where the inducements of satire make him adopt a decided attitude in favour of the dramatic rules.

Addison. His belief in the rules appears in his *Cato*. His overrated
criticism of *Paradise Lost* is little more than a laboured application
of the system of Le Bossu. But in the *Spectator* he too urges that
Shakespeare is not to be judged according to the rules. 'Our
critics do not seem sensible', he writes, 'that there is more beauty
in the works of a great genius who is ignorant of the rules of art
than in those of a little genius who knows and observes them.
Our inimitable Shakespeare is a stumbling-block to the whole
tribe of these rigid critics. Who would not rather read one of his
plays where there is not a single rule of the stage observed, than
any production of a modern critic where there is not one of them
violated?'[1] The rigid critics continued to find fault with the
structure of Shakespeare's plays. In the articles in the *Adventurer*
on the *Tempest* and *King Lear*, Joseph Warton repeats the
standard objection to tragi-comedy and underplots. In the
Biographia Britannica we still find it stated that Shakespeare set
himself to please the populace, and that the people 'had no
notion of the rules of writing, or the model of the Ancients'. But
one whose tastes were classical, both by nature and by training,
had been thinking out the matter for himself. It was only after
long reflection, and with much hesitation, that Johnson had
disavowed what had almost come to be considered the very
substance of the classical faith. In his *Irene* he had bowed to the
rules; he had, however, begun to suspect them by the time he
wrote the *Rambler*, and in the Preface to his edition of Shakespeare
suspicion has become conviction. His sturdy common sense and
independence of judgement led him to anticipate much of what
has been supposed to be the discovery of the romantic school.
His Preface has received scant justice. There is no more convincing criticism of the neo-classical doctrines.[2]

[1] No. 592. The quotation will prove the injustice of De Quincey's attitude to
Addison in his Essay on Shakespeare. De Quincey even makes the strange
statement that 'by express examination, we ascertained the curious fact that
Addison has never in one instance quoted or made any reference to Shakespeare'
(*Works*, ed. Masson, iv, p. 24).

[2] It must be noted that some of Johnson's arguments had themselves been
anticipated in *Some Remarks on the Tragedy of Hamlet*, 1736. The volume is anonymous, but has been ascribed to Sir Thomas Hanmer (see below, p. lii). It

Henceforward we hear less about the rules. Johnson had performed a great service for that class of critics whose deference to
learned opinion kept them from saying fully what they felt. The
lesser men had not been at their ease when they referred to Shakespeare. We see their difficulty in the Latin lectures of Joseph
Trapp, the first Professor of Poetry at Oxford, as well as in the
Grub Street *Essay upon English Tragedy* (1747) by William Guthrie.
They admire his genius, but they persist in regretting that his
plays are not properly constructed. Little importance attaches to
Mrs. Montagu's *Essay on the Writings and Genius of Shakespeare*
(1769).[1] It was only a well-meaning but shallow reply to
Voltaire,[2] and a reply was unnecessary. Johnson had already
vindicated the national pride in Shakespeare. That his views
soon became the commonplaces of those critics who strike the
average of current opinion, is shown by such a work as William
Cooke's *Elements of Dramatic Criticism* (1775). But traces of the
school of Rymer are still to be found, and nowhere more strongly
than in the anonymous *Cursory Remarks on Tragedy* (1774). In this
little volume of essays the dramatic rules are defended against
the criticism of Johnson by a lame repetition of the arguments
which Johnson had overthrown. Even Pope is said to have let his
partiality get the better of his usual justice and candour when he
claimed that Shakespeare was not to be judged by what were
called the rules of Aristotle. There are laws, this belated critic
urges, which bind each individual as a citizen of the world; and
once again we read that the rules of the classical drama are in

examines the play 'according to the rules of reason and nature, without having
any regard to those rules established by arbitrary dogmatising critics,' and shows
'the absurdity of such arbitrary rules' as the unities of time and place. It is a well-
written, interesting book, and is greatly superior to the *Miscellaneous Observations
on the Tragedy of Hamlet*, which appeared, likewise anonymously, in 1752.

For references to other works previous to Johnson's Preface which dispute the
authority of the classical rules, see note on p. 117.

[1] Johnson's opinion of Mrs. Montagu's *Essay* has been recorded by Boswell (ed.
Birkbeck Hill, ii, p. 88). But the book was well received. It went into a fourth
edition in 1777, in which year it was translated into French. It is praised by such
writers as Beattie and James Harris. Cf. Morgann, p. 252.

[2] See Jusserand's *Shakespeare en France*, 1898, and Lounsbury's *Shakespeare and
Voltaire*, 1902.

accordance with human reason. This book is the last direct descendant of Rymer's *Short View*. The ancestral trait appears in the question whether Shakespeare was in general even a good tragic writer. But it is a degenerate descendant. If it has learned good manners, it is unoriginal and dull; and it is so negligible that it has apparently not been thought worth while to settle the question of its authorship.[1]

II

The discussion on Shakespeare's attitude to the dramatic rules was closely connected with the long controversy on the extent of his learning. The question naturally suggested itself how far his dramatic method was due to his ignorance of the classics. Did he know the rules and ignore them, or did he write with no knowledge of the Greek and Roman models? Whichever view the critics adopted, one and all felt they were arguing for the honour of Shakespeare. If some would prove for his greater glory that parallel passages were due to direct borrowing, others held it was more to his credit to have known nothing of the classics and to have equalled or surpassed them by the mere force of unassisted genius.

The controversy proper begins with Rowe's *Account of Shakespeare*. On this subject, as on others, Rowe expresses the tradition of the seventeenth century. His view is the same as Dryden's, and Dryden had accepted Jonson's statement that Shakespeare had 'small Latin and less Greek'. Rowe believes that his acquaintance with Latin authors was such as he might have gained at

[1] This book is ascribed in Charles Knight's untrustworthy *Studies of Shakespere*, book xi, to William Richardson (1743–1814), Professor of Humanity in the University of Glasgow. Unfortunately the British Museum Catalogue lends some support to this injustice by giving it either to him or to Edward Taylor of Noan, Tipperary. The error is emphasized in the *Dictionary of National Biography*. Though Richardson upholds some of the more rigid classical doctrines, his work is of a much higher order. The book is attributed to Richardson in Watt's *Bibliotheca Britannica*, 1824, but it had been assigned to Taylor in Isaac Reed's 'List of Detached Pieces of Criticism on Shakespeare', 1803. From the evidence of the *Gentleman's Magazine* for 1797 (vol. 67, part ii, p. 1076) it would appear that the author was Edward Taylor (1741–97) of Steeple Aston, Oxfordshire.

school: he could remember tags of Horace or Mantuan, but was unable to read Plautus in the original. The plea that comparative ignorance of the classics may not have been a disadvantage, as it perhaps prevented the sacrifice of fancy to correctness, prompted a reply by Gildon in his *Essay on the Stage*, where the argument is based partly on the belief that Shakespeare had read Ovid and Plautus and had thereby neither spoiled his fancy nor confined his genius. The question was probably at this time a common topic of discussion. Dennis's abler remarks were suggested, as he tells us, by conversation in which he found himself opposed to the prevalent opinion. He is more pronounced in his views than Rowe had been. His main argument is that as Shakespeare is deficient in the 'poetical art' he could not but have been ignorant of the classics, for, had he known them, he could not have failed to profit by them. Dennis is stirred even to treat the question as one affecting the national honour. 'He who allows', he says, 'that Shakespeare had learning and a familiar acquaintance with the Ancients, ought to be looked upon as a detractor from his extraordinary merit and from the glory of Great Britain' (see p. 39 below).

The prominence of the controversy forced Pope to refer to it in his Preface, but he had apparently little interest in it. Every statement he makes is carefully guarded: there are translations from Ovid, he says, among the poems which *pass for* Shakespeare's; he will not pretend to say in what language Shakespeare read the Greek authors; Shakespeare *appears* to have been conversant in Plautus. He is glad of the opportunity to reply to Dennis's criticism of *Coriolanus* and *Julius Caesar*, but though he praises the truthful representation of the Roman spirit and manners, he discreetly refuses to say how Shakespeare came to know of them. As he had not thought out the matter for himself, he feared to tread where the lesser men rushed in. But though he records the evidence brought forward by those who believed in Shakespeare's knowledge of the Ancients, he does not fail to convey the impression that he belongs to the other party. And, indeed, in another passage of the Preface he says with definiteness, inconsistent with his other statements, that Shakespeare was 'without assistance or advice from the learned, as without the advantage of education or acquaintance among them, without that knowledge of the best models, the Ancients, to inspire him with an emulation of them'.

During the forty years between Pope's Preface and Johnson's, the controversy continued intermittently without either party gaining ground. In the Preface to the supplementary volume to Pope's edition—which is a reprint of Gildon's supplementary volume to Rowe's—Sewell declared he found evident marks through all Shakespeare's writings of knowledge of the Latin tongue. Theobald, who was bound to go astray when he ventured beyond the collation of texts, was ready to believe that similarity of idea in Shakespeare and the classics was due to direct borrowing. He had, however, the friendly advice of Warburton to make him beware of the secret satisfaction of pointing out a classical original. In its earlier form his very unequal Preface had contained the acute observation that the texture of Shakespeare's phrases indicated better than his vocabulary the extent of his knowledge of Latin. The style was submitted as 'the truest criterion to determine this long agitated question', and the conclusion was implied that Shakespeare could not have been familiar with the classics. But this interesting passage was omitted in the second edition, perhaps because it was inconsistent with a less decided utterance elsewhere in the Preface, but more probably because it had been supplied by Warburton. In his earlier days, before he had met Warburton, he had been emphatic. In the Preface to his version of *Richard II* he had tried to do Shakespeare 'some justice upon the points of his learning and acquaintance with the Ancients'. He had said that *Timon of Athens* and *Troilus and Cressida* left it without dispute or exception that Shakespeare was no inconsiderable master of the Greek story; he dared be positive that the latter play was founded directly upon Homer; he held that Shakespeare must have known Aeschylus, Lucian, and Plutarch in the Greek; and he claimed that he could, 'with the greatest ease imaginable', produce above 500 passages from the three Roman plays to prove Shakespeare's intimacy with the

Latin classics. When he came under the influence of Warburton he lost his assurance. He was then 'very cautious of declaring too positively' on either side of the question; but he was loath to give up his belief that Shakespeare knew the classics at first hand. Warburton himself did not figure creditably in the controversy. He might ridicule the discoveries of other critics, but his vanity often allured him to displays of learning as absurd as theirs. No indecision troubled Upton or Zachary Grey. They saw in Shakespeare a man of profound reading, one who might well have worn out his eyes in poring over classic tomes. They clutched at anything to show his deliberate imitation of the Ancients. There could be no better instance of the ingenious folly of this type of criticism than the passage in the *Notes on Shakespeare*, where Grey argues from Gloucester's words in *Richard III*, 'Go you before and I will follow you', that Shakespeare knew, and was indebted to, Terence's *Andria*. About the same time Peter Whalley, the editor of Ben Jonson, brought out his *Enquiry into the Learning of Shakespeare* (1748), the first formal treatise devoted directly to the subject of controversy. Therein it is claimed that Shakespeare knew Latin well enough to have acquired in it a taste and elegance of judgement, and was more indebted to the Ancients than was commonly imagined. On the whole, however, Whalley's attitude[1] was more reasonable than that of Upton or Grey, for he admitted that his list of parallel passages might not settle the point at issue.

After such a display of misapplied learning it is refreshing to meet with the common sense of one who was a greater scholar than any of these pedants. Johnson has less difficulty in giving his opinion on the extent of Shakespeare's learning than in discovering the reasons of the controversy. The evidence of Shakespeare's contemporary, he says, ought to decide the question unless some testimony of equal force can be opposed, and such testimony he refuses to find in the collections of the Uptons and Greys.

[1] See the review of Whalley in the *Gentleman's Magazine*, 1748, pp. 25–113. See also 'A Brief Enquiry into the Learning of Shakespeare' in *The Universal Visiter* for March 1756, pp. 126–32.

It is especially remarkable that Johnson, who is not considered to have been strong in research, should be the first to state that Shakespeare used North's translation of Plutarch. He is the first also to point out that there was an English translation of the play on which the *Comedy of Errors* was founded, and the first to show that it was not necessary to go back to the *Tale of Gamelyn* for the story of *As you like it*.[1] There is no evidence how he came by this knowledge. The casual and allusive manner in which he advances his information would seem to show that it was not of his own getting. He may have been indebted for it to the scholar who two years later put an end to the controversy. The edition of Shakespeare did not appear till October 1765, and early in that year Johnson had spent his 'joyous evening' at Cambridge with Richard Farmer.[2]

The *Essay on the Learning of Shakespeare* is not an independent treatise like Whalley's *Enquiry*, but rather a detailed reply to the arguments of Upton and his fellows. Farmer had once been idle enough, he tells us himself, to collect parallel passages, but he had been saved by his remarkable bibliographical knowledge. He found out that the literature of the age of Elizabeth was a better hunting ground than the classics for Shakespearian commentators. Again and again he shows that passages which had been urged as convincing proof of knowledge of Latin or Greek are either borrowed from contemporary translations or illustrated by contemporary usage. In so far as the *Essay* aims at showing the futility of the arguments advanced to prove Shakespeare's learning, it is convincing. The only criticism that can reasonably

---

[1] [Some of the statements in this paragraph would have been modified, as shown by D. N. S.'s pencilled note referring to Langbaine's mention of W. W.'s translation of the *Menaechmi* in 1595, and by the account of Farmer's discovery of Lodge's *Rosalynd* (see p. 167 below) as the probable source of Johnson's information, given in *Shakespeare in the Eighteenth Century*, 1928, p. 51: [Johnson] 'does not name it, and I suggest that he withheld the title because he did not wish to defraud another scholar of his discovery. I suspect that he heard of it during his visit to Cambridge shortly before he wrote the Preface.']

[2] It is to be noted that the three points above mentioned are dealt with at considerable length in Farmer's *Essay*.

be passed on it is that Farmer is apt to think he has proved his own case when he has merely destroyed the evidence of his opponents. His conclusion regarding Shakespeare's knowledge of French and Italian may be too extreme to be generally accepted now, and indeed it may not be logically deducible from his examination of the arguments of other critics; but on the whole the book is a remarkably able study. Though Farmer speaks expressly of acquitting 'our great poet of all piratical depredations on the Ancients', his purpose has often been misunderstood, or at least misrepresented. He aimed at giving Shakespeare the greater commendation, but certain critics of the earlier half of the nineteenth century would have it that he had tried to prove, for his own glory, that Shakespeare was a very ignorant fellow. William Maginn in particular proclaimed the *Essay* a 'piece of pedantic impertinence not paralleled in literature'. The early Variorum editions had acknowledged its value by reprinting it in its entirety, besides quoting from it liberally in the notes to the separate plays, and Maginn determined to do his best to rid them in future of this 'superfluous swelling'. So he indulged in a critical Donnybrook; but after hitting out and about at the *Essay* for three months he left it much as he found it.[1] He could not get to close quarters with Farmer's scholarship. His bluster compares ill with Farmer's gentler manner, and in some passages the quiet humour has proved too subtle for his animosity. There was more impartiality in the judgement of Johnson: 'Dr. Farmer, you have done that which was never done before; that is, you have completely finished a controversy beyond all further doubt.'[2]

III

After the publication of Farmer's *Essay* there was a change in the character of the editions of Shakespeare. Farmer is the

[1] *Fraser's Magazine*, Sept., Oct., and Dec. 1839; reprinted in *Miscellanies, Prose and Verse, by William Maginn*, 1885, vol. ii.

[2] Recorded in Northcote's *Memoirs of Sir Joshua Reynolds*, 1813, p. 90. An attempt to reopen the question has recently been made by Mr. Churton Collins in three articles in the *Fortnightly Review* (April, May, and July 1903). Mr.

forerunner of Steevens and Malone. He had a just idea of the importance of his work when he spoke of himself as the pioneer of the commentators. It did not matter whether his main contention were accepted; he had at least shown the wealth of illustration which was awaiting the scholar who cared to search in the literature of Shakespeare's age, and Steevens and Malone were not slow to follow. They had the advantage of being early in the field; but it is doubtful if any later editor has contributed as much as either of them did to the elucidation of Shakespeare's text. They have been oftener borrowed from than has been admitted, and many a learned note of later date may be found in germ in their editions. But with the advance of detailed scholarship the Prefaces deteriorate in literary merit. They concern themselves more and more with textual and bibliographical points, and hence, if they are of greater interest to the student, they are of less value as indications of the century's regard for Shakespeare. The change is already noticeable in Capell's Preface, on the literary shortcomings of which Johnson expressed himself so forcibly. Johnson is the last editor whose Preface is a piece of general criticism. It is an essay which can stand by itself.

By the time of Johnson and Capell the editor of Shakespeare has come to a clear idea of his 'true duty'. Rowe had no suspicion of the textual problems awaiting his successors. A dramatist himself, he wished merely to publish Shakespeare's plays as he would publish his own. Accordingly he modernized the spelling, divided the scenes, and added lists of dramatis personae; and the folio gave place to six octavo volumes. He was content to found his text on the fourth Folio, the last and worst; he had no idea of the superior claims of the first, though he professed to have compared the several editions. He corrected many errors and occasionally hit upon a happy emendation; but on the whole his interest in Shakespeare was that of the dramatist. Pope's interest was that of the poet. There is some truth in the criticism

Churton Collins believes that Shakespeare had a first-hand knowledge of Ovid, Plautus, Seneca, Horace, Lucretius, Cicero, Terence, and Virgil, and that he was more or less familiar with the Greek dramatists through the medium of the Latin language.

that he gave Shakespeare not as he was, but as he ought to be, though Pope might well have retorted that in his opinion the two conditions were identical. Whatever did not conform to his opinion of Shakespeare's style he treated as an interpolation. His collation of the texts, by convincing him of their corruption, only prompted him to a more liberal exercise of his own judgement. In the supplementary volume of Pope's edition, it had been suggested by Sewell that our great writers should be treated in the same way as the classics were, and the idea was put into practice by Theobald, who could say that his method of editing was 'the first assay of the kind on any modern author whatsoever'. By his careful collation of the Quartos and Folios, he pointed the way to the modern editor. But he was followed by Hanmer, who, as his chief interest was to rival Pope, was content with Pope's methods. It is easy to underestimate the value of Hanmer's edition; his happy conjectures have been prejudiced by his neglect of the older copies and his unfortunate attempt to regularize the metre; but what alone concerns us here is that he reverts to the methods which Theobald had discarded. Warburton, confident in his intellectual gifts, was satisfied with Theobald's examination of the early copies, and trusted to his own insight 'to settle the genuine text'. The critical ingenuity of editors and commentators, before the authority of the Folios was established, betrayed them into inevitable error. The amusing variety of conjectural readings was met by the exquisite satire of Fielding,[1] as well as by the heavy censure of Grub Street. 'It is to be wished', says a catchpenny publication, 'that the original text of Shakespeare were left unaltered for every English reader to understand. The numerous fry of commentators will at last explain his original meaning away.'[2] This criticism was out of date by the time of Johnson and Capell. As it has long been the fashion to decry Johnson's edition, it is well to recall two statements in his Preface, which show that

[1] *Journey from this World to the Next*, ch. viii.
[2] *The Life of Alexander Pope, Esq.*, by W. H. Dilworth, 1759, pp. 83–84. Cf. William Ayre's *Memoirs of Pope*, 1745 (on which Dilworth's *Life* is founded), vol. i, p. 273.

he had already discovered what later editors have found out for themselves:

> I collated all the folios at the beginning, but afterwards used only the first.[1]
>
> It has been my settled principle that the reading of the ancient books is probably true. . . . As I practised conjecture more, I learned to trust it less.

Johnson's collation may not have been thorough; but no modern editor can say that he proceeded on a wrong method.

Johnson has included in his Preface an account of the work of earlier editors, and it is the first attempt of the kind which is impartial. He shows that Rowe has been blamed for not performing what he did not undertake; he is severe on Pope for the allusion to the 'dull duty of an editor', as well as for the performance of it, though he also finds much to praise; he does more justice to Sir Thomas Hanmer than has commonly been done since; and he is not silent on the weaknesses of Warburton. The only thing in this unprejudiced account which is liable to criticism is his treatment of Theobald. But the censure is as just as the praise which it is now the fashion to heap on him. Though Theobald was the first to pay due respect to the original editions, we cannot, in estimating his capacity, ignore the evidence of his correspondence with Warburton. In the more detailed account of his work given below, it is shown that there was a large measure of justice in the common verdict of the eighteenth century, but it was only prejudiced critics like Pope or Warburton who would say that his Shakespearian labours were futile. Johnson is careful to state that 'what little he did was commonly right'.

It would appear that Macaulay's estimate of Johnson's own edition has been generally accepted, even by those who in other matters remark on the historian's habit of exaggeration. 'The Preface,' we read, 'though it contains some good passages, is

---

[1] It should be noted that Theobald had said that the *second* Folio 'in the generality is esteemed as the best impression of Shakespeare' (*Shakespeare Restored*, p. 70).

not in his best manner. The most valuable notes are those in which
he had an opportunity of showing how attentively he had, during many years, observed human life and human nature. The
best specimen is the note on the character of Polonius. Nothing
so good is to be found even in Wilhelm Meister's admirable examination of *Hamlet*. But here praise must end. It would be difficult to name a more slovenly, a more worthless edition of any
great classic. The reader may turn over play after play without
finding one happy conjectural emendation, or one ingenious and
satisfactory explanation of a passage which had baffled preceding
commentators.'[1] And we still find it repeated that his edition
was a failure. Johnson distrusted conjecture; but that there is not
one happy conjectural emendation is only less glaringly untrue
than the other assertion that there is not one new ingenious and
satisfactory explanation. Even though we make allowance for
Macaulay's mannerism, it is difficult to believe that he had
honestly consulted the edition. Those who have worked with it
know the force of Johnson's claim that not a single passage in the
whole work had appeared to him corrupt which he had not
attempted to restore, or obscure which he had not endeavoured
to illustrate. We may neglect the earlier eighteenth-century
editions of Shakespeare, but if we neglect Johnson's we run a
serious risk. We may now abandon his text; we must rely on later
scholarship for the explanation of many allusions; but, wherever
a difficulty can be solved by common sense, we shall never find
his notes antiquated. Other editions are distinguished by
accuracy, ingenuity, or learning; the supreme distinction of his is
sagacity. He cleared a way through a mass of misleading conjectures. In disputed passages he has an almost unerring instinct
for the explanation which alone can be right; and when the reading is corrupt beyond emendation, he gives the most helpful
statement of the probable meaning. Not only was Johnson's
edition the best which had yet appeared; it is still one of the
few editions which are indispensable.

[1] See the 'Life of Johnson' contributed to the eighth edition of the *Encyclopaedia
Brittanica*, and reprinted in the ninth.

IV

The third quarter of the eighteenth century, and not the first quarter of the nineteenth, is the true period of transition in Shakespearian criticism. The dramatic rules had been finally deposed. The corrected plays were falling into disfavour, and though Shakespeare's dramas were not yet acted as they were written, more respect was being paid to the originals. The sixty years' controversy on the extent of his learning had ended by proving that the best commentary on him is the literature of his own age. At the same time there is a far-reaching change in the literary appreciations of Shakespeare, which announces the school of Coleridge and Hazlitt: his *characters* now become the main topics of criticism.

In the five essays on the *Tempest* and *King Lear* contributed by Joseph Warton to the *Adventurer* in 1753–4, we can recognize the coming change in critical methods. He began them by giving in a sentence a summary of the common verdicts: 'As Shakespeare is sometimes blamable for the conduct of his fables, which have no unity; and sometimes for his diction, which is obscure and turgid; so his characteristical excellences may possibly be reduced to these three general heads—his lively creative imagination, his strokes of nature and passion, and his preservation of the consistency of his characters.' Warton himself believed in the dramatic conventions. He objected to the Edmund story in *King Lear* on the ground that it destroyed the unity of the fable. But he had the wisdom to recognize that irregularities in structure may be excused by the representation of the persons of the drama.[1] Accordingly, in his examination of the *Tempest* and *King Lear*, he pays most attention to the characters, and relegates to a short closing paragraph his criticism of the development of the action. Though his method has nominally much in common with that of Maurice Morgann and the romantic critics, in practice it is very different. He treats the characters from without: he lacks the intuitive sympathy which is the secret of

---

[1] This had been recognized also by Whalley (*Enquiry*, 1748, p. 17).

later criticism. To him the play is a representation of life, not a transcript from life. The characters, who are more real to us than actual persons of history, and more intimate than many an acquaintance, appear to him to be creatures of the imagination who live in a different world from his own. Warton describes the picture: he criticizes the portraits of the characters rather than the characters themselves.

The gradual change in the critical attitude is illustrated also by Lord Kames, whom Heath had reason to describe, before the appearance of Johnson's Preface, as 'the truest judge and most intelligent admirer of Shakespeare'.[1] The scheme of his *Elements of Criticism* (1762) allowed him to deal with Shakespeare only incidentally, as in the digression where he distinguishes between the presentation and the description of passion, but he gives more decisive expression to Warton's view that observance of the rules is of subordinate importance to the truthful exhibition of character. The mechanical part, he observes, in which alone Shakespeare is defective, is less the work of genius than of experience, and it is knowledge of human nature which gives him his supremacy. The same views are repeated in the periodical essays. The *Mirror* regards it as 'preposterous' to endeavour to regularize his plays, and finds the source of his superiority in his almost supernatural powers of invention, his absolute command over the passions, and his wonderful knowledge of nature; and the *Lounger* says that he presents the abstract of life in all its modes and in every time. The rules are forgotten—we cease to hear even that they are useless. But the *Elements of Criticism* gave Kames no opportunity to show that his attitude to the characters themselves was other than Warton's.

No critic had questioned Shakespeare's truth to nature. The flower of Pope's Preface is the section on his knowledge of the world and his power over the passions. Lyttelton showed his intimacy with Pope's opinion when in his *Dialogues of the Dead* he made him say: 'No author had ever so copious, so bold, so *creative* an imagination, with so perfect a knowledge of the

---

[1] See the Dedication of the *Revisal of Shakespear's Text*.

passions, the humours and sentiments of mankind. He painted all characters, from kings down to peasants, with equal truth and equal force. If human nature were destroyed, and no monument were left of it except his works, other beings might know what man was from those writings.' The same eulogy is repeated in other words by Johnson. And in Gray's *Progress of Poesy* Shakespeare is 'Nature's Darling'. It was his diction which gave most scope to the censure of the better critics. An age whose literary watchwords were simplicity and precision was bound to remark on his obscurities and plays on words, and even, as Dryden had done, on his bombast. What Shaftesbury[1] or Atterbury[2] had said at the beginning of the century is repeated, as we should expect, by the rhetoricians, such as Blair. But it was shown by Kames that the merit of Shakespeare's language lay in the absence of those abstract and general terms which were the blemish of the century's own diction. 'Shakespeare's style in that respect', says Kames, 'is excellent: every article in his descriptions is particular, as in nature.' And herein Kames gave independent expression to the views of the poet who is said to have lived in the wrong century. 'In truth,' said Gray, 'Shakespeare's language is one of his principal beauties; and he has no less advantage over your Addisons and Rowes in this, than in those other great excellencies you mention. Every word in him is a picture.'[3]

The first book devoted directly to the examination of Shakespeare's characters was by William Richardson, Professor of Humanity in the University of Glasgow. His *Philosophical Analysis and Illustration of some of Shakespeare's Remarkable Characters*, which dealt with Macbeth, Hamlet, Jaques, and Imogen, appeared in 1774; ten years later he added a second series on Richard III, King Lear, and Timon of Athens; and in 1789 he concluded his character studies with his essay on Falstaff. As the titles show, Richardson's work has a moral purpose. His intention, as he tells us, was to make poetry subservient to philosophy,

[1] *Characteristicks*, 1711, i, p. 275.
[2] See Pope's *Correspondence*, ed. Sherburn, ii, 78–79.
[3] From a letter to Richard West, written apparently in 1742: see *Correspondence*, ed. Toynbee, ii, 27–28.

and to employ it in tracing the principles of human conduct. Accordingly, he has prejudiced his claims as a literary critic. He is not interested in Shakespeare's art for its own sake; but that he should use Shakespeare's characters as the subjects of moral disquisitions is eloquent testimony to their truth to nature. His classical bias, excusable in a Professor of Latin, is best seen in his essay 'On the Faults of Shakespeare',[1] of which the title was alone sufficient to win him the contempt of later critics. His essays are the dull effusions of a clever man. Though they are not inspiriting, they are not without interest. He recognized that the source of Shakespeare's greatness is that he became for the time the person whom he represented.

Before the appearance of Richardson's *Philosophical Analysis*, Thomas Whately had written his *Remarks on Some of the Characters of Shakespeare*; but it was not published till 1785. The author, who died in 1772, had abandoned it in order to complete, in 1770, his *Observations on Modern Gardening*. The book contains only a short introduction and a comparison of Macbeth and Richard III. The fragment is sufficient, however, to indicate more clearly than the work of Richardson the coming change. The author has himself remarked on the novelty of his method. The passage must be quoted, as it is the first definite statement that the examination of Shakespeare's characters should be the main object of Shakespearian criticism:

The writers upon dramatic composition have, for the most part, confined their observations to the fable; and the maxims received

[1] Richardson believed that the greatest blemishes in Shakespeare 'proceeded from his want of consummate taste'. The same idea had been expressed more forcibly by Hume in his Appendix to the Reign of James I: 'His total ignorance of all theatrical art and conduct, however material a defect, yet, as it affects the spectator rather than the reader, we can more easily excuse than that want of taste which often prevails in his productions, and which gives way only by intervals to the irradiations of genius.' Hugh Blair, whose name is associated with the Edinburgh edition of 1753, had said in his lectures on rhetoric in the University of Edinburgh that Shakespeare was 'deficient in just taste, and altogether unassisted by knowledge or art'. And Adam Smith believed so strongly in the French doctrines that Wordsworth could call him 'the worst critic, David Hume not excepted, that Scotland, a soil to which this sort of weed seems natural, has produced'. Kames, however, was a Scot.

amongst them, for the conduct of it, are therefore emphatically called, *The Rules of the Drama*. It has been found easy to give and to apply them; they are obvious, they are certain, they are general: and poets without genius have, by observing them, pretended to fame; while critics without discernment have assumed importance from knowing them. But the regularity thereby established, though highly proper, is by no means the first requisite in a dramatic composition. Even waiving all consideration of those finer feelings which a poet's imagination or sensibility imparts, there is, within the colder provinces of judgment and of knowledge, a subject for criticism more worthy of attention than the common topics of discussion: I mean the distinction and preservation of *character*.

The earlier critics who remarked on Shakespeare's depiction of character had not suspected that the examination of it was to oust the older methods.

A greater writer, who has met with unaccountable neglect, was to express the same views independently. Maurice Morgann had apparently written his *Essay on the Dramatic Character of Sir John Falstaff* about 1774, in an interval of political employment, but he was not prevailed upon to publish it till 1777. The better we know it, the more we shall regret that it is the only critical work which he allowed to survive. He too refers to his book as a 'novelty'. He believes the task of considering Shakespeare in detail to have been 'hitherto unattempted'. But his main object, unlike Whately's or Richardson's, is a 'critique on the genius, the arts, and the conduct of Shakespeare'. He concentrates his attention on a single character, only to advance to more general criticism. 'Falstaff is the word only, Shakespeare is the theme.'

Morgann's book did not meet with the attention which it deserved, nor to this day has its importance been fully recognized. Despite his warnings, his contemporaries regarded it simply as a defence of Falstaff's courage. One spoke of him as a paradoxical critic, and others doubted if he meant what he said. All were unaccountably indifferent to his main purpose. The book was unknown even to Hazlitt, who in the preface to his *Characters of*

Shakespeare's Plays alludes only to Whately[1] and Richardson as his English predecessors. Yet it is the true forerunner of the romantic criticism of Shakespeare. Morgann's attitude to the characters is the same as Coleridge's and Hazlitt's; his criticism, neglecting all formal matters, resolves itself into a study of human nature. It was he who first said that Shakespeare's creations should be treated as historic rather than as dramatic beings. And the key-note of his criticism is that 'the impression is the fact'. He states what he *feels*, and he explains the reason in language which is barely on this side idolatry.[2]

The Essays

NICHOLAS ROWE

NICHOLAS ROWE'S *Some Account of the Life, &c., of Mr. William Shakespear* forms the introduction to his edition of Shakespeare's plays (1709, 6 vols., 8vo).

Rowe has the double honour of being the first editor of the plays of Shakespeare and the first to attempt an authoritative account of his life. The value of the biography can best be judged by comparing it with the accounts given in such books as Fuller's *Worthies of England* (1662), Phillips's *Theatrum Poetarum* (1675), Winstanley's *English Poets* (1687), Langbaine's *English Dramatick Poets* (1691), Pope Blount's *Remarks upon Poetry* (1694), or Jeremy Collier's *Historical and Poetical Dictionary* (1701). Though some of the traditions—for which he has acknowledged his debt to Betterton—are of doubtful accuracy, it is safe to say that but for Rowe they would have perished.

The *Account of Shakespeare* was the standard biography during

---

[1] Hazlitt confounds Whately with George Mason, author of *An Essay on Design in Gardening*, 1768. Whately's book was published as 'by the author of *Observations on Modern Gardening*'. His name was given in the second edition, 1808.

J. P. Kemble replied to Whately's *Remarks* in *Macbeth re-considered* (1786; republished in 1817 with the title *Macbeth and King Richard the Third*).

[2] Morgann's kinship with the romantic critics is seen even in so minor a matter as his criticism of Johnson; see p. 232.

the eighteenth century. It was reprinted by Pope, Hanmer, Warburton, Johnson, Steevens, Malone, and Reed; but they did not give it in the form in which Rowe had left it. Pope took the liberty of condensing and rearranging it, and as he did not acknowledge what he had done, his silence led other editors astray. Those who did note the alterations presumed that they had been made by Rowe himself in the second edition in 1714. Steevens, for instance, states that he publishes the life from 'Rowe's second edition, in which it had been abridged and altered by himself after its appearance in 1709'. But what Steevens reprints is Rowe's *Account of Shakespeare* as edited by Pope. In this volume the *Account* is given in its original form for the first time since 1714.

Pope omitted passages dealing only indirectly with Shakespeare, or expressing opinions with which he disagreed. He also placed the details of Shakespeare's later years (pp. 20–22) immediately after the account of his relationship with Ben Jonson (p. 8), so that the biography might form a complete portion by itself. With the exception of an occasional word, nothing occurs in the emended edition which is not to be found somewhere in the first.

A seventh and supplementary volume containing the Poems was added in 1710. It included Charles Gildon's *Remarks* on the Plays and Poems and his *Essay on the Art, Rise, and Progress of the Stage in Greece, Rome, and England.*

JOHN DENNIS

JOHN DENNIS's three letters 'on the genius and writings of Shakespear' (February 1710–11) were published together in 1712 under the title *An Essay on the Genius and Writings of Shakespear.* The volume contained also two letters on the 40th and 47th numbers of the *Spectator.* All were reprinted in Dennis's *Original Letters, Familiar, Moral and Critical,* 2 vols., 1721. The Dedication is to George Granville, then Secretary at War. 'To whom', says Dennis, 'can an Essay upon the Genius and Writings of Shakespear be so properly address'd, as to him who best understands Shakespear, and who has most improv'd him? I would not give this just encomium to the *Jew of Venice*, if I were not convinc'd, from a long experience of the penetration and force of your judgment, that no exaltation can make you asham'd of your former noble art.'

In 1693 Dennis had published the *Impartial Critick*, a reply to Rymer's *Short View of Tragedy*; but there is little about Shakespeare in its five dialogues, their main purpose being to show the absurdity of Rymer's plea for adopting the Greek methods in the English drama. Dennis had, however, great respect for Rymer's ability. In the first letter to the *Spectator* he says that Rymer 'will always pass with impartial posterity for a most learned, a most judicious, and a most useful critick'; and in the *Characters and Conduct of Sir John Edgar* he says that 'there was a great deal of good and just criticism' in the *Short View*.

In 1702 he brought out a 'corrected' version of the *Merry Wives* with the title of *The Comical Gallant or the Amours of Sir John Falstaffe*. The adaptation of *Coriolanus*, which was the occasion of the *Letters* given in this volume, appeared as *The Invader of his country, or the Fatal Resentment*. It was produced at Drury Lane in November 1719, but ran for only three nights. It was published in 1720. An account of it will be found in Genest's *English Stage*, iii, 2–5. It is the subject of Dennis's letter to Steele of 26 March 1719 (see Steele's *Theatre*, ed. Nichols, 1791, ii, pp. 542, &c.).

ALEXANDER POPE

POPE's edition of Shakespeare was published by Tonson in six quarto volumes. The first appeared in 1725, as the title-page shows; all the others are dated '1723'.

In the note to the line in the *Dunciad* in which he laments his 'ten years to comment and translate', Pope gives us to understand that he prepared his edition of Shakespeare after he had completed the translation of the *Iliad* and before he set to work on the *Odyssey*. His own correspondence, however, shows that he was engaged on Shakespeare and the *Odyssey* at the same time. There is some uncertainty as to when his edition was begun. The inference to be drawn from a letter to Pope from Atterbury is that it had been undertaken by August 1721. We have more definite information as to the date of its completion. In a letter to Broome of 31 October 1724, Pope writes: 'Shakespeare is finished. I have just written the Preface, and in less than three weeks it will be public' (ed. Sherburn, ii. 270). But it did not appear till March. Pope himself was partly to blame for the delay. In December we find Tonson 'impatient' for the return of the Preface (id. ii. 280). In the revision of the text Pope was assisted by Fenton and Gay (see Reed's Variorum edition, 1803, ii, p. 149 and Nichols, *Illustrations*, ii, p. 714).

Pope made few changes in his Preface in the second edition (1728, 8 vols., 12mo). The chief difference is the inclusion of the *Double Falshood*, which Theobald had produced in 1728 as Shakespeare's, in the list of the spurious plays.

A ninth volume was added in 1728 to this edition containing the seven spurious plays, and at the same time a tenth containing the Poems as well as the Essay and the Remarks of Gildon published in the supplementary volume of 1710, 'the whole revis'd, and corrected, with a preface, by Dr. Sewell', dated 24 November 1724.

The references in the Preface to the old actors were criticized by John Roberts in 1729 in a pamphlet entitled *An Answer to Mr. Pope's Preface to Shakespear. In a Letter to a Friend. Being a Vindication of the Old Actors who were the Publishers and Performers of that Author's Plays. . . . By a Stroling Player.*

LEWIS THEOBALD

THEOBALD's edition of Shakespeare (7 vols. 8vo) appeared in 1733. The Preface was condensed in the second edition in 1740. It is here given in its later form.

Theobald had long been interested in Shakespeare. In 1715 he had written the *Cave of Poverty*, a poem 'in imitation of Shakespeare', and in 1720 he had brought out an adaptation of *Richard II*. But it was not till 1726—though the Dedication bears the date of 18 March 1725—that he produced his first direct contribution to Shakespearian scholarship—*Shakespeare restored: or, a Specimen of the Many Errors, as well Committed, as Unamended, by Mr. Pope in his Late Edition of this Poet. Designed Not only to correct the said Edition, but to restore the True Reading of Shakespeare in all the Editions ever yet publish'd.*

We learn from a letter by Theobald dated 15 April 1729, that he had been in correspondence with Pope fully two years before the publication of this volume. (See Nichols, *Illustrations of the Literary History of the Eighteenth Century*, ii, p. 221.) Pope, however, had not encouraged his advances. In the same letter Theobald states that he had no design of commenting on Shakespeare till he saw 'how incorrect an edition Mr. Pope had given the publick'. This remark was prompted by a note in the *Dunciad* of 1729, where it was stated that 'during the space of two years, while Mr. Pope was preparing his Edition of Shakespear, and published advertisements, requesting all lovers of the author to contribute to a more perfect one; this Restorer (who had then some correspondence with him, and was solliciting favours by letters) did wholly conceal his design, 'till after its publication'. But if Theobald had not thought of issuing comments on Shakespeare's plays till Pope's edition appeared, he must have known them well already, for *Shakespeare Restored* is not a hasty piece of work.

Despite the aggressiveness of the title, Theobald protests his regard for Pope in such passages as these:

It was no small Satisfaction therefore to me, when I first heard Mr. *Pope* had taken upon him the Publication of *Shakespeare*. I very reasonably expected, from his known Talents and Abilities, from his uncommon Sagacity and Discernment, and from his unwearied Diligence and Care of informing himself by an happy and extensive Conversation, we should have had our Author come out as perfect, as the want of *Manuscripts* and *original Copies* could give us a Possibility of hoping. I may dare to say, a great Number of *Shakespeare's* Admirers, and of Mr. *Pope's* too, (both which I sincerely declare myself,) concurred in this Expectation: For there is a certain *curiosa felicitas*, as was said of an eminent *Roman* Poet, in that Gentleman's Way of working, which, we presum'd, would have laid itself out largely in such a Province; and that he would not have sate down contented with performing, as he calls it himself, the *dull Duty* of an *Editor* only.

I have so great an Esteem for Mr. *Pope*, and so high an Opinion of his Genius and Excellencies, that I beg to be excused from the least Intention of derogating from his Merits, in this Attempt to restore the true Reading of *Shakespeare*. Tho' I confess a Veneration, almost rising to Idolatry, for the writings of this inimitable Poet, I would be very loth even to do *him* Justice at the Expence of *that other* Gentleman's Character.

Whether or not these declarations were sincere, they would hardly have stayed the resentment of a less sensitive man than Pope when passage after passage was pointed out where errors were 'as well committed as unamended'. Theobald even hazarded the roguish suggestion that the bookseller had played his editor false by not sending him all the sheets to revise; and he certainly showed that the readings of Rowe's edition had occasionally been adopted without the professed collation of the older copies. The volume could raise no doubt of Theobald's own diligence. The chief part of it is devoted to an examination of the text of *Hamlet*, but there is a long appendix dealing with readings in other plays, and in it occurs the famous emendation of the line in *Henry V* describing Falstaff's death—'for his nose was as sharp as a pen, and *a' babled of green fields*'. It should be noted that the credit of this reading is not entirely Theobald's. He admits that in an edition 'with some marginal conjectures of a Gentleman sometime deceased' he found the emendation 'and *a' talked* of green fields'. Theobald's share thus amounts to the doubtful improvement of substituting *babbled* for *talked*.

Though this volume has undoubted merits, it is not difficult to understand why the name of Theobald came to convey to the eighteenth century the idea of painful pedantry, and why one so eminently just as Johnson should have dubbed him 'a man of heavy diligence, with very slender powers'. While his knowledge is indisputable, he has little or no delicacy of taste; his style is dull and lumbering; and the mere fact that he dedicated his *Shakespeare Restored* to John Rich, the Covent Garden manager who specialized in pantomime and played the part of Harlequin, may at least cast some doubt on his discretion. But he successfully attacked Pope where he was weakest and where as an editor he should have been strongest. 'From this time', in the words of Johnson, 'Pope became an enemy to editors, collators, commentators, and verbal critics; and hoped to persuade the world that he had miscarried in this undertaking only by having a mind too great for such minute employment.'

Not content with the errors pointed out in *Shakespeare Restored* —a quarto volume of 200 pages—Theobald continued his criticisms of Pope's edition in *Mist's Journal* and the *Daily Journal*, until he was ripe for the *Dunciad*. Pope enthroned him as the hero of the poem, and so he remained till he was replaced by Colley Cibber in 1742, when the alteration necessitated several omissions. In the earlier editions Theobald soliloquized thus:

> Here studious I unlucky moderns save,
> Nor sleeps one error in its father's grave,
> Old puns restore, lost blunders nicely seek,
> And crucify poor Shakespear once a week.
> For thee I dim these eyes, and stuff this head,
> With all such reading as was never read;
> For thee supplying, in the worst of days,
> Notes to dull books, and prologues to dull plays;
> For thee explain a thing till all men doubt it,
> And write about it, Goddess, and about it. (i. 161)

Theobald is introduced also in the *Art of Sinking in Poetry* among the classes of authors described as swallows and eels: the former 'are eternally skimming and fluttering up and down, but all their agility is employed to catch flies', the latter 'wrap themselves up in their own mud, but are mighty nimble and pert'.

About the same time, however, Pope brought out the second edition (1728) of his Shakespeare, and in it he incorporated some of Theobald's conjectures, though his recognition of their merit was grudging and even dishonestly inadequate. (See the preface to the various readings at the end of the eighth volume, 1728.) Yet one's sympathies with Theobald are prejudiced by his ascription to Shakespeare of the *Double Falshood, or the Distrest Lovers*, a play which was acted in 1727 and printed in the following year. Theobald professed to have revised it and adapted it to the stage. The question of authorship has not been settled, but if Theobald is relieved from the imputation of forgery, he must at least stand convicted of ignorance of the Shakespearian manner. Pope at once recognized that the play was not Shakespeare's, and added a contemptuous reference to it in the second edition of his Preface. It was the opinion of Farmer that the groundwork of the play was by Shirley (see the *Essay on the Learning of Shakespeare*, p. 169).

Theobald now sought to revenge himself on Pope, and, in his own words, he 'purposed to reply only in Shakespeare' (Nichols, id. ii, p. 248). His first plan was to publish a volume of *Remarks on Shakespeare*. On 15 April 1729, he says the volume 'will now shortly appear in the world' (id., p. 222), but on 6 November he writes to Warburton, 'I know you will not be displeased, if I should tell you in your ear, perhaps I may venture to join the *Text* to my *Remarks*' (id., p. 254). By the following March he had definitely determined upon giving an edition of Shakespeare, as appears from another letter to Warburton: 'As it is necessary I should now inform the publick that I mean to attempt to give them an edition of that Poet's [i.e. Shakespeare's] text, together with my corrections, I have concluded to give this notice, not only by advertisements, but by an occasional pamphlet, which, in order to retaliate some of our Editor's kindnesses to me, I mean to call, *An Essay upon Mr. Pope's Judgment, extracted from his own Works; and humbly addressed to him*' (id. ii, p. 551). Of this he forwards Warburton an extract. The pamphlet does not appear to have been published. The *Miscellany on Taste* which he brought out anonymously in 1732 contains a section entitled 'Of Mr. Pope's Taste of Shakespeare', but this is merely a reprint of the letter of 15 (or 16) April, which had already been printed in the *Daily Journal*. A considerable time elapsed before arrangements for publication were completed, the interval being marked by a temporary estrangement from Warburton and an unsuccessful candidature for the laureateship. Articles with Tonson were signed in November 1731 (id. ii, pp. 13, 618), and at the same time the correspondence with Warburton was renewed. The edition did not appear till 1733. The Preface had been begun about the end of 1731.

From March 1729, with the short break in 1730, Theobald had been in steady correspondence with Warburton, and most of his letters, with a few of those of Warburton, have been preserved by Nichols (see id. ii, pp. 189, 607). But it would have been more fortunate for Theobald's reputation had they perished. The cruel contempt and bitterness of Warburton's references to him after their final estrangement may be offensive, but the correspondence shows that they were not without some justification. Theobald submits his conjectures anxiously to the judgement of Warburton, and again and again Warburton saves him from himself. In one of the letters Theobald rightly condemns Pope's proposed insertion of 'Francis Drake' in the incomplete line at the end of the first scene of *Henry VI, Part I*; but not content with this flawless piece of destructive criticism he argues for inserting the words 'and Cassiopeia'. The probability is that if Warburton had not condemned the proposal it would have appeared in Theobald's edition. 'With a just deference to your most convincing reasons,' says Theobald, 'I shall with great cheerfulness banish it as a bad and unsupported conjecture' (id. ii, p. 477); and this remark is typical of the whole correspondence. A considerable share of the merit of Theobald's edition—though the share is mostly negative—belongs to Warburton, for Theobald had not taste enough to keep him right when he stepped beyond collation of the older editions or explanation by parallel passages. Indeed, the letters to Warburton, besides helping to explain his reputation in the eighteenth century, would in themselves be sufficient to justify his place in the *Dunciad*.

Warburton had undoubtedly given Theobald ungrudging assistance and was plainly interested in the success of the edition. But as he had gauged Theobald's ability, he had some fears for the Preface. So at least we gather from a letter which Theobald wrote to him on 18 November 1731:

> I am extremely obliged for the tender concern you have for my reputation in what I am *to prefix to my Edition*: and this part, as it will come last in play, I shall certainly be so kind to myself to communicate in due time to your perusal. The whole affair of *Prolegomena* I have determined to soften into *Preface*. I am so very cool as to my sentiments of my Adversary's usage, that I think the publick should not be too largely troubled with them. *Blockheadry* is the chief hinge of his satire upon me; and if my Edition do not wipe out that, I ought to be content to let the charge be fixed; if it do, the reputation gained will be a greater triumph than resentment. But, dear Sir, will you, at your leisure hours, think over for me upon the contents, topics, orders, etc., of this branch of my labour? You have a comprehensive memory, and a happiness of digesting the matter joined to it, which my head is often too much embarrassed to perform; let that be the excuse for my inability. But how unreasonable is it to expect this labour, when it is the only part in which I shall not be able to be just to my friends: for, to confess assistance in a *Preface* will, I am afraid, make me appear too naked. Rymer's extravagant rancour against our Author, under the umbrage of criticism, may, I presume, find a place here (id. ii, pp. 621, 622).

This confession of weakness is valuable in the light of Warburton's Preface to his own edition of 1747. His statement of the assistance he rendered Theobald is rude and cruel, but it is easier to impugn his taste than his truthfulness. Theobald did not merely ask for assistance in the Preface; he received it too. Warburton expressed himself on this matter, with his customary force and with a pleasing attention to detail, in a letter to the Rev. Thomas Birch on 24 November 1737. 'You will see in Theobald's heap of disjointed stuff,' he says, 'which he calls a

Preface to Shakespeare, an observation upon those poems [i.e.
L'Allegro and *Il Penseroso*] which I made to him, and which he
did not understand, and so has made it a good deal obscure by
contracting my note; for you must understand that almost all
that Preface (except what relates to Shakespeare's Life, and the
foolish Greek conjectures at the end) was made up of notes I
sent him on particular passages, and which he has there stitched
together without head or tail' (Nichols, ii, p. 81). The Preface is
indeed a poor piece of patchwork. Examination of the footnotes
throughout the edition corroborates Warburton's concluding
statement. Some of the annotations which have his name attached to them are repeated almost verbatim (e.g. the note in
Love's Labour's Lost on the use of music), while the comparison of
Addison and Shakespeare is taken from a letter written by Warburton to Concanen in 1726-7 (id. ii, pp. 195, &c.). The in-
equality of the essay—the fitful succession of limp and acute
observations—can be explained only by ill-matched collabora-
tion.

Warburton has himself indicated the extent of Theobald's debt
to him. In his own copy of Theobald's Shakespeare he marked
the passages which he had contributed to the Preface, as well
as the notes 'which Theobald deprived him of and made his
own', and the volume is now in the Capell collection in Trinity
College, Cambridge. Mr. Churton Collins, in his attempt to
prove Theobald the greatest of Shakespearian editors, has said
that 'if in this copy, which we have not had the opportunity of
inspecting, Warburton has laid claim to more than Theobald has
assigned to him, we believe him to be guilty of dishonesty even
more detestable than that of which the proofs are, as we have
shown, indisputable'.[1] An inspection of the Cambridge volume
is not necessary to show that a passage in the Preface has been
conveyed from one of Warburton's letters published by Nichols
and by Malone. Any defence of Theobald by an absolute refusal
to believe Warburton's word can be of no value unless some

[1] Essay on 'The Porson of Shakespearian Criticism', *Essays and Studies*, 1895,
p. 270.

proof be adduced that Warburton was here untruthful, and it is peculiarly inept when Theobald's own page proclaims the theft. We know that Theobald asked Warburton for assistance in the Preface, and gave warning that such assistance would not be acknowledged. Warburton could have had no evil motive in marking those passages in his *private* copy; and there is surely a strong presumption in favour of a man who deliberately goes over seven volumes, carefully indicating the material which he considered his own. It happens that one of the passages contains an unfriendly allusion to Pope. If Warburton meant to be 'dishonest'—and there could be no purpose in being dishonest before he was Theobald's enemy—why did he not disclaim this allusion some years later? The simple explanation is that he marked the passages for his own amusement while he was still on friendly terms with Theobald. They are thirteen in number, and they vary in length from a few lines to two pages. Four of them are undoubtedly his, and there is nothing to disprove that the other nine are his also.[1]

Theobald quotes also from his own correspondence. On 17 March 1729-30 he had written to Warburton a long letter dealing with Shakespeare's knowledge of languages and including a specimen of his proposed pamphlet against Pope. 'Your most necessary caution against inconsistency, with regard to my

[1] I am indebted to Dr. Aldis Wright for procuring for me the details of Warburton's claims. As a few of the passages were omitted by Theobald in the second edition, the following page references are to the edition of 1733:

(1) P. xix, *This Similitude*, to *Nature and Science*, p. xx.
(2) P. xxi, *Servetur ad imum*, to *the more wonder'd at*, p. xxii.
(3) P. xxv, *That nice Critick*, to *Truth and Nature*, p. xxvii.
(4) P. xxx, *For I shall find*, to *this long agitated Question*, p. xxxii (p. 70).
(5) P. xxxiii, *They are confessedly*, to *Force and Splendor*, p. xxxiv (p. 71).
(6) P. xxxiv, *And how great that Merit*, to *ill Appearance* (p. 72).
(7) P. xxxv, *It seems a moot Point*, to *from the spurious*, p. xxxvi (p. 73).
(8) P. xxxix, *For the late Edition*, to *have wrote so*, p. xl (p. 75).
(9) P. xl, *The Science of Criticism*, to *Editor's Labour*, p. xli (p. 76).
(10) P. xlv, *There are Obscurities*, to *antiquated and disused* (p. 78).
(11) P. xlvi, *Wit lying mostly*, to *Variety of his Ideas*, p. xlvii (pp. 79-80).
(12) P. xlviii, *as to Rymer*, to *his best Reflexions* (p. 80).
(13) P. lxii, *If the Latin*, to *Complaints of its Barbarity* (p. 83).

The passages which were retained are printed in the present text at the pages indicated above within brackets. Cf. Notes, pp. 294-5.

opinion of Shakespeare's knowledge in languages', he there says characteristically, 'shall not fail to have all its weight with me. And therefore the passages that I occasionally quote from the Classics shall not be brought as proofs that he imitated those originals, but to shew how happily he has expressed themselves upon the same topics' (Nichols, ii, pp. 564, &c.). This part of the letter is included verbatim three years afterwards in the Preface. So also is the other passage in the same letter replying to Pope on the subject of Shakespeare's anachronisms. Theobald borrows even from his own published writings. Certain passages are reproduced from the Introduction to *Shakespeare Restored*.

If Theobald could hardly acknowledge, as he said, the assistance he received in writing the Preface, he at least admitted his editorial debt to Warburton and others punctiliously and handsomely. After referring to Dr. Thirlby of Jesus College, Cambridge, and Hawley Bishop, he thus writes of his chief helper:

To these, I must add the indefatigable Zeal and Industry of my most ingenious and ever-respected Friend, the Reverend Mr. *William Warburton* of *Newark* upon *Trent*. This Gentleman, from the Motives of his frank and communicative Disposition, voluntarily took a considerable Part of my Trouble off my Hands; not only read over the whole Author for me, with the exactest Care; but enter'd into a long and laborious Epistolary Correspondence; to which I owe no small Part of my best Criticisms upon my Author.

The Number of Passages amended, and admirably Explained, which I have taken care to distinguish with his Name, will shew a Fineness of Spirit and Extent of Reading, beyond all the Commendations I can give them: Nor, indeed, would I any farther be thought to commend a Friend, than, in so doing, to give a Testimony of my own Gratitude.

So the Preface read in 1733. But by the end of 1734 Warburton had quarrelled with Theobald, and by 1740, after a passing friendship with Sir Thomas Hanmer, had become definitely attached to the party of Pope. This is probably the reason why, in the Preface to the second edition, Theobald does not repeat the detailed statement of the assistance he had received. He

wisely omits also the long and irrelevant passage of Greek conjectures, given with no other apparent reason than to parade his
learning. And several passages either claimed by Warburton
(e.g. that referring to Milton's poems) or known to be his
(e.g. the comparison of Addison and Shakespeare) are also
cancelled.

The merits of the text of Theobald's edition are undeniable;
but the text is not to be taken as the sole measure of his ability.
By his diligence in collation he restored many of the original
readings. His knowledge of Elizabethan literature was turned to
good account in the explanation and illustration of the text. He
claims to have read above 800 old English plays 'to ascertain the
obsolete and uncommon phrases'. But when we have spoken of
his diligence, we have spoken of all for which, as an editor, he
was remarkable. Pope had good reason to say of him, though he
gave the criticism a wider application, that

> Pains, reading, study are their just pretence,
> And all they want is spirit, taste, and sense.

The inner history of his Preface would prove of itself that
Theobald well deserved the notoriety which he enjoyed in the
eighteenth century.

SIR THOMAS HANMER

SIR THOMAS HANMER's edition of Shakespeare, in six
handsome quarto volumes, was printed at the Clarendon Press
in 1743–4. As it appeared anonymously it was commonly called
the 'Oxford edition'. It was well known, however, that Hanmer
was the editor. The Plays in vol. i and vols. ii, iii, and iv bear
the date 1743; the others, 1744.

Hanmer had been Speaker of the House of Commons from
1714 to 1715, and had played an important part in securing the
Protestant succession on the death of Queen Anne. He retired
from public life on the accession of George II, and thereafter
lived in 'lettered ease' at his seat of Mildenhall near Newmarket

till his death in 1746. It is not known when he undertook his edition of Shakespeare, but the idea of it was probably suggested to him by the publication of Theobald's edition in 1733. His relative and biographer, Sir Henry Bunbury, writing in 1838, refers to a copy of this edition with corrections and notes on the text of every play in Hanmer's handwriting. But there can be no doubt of the accuracy of Warburton's statement that his edition was printed from Pope's,[1] though the hastiest examination will prove the falsity of Warburton's other remark that Hanmer neglected to compare Pope's edition with Theobald's. He relied on Pope's judgement as to the authenticity of passages and on Theobald's accuracy in collation. Thus while he omits lines which Pope had omitted, or degrades them to the foot of the page, he often adopts Theobald's reading of a word or phrase.

He had certainly made considerable progress with the edition by May 1738, when he was visited by Warburton (see Nichols, *Illustrations*, ii, pp. 44, 69). It was still incomplete in March 1742, but it was sent to the printer at the end of that year, as we learn from a letter of 30 December to Zachary Grey, the editor of *Hudibras*: 'I must now acquaint you that the books are gone out of my hands, and lodged with the University of Oxford, which hath been willing to accept of them as a present from me. They intend to print them forthwith, in a fair impression adorned with sculptures; but it will be so ordered that it will be the cheapest book that ever was exposed to sale. . . . None are to go into the hands of booksellers' (Nichols, *Literary Anecdotes*, v, p. 589). Earlier in the year, in the important letter concerning his quarrel with Warburton, which will be referred to later, he had spoken of his edition in the following terms: 'As to my own particular, I have no aim to pursue in this affair; I propose neither honour, reward, or thanks, and should be very well pleased to have the books continue upon their shelf, in my own private closet. If it is thought they may be of use or pleasure to the publick, I am willing to part with them out of my hands, and

---

[1] A copy of Pope's edition, as sent to the printer, with the Preface and Notes in Hanmer's own hand, is now in the Bodleian Library.

to add, for the honour of Shakespear, some decorations and embellishments at my own expense' (id. v, p. 589). The printing of the edition was not supervised by Hanmer himself, but by Joseph Smith, Provost of Queen's College, and Robert Shippen, Principal of Brasenose. We find them receiving instructions that there must be care in the correction of the press, that the type must be as large as in Pope's edition, but the paper better.

These facts are of interest in connexion with Hanmer's inclusion in the fourth book of the *Dunciad*. In a note by Pope and Warburton he is referred to as 'an eminent person, who was about to publish a very pompous edition of a great author, *at his own expense*'; and in the poem the satire is maladroitly aimed at the handsomeness of the volumes. Warburton afterwards implied that he was responsible for the inclusion of this passage (id., p. 590), and though the claim is disputed by Hanmer's biographer, the ineffectiveness of the attack would prove that it was not spontaneous. Pope, however, would yield to Warburton's desire the more readily if, as Sir Henry Bunbury had reason to believe, the anonymous *Remarks on the Tragedy of Hamlet*, published in 1736, was the work of Hanmer,[1] for there Pope's edition was compared unfavourably, though courteously, with that of Theobald. (See the *Correspondence of Sir Thomas Hanmer*, 1838, pp. 80, &c.)

WILLIAM WARBURTON

'THE Works of Shakespear in Eight Volumes. The Genuine Text (collated with all the former Editions, and then corrected and emended) is here settled: Being restored from the *Blunders* of the first Editors, and the *Interpolations* of the two Last; with a Comment and Notes, Critical and Explanatory. By Mr. Pope and Mr. Warburton. 1747.'

[1] Lounsbury said that Hanmer's authorship of this pamphlet 'is so improbable that it may be called impossible. The sentiments expressed in it are not Hanmer's sentiments' (*Shakespeare as a Dramatic Artist*, p. 60). But he omitted to tell us how he knew what Hanmer's sentiments were.

So runs the title of what is generally known as Warburton's edition. It is professedly a revised issue of Pope's. In point of fact it is founded, not on Pope's text, but on the text of Theobald. Warburton does not follow even Pope's arrangement of the plays. With one insignificant transposition, he gives them in the identical order in which they appear in Theobald's edition. And though he has his gibe at Hanmer in the title-page, he incorporates Hanmer's glossary word for word, and almost letter for letter. But his animosity betrays him in his Preface. He complains of the trouble which he has been put to by the last two editors, for he has had 'not only their interpolations to throw out, but the genuine text to replace and establish in its stead'. He would not have had this trouble had he used Pope's edition. He may have believed that what he took from Hanmer and Theobald was very much less than what they had received from him. According to his own statements he supplied each with a large number of important emendations which had been used without acknowledgement. Yet this does not excuse the suggestion that his edition was founded on Pope's.

The explanation is Warburton's just pride in Pope's friendship—a pride which he took every opportunity of gratifying and parading. But in his earlier days he had been, all unknown to Pope, an enemy. He escaped the *Dunciad* by reason of his obscurity. He was the friend of Concanen and Theobald, and in a letter to the former, containing his earliest extant attempt at Shakespearian criticism, he observes that 'Dryden borrows for want of leisure, and Pope for want of genius'. The letter is dated 2 January 1726-7, but luckily for Warburton it was not publicly known till, in 1766, Akenside used it as a means of paying off old scores (see Nichols, *Illustrations*, ii, pp. 195-8, and Malone's *Supplement*, 1780, i, p. 223). It is of interest also from the fact that Theobald transcribed from it almost verbatim the comparison of Shakespeare and Addison in the Preface of 1733.

Theobald's deference and even humility must have confirmed Warburton's confidence in his own critical powers, but it was not till Theobald's Shakespeare was published that Warburton first hinted at an edition by himself. From 1729 to 1733 he had given Theobald loyally of his best. On the appearance of the edition he betrayed some annoyance that all his suggestions had not been accepted. 'I have transcribed about fifty emendations and remarks', he writes on 17 May 1734, 'which I have at several times sent you, omitted in the Edition of Shakespeare, which, I am sure, are better than any of mine published there. These I shall convey to you soon, and desire you to publish them (as omitted by being mislaid) in your Edition of the "Poems" which I hope you will soon make ready for the press' (Nichols, *Illustrations*, ii, p. 634). These he duly forwarded, along with a flattering criticism of the edition. He gives no hint that he may himself turn them to account, till the October of the same year, when he writes, 'I have a great number of notes, etc., on Shakespeare, *for some future Edition*' (id., p. 654). Here the correspondence ceases. Up to this time Warburton had aided Theobald's schemes of retaliating on Pope. We have his own authority for attributing to him the remark in Theobald's Preface that 'it seems a moot point whether Mr. Pope has done most injury to Shakespeare as his Editor and Encomiast; or Mr. Rymer done him service as his Rival and Censurer'. It is probable even that he had a hand in Theobald's and Concanen's *Art of a Poet's sinking in Reputation, or a Supplement to the Art of sinking in Poetry*.

Warburton then gave his services to Sir Thomas Hanmer. They had become acquainted by 1736, and they corresponded frequently till Warburton's visit to Mildenhall in May 1737. It is needless to enter into their quarrel, for the interest of it is purely personal. Hanmer told his version of it to Joseph Smith, the Provost of Queen's College, Oxford, in his letter of 28 October 1742, and Warburton gave his very different account nineteen years later, on 29 January 1761, when he discovered that Hanmer's letter was about to be published in the *Biographia Britannica*. In the absence of further evidence it is impossible to decide with whom the truth rests. The dignity of Hanmer's letter wins favour by contrast with the violence of Warburton's. Yet there must be some truth in Warburton's circumstantial

details, though his feelings may have prevented his seeing them
in proper perspective. He says that Hanmer used his notes without his knowledge. The statement is probably accurate. But
when Hanmer says that Warburton's notes were 'sometimes just
but mostly wild and out of the way', we are satisfied, from what
we know of Warburton's other work, that the criticism was
merited. Hanmer apparently found that Warburton did not give
him much help, and Warburton may have been annoyed at
failing to find Hanmer as docile as Theobald. They had quarrelled
by September 1739, when Warburton records that he has got
all his letters and papers out of Sir Thomas Hanmer's hands
(Nichols, *Illustrations*, ii. 110. See also Nichols, *Literary Anecdotes*,
v. 588–90; *Biographia Britannica*, vi (1763), pp. 3743–4, and
Appendix, p. 223; Philip Nichols, *The Castrated Letter of Sir
Thomas Hanmer*, 1763; and Bunbury, *Correspondence of Hanmer*, pp.
85–90).

During his friendship with Hanmer, Warburton had not lost
sight of his own edition. The quarrel was precipitated by Hanmer's discovery of Warburton's intention; but there is no evidence that Warburton had tried to conceal it. Everything goes to
show that each editor was so immersed in his own scheme that
he regarded the other as his collaborator. Hanmer did not know
at first that Warburton was planning an edition as a means of
making some money; and Warburton had not suspected that
Hanmer would publish an edition at all. This is the only reasonable inference to be drawn from a letter written by him to the
Rev. Thomas Birch in October 1737. 'You are pleased to enquire about Shakespeare', he writes. 'I believe (to tell it as a
secret) I shall, after I have got the whole of this work out of my
hands which I am now engaged in, give an Edition of it to the
world. Sir Thomas Hanmer has a true critical genius, and has
done great things in this Author; so you may expect to see a
very extraordinary edition of its kind. I intend to draw up and
prefix to it a just and complete critique on Shakespeare and his
Works.' This letter reads curiously in the light of after events;
but it proves, if it proves anything, that Warburton did not

suspect Hanmer's scheme, and believed that Hanmer was helping him in his edition. It is equally plain that Hanmer believed
he was being helped by Warburton.

Announcements of Warburton's forthcoming edition were
made in Birch's article on Shakespeare in the *General Dictionary,*
Historical and Critical, vol. ix, January 1739–40, and in the
History of the Works of the Learned for 1740 (Nichols, *Illustrations,*
ii, pp. 72–74, and *Lit. Anecdotes,* v, p. 559). But there were no
signs of its appearance, and Hanmer had good reason to say in
October 1742, in his letter to Joseph Smith, 'I am satisfied there
is no edition coming or likely to come from Warburton; but it is
a report raised to support some little purpose or other, of which
I see there are many on foot'. Up to this time Warburton had
merely suggested emendations and puzzled out explanations: he
had not set to work seriously on the complete text. Since 1740,
when he published the *Vindication of the Essay on Man,* his critical
and polemical talents had been devoted to the service of Pope.
To judge from what he says in his Preface, his project of an
edition of Shakespeare might have been abandoned had not Pope
persuaded him to proceed with it by the offer of making it appear
their joint work. Pope had nothing to do with it, for it was not
begun till after his death. But it was a cruel fate that what professed to be a new edition of his 'Shakespeare' should really be
founded on Theobald's. The knowledge of Theobald's use of the
Quartos and Folios led Warburton to commit a detestable
quibble on his title-page. There is said to be no evidence that
Warburton himself had consulted them. Yet the statement that
his text is 'collated with all the former editions' is not absolutely
without the bounds of truth: Theobald had consulted them, and
Warburton does not say that he had consulted them himself.
What Warburton did was to give full play to his talent for
emendation, and to indulge what Johnson called his rage for
saying something when there is nothing to be said. Yet we are
too prone to depreciate Warburton. He has prejudiced his
reputation by his arrogance and his contemptuous malignity;
but we do him an injustice if we endeavour to gauge his merit

only by comparing his edition with those of his immediate predecessors. No early editor of Shakespeare has gained more than Theobald and suffered more than Warburton by the custom of attributing the whole merit of an edition to him whose name is on the title-page. When we read their correspondence and see their editions in the making, it is not difficult to realize what Johnson meant when he said that Warburton as a critic would make 'two and fifty Theobalds, cut into slices'.

SAMUEL JOHNSON[1]

WHEN recording the publication of Johnson's edition of Shakespeare *The Gentleman's Magazine* (October 1765, p. 479) mentioned 'the rapid sale of the impression which has already made a second necessary, though it has not been published a month'. This new impression was reset and is strictly a new edition. The differences in the two texts of the Preface are not serious enough to give independent authority to the later one; it is a reprint of the other and was itself reprinted in the edition of 1768. The original edition has been followed in the present volume, but corrections made by Johnson in the editions of 1773 and 1778 have been incorporated, and are pointed out in the notes.

In 1745 Johnson had published his *Miscellaneous Observations on the Tragedy of Macbeth: with Remarks on Sir T. H.'s Edition of Shakespear. To which is affix'd, Proposals for a new Edition of Shakespear, with a Specimen.* This anonymous edition was to be in ten volumes printed by Edward Cave, but it met with no encouragement. It was opposed in an angry letter to Cave from Jacob Tonson, who claimed copyright in the text of Shakespeare with 'all the emendations to this time' (see Samuel Pegge, *Anonymiana*, 1818, p. 23); and Warburton's edition, which had been announced in 1740, might still be expected. Johnson waited till he had completed his labours on the *Dictionary* and issued

---

[1] This section was rewritten in May 1961.

new Proposals on 1 June 1756. In the interval he had written about Shakespeare in the famous Prologue which inaugurated Garrick's rule at Drury Lane, and had shadowed in *Rambler* essays and in the Dedication of Mrs. Charlotte Lennox's *Shakespear Illustrated*, 1753, much of what was to appear in final form in the Preface of 1765. It was one of the conditions of the Proposals that the edition was to be published by Christmas 1757. As in the case of the *Dictionary* Johnson underestimated the labour which was involved. In December 1757 we find him saying that he will publish about March, and in March he says before summer. He must have made considerable progress at this time, as, according to his own statement, 'many of the plays' were then printed. But its preparation was interrupted by *The Idler* (April 1758 to April 1760). Thereafter Johnson would appear to have done little to it till he was stirred to activity by the attack on his integrity in Churchill's *Ghost* (Book iii, October 1762):

> He for Subscribers baits his hook,
> And takes their cash—but where's the Book?

Good progress was mentioned by Thomas Percy to Richard Farmer in a letter written on 31 December 1763: 'By the bye Johnson's Edition will soon make its appearance: he has for these five or six weeks past retired to a Country-house at Twickenham belonging to Reynolds the Painter, where he is busily employed in putting the finishing hand to that work; resolved not to return to London till he has compleated it.' The edition at length appeared on 10 October 1765. 'In 1764 and 1765', says Boswell, 'it should seem that Dr. Johnson was so busily employed with his edition of Shakespeare as to have had little leisure for any other literary exertion, or indeed even for private correspondence.' The Preface as set in the later edition of 1765 was published by itself with the title *Mr. Johnson's Preface To his Edition of Shakespear's Plays*.

It immediately attracted great attention. The *Monthly Review* lost no time in devoting two articles (October and November) to an attack which examines Johnson's arguments against 'the unities', and maintains that there is hardly one of them that does not seem false, or foreign to the purpose. The *Critical Review*, on the other hand, pronounces them 'worthy of Mr. Johnson's pen'; and the *London Magazine* admits their force, though it wishes that Johnson had 'rather retained the character of a reasoner than assumed that of a pleader'. The writer of the articles in the *Monthly Review* was William Kenrick, who at the very same time published under his own name a substantial pamphlet on the 'most glaring blunders' in the notes on the plays, *A Review of Doctor Johnson's New Edition of Shakespeare: in which the Ignorance or Inattention of that Editor is exposed, and the Poet defended from the Persecution of his Commentators. By W. Kenrick*, 1765 (reviewed in *The Gentleman's Magazine* for November). Johnson was 'above answering for himself', but James Barclay, an Oxford undergraduate of Balliol College, replied for him, to his annoyance, in *An Examination of Mr. Kenrick's Review*, 1766; and this was followed by *A Defence of Mr. Kenrick's Review . . . By a Friend*, which was written by Kenrick himself, in reply to his critics in general. Of the many reviews, notices, and pamphlets perhaps none is better known now than *Observations and Conjectures upon some Passages of Shakespeare*, 1766, an anonymous pamphlet published by the Clarendon Press in which Thomas Tyrwhitt anticipated his great work as a Chaucerian and Aristotelian scholar. Though he declares that he did not 'mean to enter into the merits of Mr. Johnson's performance', the little book is in effect an examination of Johnson's edition. But no less important at the time were George Colman's contributions to *The St. James's Chronicle* beginning with a review of the Preface and leading to comments on the notes. Explanations and conjectures soon became a regular feature of this newspaper, and on 8 March 1766 Johnson could say in a private letter that he had 'maintained the newspapers these many weeks' (see George Colman, *Prose on Several Occasions*, 1787, vol. ii, p. 59, and Johnson, *Letters*, ed. R. W. Chapman, 1952, vol. i, pp. 182 and 426).

RICHARD FARMER

FARMER'S *Essay on the Learning of Shakespeare* was published at Cambridge early in January 1767. In the Preface to the second and enlarged edition, which appeared in the same year, Farmer says that 'the few who have been pleased to controvert any part of his doctrine have favoured him with better manners than arguments'. This remark, like most of the Preface, appears to be directed chiefly at the prejudiced notice which appeared in the *Critical Review* for January 1767. The writer of it was well versed in the controversy, for he had expressed his opinion unhesitatingly in an earlier number, and he lost no time in advancing new evidence in opposition to Farmer's doctrine; but he only provided Farmer with new proofs, which were at once incorporated in the text of the Essay. The third edition, which was called for in 1789, differs from the second only by the inclusion of a short 'advertisement' and a final note explaining that Farmer had abandoned his intention of publishing the *Antiquities of Leicester*. In the 'Advertisement' he admits that 'a few corrections might probably be made, and many additional proofs of the argument have necessarily occurred in more than twenty years'; but he did not think it necessary to make any changes. He was content to leave the book in the hands of the printers, and accordingly he is still described on the title-page as 'Fellow of Emmanuel College, Cambridge', though he had succeeded to the mastership of his college in 1775.

Farmer had, however, already supplemented his Essay by a letter to Steevens, who printed it as an appendix to his edition of Johnson's Shakespeare in 1773. 'The track of reading', says Farmer, 'which I sometime ago endeavoured to prove more immediately necessary to a commentator on Shakespeare, you have very successfully followed, and have consequently superseded some remarks which I might otherwise have troubled you with. Those I now send you are such as I marked on the margin of the copy you were so kind to communicate to me, and

bear a very small proportion to the miscellaneous collections of
this sort which I may probably put together some time or other.'
Farmer did not carry out this intention, and the *Essay on the
Learning of Shakespeare* remains his only independent publication.

MAURICE MORGANN

MORGANN has himself told us in his Preface all that we know
about the composition of his *Essay on the Dramatic Character of Sir
John Falstaff*. The result of a challenge arising out of a friendly
conversation, it was written 'in a very short time' in 1774, and
then laid aside and almost forgotten. But for the advice of friends
it would probably have remained in manuscript, and been
destroyed, like his other critical works, at his death. On their
suggestion he revised and enlarged it, as hastily as he had written
it; and it appeared anonymously in the spring of 1777. The
original purpose of the Essay is indicated by the motto on the
title-page: 'I am not John of Gaunt your grandfather, but yet
no Coward, Hal'; but as Morgann wrote he passed from Falstaff
to the greater theme of Falstaff's creator. He was persuaded to
publish his Essay because, though it dealt nominally with one
character, its main subject was the art of Shakespeare. For the
same reason it finds a place in this volume.

In 1744 Corbyn Morris had briefly analysed the character of
Falstaff in his *Essay towards fixing the true standards of Wit, Humour,
Raillery, Satire, and Ridicule*; Mrs. Montagu had expressed the
common opinion of his cowardice in her *Essay on the Writings and
Genius of Shakespeare*; the *Biographia Britannica* had declared him
to be Shakespeare's masterpiece; while his popularity had led
Kenrick to produce in 1766 *Falstaff's Wedding* as a sequel to the
second part of *Henry IV*; but Morgann's Essay is the first detailed
examination of his character. He was afterwards the subject of
papers by Cumberland in the *Observer* (1785, No. 73), and by
Henry Mackenzie in the *Lounger* (1786, Nos. 68, 69), and in
1789 he was described by Richardson in an essay which

reproduced Morgann's title. None of these later works have the interest attaching to James White's *Falstaff's Letters* (1796).

The *Essay on Falstaff* was republished, with a short biographical preface, in 1820, and a third and last edition came out in 1825. What is apparently the first detailed criticism of it occurs in the *London Magazine* for February 1820.

NICHOLAS ROWE

Some Account of the Life *&c.* of Mr. William Shakespear

1709

IT seems to be a kind of Respect due to the Memory of Excellent Men, especially of those whom their Wit and Learning have made Famous, to deliver some Account of themselves, as well as their Works, to Posterity. For this Reason, how fond do we see some People of discovering any little Personal Story of the great Men of Antiquity, their Families, the common Accidents of their Lives, and even their Shape, Make and Features have been the Subject of critical Enquiries. How trifling soever this Curiosity may seem to be, it is certainly very Natural; and we are hardly satisfy'd with an Account of any remarkable Person, 'till we have heard him describ'd even to the very Cloaths he wears. As for what relates to Men of Letters, the knowledge of an Author may sometimes conduce to the better understanding his Book: And tho' the Works of Mr. *Shakespear* may seem to many not to want a Comment, yet I fancy some little Account of the Man himself may not be thought improper to go along with them.

He was the Son of Mr. *John Shakespear*, and was Born at *Stratford* upon *Avon*, in *Warwickshire*, in *April* 1564. His Family, as appears by the Register and Publick Writings relating to that Town, were of good Figure and Fashion there, and are mention'd as Gentlemen. His Father, who was a considerable Dealer in Wool, had so large a Family, ten Children in all, that tho' he was his eldest Son, he could give him no better Education than his own Employment. He had bred him, 'tis true, for some time at a Free-School, where 'tis probable he acquir'd that little *Latin* he was Master of: But the narrowness of his Circumstances, and

the want of his assistance at Home, forc'd his Father to withdraw him from thence, and unhappily prevented his further
Proficiency in that Language. It is without Controversie, that he
had no knowledge of the Writings of the Antient Poets, not only
from this Reason, but from his Works themselves, where we
find no traces of any thing that looks like an Imitation of 'em;
the Delicacy of his Taste, and the natural Bent of his own Great
Genius, equal, if not superior to some of the best of theirs, would
certainly have led him to Read and Study 'em with so much
Pleasure, that some of their fine Images would naturally have
insinuated themselves into, and been mix'd with his own
Writings; so that his not copying at least something from them,
may be an Argument of his never having read 'em. Whether his
Ignorance of the Antients were a disadvantage to him or no, may
admit of a Dispute: For tho' the knowledge of 'em might have
made him more Correct, yet it is not improbable but that the
Regularity and Deference for them, which would have attended
that Correctness, might have restrain'd some of that Fire,
Impetuosity, and even beautiful Extravagance which we admire
in *Shakespear:* And I believe we are better pleas'd with those
Thoughts, altogether New and Uncommon, which his own
Imagination supply'd him so abundantly with, than if he had
given us the most beautiful Passages out of the *Greek* and *Latin*
Poets, and that in the most agreeable manner that it was possible
for a Master of the *English* Language to deliver 'em. Some *Latin*
without question he did know, and one may see up and down in
his Plays how far his Reading that way went: In *Love's Labour
lost*, the Pedant comes out with a Verse of *Mantuan*; and in
Titus Andronicus, one of the *Gothick* Princes, upon reading

> *Integer vitæ scelerisque purus*
> *Non eget Mauri jaculis nec arcu—*

says, *'Tis a Verse in* Horace, *but he remembers it out of his* Grammar:
Which, I suppose, was the Author's Case. Whatever *Latin* he
had, 'tis certain he understood *French*, as may be observ'd from
many Words and Sentences scatter'd up and down his Plays in

that Language; and especially from one Scene in *Henry* the Fifth written wholly in it. Upon his leaving School, he seems to have given intirely into that way of Living which his Father propos'd to him; and in order to settle in the World after a Family manner, he thought fit to marry while he was yet very Young. His Wife was the Daughter of one *Hathaway*, said to have been a substantial Yeoman in the Neighbourhood of *Stratford*. In this kind of Settlement he continu'd for some time, 'till an Extravagance that he was guilty of, forc'd him both out of his Country and that way of Living which he had taken up; and tho' it seem'd at first to be a Blemish upon his good Manners, and a Misfortune to him, yet it afterwards happily prov'd the occasion of exerting one of the greatest *Genius's* that ever was known in Dramatick Poetry. He had, by a Misfortune common enough to young Fellows, fallen into ill Company; and amongst them, some that made a frequent practice of Deer-stealing, engag'd him with them more than once in robbing a Park that belong'd to Sir *Thomas Lucy* of *Cherlecot*, near *Stratford*. For this he was prosecuted by that Gentleman, as he thought, somewhat too severely; and in order to revenge that ill Usage, he made a Ballad upon him. And tho' this, probably the first Essay of his Poetry, be lost, yet it is said to have been so very bitter, that it redoubled the Prosecution against him to that degree, that he was oblig'd to leave his Business and Family in *Warwickshire*, for some time, and shelter himself in *London*.

It is at this Time, and upon this Accident, that he is said to have made his first Acquaintance in the Play-house. He was receiv'd into the Company then in being, at first in a very mean Rank; But his admirable Wit, and the natural Turn of it to the Stage, soon distinguish'd him, if not as an extraordinary Actor, yet as an excellent Writer. His Name is Printed, as the Custom was in those Times, amongst those of the other Players, before some old Plays, but without any particular Account of what sort of Parts he us'd to play; and tho' I have inquir'd, I could never meet with any further Account of him this way, than that the top of his Performance was the Ghost in his own *Hamlet*. I should have been much more pleas'd, to have learn'd from some certain Authority, which was the first Play he wrote; it would be without doubt a pleasure to any Man, curious in Things of this Kind, to see and know what was the first Essay of a Fancy like *Shakespear*'s. Perhaps we are not to look for his Beginnings, like those of other Authors, among their least perfect Writings; Art had so little, and Nature so large a Share in what he did, that, for ought I know, the Performances of his Youth, as they were the most vigorous, and had the most fire and strength of Imagination in 'em, were the best. I would not be thought by this to mean, that his Fancy was so loose and extravagant, as to be Independent on the Rule and Government of Judgment; but that what he thought, was commonly so Great, so justly and rightly Conceiv'd in it self, that it wanted little or no Correction, and was immediately approv'd by an impartial Judgment at the first sight. Mr. *Dryden* seems to think that *Pericles* is one of his first Plays; but there is no judgment to be form'd on that, since there is good Reason to believe that the greatest part of that Play was not written by him; tho' it is own'd, some part of it certainly was, particularly the last Act. But tho' the order of Time in which the several Pieces were written be generally uncertain, yet there are Passages in some few of them which seem to fix their Dates. So the *Chorus* in the beginning of the fifth Act of *Henry* V. by a Compliment very handsomly turn'd to the Earl of *Essex*, shews the Play to have been written when that Lord was General for the Queen in *Ireland:* And his Elogy upon Q. *Elizabeth*, and her Successor K. *James*, in the latter end of his *Henry* VIII, is a Proof of that Play's being written after the Accession of the latter of those two Princes to the Crown of *England*. Whatever the particular Times of his Writing were, the People of his Age, who began to grow wonderfully fond of Diversions of this kind, could not but be highly pleas'd to see a *Genius* arise amongst 'em of so pleasurable, so rich a Vein, and so plentifully capable of furnishing their favourite Entertainments. Besides the advantages of his Wit, he was in himself a good-natur'd Man, of great sweetness in his Manners, and a most agreeable Companion; so that it is no wonder if with so many good Qualities he made himself acquainted with the best Conversations of those Times. Queen *Elizabeth* had several of his Plays Acted before her, and without doubt gave him many gracious Marks of her Favour: It is that Maiden Princess plainly, whom he intends by

—*A fair Vestal, Throned by the West.*
Midsummer Night's Dream, Vol. 2. p. 480.

And that whole Passage is a Compliment very properly brought in, and very handsomly apply'd to her. She was so well pleas'd with that admirable Character of *Falstaff*, in the two Parts of *Henry* the Fourth, that she commanded him to continue it for one Play more, and to shew him in Love. This is said to be the Occasion of his Writing *The Merry Wives of* Windsor. How well she was obey'd, the Play it self is an admirable Proof. Upon this Occasion it may not be improper to observe, that this Part of *Falstaff* is said to have been written originally under the Name of *Oldcastle*; some of that Family being then remaining, the Queen was pleas'd to command him to alter it; upon which he made use of *Falstaff*. The present Offence was indeed avoided; but I don't know whether the Author may not have been somewhat to blame in his second Choice, since it is certain that Sir *John Falstaff*, who was a Knight of the Garter, and a Lieutenant-General, was a Name of distinguish'd Merit in the Wars in *France* in *Henry* the Fifth's and *Henry* the Sixth's Times. What Grace soever the Queen confer'd upon him, it was not to her only he ow'd the Fortune which the Reputation of his Wit made. He had the Honour to meet with many great and uncommon Marks of Favour and Friendship from the Earl of *Southampton*, famous in the Histories of that Time for his Friendship to the unfortunate Earl of *Essex*. It was to that Noble Lord that he Dedicated his *Venus* and *Adonis*, the only Piece of his Poetry which he ever publish'd himself, tho' many of his Plays were surrepticiously and lamely Printed in his Life-time. There is one Instance so singular in the Magnificence of this Patron of *Shakespear*'s, that if I had not been assur'd that the Story was handed down by Sir

William D'Avenant, who was probably very well acquainted with his Affairs, I should not have ventur'd to have inserted, that my Lord *Southampton*, at one time, gave him a thousand Pounds, to enable him to go through with a Purchase which he heard he had a mind to. A Bounty very great, and very rare at any time, and almost equal to that profuse Generosity the present Age has shewn to *French* Dancers and *Italian* Eunuchs.

What particular Habitude or Friendships he contracted with private Men, I have not been able to learn, more than that every one who had a true Taste of Merit, and could distinguish Men, had generally a just Value and Esteem for him. His exceeding Candor and good Nature must certainly have inclin'd all the gentler Part of the World to love him, as the power of his Wit oblig'd the Men of the most delicate Knowledge and polite Learning to admire him. Amongst these was the incomparable Mr. *Edmond Spencer*, who speaks of him in his *Tears of the Muses*, not only with the Praises due to a good Poet, but even lamenting his Absence with the tenderness of a Friend. The Passage is in *Thalia*'s Complaint for the Decay of Dramatick Poetry, and the Contempt the Stage then lay under, amongst his Miscellaneous Works, *p.* 147.

> *And he the Man, whom Nature's self had made*
> *To mock her self, and Truth to imitate*
> *With kindly Counter under mimick Shade,*
> *Our pleasant* Willy, *ah! is dead of late:*
> *With whom all Joy and jolly Merriment*
> *Is also deaded, and in Dolour drent.*
>
> *Instead thereof, scoffing Scurrility*
> *And scorning Folly with Contempt is crept,*
> *Rolling in Rhimes of shameless Ribaudry,*
> *Without Regard or due Decorum kept;*
> *Each idle Wit at will presumes to make,*
> *And doth the Learned's Task upon him take.*
>
> *But that same gentle Spirit, from whose Pen*
> *Large Streams of Honey and sweet Nectar flow,*
> *Scorning the Boldness of such base-born Men,*
> *Which dare their Follies forth so rashly throw;*

Doth rather choose to sit in idle Cell,
Than so himself to Mockery to sell.

I know some People have been of Opinion, that *Shakespear* is
not meant by *Willy* in the first *Stanza* of these Verses, because
Spencer's Death happen'd twenty Years before *Shakespear*'s. But,
besides that the Character is not applicable to any Man of that
time but himself, it is plain by the last *Stanza* that Mr. *Spencer*
does not mean that he was then really Dead, but only that
he had with-drawn himself from the Publick, or at least withheld his Hand from Writing, out of a disgust he had taken at the
then ill taste of the Town, and the mean Condition of the Stage.
Mr. *Dryden* was always of Opinion these Verses were meant of
Shakespear; and 'tis highly probable they were so, since he was
three and thirty Years old at *Spencer*'s Death; and his Reputation
in Poetry must have been great enough before that Time to
have deserv'd what is here said of him. His Acquaintance with
Ben Johnson began with a remarkable piece of Humanity and
good Nature; Mr. *Johnson*, who was at that Time altogether
unknown to the World, had offer'd one of his Plays to the Players,
in order to have it Acted; and the Persons into whose Hands it
was put, after having turn'd it carelessly and superciliously over,
were just upon returning it to him with an ill-natur'd Answer,
that it would be of no service to their Company, when *Shakespear*
luckily cast his Eye upon it, and found something so well in it as
to engage him first to read it through, and afterwards to recommend Mr. *Johnson* and his Writings to the Publick. After this
they were profess'd Friends; tho' I don't know whether the other
ever made him an equal return of Gentleness and Sincerity. *Ben*
was naturally Proud and Insolent, and in the Days of his Reputation did so far take upon him the Supremacy in Wit, that he
could not but look with an evil Eye upon any one that seem'd to
stand in Competition with him. And if at times he has affected
to commend him, it has always been with some Reserve, insinuating his Uncorrectness, a careless manner of Writing, and
want of Judgment; the Praise of seldom altering or blotting out
what he writ, which was given him by the Players who were the

first Publishers of his Works after his Death, was what *Johnson* could not bear; he thought it impossible, perhaps, for another Man to strike out the greatest Thoughts in the finest Expression, and to reach those Excellencies of Poetry with the Ease of a first Imagination, which himself with infinite Labour and Study could but hardly attain to. *Johnson* was certainly a very good Scholar, and in that had the advantage of *Shakespear*; tho' at the same time I believe it must be allow'd, that what Nature gave the latter, was more than a Ballance for what Books had given the former; and the Judgment of a great Man upon this occasion was, I think, very just and proper. In a Conversation between Sir *John Suckling*, Sir *William D'Avenant*, *Endymion Porter*, Mr. *Hales* of *Eaton*, and *Ben Johnson*; Sir *John Suckling*, who was a profess'd Admirer of *Shakespear*, had undertaken his Defence against *Ben Johnson* with some warmth; Mr. *Hales*, who had sat still for some time, hearing *Ben* frequently reproaching him with the want of Learning, and Ignorance of the Antients, told him at last, *That if Mr.* Shakespear *had not read the Antients, he had likewise not stollen any thing from 'em;* (a Fault the other made no Conscience of) *and that if he would produce any one Topick finely treated by any of them, he would undertake to shew something upon the same Subject at least as well written by* Shakespear. *Johnson* did indeed take a large liberty, even to the transcribing and translating of whole Scenes together; and sometimes, with all Deference to so great a Name as his, not altogether for the advantage of the Authors of whom he borrow'd. And if *Augustus* and *Virgil* were really what he has made 'em in a Scene of his *Poetaster*, they are as odd an Emperor and a Poet as ever met. *Shakespear*, on the other Hand, was beholding to no body farther than the Foundation of the Tale, the Incidents were often his own, and the Writing intirely so. There is one Play of his, indeed, *The Comedy of Errors*, in a great measure taken from the *Menæchmi* of *Plautus*. How that happen'd, I cannot easily Divine, since, as I hinted before, I do not take him to have been Master of *Latin* enough to read it in the Original, and I know of no Translation of *Plautus* so Old as his Time.

As I have not propos'd to my self to enter into a Large and Compleat Criticism upon Mr. *Shakespear*'s Works, so I suppose it will neither be expected that I should take notice of the severe Remarks that have been formerly made upon him by Mr. *Rhymer*. I must confess, I can't very well see what could be the Reason of his animadverting with so much Sharpness, upon the Faults of a Man Excellent on most Occasions, and whom all the World ever was and will be inclin'd to have an Esteem and Veneration for. If it was to shew his own Knowledge in the Art of Poetry, besides that there is a Vanity in making that only his Design, I question if there be not many Imperfections as well in those Schemes and Precepts he has given for the Direction of others, as well as in that Sample of Tragedy which he has written to shew the Excellency of his own *Genius*. If he had a Pique against the Man, and wrote on purpose to ruin a Reputation so well establish'd, he has had the Mortification to fail altogether in his Attempt, and to see the World at least as fond of *Shakespear* as of his Critique. But I won't believe a Gentleman, and a good-natur'd Man, capable of the last Intention. Whatever may have been his Meaning, finding fault is certainly the easiest Task of Knowledge, and commonly those Men of good Judgment, who are likewise of good and gentle Dispositions, abandon this un-grateful Province to the Tyranny of Pedants. If one would enter into the Beauties of *Shakespear*, there is a much larger, as well as a more delightful Field; but as I won't prescribe to the Tastes of other People, so I will only take the liberty, with all due Submis-sion to the Judgment of others, to observe some of those Things I have been pleas'd with in looking him over.

His Plays are properly to be distinguish'd only into Comedies and Tragedies. Those which are called Histories, and even some of his Comedies, are really Tragedies, with a run or mixture of Comedy amongst 'em. That way of Trage-Comedy was the common Mistake of that Age, and is indeed become so agreeable to the *English* Tast, that tho' the severer Critiques among us cannot bear it, yet the generality of our Audiences seem to be better pleas'd with it than with an exact Tragedy. *The Merry*

Wives of Windsor, *The Comedy of Errors,* and *The Taming of the Shrew,* are all pure Comedy; the rest, however they are call'd, have something of both Kinds. 'Tis not very easie to determine which way of Writing he was most Excellent in. There is certainly a great deal of Entertainment in his Comical Humours; and tho' they did not then strike at all Ranks of People, as the Satyr of the present Age has taken the Liberty to do, yet there is a pleasing and a well-distinguish'd Variety in those Characters which he thought fit to meddle with. *Falstaff* is allow'd by every body to be a Master-piece; the Character is always well-sustain'd, tho' drawn out into the length of three Plays; and even the Account of his Death, given by his Old Landlady Mrs. *Quickly,* in the first Act of *Henry* V. tho' it be extremely Natural, is yet as diverting as any Part of his Life. If there be any Fault in the Draught he has made of this lewd old Fellow, it is, that tho' he has made him a Thief, Lying, Cowardly, Vain-glorious, and in short every way Vicious, yet he has given him so much Wit as to make him almost too agreeable; and I don't know whether some People have not, in remembrance of the Diversion he had formerly afforded 'em, been sorry to see his Friend *Hal* use him so scurvily, when he comes to the Crown in the End of the Second Part of *Henry* the Fourth. Amongst other Extravagances, in *The Merry Wives of* Windsor, he has made him a Deer-stealer, that he might at the same time remember his *Warwickshire* Prosecutor, under the Name of Justice *Shallow*; he has given him very near the same Coat of Arms which *Dugdale,* in his Antiquities of that County, describes for a Family there, and makes the *Welsh* Parson descant very pleasantly upon 'em. That whole Play is admirable; the Humours are various and well oppos'd; the main Design, which is to cure *Ford* of his unreasonable Jealousie, is extremely well conducted. *Falstaff's Billet-doux,* and Master *Slender's*

Ah! Sweet Ann Page!

are very good Expressions of Love in their Way. In *Twelfth-Night* there is something singularly Ridiculous and Pleasant in the fantastical Steward *Malvolio*. The Parasite and the Vain-glorious in *Parolles*, in *All's Well that ends Well*, is as good as any thing of that Kind in *Plautus* or *Terence*. *Petruchio*, in *The Taming of the Shrew*, is an uncommon Piece of Humour. The Conversation of *Benedick* and *Beatrice*, in *Much ado about Nothing*, and of *Rosalind* in *As you like it*, have much Wit and Sprightliness all along. His Clowns, without which Character there was hardly any Play writ in that Time, are all very entertaining: And, I believe, *Thersites* in *Troilus* and *Cressida*, and *Apemantus* in *Timon*, will be allow'd to be Master-Pieces of ill Nature, and satyrical Snarling. To these I might add, that incomparable Character of *Shylock* the *Jew*, in *The Merchant of* Venice; but tho' we have seen that Play Receiv'd and Acted as a Comedy, and the Part of the *Jew* perform'd by an Excellent Comedian, yet I cannot but think it was design'd Tragically by the Author. There appears in it such a deadly Spirit of Revenge, such a savage Fierceness and Fellness, and such a bloody designation of Cruelty and Mischief, as cannot agree either with the Stile or Characters of Comedy. The Play it self, take it all together, seems to me to be one of the most finish'd of any of *Shakespear*'s. The Tale indeed, in that Part relating to the Caskets, and the extravagant and unusual kind of Bond given by *Antonio*, is a little too much remov'd from the Rules of Probability: But taking the Fact for granted, we must allow it to be very beautifully written. There is something in the Friendship of *Antonio* to *Bassanio* very Great, Generous and Tender. The whole fourth Act, supposing, as I said, the Fact to be probable, is extremely Fine. But there are two Passages that deserve a particular Notice. The first is, what *Portia* says in praise of Mercy, *pag.* 577; and the other on the Power of Musick, *pag.* 587. The Melancholy of *Jaques*, in *As you like it*, is as singular and odd as it is diverting. And if what *Horace* says

Difficile est proprie communia Dicere,

'Twill be a hard Task for any one to go beyond him in the Description of the several Degrees and Ages of Man's Life, tho' the Thought be old, and common enough.

><u>All the World's a Stage</u>,
><u>And all the Men and Women meerly Players</u>;
><u>They have their Exits and their Entrances</u>,
><u>And one Man in his time plays many Parts</u>,
><u>His Acts being seven Ages. At first the Infant</u>
><u>Mewling and puking in the Nurse's Arms</u>:
><u>And then, the whining School-boy with his Satchel</u>,
><u>And shining Morning-face, creeping like Snail</u>
><u>Unwillingly to School. And then the Lover</u>
><u>Sighing like Furnace, with a woful Ballad</u>
><u>Made to his Mistress' Eye-brow. Then a Soldier</u>
><u>Full of strange Oaths, and bearded like the Pard</u>,
><u>Jealous in Honour, sudden and quick in Quarrel</u>,
><u>Seeking the bubble Reputation</u>
><u>Ev'n in the Cannon's Mouth. And then the Justice</u>
><u>In fair round Belly, with good Capon lin'd</u>,
><u>With Eyes severe, and Beard of formal Cut</u>,
><u>Full of wise Saws and modern Instances</u>;
><u>And so he plays his Part. The sixth Age shifts</u>
><u>Into the lean and slipper'd Pantaloon</u>,
><u>With Spectacles on Nose, and Pouch on Side</u>;
><u>His youthful Hose, well sav'd, a world too wide</u>
><u>For his shrunk Shank; and his big manly Voice</u>
><u>Turning again tow'rd childish treble Pipes</u>,
><u>And Whistles in his Sound. Last Scene of all</u>,
><u>That ends this strange eventful History</u>,
><u>Is second Childishness and meer Oblivion</u>,
><u>Sans Teeth, sans Eyes, sans Tast, sans ev'ry thing</u>.
>
>   p. 625.

His Images are indeed ev'ry where so lively, that the Thing
he would represent stands full before you, and you possess ev'ry
Part of it. I will venture to point out one more, which is, I think,
as strong and as uncommon as any thing I ever saw; 'tis an
Image of Patience. Speaking of a Maid in Love, he says,

><u>She never told her Love</u>,
><u>But let Concealment, like a Worm i'th' Bud</u>
><u>Feed on her Damask Cheek: She pin'd in Thought</u>,

And sate like Patience *on a Monument,*
Smiling at Grief.

What an Image is here given! and what a Task would it have
been for the greatest Masters of *Greece* and *Rome* to have express'd
the Passions design'd by this Sketch of Statuary? The Stile of
his Comedy is, in general, Natural to the Characters, and easie
in it self; and the Wit most commonly sprightly and pleasing,
except in those places where he runs into Dogrel Rhymes, as in
The Comedy of Errors, and a Passage or two in some other Plays. As
for his Jingling sometimes, and playing upon Words, it was the
common Vice of the Age he liv'd in: And if we find it in the
Pulpit, made use of as an Ornament to the Sermons of some of
the Gravest Divines of those Times; perhaps it may not be
thought too light for the Stage.

But certainly the greatness of this Author's Genius do's no
where so much appear, as where he gives his Imagination an
entire Loose, and raises his Fancy to a flight above Mankind
and the Limits of the visible World. Such are his Attempts in
The Tempest, Midsummer-Night's Dream, Macbeth and *Hamlet*. Of
these, *The Tempest*, however it comes to be plac'd the first by the
former Publishers of his Works, can never have been the first
written by him: It seems to me as perfect in its Kind, as almost
any thing we have of his. One may observe, that the Unities are
kept here with an Exactness uncommon to the Liberties of his
Writing: Tho' that was what, I suppose, he valu'd himself least
upon, since his Excellencies were all of another Kind. I am very
sensible that he do's, in this Play, depart too much from that
likeness to Truth which ought to be observ'd in these sort of
Writings; yet he do's it so very finely, that one is easily drawn
in to have more Faith for his sake, than Reason does well allow
of. His Magick has something in it very Solemn and very Poetical:
And that extravagant Character of *Caliban* is mighty well sustain'd, shews a wonderful Invention in the Author, who could
strike out such a particular wild Image, and is certainly one of the
finest and most uncommon Grotesques that was ever seen. The

Observation, which I have been inform'd *three very great Men concurr'd in making upon this Part, was extremely just. *That Shakespear had not only found out a new Character in his Caliban, but had also devis'd and adapted a new manner of Language for that Character.* Among the particular Beauties of this Piece, I think one may be allow'd to point out the Tale of *Prospero* in the First Act; his Speech to *Ferdinand* in the Fourth, upon the breaking up the Masque of *Juno* and *Ceres*; and that in the Fifth, where he dissolves his Charms, and resolves to break his Magick Rod. This Play has been alter'd by Sir *William D'Avenant* and Mr. *Dryden*; and tho' I won't Arraign the Judgment of those two great Men, yet I think I may be allow'd to say, that there are some things left out by them, that might, and even ought to have been kept in. Mr. *Dryden* was an Admirer of our Author, and, indeed, he owed him a great deal, as those who have read them both may very easily observe. And, I think, in Justice to 'em both, I should not on this Occasion omit what Mr. *Dryden* has said of him.

> *Shakespear, who, taught by none, did first impart*
> *To* Fletcher *Wit, to lab'ring* Johnson *Art.*
> *He,* Monarch-like, *gave those his Subjects Law,*
> *And is that Nature which they Paint and Draw.*
> Fletcher *reach'd that which on his heights did grow,*
> *Whilst* Johnson *crept and gather'd all below:*
> *This did his Love, and this his Mirth digest,*
> *One imitates him most, the other best.*
> *If they have since out-writ all other Men,*
> *'Tis with the Drops which fell from* Shakespear's *Pen.*
> *The* †*Storm which vanish'd on the neighb'ring Shoar,*
> *Was taught by* Shakespear's *Tempest first to roar.*
> *That Innocence and Beauty which did smile*
> *In* Fletcher, *grew on this Enchanted Isle.*
> *But* Shakespear's *Magick could not copied be,*
> *Within that Circle none durst walk but he.*
> *I must confess 'twas bold, nor would you now*
> *That Liberty to vulgar Wits allow,*

* Ld. Falkland, Ld. C. J. Vaughan, *and* Mr. Selden.
† Alluding to the Sea-Voyage of *Fletcher*.

Which works by Magick supernatural things:
But Shakespear's *Pow'r is Sacred as a King's.*

Prologue to The *Tempest,* as it is alter'd by Mr. *Dryden.*

It is the same Magick that raises the Fairies in *Midsummer Night's Dream,* the Witches in *Macbeth,* and the Ghost in *Hamlet,* with Thoughts and Language so proper to the Parts they sustain, and so peculiar to the Talent of this Writer. But of the two last of these Plays I shall have occasion to take notice, among the Tragedies of Mr. *Shakespear.* If one undertook to examine the greatest part of these by those Rules which are establish'd by *Aristotle,* and taken from the Model of the *Grecian* Stage, it would be no very hard Task to find a great many Faults: But as *Shakespear* liv'd under a kind of mere Light of Nature, and had never been made acquainted with the Regularity of those written Precepts, so it would be hard to judge him by a Law he knew nothing of. We are to consider him as a Man that liv'd in a State of almost universal License and Ignorance: There was no establish'd Judge, but every one took the liberty to Write according to the Dictates of his own Fancy. When one considers, that there is not one Play before him of a Reputation good enough to entitle it to an Appearance on the present Stage, it cannot but be a Matter of great Wonder that he should advance Dramatick Poetry so far as he did. The Fable is what is generally plac'd the first, among those that are reckon'd the constituent Parts of a Tragick or Heroick Poem; not, perhaps, as it is the most Difficult or Beautiful, but as it is the first properly to be thought of in the Contrivance and Course of the whole; and with the Fable ought to be consider'd, the fit Disposition, Order and Conduct of its several Parts. As it is not in this Province of the *Drama* that the Strength and Mastery of *Shakespear* lay, so I shall not undertake the tedious and ill-natur'd Trouble to point out the several Faults he was guilty of in it. His Tales were seldom invented, but rather taken either from true History, or Novels and Romances: And he commonly made use of 'em in that Order, with those Incidents, and that extent of Time in which he found 'em in the Authors from whence he borrow'd them. So *The Winter's Tale*, which is taken from an old Book, call'd, *The Delectable History of* Dorastus *and* Faunia, contains the space of sixteen or seventeen Years, and the Scene is sometimes laid in *Bohemia*, and sometimes in *Sicily*, according to the original Order of the Story. Almost all his Historical Plays comprehend a great length of Time, and very different and distinct Places: And in his *Antony and Cleopatra*, the Scene travels over the greatest Part of the *Roman* Empire. But in Recompence for his Carelessness in this Point, when he comes to another Part of the *Drama*, *The Manners of his Characters, in Acting or Speaking what is proper for them, and fit to be shown by the Poet*, he may be generally justify'd, and in very many places greatly commended. For those Plays which he has taken from the *English* or *Roman* History, let any Man compare 'em, and he will find the Character as exact in the Poet as the Historian. He seems indeed so far from proposing to himself any one Action for a Subject, that the Title very often tells you, 'tis *The Life of King* John, *King* Richard, &c. What can be more agreeable to the Idea our Historians give of *Henry* the Sixth, than the Picture *Shakespear* has drawn of him! His Manners are every where exactly the same with the Story; one finds him still describ'd with Simplicity, passive Sanctity, want of Courage, weakness of Mind, and easie Submission to the Governance of an imperious Wife, or prevailing Faction: Tho' at the same time the Poet do's Justice to his good Qualities, and moves the Pity of his Audience for him, by showing him Pious, Disinterested, a Contemner of the Things of this World, and wholly resign'd to the severest Dispensations of God's Providence. There is a short Scene in the Second Part of *Henry* VI. *Vol. III. pag.* 1504. which I cannot but think admirable in its Kind. Cardinal *Beaufort*, who had murder'd the Duke of *Gloucester*, is shewn in the last Agonies on his Death-Bed, with the good King praying over him. There is so much Terror in one, so much Tenderness and moving Piety in the other, as must touch any one who is capable either of Fear or Pity. In his *Henry* VIII. that Prince is drawn with that Greatness of Mind, and all those good Qualities which are attributed to him in any Account of his Reign. If his Faults are not shewn in an equal degree, and the Shades in this Picture do not bear a just Proportion to the Lights, it is not that the Artist wanted either Colours or Skill in the Disposition of 'em; but the truth, I believe, might be, that he forbore doing it out of regard to Queen *Elizabeth*, since it could have been no very great Respect to the Memory of his Mistress, to have expos'd some certain Parts of her Father's Life upon the Stage. He has dealt much more freely with the Minister of that Great King, and certainly nothing was ever more justly written, than the Character of Cardinal *Wolsey*. He has shewn him Tyrannical, Cruel, and Insolent in his Prosperity; and yet, by a wonderful Address, he makes his Fall and Ruin the Subject of general Compassion. The whole Man, with his Vices and Virtues, is finely and exactly describ'd in the second Scene of the fourth Act. The Distresses likewise of Queen *Katherine*, in this Play, are very movingly touch'd; and tho' the Art of the Poet has skreen'd King *Henry* from any gross Imputation of Injustice, yet one is inclin'd to wish, the Queen had met with a Fortune more worthy of her Birth and Virtue. Nor are the Manners, proper to the Persons represented, less justly observ'd, in those Characters taken from the *Roman* History; and of this, the Fierceness and Impatience of *Coriolanus*, his Courage and Disdain of the common People, the Virtue and Philosophical Temper of *Brutus*, and the irregular Greatness of Mind in *M. Antony*, are beautiful Proofs. For the two last especially, you find 'em exactly as they are describ'd by *Plutarch*, from whom certainly *Shakespear* copy'd 'em. He has indeed follow'd his Original pretty close, and taken in several little Incidents that might have been spar'd in a Play. But, as I hinted before, his Design seems most commonly rather to describe those great Men in the several Fortunes and Accidents of their Lives, than to take any single great Action, and form his Work simply upon that. However, there are some of his Pieces, where the Fable is founded upon one Action only. Such are more especially, *Romeo* and *Juliet*, *Hamlet*, and *Othello*. The Design in *Romeo* and *Juliet*, is plainly the Punishment of their

C

two Families, for the unreasonable Feuds and Animosities that had been so long kept up between 'em, and occasion'd the Effusion of so much Blood. In the management of this Story, he has shewn something wonderfully Tender and Passionate in the Love-part, and very Pitiful in the Distress. *Hamlet* is founded on much the same Tale with the *Electra* of *Sophocles*. In each of 'em a young Prince is engag'd to Revenge the Death of his Father, their Mothers are equally Guilty, are both concern'd in the Murder of their Husbands, and are afterwards married to the Murderers. There is in the first Part of the *Greek* Trajedy, something very moving in the Grief of *Electra*; but as Mr. *D'Acier* has observ'd, there is something very unnatural and shocking in the Manners he has given that Princess and *Orestes* in the latter Part. *Orestes* embrues his Hands in the Blood of his own Mother; and that barbarous Action is perform'd, tho' not immediately upon the Stage, yet so near, that the Audience hear *Clytemnestra* crying out to *Æghystus* for Help, and to her Son for Mercy: While *Electra*, her Daughter, and a Princess, both of them Characters that ought to have appear'd with more Decency, stands upon the Stage and encourages her Brother in the Parricide. What Horror does this not raise! *Clytemnestra* was a wicked Woman, and had deserv'd to Die; nay, in the truth of the Story, she was kill'd by her own Son; but to represent an Action of this Kind on the Stage, is certainly an Offence against those Rules of Manners proper to the Persons that ought to be observ'd there. On the contrary, let us only look a little on the Conduct of *Shakespear*. *Hamlet* is represented with the same Piety towards his Father, and Resolution to Revenge his Death, as *Orestes*; he has the same Abhorrence for his Mother's Guilt, which, to provoke him the more, is heighten'd by Incest: But 'tis with wonderful Art and Justness of Judgment, that the Poet restrains him from doing Violence to his Mother. To prevent any thing of that Kind, he makes his Father's Ghost forbid that part of his Vengeance.

> *But howsoever thou pursu'st this Act,*
> *Taint not thy Mind; nor let thy Soul contrive*
> *Against thy Mother ought; leave her to Heav'n,*

And to those Thorns that in her Bosom lodge,
To prick and sting her.   Vol. V. p. 2386.

This is to distinguish rightly between *Horror* and *Terror*. The
latter is a proper Passion of Tragedy, but the former ought
always to be carefully avoided. And certainly no Dramatick
Writer ever succeeded better in raising *Terror* in the Minds of
an Audience than *Shakespear* has done. The whole Tragedy of
Macbeth, but more especially the Scene where the King is murder'd, in the second Act, as well as this Play, is a noble Proof of
that manly Spirit with which he writ; and both shew how
powerful he was, in giving the strongest Motions to our Souls
that they are capable of. I cannot leave *Hamlet*, without taking
notice of the Advantage with which we have seen this Master-
piece of *Shakespear* distinguish it self upon the Stage, by Mr.
Betterton's fine Performance of that Part. A Man, who tho' he
had no other good Qualities, as he has a great many, must have
made his way into the Esteem of all Men of Letters, by this only
Excellency. No Man is better acquainted with *Shakespear*'s manner of Expression, and indeed he has study'd him so well, and is
so much a Master of him, that whatever Part of his he performs,
he does it as if it had been written on purpose for him, and that
the Author had exactly conceiv'd it as he plays it. I must own a
particular Obligation to him, for the most considerable part of
the Passages relating to his Life, which I have here transmitted
to the Publick; his Veneration for the Memory of *Shakespear*
having engag'd him to make a Journey into *Warwickshire*, on
purpose to gather up what Remains he could of a Name for which
he had so great a Value. Since I had at first resolv'd not to enter
into any Critical Controversie, I won't pretend to enquire into
the Justness of Mr. *Rhymer*'s Remarks on *Othello*; he has certainly pointed out some Faults very judiciously; and indeed they
are such as most People will agree, with him, to be Faults: But
I wish he would likewise have observ'd some of the Beauties too;
as I think it became an Exact and Equal Critique to do. It seems
strange that he should allow nothing Good in the whole: If the
Fable and Incidents are not to his Taste, yet the Thoughts are

almost every where very Noble, and the Diction manly and proper. These last, indeed, are Parts of *Shakespear*'s Praise, which it would be very hard to Dispute with him. His Sentiments and Images of Things are Great and Natural; and his Expression (tho' perhaps in some Instances a little Irregular) just, and rais'd in Proportion to his Subject and Occasion. It would be even endless to mention the particular Instances that might be given of this Kind: But his Book is in the Possession of the Publick, and 'twill be hard to dip into any Part of it, without finding what I have said of him made good.

The latter Part of his Life was spent, as all Men of good Sense will wish theirs may be, in Ease, Retirement, and the Conversation of his Friends. He had the good Fortune to gather an Estate equal to his Occasion, and, in that, to his Wish; and is said to have spent some Years before his Death at his native *Stratford*. His pleasurable Wit, and good Nature, engag'd him in the Acquaintance, and entitled him to the Friendship of the Gentlemen of the Neighbourhood. Amongst them, it is a Story almost still remember'd in that Country, that he had a particular Intimacy with Mr. *Combe*, an old Gentleman noted thereabouts for his Wealth and Usury: It happen'd, that in a pleasant Conversation amongst their common Friends, Mr. *Combe* told *Shakespear* in a laughing manner, that he fancy'd, he intended to write his Epitaph, if he happen'd to out-live him; and since he could not know what might be said of him when he was dead, he desir'd it might be done immediately: Upon which *Shakespear* gave him these four Verses.

> *Ten in the Hundred lies here ingrav'd,*
> *'Tis a Hundred to Ten, his Soul is not sav'd:*
> *If any Man ask, Who lies in this Tomb?*
> *Oh! ho! quoth the Devil, 'tis my* John-a-Combe.

But the Sharpness of the Satyr is said to have stung the Man so severely, that he never forgave it.

He Dy'd in the 53d Year of his Age, and was bury'd on the North side of the Chancel, in the Great Church at *Stratford*, where a Monument, as engrav'd in the Plate, is plac'd in the Wall. On his Grave-Stone underneath is,

> Good Friend, for Jesus sake, forbear
> To dig the Dust inclosed here.
> Blest be the Man that spares these Stones,
> And Curst be he that moves my Bones.

He had three Daughters, of which two liv'd to be marry'd; *Judith*, the Elder, to one Mr. *Thomas Quiney*, by whom she had three Sons, who all dy'd without Children; and *Susannah*, who was his Favourite, to Dr. *John Hall*, a Physician of good Reputation in that Country. She left one Child only, a Daughter, who was marry'd first to *Thomas Nash*, Esq; and afterwards to Sir *John Bernard* of *Abbington*, but dy'd likewise without Issue.

This is what I could learn of any Note, either relating to himself or Family: The Character of the Man is best seen in his Writings. But since *Ben Johnson* has made a sort of an Essay towards it in his *Discoveries*, tho', as I have before hinted, he was not very Cordial in his Friendship, I will venture to give it in his Words.

'I remember the Players have often mention'd it as an Honour 'to *Shakespear*, that in Writing (whatsoever he penn'd) he never 'blotted out a Line. My Answer hath been, *Would he had blotted* '*a thousand*, which they thought a malevolent Speech. I had not 'told Posterity this, but for their Ignorance, who chose that 'Circumstance to commend their Friend by, wherein he most 'faulted. And to justifie mine own Candor, (for I lov'd the Man, 'and do honour his Memory, on this side Idolatry, as much as 'any.) He was, indeed, Honest, and of an open and free Nature, 'had an Excellent Fancy, brave Notions, and gentle Expressions; 'wherein he flow'd with that Facility, that sometimes it was 'necessary he should be stopp'd: *Sufflaminandus erat*, as *Augustus* 'said of *Haterius*. His Wit was in his own Power, would the Rule 'of it had been so too. Many times he fell into those things could 'not escape Laughter; as when he said in the Person of *Cæsar*, 'one speaking to him,

'Cæsar *thou dost me Wrong.*

'He reply'd:

'Cæsar *did never Wrong, but with just Cause.*

'and such like, which were ridiculous. But he redeem'd his Vices 'with his Virtues: There was ever more in him to be Prais'd 'than to be Pardon'd.

As for the Passage which he mentions out of *Shakespear*, there is somewhat like it in *Julius Cæsar*, Vol. V. p. 2260. but without the Absurdity; nor did I ever meet with it in any Edition that I have seen, as quoted by Mr. *Johnson*. Besides his Plays in this Edition, there are two or three ascrib'd to him by Mr. *Langbain*, which I have never seen, and know nothing of. He writ likewise, *Venus* and *Adonis*, and *Tarquin* and *Lucrece*, in Stanza's, which have been printed in a late Collection of Poems. As to the Character given of him by *Ben Johnson*, there is a good deal true in it: But I believe it may be as well express'd by what *Horace* says of the first *Romans*, who wrote Tragedy upon the *Greek* Models, (or indeed translated 'em) in his Epistle to *Augustus*.

——*Naturâ sublimis & Acer*
Nam spirat Tragicum satis & fæliciter Audet,
Sed turpem putat in Chartis metuitq; Lituram.

There is a Book of Poems, publish'd in 1640, under the Name of Mr. *William Shakespear*, but as I have but very lately seen it, without an Opportunity of making any Judgment upon it, I won't pretend to determine, whether it be his or no.

JOHN DENNIS

On the Genius and Writings of Shakespear

1712

To Mr.——

LETTER I.

SIR, *Feb.* I. 17$\frac{10}{11}$.

I HERE send you the Tragedy of *Coriolanus*, which I have alter'd from the Original of *Shakespear*, and with it a short Account of the Genius and Writings of that Author, both which you desired me to send to you the last time I had the good Fortune to see you. But I send them both upon this condition, that you will with your usual Sincerity tell me your Sentiments both of the Poem and of the Criticism.

Shakespear was one of the greatest Genius's that the World e'er saw for the Tragick Stage. Tho' he lay under greater Disadvantages than any of his Successors, yet had he greater and more genuine Beauties than the best and greatest of them. And what makes the brightest Glory of his Character, those Beauties were entirely his own, and owing to the Force of his own Nature; whereas his Faults were owing to his Education, and to the Age that he liv'd in. One may say of him as they did of *Homer*, that he had none to imitate, and is himself inimitable. His Imaginations were often as just, as they were bold and strong. He had a natural Discretion which never cou'd have been taught him, and his Judgment was strong and penetrating. He seems to have wanted nothing but Time and Leisure for Thought, to have found out those Rules of which he appears so ignorant. His Characters are always drawn justly, exactly, graphically, except where he fail'd by not knowing History or the Poetical Art. He has for the most part more fairly distinguish'd them than any of his Successors have done, who have falsified them, or confounded them, by making Love the predominant Quality in all. He had so fine a Talent for touching the Passions, and they are so lively in him, and so truly in Nature, that they often touch us more without their due Preparations, than those of other Tragick Poets, who have all the Beauty of Design and all the Advantage of Incidents. His Master-Passion was Terror, which he has often mov'd so powerfully and so wonderfully, that we may justly conclude, that if he had had the Advantage of Art and Learning, he wou'd have surpass'd the very best and strongest of the Ancients. His Paintings are often so beautiful and so lively, so graceful and so powerful, especially where he uses them in order to move Terror, that there is nothing perhaps more accomplish'd in our *English* Poetry. His Sentiments for the most part in his best Tragedies, are noble, generous, easie and natural, and adapted to the Persons who use them. His Expression is in many Places good and pure after a hundred Years; simple tho' elevated, graceful tho' bold, and easie tho' strong. He seems to have been the very Original of our *English* Tragical Harmony; that is the Harmony of Blank Verse, diversifyed often by Dissyllable and Trissyllable Terminations. For that Diversity distinguishes it from Heroick Harmony, and, bringing it nearer to common Use, makes it more proper to gain Attention, and more fit for Action and Dialogue. Such Verse we make when we are writing Prose; we make such Verse in common Conversation.

If *Shakespear* had these great Qualities by Nature, what would he not have been, if he had join'd to so happy a Genius Learning and the Poetical Art? For want of the latter, our Author has sometimes made gross Mistakes in the Characters which he has drawn from History, against the Equality and Conveniency of Manners of his Dramatical Persons. Witness *Menenius* in the following Tragedy, whom he has made an errant Buffoon, which is a great Absurdity. For he might as well have imagin'd a grave majestick *Jack-Pudding*, as a Buffoon in a *Roman* Senator. *Aufidius* the General of the *Volscians* is shewn a base and a profligate Villain. He has offended against the Equality of the Manners even in his Hero himself. For *Coriolanus* who in the first part of the Tragedy is shewn so open, so frank, so violent, and so magnanimous, is represented in the latter part by *Aufidius*, which is contradicted by no one, a flattering, fawning, cringing, insinuating Traytor.

For want of this Poetical Art, *Shakespear* has introduced things into his Tragedies, which are against the Dignity of that noble Poem, as the Rabble in *Julius Cæsar*, and that in *Coriolanus*; tho' that in *Coriolanus* offends not only against the Dignity of Tragedy, but against the Truth of History likewise, and the Customs of Ancient *Rome*, and the Majesty of the *Roman* People, as we shall have occasion to shew anon.

For want of this Art, he has made his Incidents less moving, less surprizing, and less wonderful. He has been so far from seeking those fine Occasions to move with which an Action furnish'd according to Art would have furnish'd him, that he seems rather to have industriously avoided them. He makes *Coriolanus*, upon his Sentence of Banishment, take his leave of his Wife and his Mother out of sight of the Audience, and so has purposely as it were avoided a great occasion to move.

If we are willing to allow that *Shakespear*, by sticking to the bare Events of History, has mov'd more than any of his Successors, yet his just Admirers must confess, that if he had had the Poetical Art, he would have mov'd ten times more. For 'tis impossible that by a bare Historical Play he could move so much as he would have done by a Fable.

We find that a Romance entertains the generality of Mankind with more Satisfaction than History, if they read only to be entertain'd; but if they read History thro' Pride or Ambition, they bring their Passions along with them, and that alters the case. Nothing is more plain than that even in an Historical Relation some Parts of it, and some Events, please more than others. And therefore a Man of Judgment, who sees why they do so, may in forming a Fable, and disposing an Action, please more than an Historian can do. For the just Fiction of a Fable moves us more than an Historical Relation can do, for the two following Reasons: First, by reason of the Communication and mutual Dependence of its Parts. For if Passion springs from Motion, then the Obstruction of that Motion or a counter Motion must obstruct and check the Passion: And therefore an Historian and a Writer of Historical Plays, passing from Events of one nature to Events of another nature without a due Preparation, must of necessity stifle and confound one Passion by another. The second Reason why the Fiction of a Fable pleases us more than an Historical Relation can do, is, because in an Historical Relation we seldom are acquainted with the true Causes of Events; whereas in a feign'd Action which is duly constituted, that is, which has a just beginning, those Causes always appear. For 'tis observable, that both in a Poetical Fiction and an Historical Relation, those Events are the most entertaining, the most surprizing, and the most wonderful, in which Providence most plainly appears. And 'tis for this Reason that the Author of a just Fable must please more than the Writer of an Historical Relation. The Good must never fail to prosper, and the Bad must be always punish'd: Otherwise the Incidents, and particularly the Catastrophe which is the grand Incident, are liable to be imputed rather to Chance, than to Almighty Conduct and to Sovereign Justice. The want of this impartial Distribution of Justice makes the *Coriolanus* of *Shakespear* to be without Moral. 'Tis true indeed *Coriolanus* is kill'd by those Foreign Enemies with whom he had openly sided against his Country, which seems to be an Event worthy of Providence, and would look as if it were contriv'd by infinite Wisdom, and executed by supreme Justice, to make *Coriolanus* a dreadful Example to all who lead on Foreign Enemies to the Invasion of their native Country; if there were not something in the Fate of the other Characters, which gives occasion to doubt of it, and which suggests to the Sceptical Reader that this might happen by accident. For *Aufidius* the principal Murderer of *Coriolanus*, who in cold Blood gets him assassinated by Ruffians, instead of leaving him to the Law of the Country, and the Justice of the *Volscian* Senate, and who commits so black a Crime, not by any erroneous Zeal, or a mistaken publick Spirit, but thro' Jealousy, Envy, and inveterate Malice; this Assassinator not only survives, and survives un-unpunish'd, but seems to be rewarded for so detestable an Action, by engrossing all those Honours to himself which *Coriolanus* before had shar'd with him. But not only *Aufidius*, but the *Roman* Tribunes, *Sicinius* and *Brutus*, appear to me to cry aloud for Poetick Vengeance. For they are guilty of two Faults, neither of which ought to go unpunish'd: The first in procuring the Banishment of *Coriolanus*. If they were really jealous that *Coriolanus* had a Design on their Liberties, when he stood for the Consul-ship, it was but just that they should give him a Repulse; but to get the Champion and Defender of their Country banish'd upon a pretended Jealousy was a great deal too much, and could proceed from nothing but that Hatred and Malice which they had conceiv'd against him, for opposing their Institution. Their second Fault lay in procuring this Sentence by indirect Methods, by exasperating and inflaming the People by Artifices and In-sinuations, by taking a base Advantage of the Open-heartedness and Violence of *Coriolanus*, and by oppressing him with a Soph-istical Argument, that he aim'd at Sovereignty, because he had not deliver'd into the Publick Treasury the Spoils which he had taken from the *Antiates*. As if a Design of Sovereignty could be reasonably concluded from any one Act; or any one could think of bringing to pass such a Design, by eternally favouring the Patricians, and disobliging the Populace. For we need make no doubt, but that it was among the young Patricians that *Coriolanus* distributed the Spoils which were taken from the *Antiates*; whereas nothing but caressing the Populace could enslave the *Roman* People, as *Cæsar* afterwards very well saw and experi-enc'd. So that this Injustice of the Tribunes was the original Cause of the Calamity which afterwards befel their Country, by the Invasion of the *Volscians*, under the Conduct of *Coriolanus*. And yet these Tribunes at the end of the Play, like *Aufidius*,

remain unpunish'd. But indeed *Shakespear* has been wanting in the
exact Distribution of Poetical Justice not only in his *Coriolanus*,
but in most of his best Tragedies, in which the Guilty and the
Innocent perish promiscuously; as *Duncan* and *Banquo* in *Mack-
beth*, as likewise Lady *Macduffe* and her Children; *Desdemona* in
Othello; *Cordelia*, *Kent*, and King *Lear*, in the Tragedy that bears
his Name; *Brutus* and *Porcia* in *Julius Cæsar*; and young *Hamlet*
in the Tragedy of *Hamlet*. For tho' it may be said in Defence of
the last, that *Hamlet* had a Design to kill his Uncle who then
reign'd; yet this is justify'd by no less than a Call from Heaven,
and raising up one from the Dead to urge him to it. The Good
and the Bad then perishing promiscuously in the best of *Shakespear*'s Tragedies, there can be either none or very weak Instruction in them: For such promiscuous Events call the Government of Providence into Question, and by Scepticks and Liber-
tines are resolv'd into Chance. I humbly conceive therefore that
this want of Dramatical Justice in the Tragedy of *Coriolanus* gave
occasion for a just Alteration, and that I was oblig'd to sacrifice
to that Justice *Aufidius* and the Tribunes, as well as *Coriolanus*.

Thus have we endeavour'd to shew that, for want of the
Poetical Art, *Shakespear* lay under very great Disadvantages. At
the same time we must own to his Honour, that he has often
perform'd Wonders without it, in spight of the Judgment of so
great a Man as *Horace*.

> *Natura fieret laudabile carmen, an arte,*
> *Quæsitum est: ego nec studium sine divite vena,*
> *Nec rude quid prosit video ingenium; alterius sic*
> *Altera poscit opem res, & conjurat amice.*

But from this very Judgment of *Horace* we may justly conclude
that *Shakespear* would have wonderfully surpass'd himself, if Art
had been join'd to Nature. There never was a greater Genius in
the World than *Virgil*: He was one who seems to have been
born for this glorious End, that the *Roman* Muse might exert in
him the utmost Force of her Poetry: And his admirable and
divine Beauties are manifestly owing to the happy Confederacy

of Art and Nature. It was Art that contriv'd that incomparable
Design of the *Æneis*, and it was Nature that executed it. Could
the greatest Genius that ever was infus'd into Earthly Mold by
Heaven, if it had been unguided and unassisted by Art, have
taught him to make that noble and wonderful Use of the
Pythagorean Transmigration, which he makes in the Sixth Book
of his Poem? Had *Virgil* been a circular Poet, and closely adher'd
to History, how could the *Romans* have been transported with
that inimitable Episode of *Dido*, which brought a-fresh into their
Minds the *Carthaginian* War, and the dreadful *Hannibal*? When
'tis evident that that admirable Episode is so little owing to a
faithful observance of History, and the exact order of Time, that
'tis deriv'd from a very bold but judicious Violation of these; it
being undeniable that *Dido* liv'd almost 300 Years after *Æneas*.
Yet is it that charming Episode that makes the chief Beauties of
a third Part of the Poem. For the Destruction of *Troy* it self,
which is so divinely related, is still more admirable by the
Effect it produces, which is the Passion of *Dido*.

I should now proceed to shew under what Disadvantages
Shakespear lay for want of being conversant with the Ancients.
But I have already writ a long Letter, and am desirous to know
how you relish what has been already said before I go any
farther: For I am unwilling to take more Pains before I am sure of
giving you some Pleasure. I am,

SIR,

Your most humble, faithful Servant.

LETTER II.

SIR,   Feb. 6. 17$\frac{10}{11}$.
UPON the Encouragement I have receiv'd from you, I shall
proceed to shew under what Disadvantages *Shakespear* lay for
want of being conversant with the Ancients. But because I
have lately been in some Conversation, where they would not
allow but that he was acquainted with the Ancients, I shall

endeavour to make it appear that he was not; and the shewing
that in the Method in which I pretend to convince the Reader of
it, will sufficiently prove what Inconveniencies he lay under, and
what Errors he committed for want of being conversant with
them. But here we must distinguish between the several kinds
of Acquaintance: A Man may be said to be acquainted with another who never was but twice in his Company; but that is at
the best a superficial Acquaintance, from which neither very
great Pleasure nor Profit can be deriv'd. Our Business is here to
shew that *Shakespear* had no familiar Acquaintance with the
Græcian and *Roman* Authors. For if he was familiarly conversant
with them, how comes it to pass that he wants Art? Is it that he
studied to know them in other things, and neglected that only
in them, which chiefly tends to the Advancement of the Art of
the Stage? Or is it that he wanted Discernment to see the
Justness, and the Greatness, and the Harmony of their Designs,
and the Reasonableness of those Rules upon which those Designs
are founded? Or how come his Successors to have that Discernment which he wanted, when they fall so much below him in
other things? How comes he to have been guilty of the grossest
Faults in Chronology, and how come we to find out those Faults?
In his Tragedy of *Troylus* and *Cressida*, he introduces *Hector*
speaking of *Aristotle*, who was born a thousand Years after the
Death of *Hector*. In the same Play mention is made of *Milo*,
which is another very great Fault in Chronology. *Alexander* is
mention'd in *Coriolanus*, tho' that Conqueror of the Orient liv'd
about two hundred Years after him. In this last Tragedy he has
mistaken the very Names of his Dramatick Persons, if we give
Credit to *Livy*. For the Mother of *Coriolanus* in the *Roman*
Historian is *Vetturia*, and the Wife is *Volumnia*. Whereas in
Shakespear the Wife is *Virgilia*, and the Mother *Volumnia*. And the
Volscian General in *Shakespear* is *Tullus Aufidius*, and *Tullus Attius*
in *Livy*. How comes it that he takes *Plutarch's* Word, who was by
Birth a *Græcian*, for the Affairs of *Rome*, rather than that of the
Roman Historian, if so be that he had read the latter? Or what
Reason can be given for his not reading him, when he wrote upon

a *Roman* Story, but that in *Shakespear's* time there was a Translation of *Plutarch*, and there was none of *Livy*? If *Shakespear* was
familiarly conversant with the *Roman* Authors, how came he to
introduce a Rabble into *Coriolanus*, in which he offended not
only against the Dignity of Tragedy, but the Truth of Fact, the
Authority of all the *Roman* Writers, the Customs of Ancient
Rome, and the Majesty of the *Roman* People? By introducing a
Rabble into *Julius Cæsar*, he only offended against the Dignity of
Tragedy. For that part of the People who ran about the Streets
upon great Festivals, or publick Calamities, or publick Rejoic-
ings, or Revolutions in Government, are certainly the Scum of
the Populace. But the Persons who in the Time of *Coriolanus* rose
in Vindication of their just Rights, and extorted from the
Patricians the Institution of the Tribunes of the People, and the
Persons by whom afterwards *Coriolanus* was tried, were the whole
Body of the *Roman* People to the Reserve of the Patricians, which
Body included the *Roman* Knights, and the wealthy substantial
Citizens, who were as different from the Rabble as the Patricians
themselves, as qualify'd as the latter to form a right Judgment of
Things, and to contemn the vain Opinions of the Rabble. So at
least *Horace* esteems them, who very well knew his Countrymen.

> *Offenduntur enim, quibus est equus, aut pater, aut res,*
> *Nec, si quid fricti ciceris probat aut nucis emptor,*
> *Æquis accipiunt animis donantve Corona.*

Where we see the Knights and the substantial Citizens are
rank'd in an equal Degree of Capacity with the *Roman* Senators,
and are equally distinguish'd from the Rabble.

If *Shakespear* was so conversant with the Ancients, how comes
he to have introduc'd some Characters into his Plays so unlike
what they are to be found in History? In the Character of
Menenius in the following Tragedy, he has doubly offended
against that Historical Resemblance. For first whereas *Menenius*
was an eloquent Person, *Shakespear* has made him a downright
Buffoon. And how is it possible for any Man to conceive a
Ciceronian Jack-pudding? Never was any Buffoon eloquent, or wise,

or witty, or virtuous. All the good and ill Qualities of a Buffoon are summ'd up in one Word, and that is a Buffoon. And secondly, whereas *Shakespear* has made him a Hater and Contemner and Villifier of the People, we are assur'd by the *Roman* Historian that *Menenius* was extremely popular. He was so very far from opposing the Institution of the Tribunes, as he is represented in *Shakespear*, that he was chiefly instrumental in it. After the People had deserted the City, and sat down upon the sacred Mountain, he was the chief of the Delegates whom the Senate deputed to them, as being look'd upon to be the Person who would be most agreeable to them. In short, this very *Menenius* both liv'd and dy'd so very much their Favourite, that dying poor he had pompous Funerals at the Expence of the *Roman* People.

Had *Shakespear* read either *Sallust* or *Cicero*, how could he have made so very little of the first and greatest of Men, as that *Cæsar* should be but a Fourth-rate Actor in his own Tragedy? How could it have been that seeing *Cæsar*, we should ask for *Cæsar*? That we should ask, where is his unequall'd Greatness of Mind, his unbounded Thirst of Glory, and that victorious Eloquence, with which he triumph'd over the Souls of both Friends and Enemies, and with which he rivall'd *Cicero* in Genius as he did *Pompey* in Power? How fair an Occasion was there to open the Character of *Cæsar* in the first Scene between *Brutus* and *Cassius*? For when *Cassius* tells *Brutus* that *Cæsar* was but a Man like them, and had the same natural Imperfections which they had, how natural had it been for *Brutus* to reply, that *Cæsar* indeed had their Imperfections of Nature, but neither he nor *Cassius* had by any means the great Qualities of *Cæsar*: neither his Military Virtue, nor Science, nor his matchless Renown, nor his unparallell'd Victories, his unwearied Bounty to his Friends, nor his Godlike Clemency to his Foes, his Beneficence, his Munificence, his Easiness of Access to the meanest *Roman*, his indefatigable Labours, his incredible Celerity, the Plausibleness if not Justness of his Ambition, that knowing himself to be the greatest of Men, he only sought occasion to make the World confess him such. In short, if *Brutus*, after enumerating all the wonderful Qualities of *Cæsar*, had resolv'd in spight of them all to sacrifice him to publick Liberty, how had such a Proceeding heighten'd the Virtue and the Character of *Brutus*? But then indeed it would have been requisite that *Cæsar* upon his Appearance should have made all this good. And as we know no Principle of human Action but human Sentiment only, *Cæsar*, who did greater Things, and had greater Designs than the rest of the *Romans*, ought certainly to have outshin'd by many Degrees all the other Characters of his Tragedy. *Cæsar* ought particularly to have justified his Actions, and to have heighten'd his Character, by shewing that what he had done, he had done by Necessity; that the *Romans* had lost their *Agrarian*, lost their Rotation of Magistracy, and that consequently nothing but an empty Shadow of publick Liberty remain'd; that the *Gracchi* had made the last noble but unsuccessful Efforts for the restoring the Commonwealth, that they had fail'd for want of arbitrary irresistible Power, the Restoration of the *Agrarian* requiring too vast a Retrospect to be done without it; that the Government, when *Cæsar* came to publick Affairs, was got into the Hands of a few, and that those few were factious, and were contending among themselves, and, if you will pardon so mean an Expression, scrambling as it were for Power; that *Cæsar* was reduc'd to the Necessity of ruling, or himself obeying a Master; and that apprehending that another would exercise the supreme Command without that Clemency and Moderation which he did, he had rather chosen to rule than to obey. So that *Cæsar* was faulty not so much in seizing upon the Sovereignty, which was become in a manner necessary, as in not re-establishing the Commonwealth, by restoring the *Agrarian* and the Rotation of Magistracies, after he had got absolute and uncontroulable Power. And if *Cæsar* had seiz'd upon the Sovereignty only with a View of re-establishing Liberty, he had surpass'd all Mortals in Godlike Goodness as much as he did in the rest of his astonishing Qualities. I must confess, I do not remember that we have any Authority from the *Roman* Historians which may induce us to believe that *Cæsar* had any such Design. Nor if he had had any such View, could he, who was the most secret, the most prudent, and the most discerning of Men, have discover'd it before his *Parthian* Expedition was over, for fear of utterly disobliging his Veterans. And *Cæsar* believ'd that Expedition necessary for the Honour and Interest of the State, and for his own Glory.

But of this we may be sure, that two of the most discerning of all the *Romans*, and who had the deepest Insight into the Soul of *Cæsar*, *Sallust* and *Cicero*, were not without Hopes that *Cæsar* would really re-establish Liberty, or else they would not have attack'd him upon it; the one in his Oration for *Marcus Marcellus*, the other in the Second Part of that little Treatise *De Republica ordinanda*, which is address'd to *Cæsar*. *Hæc igitur tibi reliqua pars*, says *Cicero*, *Hic restat Actus, in hoc elaborandum est, ut Rempublicam constituas, eaque tu in primis composita, summa Tranquillitate & otio perfruare.* *Cicero* therefore was not without Hope that *Cæsar* would re-establish the Commonwealth; and any one who attentively peruses that Oration of *Cicero*, will find that that Hope was reasonably grounded, upon his knowledge of the great Qualities of *Cæsar*, his Clemency, his Beneficence, his admirable Discernment; and that avoidless Ruine in which the whole Empire would be soon involv'd, if *Cæsar* did not effect this. *Sallust* urges it still more home to him and with greater vehemence; he has recourse to every Motive that may be thought to be powerful over so great a Soul. He exhorts him by the Memory of his matchless Conquests, not to suffer the invincible Empire of the *Roman* People to be devour'd by Time, or to be torn in pieces by Discord; one of which would soon and infallibly happen, if Liberty was not restor'd.

He introduces his Country and his Progenitors urging him in a noble Prosopopeia, by all the mighty Benefits which they had conferr'd upon him, with so little Pains of his own, not to deny them that just and easy Request of the Restoration of Liberty. He adjures him by those Furies which will eternally haunt his Soul upon his impious Refusal: He implores him by the foresight of those dismal Calamities, that horrible Slaughter, those endless Wars, and that unbounded Devastation, which will certainly fall upon Mankind, if the Restoration of Liberty is prevented by his Death, or his incurable Sickness: And lastly, he entreats him by his Thirst of immortal Glory, that Glory in which he now has Rivals, if he has not Equals; but which, if he re-establishes Liberty, will be acknowledg'd by consenting Nations to have neither Equal nor Second.

I am apt to believe that if *Shakespear* had been acquainted with all this, we had had from him quite another Character of *Cæsar* than that which we now find in him. He might then have given us a Scene something like that which *Corneille* has so happily us'd in his *Cinna*; something like that which really happen'd between *Augustus*, *Mecænas*, and *Agrippa*. He might then have introduc'd *Cæsar* consulting *Cicero* on the one side, and on the other *Anthony*, whether he should retain that absolute Sovereignty which he had acquir'd by his Victory, or whether he should re-establish and immortalize Liberty. That would have been a Scene which might have employ'd the finest Art and the utmost force of a Writer. That had been a Scene in which all the great Qualities of *Cæsar* might have been display'd. I will not pretend to determine here how that Scene might have been turn'd; and what I have already said on this Subject, has been spoke with the utmost Caution and Diffidence. But this I will venture to say, that if that Scene had been manag'd so, as, by the powerful Motives employ'd in it, to have shaken the Soul of *Cæsar*, and to have left room for the least Hope, for the least Doubt, that *Cæsar* would have re-establish'd Liberty, after his *Parthian* Expedition; and if this Conversation had been kept secret till the Death of *Cæsar*, and then had been discover'd by *Anthony*, then had *Cæsar* fall'n, so belov'd and lamented by the *Roman* People, so pitied and so bewail'd even by the Conspirators themselves, as never Man fell. Then there would have been a Catastrophe the most dreadful and the most deplorable that ever was beheld upon the Tragick Stage. Then had we seen the noblest of the Conspirators cursing their temerarious Act, and the most apprehensive of them in dreadful expectation of those horrible Calamities which fell upon the *Romans* after the Death of *Cæsar*. But, Sir, when I write this to you, I write it with the utmost Deference to the extraordinary Judgment of that great Man who some Years ago, I hear, alter'd the *Julius Cæsar*. And I make no doubt but that his fine Discernment and the rest of his great Qualities have amply supply'd the Defects which are found in the Character of *Shakespear*'s *Cæsar*.

I should here answer an Argument, by which some People pretend to prove, and especially those with whom I lately convers'd, that *Shakespear* was conversant with the Ancients. But besides that the Post is about to be gone, I am heartily tir'd with what I have already writ, and so doubtless are you; I shall therefore defer the rest to the next opportunity, and remain

Your, *&c.*

LETTER III.

SIR,   *Feb.* 8.

I COME now to the main Argument, which some People urge to prove that *Shakespear* was conversant with the Ancients. For there is, say they, among *Shakespear*'s Plays, one call'd *The Comedy of Errors*, which is undeniably an Imitation of the *Menechmi* of *Plautus*. Now *Shakespear*, say they, being conversant with *Plautus*, it undeniably follows that he was acquainted with the Ancients; because no *Roman* Author could be hard to him who had conquer'd *Plautus*. To which I answer, that the Errors which we have mention'd above are to be accounted for no other way but by the want of knowing the Ancients, or by downright want of Capacity. But nothing can be more absurd or more unjust than to impute it to want of Capacity. For the very Sentiments of *Shakespear* alone are sufficient to shew that he had a great Understanding: And therefore we must account some other way for his Imitation of the *Menechmi*. I remember to have seen, among the Translations of *Ovid*'s Epistles printed by Mr. *Tonson*, an Imitation of that from *Œnone* to *Paris*, which Mr. *Dryden* tells us in his Preface to those Epistles was imitated by one of the Fair Sex who understood no *Latin*, but that she had done enough to make those blush who understood it the best. There are at this day several Translators, who, as *Hudibrass* has it,

> *Translate from Languages of which*
> *They understand no part of Speech.*

I will not affirm that of *Shakespear*; I believe he was able to do what Pedants call construe, but that he was able to read *Plautus* without Pain and Difficulty I can never believe. Now I appeal to you, Sir, what time he had between his Writing and his Acting, to read any thing that could not be read with Ease and Pleasure. We see that our Adversaries themselves acknowledge, that if *Shakespear* was able to read *Plautus* with Ease, nothing in Latinity could be hard to him. How comes it to pass then, that he has given us no Proofs of his familiar Acquaintance with the Ancients, but this Imitation of the *Menechmi*, and a Version of two Epistles of *Ovid*? How comes it that he had never read *Horace*, of a superiour Merit to either, and particularly his Epistle to the *Piso's*, which so much concern'd his Art? Or if he had read that Epistle, how comes it that in his *Troylus* and *Cressida* [we must observe by the way, that when *Shakespear* wrote that Play, *Ben Johnson* had not as yet translated that Epistle] he runs counter to the Instructions which *Horace* has given for the forming the Character of *Achilles*?

> *Scriptor: Honoratum si forte reponis Achillem,*
> *Impiger, Iracundus, Inexorabilis, Acer,*
> *Jura neget sibi nata.*

Where is the *Impiger*, the *Iracundus*, or the *Acer*, in the Character of *Shakespear's Achilles*? who is nothing but a drolling, lazy, conceited, overlooking Coxcomb; so far from being the honour'd *Achilles*, the Epithet that *Homer* and *Horace* after him give him, that he is deservedly the Scorn and the Jest of the rest of the Characters, even to that Buffoon *Thersites*.

Tho' *Shakespear* succeeded very well in Comedy, yet his principal Talent and his chief Delight was Tragedy. If then *Shakespear* was qualify'd to read *Plautus* with Ease, he could read with a great deal more Ease the Translations of *Sophocles* and *Euripides*. And tho' by these Translations he would not have been able to have seen the charming colouring of those great Masters, yet would he have seen all the Harmony and the Beauty of their great and their just Designs. He would have seen enough to have stirr'd up a noble Emulation in so exalted a Soul as his. How comes it then that we hear nothing from him of the *Œdipus*, the *Electra*, the *Antigone* of *Sophocles*, of the *Iphigenia's*, the *Orestes*, the *Medea*, the *Hecuba* of *Euripides*? How comes it that we see nothing in the Conduct of his Pieces, that shews us that he had the least Acquaintance with any of these great Master-pieces? Did *Shakespear* appear to be so nearly touch'd with the Affliction of *Hecuba* for the Death of *Priam*, which was but daub'd and bungled by one of his Countrymen, that he could not forbear introducing it as it were by Violence into his own *Hamlet*, and would he make no Imitation, no Commendation, not the least Mention of the unparallell'd and inimitable Grief of the *Hecuba* of *Euripides*? How comes it that we find no Imitation of any ancient Play in Him but the *Menechmi* of *Plautus*? How came he to chuse a Comick preferably to the Tragick Poets? Or how comes he to chuse *Plautus* preferably to *Terence*, who is so much more just, more graceful, more regular, and more natural? Or how comes he to chuse the *Menechmi* of *Plautus*, which is by no means his Master-piece, before all his other Comedies? I vehemently suspect that this Imitation of the *Menechmi* was either from a printed Translation of that Comedy which is lost, or some Version in Manuscript brought him by a Friend, or sent him perhaps by a Stranger, or from the original Play it self recommended to him, and read to him by some learned Friend. In short, I had rather account for this by what is not absurd than by what is, or by a less Absurdity than by a greater. For nothing can be more wrong than to conclude from this that *Shakespear* was conversant with the Ancients; which contradicts the Testimony of his Contemporary

and his familiar Acquaintance *Ben Johnson*, and of his Successor
Milton;

> *Lo* Shakespear, *Fancy's sweetest Child,*
> *Warbles his native Wood-Notes wild.*

and of Mr. *Dryden* after them both; and which destroys the most
glorious Part of *Shakespear's* Merit immediately. For how can he
be esteem'd equal by Nature, or superior to the Ancients, when
he falls so far short of them in Art, tho' he had the Advantage of
knowing all that they did before him? Nay it debases him below
those of common Capacity, by reason of the Errors which we
mention'd above. Therefore he who allows that *Shakespear* had
Learning and a familiar Acquaintance with the Ancients, ought
to be look'd upon as a Detractor from his extraordinary Merit,
and from the Glory of *Great Britain*. For whether is it more
honourable for this Island to have produc'd a Man who, without
having any Acquaintance with the Ancients, or any but a slender
and a superficial one, appears to be their Equal or their Superiour
by the Force of Genius and Nature, or to have bred one who,
knowing the Ancients, falls infinitely short of them in Art, and
consequently in Nature it self? *Great Britain* has but little
Reason to boast of its Natives Education, since the same that
they had here, they might have had in another place. But it may
justly claim a very great share in their Nature and Genius, since
these depend in a great measure on the Climate; and therefore
Horace in the Instruction which he gives for the forming the
Characters, advises the noble *Romans* for whose Instruction he
chiefly writes to consider whether the Dramatick Person whom
they introduce is

> *Colchus an Assyrius, Thebis nutritus an Argis.*

Thus, Sir, I have endeavour'd to shew under what great Disadvantages *Shakespear* lay, for want of the Poetical Art, and for
want of being conversant with the Ancients.

But besides this, he lay under other very great Inconveniencies. For he was neither Master of Time enough to consider,

correct, and polish what he wrote, to alter it, to add to it, and to
retrench from it, nor had he Friends to consult upon whose
Capacity and Integrity he could depend. And tho' a Person of
very good Judgment may succeed very well without consulting
his Friends, if he takes time enough to correct what he writes;
yet even the greatest Man that Nature and Art can conspire to
accomplish, can never attain to Perfection, without either
employing a great deal of time, or taking the Advice of judicious
Friends. Nay, 'tis the Opinion of *Horace* that he ought to do both.

> *Si quid tamen olim*
> *Scripseris, in Metii descendat Judicis aures,*
> *Et Patris, & nostras; nonumque prematur in Annum.*

Now we know very well that *Shakespear* was an Actor, at a time
when there were seven or eight Companies of Players in the
Town together, who each of them did their utmost Endeavours
to get the Audiences from the rest, and consequently that our
Author was perpetually call'd upon, by those who had the Direction and Management of the Company to which he belong'd, for
new Pieces which might be able to support them, and give them
some Advantage over the rest. And 'tis easie to judge what
Time he was Master of, between his laborious Employment of
Acting, and his continual Hurry of Writing. As for Friends, they
whom in all likelihood *Shakespear* consulted most were two or
three of his Fellow-Actors, because they had the Care of publishing his Works committed to them. Now they, as we are told
by *Ben Johnson* in his *Discoveries*, were extremely pleas'd with their
Friend for scarce ever making a Blot; and were very angry with
Ben for saying he wish'd that he had made a thousand. The
Misfortune of it is that *Horace* was perfectly of *Ben*'s mind.

> *—Vos, O*
> *Pompilius sanguis, carmen reprehendite, quod non*
> *Multa dies & multa litura coercuit, atque*
> *Præsectum decies non castigavit ad unguem.*

And so was my Lord *Roscommon*.

Poets lose half the Praise they should have got,
Could it be known what they discreetly blot.

These Friends then of *Shakespear* were not qualify'd to advise him. As for *Ben Johnson*, besides that *Shakespear* began to know him late, and that *Ben* was not the most communicative Person in the World of the Secrets of his Art, he seems to me to have had no right Notion of Tragedy. Nay, so far from it, that he who was indeed a very great Man, and who has writ Comedies, by which he has born away the Prize of Comedy both from Ancients and Moderns, and been an Honour to *Great Britain*; and who has done this without any Rules to guide him, except what his own incomparable Talent dictated to him; This extraordinary Man has err'd so grossly in Tragedy, of which there were not only stated Rules, but Rules which he himself had often read, and had even translated, that he has chosen two Subjects, which, according to those very Rules, were utterly incapable of exciting either Compassion or Terror for the principal Characters, which yet are the chief Passions that a Tragick Poet ought to endeavour to excite. So that *Shakespear* having neither had Time to correct, nor Friends to consult, must necessarily have frequently left such faults in his Writings, for the Correction of which either a great deal of Time or a judicious and a well-natur'd Friend is indispensably necessary.

> *Vir bonus & prudens versus reprehendet inertes,*
> *Culpabit duros, incomptis allinet atrum*
> *Transverso calamo signum, ambitiosa recidet*
> *Ornamenta, parum claris lucem dare coget,*
> *Arguet ambigue dictum, mutanda notabit.*

There is more than one Example of every kind of these Faults in the Tragedies of *Shakespear*, and even in the *Coriolanus*. There are Lines that are utterly void of that celestial Fire of which *Shakespear* is sometimes Master in so great a Degree. And consequently there are Lines that are stiff and forc'd, and harsh and unmusical, tho' *Shakespear* had naturally an admirable Ear for the Numbers. But no Man ever was very musical who did not write with Fire, and no Man can always write with Fire, unless he is so far Master of his Time, as to expect those Hours when his Spirits are warm and volatile. *Shakespear* must therefore sometimes have Lines which are neither strong nor graceful: For who ever had Force or Grace that had not Spirit? There are in his *Coriolanus*, among a great many natural and admirable Beauties, three or four of those Ornaments which *Horace* would term ambitious; and which we in *English* are apt to call Fustian or Bombast. There are Lines in some Places which are very obscure, and whole Scenes which ought to be alter'd.

I have, Sir, employ'd some Time and Pains, and that little Judgment which I have acquir'd in these Matters by a long and a faithful reading both of Ancients and Moderns, in adding, retrenching, and altering several Things in the *Coriolanus* of *Shakespear*, but with what Success I must leave to be determin'd by you. I know very well that you will be surpriz'd to find, that after all that I have said in the former Part of this Letter, against *Shakespear*'s introducing the Rabble into *Coriolanus*, I have not only retain'd in the second Act of the following Tragedy the Rabble which is in the Original, but deviated more from the *Roman* Customs than *Shakespear* had done before me. I desire you to look upon it as a voluntary Fault and a Trespass against Conviction: 'Tis one of those Things which are *ad Populum Phaleræ*, and by no means inserted to please such Men as you.

Thus, Sir, have I laid before you a short but impartial Account of the Beauties and Defects of *Shakespear*, with an Intention to make these Letters publick if they are approv'd by you; to teach some People to distinguish between his Beauties and his Defects, that while they imitate the one, they may with Caution avoid the other [there being nothing of more dangerous Contagion to Writers, and especially to young ones, than the Faults of great Masters] and while with *Milton* they applaud the great Qualities which *Shakespear* had by Nature, they may follow his wise Example, and form themselves as he assures us that he himself did, upon the Rules and Writings of the Ancients.

Sir, if so candid and able a Judge as your self shall happen to approve of this Essay in the main, and to excuse and correct my Errors, that Indulgence and that Correction will not only encourage me to make these Letters publick, but will enable me to bear the Reproach of those who would fix a Brand even upon the justest Criticism, as the Effect of Envy and Ill-nature; as if there could possibly be any Ill-nature in the doing Justice, or in the endeavouring to advance a very noble and a very useful Art, and consequently to prove beneficent to Mankind. As for those who may accuse me of the want of a due Veneration for the Merit of an Author of so establish'd a Reputation as *Shakespear*, I shall beg leave to tell them, that they chuse the wrongest time that they could possibly take for such an Accusation as that. For I appeal to you, Sir, who shews most Veneration for the Memory of *Shakespear*, he who loves and admires his Charms and makes them one of his chief Delights, who sees him and reads him over and over and still remains unsatiated, and who mentions his Faults for no other Reason but to make his Excellency the more conspicuous, or he who pretending to be his blind Admirer, shews in Effect the utmost Contempt for him, preferring empty effeminate Sound to his solid Beauties and manly Graces, and deserting him every Night for an execrable *Italian* Ballad, so vile that a Boy who should write such lamentable Dogrel, would be turn'd out of *Westminster*-School for a desperate Blockhead, too stupid to be corrected and amended by the harshest Discipline of the Place.

I am,

SIR,

Yours, &c.

ALEXANDER POPE

Preface to 'The Works of Shakespear'

1725

IT is not my design to enter into a Criticism upon this Author; tho' to do it effectually and not superficially would be the best occasion that any just Writer could take, to form the judgment and taste of our nation. For of all *English* Poets *Shakespear* must be confessed to be the fairest and fullest subject for Criticism, and to afford the most numerous as well as most conspicuous instances, both of Beauties and Faults of all sorts. But this far exceeds the bounds of a Preface, the business of which is only to give an account of the fate of his Works, and the disadvantages under which they have been transmitted to us. We shall hereby extenuate many faults which are his, and clear him from the imputation of many which are not: A design, which tho' it can be no guide to future Criticks to do him justice in one way, will at least be sufficient to prevent their doing him an injustice in the other.

I cannot however but mention some of his principal and characteristic Excellencies, for which (notwithstanding his defects) he is justly and universally elevated above all other Dramatic Writers. Not that this is the proper place of praising him, but because I would not omit any occasion of doing it.

If ever any Author deserved the name of an *Original*, it was *Shakespear*. *Homer* himself drew not his art so immediately from the fountains of Nature, it proceeded thro' *Ægyptian* strainers and channels, and came to him not without some tincture of the learning, or some cast of the models, of those before him. The Poetry of *Shakespear* was Inspiration indeed: he is not so much an Imitator, as an Instrument, of Nature; and 'tis not so just to say that he speaks from her, as that she speaks thro' him.

His *Characters* are so much Nature her self, that 'tis a sort of injury to call them by so distant a name as Copies of her. Those of other Poets have a constant resemblance, which shews that they receiv'd them from one another, and were but multiplyers of the same image: each picture like a mock-rainbow is but the reflexion of a reflexion. But every single character in *Shakespear* is as much an Individual as those in Life itself; it is as impossible to find any two alike; and such as from their relation or affinity in any respect appear most to be Twins, will upon comparison be found remarkably distinct. To this life and variety of Character, we must add the wonderful Preservation of it; which is such throughout his plays, that had all the Speeches been printed without the very names of the Persons, I believe one might have apply'd them with certainty to every speaker.

The *Power* over our *Passions* was never possess'd in a more eminent degree, or display'd in so different instances. Yet all along, there is seen no labour, no pains to raise them; no preparation to guide our guess to the effect, or be perceiv'd to lead toward it: But the heart swells, and the tears burst out, just at the proper places: We are surpriz'd, the moment we weep; and yet upon reflection find the passion so just, that we shou'd be surpriz'd if we had not wept, and wept at that very moment.

How astonishing is it again, that the passions directly opposite to these, Laughter and Spleen, are no less at his command! that he is not more a master of the *Great*, than of the *Ridiculous* in human nature; of our noblest tendernesses, than of our vainest foibles; of our strongest emotions, than of our idlest sensations!

Nor does he only excell in the Passions: In the coolness of Reflection and Reasoning he is full as admirable. His *Sentiments* are not only in general the most pertinent and judicious upon every subject; but by a talent very peculiar, something between Penetration and Felicity, he hits upon that particular point on which the bent of each argument turns, or the force of each motive depends. This is perfectly amazing, from a man of no education or experience in those great and publick scenes of life which are usually the subject of his thoughts: So that he seems to have known the world by Intuition, to have look'd thro' humane nature at one glance, and to be the only Author that gives ground for a very new opinion, That the Philosopher and even the Man of the world, may be *Born*, as well as the Poet.

It must be own'd that with all these great excellencies he has almost as great defects; and that as he has certainly written better, so he has perhaps written worse, than any other. But I think I can in some measure account for these defects, from several causes and accidents; without which it is hard to imagine that so large and so enlighten'd a mind could ever have been susceptible of them. That all these Contingencies should unite to his disadvantage seems to me almost as singularly unlucky, as that so many various (nay contrary) Talents should meet in one man, was happy and extraordinary.

It must be allowed that Stage-Poetry of all other, is more particularly levell'd to please the *Populace*, and its success more immediately depending upon the *Common Suffrage*. One cannot therefore wonder, if *Shakespear* having at his first appearance no other aim in his writings than to procure a subsistance, directed his endeavours solely to hit the taste and humour that then prevailed. The Audience was generally composed of the meaner sort of people; and therefore the Images of Life were to be drawn from those of their own rank: accordingly we find, that not our Author's only but almost all the old Comedies have their Scene among *Tradesmen* and *Mechanicks:* And even their Historical Plays strictly follow the common *Old Stories* or *Vulgar Traditions* of that kind of people. In Tragedy, nothing was so sure to *Surprize* and cause *Admiration*, as the most strange, unexpected, and consequently most unnatural, Events and Incidents; the most exaggerated Thoughts; the most verbose and bombast Expression; the most pompous Rhymes, and thundering Versification. In Comedy, nothing was so sure to *please*, as mean buffoonry, vile ribaldry, and unmannerly jests of fools and clowns. Yet even in these our Author's Wit buoys up, and is born above his subject: his Genius in those low parts is like some Prince of a

Romance in the disguise of a Shepherd or Peasant; a certain Greatness and Spirit now and then break out, which manifest his higher extraction and qualities.

It may be added, that not only the common Audience had no notion of the rules of writing, but few even of the better sort piqu'd themselves upon any great degree of knowledge or nicety that way; till *Ben Johnson* getting possession of the Stage, brought critical learning into vogue: And that this was not done without difficulty, may appear from those frequent lessons (and indeed almost Declamations) which he was forced to prefix to his first plays, and put into the mouth of his Actors, the *Grex*, *Chorus*, &c. to remove the prejudices, and inform the judgment of his hearers. Till then, our Authors had no thoughts of writing on the model of the Ancients: their Tragedies were only Histories in Dialogue; and their Comedies follow'd the thread of any Novel as they found it, no less implicitly than if it had been true History.

To judge therefore of *Shakespear* by *Aristotle*'s rules, is like trying a man by the Laws of one Country, who acted under those of another. He writ to the *People;* and writ at first without patronage from the better sort, and therefore without aims of pleasing them: without assistance or advice from the Learned, as without the advantage of education or acquaintance among them: without that knowledge of the best models, the Ancients, to inspire him with an emulation of them; in a word, without any views of Reputation, and of what Poets are pleas'd to call Immortality: Some or all of which have encourag'd the vanity, or animated the ambition, of other writers.

Yet it must be observ'd, that when his performances had merited the protection of his Prince, and when the encouragement of the Court had succeeded to that of the Town, the works of his riper years are manifestly raised above those of his former. The Dates of his plays sufficiently evidence that his productions improved, in proportion to the respect he had for his auditors. And I make no doubt this observation would be found true in every instance, were but Editions extant from which we might learn the exact time when every piece was composed, and whether writ for the Town or the Court.

Another Cause (and no less strong than the former) may be deduced from our Author's being a *Player*, and forming himself first upon the judgments of that body of men whereof he was a member. They have ever had a Standard to themselves, upon other principles than those of *Aristotle*. As they live by the Majority, they know no rule but that of pleasing the present humour, and complying with the wit in fashion; a consideration which brings all their judgment to a short point. Players are just such judges of what is *right*, as Taylors are of what is *graceful*. And in this view it will be but fair to allow, that most of our Author's faults are less to be ascribed to his wrong judgment as a Poet, than to his right judgment as a Player.

By these men it was thought a praise to *Shakespear*, that he scarce ever *blotted a line*. This they industriously propagated, as appears from what we are told by *Ben Johnson* in his *Discoveries*, and from the preface of *Heminges* and *Condell* to the first folio Edition. But in reality (however it has prevailed) there never was a more groundless report, or to the contrary of which there are more undeniable evidences: As, the Comedy of the *Merry Wives* of *Windsor*, which he entirely new writ; the *History of* Henry *the 6th*, which was first published under the Title of the *Contention of* York *and* Lancaster; and that of *Henry the 5th*, extreamly improved; that of *Hamlet* enlarged to almost as much again as at first, and many others. I believe the common opinion of his want of Learning proceeded from no better ground. This too might be thought a Praise by some; and to this his Errors have as injudiciously been ascribed by others. For 'tis certain, were it true, it would concern but a small part of them; the most are such as are not properly Defects, but Superfœtations: and arise not from want of learning or reading, but from want of thinking or judging: or rather (to be more just to our Author) from a compliance to those wants in others. As to a wrong choice of the subject, a wrong conduct of the incidents, false thoughts, forc'd expressions, &c. if these are not to be ascrib'd to the foresaid accidental reasons, they must be charg'd upon the Poet himself, and there is no help for it. But I think the two Disadvantages which I have mentioned (to be obliged to please the lowest of people, and to keep the worst of company) if the consideration be extended as far as it reasonably may, will appear sufficient to mis-lead and depress the greatest Genius upon earth. Nay the more modesty with which such a one is endued, the more he is in danger of submitting and conforming to others, against his own better judgment.

But as to his *Want of Learning*, it may be necessary to say something more: There is certainly a vast difference between *Learning* and *Languages*. How far he was ignorant of the latter, I cannot determine; but 'tis plain he had much Reading at least, if they will not call it Learning. Nor is it any great matter, if a man has Knowledge, whether he has it from one language or from another. Nothing is more evident than that he had a taste of natural Philosophy, Mechanicks, ancient and modern History, Poetical learning and Mythology: We find him very knowing in the customs, rites, and manners of Antiquity. In *Coriolanus* and *Julius Cæsar*, not only the Spirit, but Manners, of the *Romans* are exactly drawn; and still a nicer distinction is shown, between the manners of the *Romans* in the time of the former and of the latter. His reading in the ancient Historians is no less conspicuous, in many references to particular passages: and the speeches copy'd from *Plutarch* in *Coriolanus* may, I think, as well be made an instance of his learning, as those copy'd from *Cicero* in *Catiline*, of *Ben Johnson*'s. The manners of other nations in general, the *Egyptians*, *Venetians*, *French*, &c. are drawn with equal propriety. Whatever object of nature, or branch of science, he either speaks of or describes, it is always with competent, if not extensive knowledge: his descriptions are still exact; all his metaphors appropriated, and remarkably drawn from the true nature and inherent qualities of each subject. When he treats of Ethic or Politic, we may constantly observe a wonderful justness of distinction, as well as extent of comprehension. No one is more a master of the Poetical story, or has more frequent allusions to the various parts of it: Mr. *Waller* (who has been celebrated for this last particular) has not shown more learning this way than *Shakespear*. We have Translations from *Ovid* published in his name, among those Poems which pass for his, and for some of which we have undoubted authority, (being published by himself, and dedicated to his noble Patron the Earl of *Southampton*:) He appears also to have been conversant in *Plautus*, from whom he has taken the plot of one of his plays: he follows the *Greek* Authors, and particularly *Dares Phrygius*, in another: (altho' I will not pretend to say in what language he read them.) The modern *Italian* writers of Novels he was manifestly acquainted with; and we may conclude him to be no less conversant with the Ancients of his own country, from the use he has made of *Chaucer* in *Troilus* and *Cressida*, and in the *Two Noble Kinsmen*, if that Play be his, as there goes a Tradition it was, (and indeed it has little resemblance of *Fletcher*, and more of our Author than some of those which have been received as genuine.)

I am inclined to think, this opinion proceeded originally from the zeal of the Partizans of our Author and *Ben Johnson*; as they endeavoured to exalt the one at the expence of the other. It is ever the nature of Parties to be in extremes; and nothing is so probable, as that because *Ben Johnson* had much the most learning, it was said on the one hand that *Shakespear* had none at all; and because *Shakespear* had much the most wit and fancy, it was retorted on the other, that *Johnson* wanted both. Because *Shakespear* borrowed nothing, it was said that *Ben Johnson* borrowed every thing. Because *Johnson* did not write extempore, he was reproached with being a year about every piece; and because *Shakespear* wrote with ease and rapidity, they cryed, he never once made a blot. Nay the spirit of opposition ran so high, that whatever those of the one side objected to the other, was taken at the rebound, and turned into Praises; as injudiciously as their antagonists before had made them Objections.

Poets are always afraid of Envy; but sure they have as much reason to be afraid of Admiration. They are the *Scylla* and *Charybdis* of Authors; those who escape one, often fall by the other. *Pessimum genus inimicorum Laudantes*, says *Tacitus*: and *Virgil* desires to wear a charm against those who praise a Poet without rule or reason.

—*Si ultra placitum laudarit, baccare frontem
Cingite, ne Vati noceat—*

But however this contention might be carried on by the Partizans on either side, I cannot help thinking these two great Poets were good friends, and lived on amicable terms and in offices of society with each other. It is an acknowledged fact, that *Ben Johnson* was introduced upon the Stage, and his first works encouraged, by *Shakespear*. And after his death, that Author writes *To the memory of his beloved Mr.* William Shakespear, which shows as if the friendship had continued thro' life. I cannot for my own part find any thing *Invidious* or *Sparing* in those verses, but wonder Mr. *Dryden* was of that opinion. He exalts him not only above all his Contemporaries, but above *Chaucer* and *Spenser*, whom he will not allow to be great enough to be rank'd with him; and challenges the names of *Sophocles*, *Euripides*, and *Æschylus*, nay all *Greece* and *Rome* at once, to equal him: And (which is very particular) expressly vindicates him from the imputation of wanting *Art*, not enduring that all his excellencies shou'd be attributed to *Nature*. It is remarkable too, that the praise he gives him in his *Discoveries* seems to proceed from a *personal kindness*; he tells us that he lov'd the man, as well as honoured his memory; celebrates the honesty, openness, and frankness of his temper; and only distinguishes, as he reasonably ought, between the real merit of the Author, and the silly and derogatory applauses of the Players. *Ben Johnson* might indeed be sparing in his Commendations (tho' certainly he is not so in this instance) partly from his own nature, and partly from judgment. For men of judgment think they do any man more service in praising him justly, than lavishly. I say, I would fain believe they were Friends, tho' the violence and ill-breeding of their Followers and Flatterers were enough to give rise to the contrary report. I would hope that it may be with *Parties*, both in Wit and State, as with those Monsters described by the Poets; and that their *Heads* at least may have something humane, tho' their *Bodies* and *Tails* are wild beasts and serpents.

As I believe that what I have mentioned gave rise to the opinion of *Shakespear*'s want of learning; so what has continued it down to us may have been the many blunders and illiteracies of the first Publishers of his works. In these Editions their ignorance shines almost in every page; nothing is more common than *Actus tertia. Exit Omnes. Enter three Witches solus.* Their *French* is as bad as their *Latin*, both in construction and spelling: Their very *Welsh* is false. Nothing is more likely than that those palpable blunders of *Hector*'s quoting *Aristotle*, with others of that gross kind, sprung from the same root: It not being at all credible that these could be the errors of any man who had the least tincture of a School, or the least conversation with such as had. *Ben Johnson* (whom they will not think partial to him) allows him at least to have had *some Latin*; which is utterly inconsistent with mistakes like these. Nay the constant blunders in proper names of persons and places, are such as must have proceeded from a man who had not so much as read any history, in any language: so could not be *Shakespear*'s.

I shall now lay before the reader some of those almost innumerable Errors which have risen from one source, the ignorance of the Players, both as his actors, and as his editors. When the nature and kinds of these are enumerated and considered, I dare to say that not *Shakespear* only, but *Aristotle* or *Cicero*, had their works undergone the same fate, might have appear'd to want sense as well as learning.

It is not certain that any one of his Plays was published by himself. During the time of his employment in the Theatre, several of his pieces were printed separately in Quarto. What makes me think that most of these were not publish'd by him, is the excessive carelessness of the press: every page is so scandalously false spelled, and almost all the learned or unusual words so intolerably mangled, that it's plain there either was no Corrector to the press at all, or one totally illiterate. If any were

supervised by himself, I should fancy the two parts of *Henry the
4th* and *Midsummer-Night's Dream* might have been so: because I
find no other printed with any exactness; and (contrary to the
rest) there is very little variation in all the subsequent editions
of them. There are extant two Prefaces, to the first quarto edition
of *Troilus* and *Cressida* in 1609, and to that of *Othello*; by which it
appears, that the first was publish'd without his knowledge or
consent, and even before it was acted, so late as seven or eight
years before he died: and that the latter was not printed till
after his death. The whole number of genuine plays which we
have been able to find printed in his life-time, amounts but to
eleven. And of some of these, we meet with two or more editions
by different printers, each of which has whole heaps of trash
different from the other: which I should fancy was occasion'd by
their being taken from different copies, belonging to different
Play-houses.

The folio edition (in which all the plays we now receive as his
were first collected) was published by two Players, *Heming* and
Condell, in 1623, seven years after his decease. They declare, that
all the other editions were stolen and surreptitious, and affirm
theirs to be purged from the errors of the former. This is true as
to the literal errors, and no other; for in all respects else it is far
worse than the Quarto's:

First, because the additions of trifling and bombast passages
are in this edition far more numerous. For whatever had been
added, since those Quarto's, by the actors, or had stolen from
their mouths into the written parts, were from thence conveyed into the printed text, and all stand charged upon the
Author. He himself complained of this usage in *Hamlet*, where he
wishes that *those who play the Clowns wou'd speak no more than is set
down for them.* (Act 3. Sc. 4.) But as a proof that he could not
escape it, in the old editions of *Romeo* and *Juliet* there is no hint
of a great number of the mean conceits and ribaldries now to be
found there. In others, the low scenes of Mobs, Plebeians and
Clowns, are vastly shorter than at present: And I have seen one
in particular (which seems to have belonged to the Playhouse,

by having the parts divided with lines, and the Actors names in the margin) where several of those very passages were added in a written hand, which are since to be found in the folio.

In the next place, a number of beautiful passages which are extant in the first single editions, are omitted in this: as it seems, without any other reason than their willingness to shorten some scenes: These men (as it was said of *Procrustes*) either lopping or stretching an Author, to make him just fit for their Stage.

This edition is said to be printed from the *Original Copies*; I believe they meant those which had lain ever since the Author's days in the play-house, and had from time to time been cut, or added to, arbitrarily. It appears that this edition, as well as the Quarto's, was printed (at least partly) from no better copies than the *Prompter's Book*, or *Piece-meal Parts* written out for the use of the actors: For in some places their very[1] names are thro' carelessness set down instead of the *Personæ Dramatis*: And in others the notes of direction to the *Property-men* for their *Moveables*, and to the *Players* for their *Entries*,[2] are inserted into the Text, thro' the ignorance of the Transcribers.

The Plays not having been before so much as distinguish'd by *Acts* and *Scenes*, they are in this edition divided according as they play'd them; often when there is no pause in the action, or where they thought fit to make a breach in it, for the sake of Musick, Masques, or Monsters.

Sometimes the scenes are transposed and shuffled backward and forward; a thing which could no otherwise happen, but by their being taken from seperate and piecemeal-written parts.

Many verses are omitted intirely, and others transposed; from whence invincible obscurities have arisen, past the guess of

---

[1] Much ado about nothing, *Act* 2. *Enter* Prince, Leonato, Claudio, *and* Jack Wilson, *instead of* Balthasar. *And in Act* 4. Cowley, *and* Kemp, *constantly thro' a whole Scene*. Edit. Fol. of 1623, and 1632.

[2] *Such as,*
—My Queen is murder'd! *Ring the little Bell*—
—His nose grew as sharp as a pen, and *a table of Greenfield's*, &c.

any Commentator to clear up, but just where the accidental glympse of an old edition enlightens us.

Some Characters were confounded and mix'd, or two put into one, for want of a competent number of actors. Thus in the Quarto edition of *Midsummer-Night's Dream*, Act 5, *Shakespear* introduces a kind of Master of the Revels called *Philostratus*: all whose part is given to another character (that of *Ægeus*) in the subsequent editions: So also in *Hamlet* and *King Lear*. This too makes it probable that the Prompter's Books were what they call'd the Original Copies.

From liberties of this kind, many speeches also were put into the mouths of wrong persons, where the Author now seems chargeable with making them speak out of character: Or sometimes perhaps for no better reason than that a governing Player, to have the mouthing of some favourite speech himself, would snatch it from the unworthy lips of an Underling.

Prose from verse they did not know, and they accordingly printed one for the other throughout the volume.

Having been forced to say so much of the Players, I think I ought in justice to remark, that the Judgment, as well as Condition, of that class of people was then far inferior to what it is in our days. As then the best Playhouses were Inns and Taverns (the *Globe*, the *Hope*, the *Red Bull*, the *Fortune*, &c.), so the top of the profession were then meer Players, not Gentlemen of the stage: They were led into the Buttery by the Steward, not plac'd at the Lord's table, or Lady's toilette: and consequently were intirely depriv'd of those advantages they now enjoy, in the familiar conversation of our Nobility, and an intimacy (not to say dearness) with people of the first condition.

From what has been said, there can be no question but had *Shakespear* published his works himself (especially in his latter time, and after his retreat from the stage) we should not only be certain which are genuine; but should find in those that are, the errors lessened by some thousands. If I may judge from all the distinguishing marks of his style, and his manner of thinking and writing, I make no doubt to declare that those wretched plays,

Pericles, Locrine, Sir John Oldcastle, Yorkshire Tragedy, Lord Crom-well, The Puritan, and *London Prodigal,* cannot be admitted as his. And I should conjecture of some of the others (particularly *Love's Labour Lost, The Winter's Tale,* and *Titus Andronicus*) that only some characters, single scenes, or perhaps a few particular passages, were of his hand. It is very probable what occasion'd some Plays to be supposed *Shakespear's* was only this; that they were pieces produced by unknown authors, or fitted up for the Theatre while it was under his administration: and no owner claiming them, they were adjudged to him, as they give Strays to the Lord of the Manor. A mistake which (one may also observe) it was not for the interest of the House to remove. Yet the Players themselves, *Hemings* and *Condell,* afterwards did *Shakespear* the justice to reject those eight plays in their edition; tho' they were then printed in his name, in every body's hands, and acted with some applause; (as we learn from what *Ben Johnson* says of *Pericles* in his Ode on the *New Inn.*) That *Titus Andronicus* is one of this class I am the rather induced to believe, by finding the same Author openly express his contempt of it in the *Induction* to *Bartholomew-Fair,* in the year 1614, when *Shakespear* was yet living. And there is no better authority for these latter sort, than for the former, which were equally published in his life-time.

If we give into this opinion, how many low and vicious parts and passages might no longer reflect upon this great Genius, but appear unworthily charged upon him? And even in those which are really his, how many faults may have been unjustly laid to his account from arbitrary Additions, Expunctions, Transpositions of scenes and lines, confusion of Characters and Persons, wrong application of Speeches, corruptions of innumerable Passages by the Ignorance, and wrong Corrections of 'em again by the Impertinence, of his first Editors? From one or other of these considerations, I am verily perswaded, that the greatest and the grossest part of what are thought his errors would vanish, and leave his character in a light very different from that disadvantageous one, in which it now appears to us.

This is the state in which *Shakespear's* writings lye at present;

for since the above-mentioned Folio Edition, all the rest have implicitly followed it, without having recourse to any of the former, or ever making the comparison between them. It is impossible to repair the Injuries already done him; too much time has elaps'd, and the materials are too few. In what I have done I have rather given a proof of my willingness and desire, than of my ability, to do him justice. I have discharg'd the dull duty of an Editor, to my best judgment, with more labour than I expect thanks, with a religious abhorrence of all Innovation, and without any indulgence to my private sense or conjecture. The method taken in this Edition will show it self. The various Readings are fairly put in the margin, so that every one may compare 'em; and those I have prefer'd into the Text are constantly *ex fide Codicum*, upon authority. The Alterations or Additions which *Shakespear* himself made, are taken notice of as they occur. Some suspected passages which are excessively bad (and which seem Interpolations by being so inserted that one can intirely omit them without any chasm or deficience in the context) are degraded to the bottom of the page; with an Asterisk referring to the places of their insertion. The Scenes are mark'd so distinctly that every removal of place is specify'd; which is more necessary in this Author than any other, since he shifts them more frequently: and sometimes without attending to this particular, the reader would have met with obscurities. The more obsolete or unusual words are explained. Some of the most shining passages are distinguish'd by comma's in the margin; and where the beauty lay not in particulars but in the whole, a star is prefix'd to the scene. This seems to me a shorter and less ostentatious method of performing the better half of Criticism (namely the pointing out an Author's excellencies) than to fill a whole paper with citations of fine passages, with *general Applauses*, or *empty Exclamations* at the tail of them. There is also subjoin'd a Catalogue of those first Editions by which the greater part of the various readings and of the corrected passages are authorised, (most of which are such as carry their own evidence along with them.) These Editions now hold the place of Originals, and are the only materials left to repair the deficiences or restore the corrupted sense of the Author: I can only wish that a greater number of them (if a greater were ever published) may yet be found, by a search more successful than mine, for the better accomplishment of this end.

I will conclude by saying of *Shakespear*, that with all his faults, and with all the irregularity of his *Drama*, one may look upon his works, in comparison of those that are more finish'd and regular, as upon an ancient majestick piece of *Gothick* Architecture, compar'd with a neat Modern building: The latter is more elegant and glaring, but the former is more strong and more solemn. It must be allow'd, that in one of these there are materials enough to make many of the other. It has much the greater variety, and much the nobler apartments; tho' we are often conducted to them by dark, odd, and uncouth passages. Nor does the Whole fail to strike us with greater reverence, tho' many of the Parts are childish, ill-plac'd, and unequal to its grandeur.

LEWIS THEOBALD

Preface to 'The Works of Shakespeare', 1733

SECOND EDITION 1740

THE Attempt to write upon SHAKESPEARE is like going into a
large, a spacious, and a splendid Dome thro' the Conveyance of
a narrow and obscure Entry. A Glare of Light suddenly breaks
upon you, beyond what the Avenue at first promis'd: and a
thousand Beauties of Genius and Character, like so many gaudy
Apartments pouring at once upon the Eye, diffuse and throw
themselves out to the Mind. The Prospect is too wide to come
within the Compass of a single View: 'tis a gay Confusion of
pleasing Objects, too various to be enjoyed but in a general
Admiration; and they must be separated, and ey'd distinctly, in
order to give the proper Entertainment.

And as in great Piles of Building, some Parts are often finish'd
up to hit the Taste of the *Connoisseur*; others more negligently
put together, to strike the Fancy of a common and unlearned
Beholder: Some Parts are made stupendiously magnificent and
grand, to surprize with the vast Design and Execution of the
Architect; others are contracted, to amuse you with his Neatness
and Elegance in little. So, in *Shakespeare*, we may find *Traits* that
will stand the Test of the severest Judgment; and Strokes as
carelesly hit off, to the Level of the more ordinary Capacities:
Some Descriptions rais'd to that Pitch of Grandeur, as to astonish
you with the Compass and Elevation of his Thought: and others
copying Nature within so narrow, so confined a Circle, as if the
Author's Talent lay only at drawing in Miniature.

In how many Points of Light must we be oblig'd to gaze at
this great Poet! In how many Branches of Excellence to consider,
and admire him! Whether we view him on the Side of Art or

Nature, he ought equally to engage our Attention: Whether we
respect the Force and Greatness of his Genius, the Extent of his
Knowledge and Reading, the Power and Address with which he
throws out and applies either Nature, or Learning, there is
ample Scope both for our Wonder and Pleasure. If his Diction,
and the cloathing of his Thoughts attract us, how much more
must we be charm'd with the Richness, and Variety, of his
Images and Ideas! If his Images and Ideas steal into our Souls,
and strike upon our Fancy, how much are they improv'd in
Price, when we come to reflect with what Propriety and Justness
they are apply'd to Character! If we look into his Characters,
and how they are furnish'd and proportion'd to the Employment he cuts out for them, how are we taken up with the
Mastery of his Portraits! What Draughts of Nature! What
Variety of Originals, and how differing each from the other! How
are they dress'd from the Stores of his own luxurious Imagination;
without being the Apes of Mode, or borrowing from any foreign
Wardrobe! Each of them are the Standards of Fashion for themselves: like Gentlemen that are above the Direction of their
Tailors, and can adorn themselves without the Aid of Imitation.
If other Poets draw more than one Fool or Coxcomb, there is the
same Resemblance in them, as in that Painter's Draughts, who
was happy only at forming a Rose: you find them all younger
Brothers of the same Family, and all of them have a Pretence to
give the same Crest: But *Shakespeare*'s Clowns and Fops come all
of a different House: they are no farther allied to one another
than as Man to Man, Members of the same Species: but as
different in Features and Lineaments of Character, as we are
from one another in Face, or Complexion. But I am unawares
launching into his Character as a Writer, before I have said what
I intended of him as a private Member of the Republick.

    Mr. *Rowe* has very justly observ'd, that People are fond of
discovering any little personal Story of the Great Men of Antiquity: and that the common Accidents of their Lives naturally
become the Subject of our critical Enquiries: That however trifling such a Curiosity at the first View may appear, yet, as for

what relates to Men of Letters, the Knowledge of an Author may, perhaps, sometimes conduce to the better understanding his Works: And, indeed, this Author's Works, from the bad Treatment he has met with from Copyists and Editors, have so long wanted a Comment, that one would zealously embrace every Method of Information, that could contribute to recover them from the Injuries with which they have so long lain o'erwhelm'd.

'Tis certain, that if we have first admir'd the Man in his Writings, his Case is so circumstanc'd, that we must naturally admire the Writings in the Man: That if we go back to take a View of his Education, and the Employment in Life which Fortune had cut out for him, we shall retain the stronger Ideas of his extensive Genius.

His Father, we are told, was a considerable Dealer in Wool; but having no fewer than ten Children, of whom our *Shakespeare* was the eldest, the best Education he could afford him was no better than to qualify him for his own Business and Employment. I cannot affirm with any Certainty how long his Father liv'd; but I take him to be the same Mr. *John Shakespeare* who was living in the Year 1599, and who then, in Honour of his Son, took out an Extract of his Family-Arms from the Herald's Office; by which it appears, that he had been Officer and Bailiff of *Stratford* upon *Avon* in *Warwickshire*; and that he enjoy'd some hereditary Lands and Tenements, the Reward of his Great Grandfather's faithful and approved Service to King *Henry* VII.

Be this as it will, our *Shakespeare*, it seems, was bred for some Time at a Free-School; the very Free-School, I presume, founded at *Stratford*: where, we are told, he acquired what *Latin* he was Master of: but, that his Father being oblig'd, thro' Narrowness of Circumstance, to withdraw him too soon from thence, he was thereby unhappily prevented from making any Proficiency in the Dead Languages: A Point, that will deserve some little Discussion in the Sequel of this Dissertation.

How long he continued in his Father's Way of Business, either as an Assistant to him, or on his own proper Account, no Notices are left to inform us: nor have I been able to learn precisely at what Period of Life he quitted his native *Stratford*, and began his Acquaintance with *London*, and the *Stage*.

In order to settle in the World after a Family-manner, he thought fit, Mr. *Rowe* acquaints us, to marry while he was yet very young. It is certain, he did so: for by the Monument, in *Stratford* Church, erected to the Memory of his Daughter *Susanna*, the Wife of *John Hall*, Gentleman, it appears, that she died on the 2d Day of *July*, in the Year 1649, aged 66. So that she was born in 1583, when her Father could not be full 19 Years old; who was himself born in the Year 1564. Nor was she his eldest Child, for he had another Daughter, *Judith*, who was born before her, and who was married to one Mr. *Thomas Quiney*. So that *Shakespeare* must have entred into Wedlock, by that time he was turn'd of seventeen Years.

Whether the Force of Inclination merely, or some concurring Circumstances of Convenience in the Match, prompted him to marry so early, is not easy to be determin'd at this Distance: but 'tis probable, a View of Interest might partly sway his Conduct in this Point: for he married the Daughter of one *Hathaway*, a substantial Yeoman in his Neighbourhood, and she had the Start of him in Age no less than 8 years. She surviv'd him, notwithstanding, seven Seasons, and dy'd that very Year in which the *Players* publish'd the first Edition of his Works in *Folio*, Anno Dom. 1623, at the Age of 67 Years, as we likewise learn from her Monument in *Stratford*-Church.

How long he continued in this kind of Settlement, upon his own Native Spot, is not more easily to be determin'd. But if the Tradition be true, of that Extravagance which forc'd him both to quit his Country and Way of Living; to wit, his being engag'd, with a Knot of young Deer-stealers, to rob the Park of Sir *Thomas Lucy* of *Cherlecot* near *Stratford:* the Enterprize savours so much of Youth and Levity, we may reasonably suppose it was before he could write full Man. Besides, considering he has left us six and thirty Plays, at least, avow'd to be genuine; and considering too, that he had retir'd from the Stage, to spend the latter Part of his

Days at his own Native *Stratford*; the Interval of Time, necessarily required for the finishing so many Dramatic Pieces, obliges
us to suppose he threw himself very early upon the Play-house.
And as he could, probably, contract no Acquaintance with the
Drama, while he was driving on the Affair of Wool at home; some
Time must be lost, even after he had commenc'd Player, before
he could attain Knowledge enough in the Science to qualify himself for turning Author.

It has been observ'd by Mr. *Rowe*, that, amongst other Extravagancies which our Author has given to his Sir *John Falstaffe*,
in the *Merry Wives* of *Windsor*, he has made him a Deer-stealer;
and that he might at the same time remember his *Warwickshire*
Prosecutor, under the Name of *Justice Shallow*, he has given him
very near the same Coat of Arms, which *Dugdale*, in his Antiquities of that County, describes for a Family there. There
are two Coats, I observe, in *Dugdale*, where three Silver Fishes
are borne in the Name of *Lucy*; and another Coat, to the Monument of *Thomas Lucy*, Son of Sir *William Lucy*, in which are
quarter'd in four several Divisions, twelve little Fishes, three in
each Division, probably *Luces*. This very Coat, indeed, seems
alluded to in *Shallow*'s giving the *dozen* White *Luces*, and in *Slender*
saying, *he may quarter*. When I consider the exceeding Candour
and Good-nature of our Author, (which inclin'd all the gentler
Part of the World to love him; as the Power of his Wit obliged
the Men of the most delicate Knowledge and polite Learning to
admire him;) and that he should throw this humorous Piece of
Satire at his Prosecutor, at least twenty Years after the Provocation given; I am confidently persuaded it must be owing to an
unforgiving Rancour on the Prosecutor's Side: and if This was
the Case, it were Pity but the Disgrace of such an Inveteracy
should remain as a lasting Reproach, and *Shallow* stand as a
Mark of Ridicule to stigmatize his Malice.

It is said, our Author spent some Years before his Death, in
Ease, Retirement, and the Conversation of his Friends, at his
Native *Stratford*. I could never pick up any certain Intelligence,
when He relinquish'd the Stage. I know, it has been mistakenly

thought by some, that *Spenser*'s *Thalia*, in his *Tears of his Muses*, where she laments the Loss of her *Willy* in the Comic Scene, has been apply'd to our Author's quitting the Stage. But *Spenser* himself, 'tis well known, quitted the Stage of Life in the Year 1598; and, five Years after this, we find *Shakespeare*'s Name among the Actors in *Ben Jonson*'s *Sejanus*, which first made its Appearance in the Year 1603. Nor, surely, could he then have any Thoughts of retiring, since, that very Year, a Licence under the Privy-Seal was granted by K. *James* I. to him and *Fletcher, Burbage, Phillippes, Hemings, Condel,* &c. authorizing them to exercise the Art of playing Comedies, Tragedies, *&c.* as well at their usual House call'd the *Globe* on the other Side of the Water, as in any other Parts of the Kingdom, during his Majesty's Pleasure: (A Copy of which Licence is preserv'd in *Rymer*'s *Fœdera*.) Again, 'tis certain, that *Shakespeare* did not exhibit his *Macbeth*, till after the Union was brought about, and till after K. *James* I. had begun to touch for the *Evil:* for 'tis plain, he has inserted Compliments, on both those Accounts, upon his Royal Master in that Tragedy. Nor, indeed, could the Number of the Dramatic Pieces, he produced, admit of his retiring near so early as that Period. So that what *Spenser* there says, if it relate at all to *Shakespeare*, must hint at some occasional Recess he made for a time upon a Disgust taken: or the *Willy*, there mention'd, must relate to some other favourite Poet. I believe, we may safely determine that he had not quitted in the Year 1610. For in his *Tempest*, our Author makes mention of the *Bermuda* Islands, which were unknown to the *English*, till, in 1609, Sir *John Summers* made a Voyage to *North-America*, and discover'd them: and afterwards invited some of his Countrymen to settle a Plantation there. That he became the private Gentleman, at least three Years before his Decease, is pretty obvious from another Circumstance: I mean, from that remarkable and well-known Story, which Mr. *Rowe* has given us of our Author's Intimacy with Mr. *John Combe*, an old Gentleman noted thereabouts for his Wealth and Usury: and upon whom *Shakespeare* made the following facetious Epitaph.

Ten in the hundred lies here ingrav'd,
'Tis a hundred to ten his Soul is not sav'd;
If any Man ask who lies in this Tomb,
Oh! oh! quoth the Devil, 'tis my John-a-Combe.

This sarcastical Piece of Wit was, at the Gentleman's own Request, thrown out extemporally in his Company. And this Mr. *John Combe* I take to be the same, who, by *Dugdale* in his Antiquities of *Warwickshire*, is said to have dy'd in the Year 1614, and for whom at the upper end of the Quire, of the Guild of the Holy Cross at *Stratford*, a fair Monument is erected, having a Statue thereon cut in Alabaster, and in a Gown, with this Epitaph. 'Here lyeth enterr'd the Body of *John Combe* Esq; who 'dy'd the 10th of *July*, 1614, who bequeathed several Annual 'Charities to the Parish of *Stratford*, and 100*l.* to be lent to fifteen 'poor Tradesmen from three years to three years, changing the 'Parties every third Year, at the Rate of fifty Shillings *per Annum*, the Increase to be distributed to the Almes-poor there.'— The Donation has all the Air of a rich and sagacious Usurer.

Shakespeare himself did not survive Mr. *Combe* long, for he dy'd in the Year 1616, the 53d of his Age. He lies buried on the North Side of the Chancel in the great Church at *Stratford*; where a Monument, decent enough for the Time, is erected to him, and plac'd against the Wall. He is represented under an Arch in a sitting Posture, a Cushion spread before him, with a Pen in his Right Hand, and his Left rested on a Scrowl of Paper. The *Latin* Distich, which is placed under the Cushion, has been given us by Mr. *Pope*, or his Graver, in this Manner.

INGENIO Pylium, *Genio* Socratem, *Arte* Maronem,
Terra tegit, Populus mæret, Olympus habet.

I confess I don't conceive the Difference betwixt *Ingenio* and *Genio* in the first Verse. They seem to me intirely synonomous Terms; nor was the *Pylian* Sage *Nestor* celebrated for his Ingenuity, but for an Experience and Judgment owing to his long Age. *Dugdale*, in his Antiquities of *Warwickshire*, has copied this Distich with a Distinction which Mr. *Rowe* has follow'd,

and which certainly restores us the true Meaning of the Epitaph.

JUDICIO Pylium, Genio *Socratem*, &c.

In 1614, the greater part of the Town of *Stratford* was consumed by Fire; but our *Shakespeare*'s House, among some others,
escap'd the Flames. This House was first built by Sir *Hugh
Clopton*, a younger Brother of an ancient Family in that Neighbourhood, who took their Name from the Manor of *Clopton*. Sir
Hugh was Sheriff of *London* in the Reign of *Richard* III, and Lord
Mayor in the Reign of King *Henry* VII. To this Gentleman the
Town of *Stratford* is indebted for the fine Stone-bridge, con-
sisting of fourteen Arches, which at an extraordinary Expence
he built over the *Avon*, together with a Cause-way running at
the West-end thereof; as also for rebuilding the Chapel adjoining
to his House, and the Cross-Isle in the Church there. It is remarkable of him, that, tho' he liv'd and dy'd a Batchelor, among
the other extensive Charities which he left both to the City of
London and Town of *Stratford*, he bequeath'd considerable
Legacies for the Marriage of poor Maidens of good Name and
Fame both in *London* and at *Stratford*. Notwithstanding which
large Donations in his Life, and Bequests at his Death, as he had
purchased the Manor of *Clopton*, and all the Estate of the Family,
so he left the same again to his Elder Brother's Son with a very
great Addition: (a Proof, how well Beneficence and Oeconomy may
walk hand in hand in wise Families:) Good part of which Estate
is yet in the Possession of *Edward Clopton*, Esq; and Sir *Hugh
Clopton*, Knt. lineally descended from the Elder Brother of the
first Sir *Hugh:* Who particularly bequeathed to his Nephew, by
his Will, his House, by the Name of his *Great-House* in *Stratford*.

The Estate had now been sold out of the *Clopton* Family for
above a Century, at the Time when *Shakespeare* became the
Purchaser: who, having repair'd and modell'd it to his own
Mind, chang'd the Name to *New-place*; which the Mansion-house,
since erected upon the same Spot, at this day retains. The
House and Lands, which attended it, continued in *Shakespeare*'s

Descendants to the Time of the *Restoration:* when they were
repurchased by the *Clopton* Family, and the Mansion now belongs
to Sir *Hugh Clopton*, Knt. To the Favour of this worthy Gentleman I owe the Knowledge of one Particular, in Honour of our
Poet's once Dwelling-house, of which, I presume, Mr. ROWE
never was appriz'd. When the Civil War raged in *England*, and
K. *Charles* the *First's* Queen was driven by the Necessity of
Affairs to make a Recess in *Warwickshire*, She kept her Court
for three Weeks in *New-place*. We may reasonably suppose it
then the best private House in the Town; and her Majesty pre-
ferr'd it to the *College*, which was in the Possession of the *Combe-*
Family, who did not so strongly favour the King's Party.

How much our Author employ'd himself in Poetry, after his
Retirement from the Stage, does not so evidently appear: Very
few posthumous Sketches of his Pen have been recover'd to
ascertain that Point. We have been told, indeed, in Print, but
not till very lately, That two large Chests full of this Great
Man's loose Papers and Manuscripts, in the Hands of an ignorant Baker of *Warwick*, (who married one of the Descendants
from our *Shakespeare*) were carelesly scatter'd and thrown about,
as Garret-Lumber, and Litter, to the particular Knowledge of the
late Sir *William Bishop*, till they were all consumed in the general
Fire and Destruction of that Town. I cannot help being a little
apt to distrust the Authority of this Tradition; because his
Wife surviv'd him seven Years, and as his Favourite Daughter
Susanna surviv'd her twenty six Years, 'tis very improbable, they
should suffer such a Treasure to be remov'd, and translated into
a remoter Branch of the Family, without a Scrutiny first made
into the Value of it. This, I say, inclines me to distrust the
Authority of the Relation: but, notwithstanding such an apparent Improbability, if we really lost such a Treasure, by whatever Fatality or Caprice of Fortune they came into such ignorant
and neglectful Hands, I agree with the *Relater*, the Misfortune is
wholly irreparable.

To these Particulars, which regard his Person and private
Life, some few more are to be glean'd from Mr. ROWE's Account

of his *Life* and *Writings:* Let us now take a short View of him in his publick Capacity, as a *Writer:* and, from thence, the Transition will be easy to the *State* in which his *Writings* have been handed down to us.

No Age, perhaps, can produce an Author more various from himself, than *Shakespeare* has been universally acknowledg'd to be. The Diversity in Stile, and other Parts of Composition, so obvious in him, is as variously to be accounted for. His Education, we find, was at best but begun: and he started early into a Science from the Force of Genius, unequally assisted by acquir'd Improvements. His Fire, Spirit, and Exuberance of Imagination gave an Impetuosity to his Pen: His Ideas flow'd from him in a Stream rapid, but not turbulent; copious, but not ever overbearing its Shores. The Ease and Sweetness of his Temper might not a little contribute to his Facility in Writing: as his Employment, as a *Player*, gave him an Advantage and Habit of fancying himself the very Character he meant to delineate. He used the Helps of his Function in forming himself to create and express that *Sublime*, which other Actors can only copy, and throw out, in Action and graceful Attitude. But *Nullum sine Venia placuit Ingenium*, says *Seneca*. The Genius, that gives us the greatest Pleasure, sometimes stands in Need of our Indulgence. Whenever this happens with regard to *Shakespeare* I would willingly impute it to a Vice of *his Times*. We see Complaisance enough, in our Days, paid to a *bad Taste*. So that his *Clinches, false Wit*, and descending beneath himself, may have proceeded from a Deference paid to the then *reigning Barbarism*.

I have not thought it out of my Province, whenever Occasion offer'd, to take notice of some of our Poet's grand Touches of Nature: Some, that do not appear superficially such; but in which he seems the most deeply instructed; and to which, no doubt, he has so much ow'd that happy Preservation of his *Characters*, for which he is justly celebrated. Great Genius's, like his, naturally unambitious, are satisfy'd to conceal their Art in these Points. 'Tis the Foible of your worser Poets to make a Parade and Ostentation of that little Science they have; and to throw it out in the most ambitious Colours. And whenever a Writer of this Class shall attempt to copy these artful Concealments of our Author, and shall either think them easy, or practised by a Writer for his Ease, he will soon be convinced of his Mistake by the Difficulty of reaching the Imitation of them.

Speret idem, sudet multùm; frustráq; laboret,
Ausus idem:—

Indeed, to point out, and exclaim upon, all the Beauties of *Shakespeare*, as they come singly in Review, would be as insipid, as endless; as tedious, as unnecessary: But the Explanation of those Beauties, that are less obvious to common Readers, and whose Illustration depends on the Rules of just Criticism, and an exact Knowledge of human Life, should deservedly have a Share in a general Critic upon the Author. But, to pass over at once to another Subject:—

It has been allow'd on all hands, how far our Author was indebted to *Nature*; it is not so well agreed, how much he ow'd to *Languages* and acquir'd *Learning*. The Decisions on this Subject were certainly set on Foot by the Hint from *Ben Jonson*, that he had small *Latin* and less *Greek:* And from this Tradition, as it were, Mr. *Rowe* has thought fit peremptorily to declare, that, 'It is without Controversy, he had no Knowledge of the Writings 'of the ancient Poets, for that in his Works we find no Traces of 'any thing which looks like an Imitation of the Ancients. For 'the Delicacy of his Taste (*continues He,*) and the natural Bent of 'his own great Genius (equal, if not superior, to some of the Best 'of theirs;) would certainly have led him to read and study them 'with so much Pleasure, that some of their fine Images would 'naturally have insinuated themselves into, and been mix'd with, 'his own Writings: and so his not copying, at least, something 'from them, may be an Argument of his never having read them.' I shall leave it to the Determination of my Learned Readers, from the numerous Passages, which I have occasionally quoted in my Notes, in which our Poet seems closely to have imitated the Classics, whether Mr. *Rowe*'s Assertion be so absolutely to be depended on. The Result of the Controversy must certainly, either way, terminate to our Author's Honour: how happily he could imitate them, if that Point be allow'd; or how gloriously he could think like them, without owing any thing to Imitation.

Tho' I should be very unwilling to allow *Shakespeare* so poor a Scholar, as Many have labour'd to represent him, yet I shall be very cautious of declaring too positively on the other side of the Question: that is, with regard to my Opinion of his Knowledge in the dead Languages. And therefore the Passages, that I occasionally quote from the *Classics*, shall not be urged as Proofs that he knowingly imitated those Originals; but brought to shew how happily he has express'd himself upon the same Topicks. A very learned Critick of our own Nation has declar'd, that a Sameness of Thought and Sameness of Expression too, in Two Writers of a different Age, can hardly happen, without a violent Suspicion of the Latter copying from his Predecessor. I shall not therefore run any great Risque of a Censure, tho' I should venture to hint, that the Resemblance, in Thought and Expression, of our Author and an Ancient (which we should allow to be Imitation in One, whose Learning was not question'd) may sometimes take its Rise from Strength of Memory, and those Impressions which he ow'd to the School. And if we may allow a Possibility of This, considering that, when he quitted the School, he gave into his Father's Profession and way of Living, and had, 'tis likely, but a slender Library of Classical Learning; and considering what a Number of Translations, Romances, and Legends, started about his Time, and a little before; (most of which, 'tis very evident, he read;) I think, it may easily be reconcil'd why he rather schemed his *Plots* and *Characters* from these more latter Informations, than went back to those Fountains, for which he might entertain a sincere Veneration, but to which he could not have so ready a Recourse.

In touching on another Part of his Learning, as it related to the Knowledge of *History*, and *Books*, I shall advance something, that, at first sight, will very much wear the Appearance of a Paradox. For I shall find it no hard Matter to prove, that, from the grossest Blunders in History, we are not to infer his real Ignorance of it: Nor from a greater Use of *Latin* Words, than ever any other *English* Author used, must we infer his intimate Acquaintance with that Language.

A Reader of Taste may easily observe, that tho' *Shakespeare*, almost in every Scene of his historical Plays, commits the grossest Offences against Chronology, History, and Ancient Politicks; yet This was not thro' Ignorance, as is generally supposed, but thro' the too powerful Blaze of his Imagination; which, when once raised, made all acquired Knowledge vanish and disappear before it. But this Licence in him, as I have said, must not be imputed to Ignorance: since as often we may find him, when Occasion serves, reasoning up to the Truth of History; and throwing out Sentiments as justly adapted to the Circumstances of his Subject, as to the Dignity of his Characters, or Dictates of Nature in general.

Then, to come to his Knowledge of the *Latin* Tongue, 'tis certain, there is a surprising Effusion of *Latin* Words made *English*, far more than in any one *English* Author I have seen; but we must be cautious to imagine, this was of his own doing. For the *English* Tongue, in his Age, began extremely to suffer by an Inundation of *Latin*: And this, to be sure, was occasion'd by the Pedantry of those two Monarchs, *Elizabeth* and *James*, Both great *Latinists*. For it is not to be wonder'd at, if both the Court and Schools, equal Flatterers of Power, should adapt themselves to the Royal Taste.

But now I am touching on the Question, (which has been so frequently agitated, yet so entirely undecided) of his Learning and Acquaintance with the Languages; an additional Word or two naturally falls in here upon the Genius of our Author, as compared with that of *Jonson* his Contemporary. They are confessedly the greatest Writers our Nation could ever boast of in the *Drama*. The first, we say, owed all to his prodigious natural Genius; and the other a great deal to his Art and Learning. This, if attended to, will explain a very remarkable Appearance in their Writings. Besides those wonderful Masterpieces of Art and Genius, which each has given Us; They are the Authors of other Works very unworthy of them: But with this Difference; that in *Jonson*'s bad Pieces we don't discover one single Trace of the Author of the *Fox* and *Alchemist:* but in the wild extravagant Notes of *Shakespeare*, you every now and then encounter Strains that recognize the divine Composer. This Difference may be thus accounted for. *Jonson*, as we said before, owing all his Excellence to his Art, by which he sometimes strain'd himself to an uncommon Pitch, when at other times he unbent and play'd with his Subject, having nothing then to support him, it is no wonder he wrote so far beneath himself. But *Shakespeare*, indebted more largely to Nature, than the Other to acquired Talents, in his most negligent Hours could never so totally divest himself of his Genius, but that it would frequently break out with astonishing Force and Splendor.

As I have never propos'd to dilate farther on the Character of my Author, than was necessary to explain the Nature and Use of this Edition, I shall proceed to consider him as a Genius in Possession of an everlasting Name. And how great that Merit must be, which could gain it against all the Disadvantages of the horrid Condition in which he has hitherto appear'd! Had *Homer*, or any other admir'd Author, first started into Publick so maim'd and deform'd, we cannot determine whether they had not sunk for ever under the Ignominy of such an ill Appearance. The mangled Condition of *Shakespeare* has been acknowledg'd by Mr. *Rowe*, who publish'd him indeed, but neither corrected his Text, nor collated the old Copies. This Gentleman had Abilities, and a sufficient Knowledge of his Author, had but his Industry been equal to his Talents. The same mangled Condition has been acknowledg'd too by Mr. *Pope*, who publish'd him likewise, pretended to have collated the old Copies, and yet seldom has corrected the Text but to its Injury. I congratulate with the *Manes* of our Poet, that this Gentleman has been sparing in *indulging his private Sense*, as he phrases it; for He, who tampers with an Author whom he does not understand, must do it at the Expence of his Subject. I have made it evident throughout my Remarks, that he has frequently inflicted a Wound where he intended a Cure. He has acted with regard to our Author, as an

Editor, whom LIPSIUS mentions, did with regard to MARTIAL; *Inventus est nescio quis* Popa, *qui non* vitia *ejus, sed* ipsum *excidit*. He has attack'd him like an unhandy *Slaughterman*; and not lopp'd off the *Errors*, but the *Poet*.

When this is found to be the Fact, how absurd must appear the Praises of such an Editor? It seems a moot Point, whether Mr. *Pope* has done most Injury to *Shakespeare* as his Editor and Encomiast; or Mr. *Rymer* done him Service as his Rival and Censurer. They have Both shewn themselves in an equal *Impuissance* of suspecting, or amending, the corrupted Passages: and tho' it be neither Prudence to censure, or commend, what one does not understand; yet if a man must do one when he plays the Critick, the latter is the more ridiculous Office: And by That *Shakespeare* suffers most. For the natural Veneration, which we have for him, makes us apt to swallow whatever is given us as *his*, and set off with Encomiums; and hence we quit all Suspicions of Depravity: On the contrary, the Censure of so divine an Author sets us upon his Defence; and this produces an exact Scrutiny and Examination, which ends in finding out and discriminating the true from the spurious.

It is not with any secret Pleasure, that I so frequently animadvert on Mr. *Pope* as a Critick; but there are Provocations, which a Man can never quite forget. His Libels have been thrown out with so much Inveteracy, that, not to dispute whether they *should* come from a *Christian*, they leave it a Question whether they *could* come from a *Man*. I should be loth to doubt, as *Quintus Serenus* did in a like Case,

> *Sive homo, seu similis turpissima bestia nobis,*
> *Vulnera dente dedit.*

The Indignation, perhaps, for being represented a *Blockhead*, may be as strong in us as it is in the Ladies for a Reflexion on their *Beauties*. It is certain, I am indebted to Him for some *flagrant Civilities*; and I shall willingly devote a part of my Life to the honest Endeavour of quitting Scores: with this Exception however, that I will not return those Civilities in his *peculiar*

Strain, but confine myself, at least, to the Limits of *common Decency*. I shall ever think it better to want *Wit*, than to want *Humanity*: and impartial Posterity may, perhaps, be of my Opinion.

But, to return to my Subject; which now calls upon me to inquire into those Causes, to which the Depravations of my Author originally may be assign'd. We are to consider him as a Writer, of whom no authentic Manuscript was left extant; as a Writer, whose Pieces were dispersedly perform'd on the several *Stages* then in Being. And it was the Custom of those Days for the Poets to take a Price of the *Players* for the Pieces They from time to time furnish'd; and thereupon it was suppos'd, they had no farther Right to print them without the Consent of the *Players*. As it was the Interest of the *Companies* to keep their Plays un-publish'd, when any one succeeded, there was a Contest be-twixt the Curiosity of the Town, who demanded to see it in Print, and the Policy of the *Stagers*, who wish'd to secrete it within their own Walls. Hence, many Pieces were taken down in Short-hand, and imperfectly copied by Ear, from a *Representation:* Others were printed from piece-meal Parts surreptitiously obtain'd from the Theatres, uncorrect, and without the Poet's Knowledge. To some of these Causes we owe the Train of Blemishes, that deform those Pieces which stole singly into the World in our Author's Life-time.

There are still other Reasons, which may be suppos'd to have affected the whole Set. When the *Players* took upon them to publish his Works intire, every Theatre was ransack'd to supply the Copy; and *Parts* collected, which had gone thro' as many Changes as Performers, either from Mutilations or Additions made to them. Hence we derive many Chasms and Incoherences in the Sense and Matter. Scenes were frequently transposed, and shuffled out of their true Place, to humour the Caprice, or suppos'd Convenience, of some particular Actor. Hence much Confusion and Impropriety has attended, and embarras'd, the Business and Fable. To these obvious Causes of Corruption it must be added, that our Author has lain under the Disadvantage of having his Errors propagated and multiplied by Time: because, for near a Century, his Works were republish'd from the faulty Copies, without the Assistance of any intelligent Editor: which has been the Case likewise of many a *Classic* Writer.

The Nature of any Distemper once found has generally been the immediate Step to a Cure. *Shakespeare*'s Case has in a great measure resembled That of a corrupt *Classic*; and, consequently, the Method of Cure was likewise to bear a Resemblance. By what Means, and with what Success, this Cure has been effected on ancient Writers, is too well known, and needs no formal Illustration. The Reputation, consequent on Tasks of that na-ture, invited me to attempt the Method here; with this View, the Hopes of restoring to the Publick their greatest Poet in his Original Purity: after having so long lain in a Condition that was a Disgrace to common Sense. To this end I have ventur'd on a Labour, that is the first Assay of the kind on any modern Author whatsoever. For the late Edition of *Milton* by the Learned Dr. *Bentley* is, in the main, a Performance of another Species. It is plain, it was the Intention of that Great Man rather to correct and pare off the Excrescencies of the *Paradise Lost*, in the manner that *Tucca* and *Varius* were employ'd to criticize the *Æneis* of *Virgil*, than to restore corrupted Passages. Hence, therefore, may be seen either the Iniquity or Ignorance of his Censurers, who, from some Expressions, would make us believe, the *Doctor* every where gives us his Corrections as the Original Text of the Author; whereas the chief Turn of his Criticism is plainly to shew the World, that if *Milton* did not write as He would have him, he ought to have wrote so.

I thought proper to premise this Observation to the Readers, as it will shew that the Critic on *Shakespeare* is of a quite different Kind. His genuine Text is for the most part religiously adher'd to, and the numerous Faults and Blemishes, purely his own, are left as they were found. Nothing is alter'd, but what by the clearest Reasoning can be proved a Corruption of the true Text; and the Alteration, a real Restoration of the genuine Reading. Nay, so strictly have I strove to give the true Reading, tho' sometimes not to the Advantage of my Author, that I have been ridiculously ridicul'd for it by Those, who either were iniquitously for turning every thing to my Disadvantage; or else were totally ignorant of the true Duty of an Editor.

The Science of Criticism, as far as it affects an Editor, seems to be reduced to these three Classes; the Emendation of corrupt Passages; the Explanation of obscure and difficult ones; and an Inquiry into the Beauties and Defects of Composition. This Work is principally confin'd to the two former Parts: tho' there are some Specimens interspers'd of the latter Kind, as several of the Emendations were best supported, and several of the Difficulties best explain'd, by taking notice of the Beauties and Defects of the Composition peculiar to this Immortal Poet. But This was but occasional, and for the sake only of perfecting the two other Parts, which were the proper Objects of the Editor's Labour. The third lies open for every willing Undertaker: and I shall be pleas'd to see it the Employment of a masterly Pen.

It must necessarily happen, as I have formerly observ'd, that where the Assistance of Manuscripts is wanting to set an Author's Meaning right, and rescue him from those Errors which have been transmitted down thro' a Series of incorrect Editions, and a long Intervention of Time, many Passages must be desperate, and past a Cure; and their true Sense irretrievable either to Care or the Sagacity of Conjecture. But is there any Reason therefore to say, That because All cannot be retriev'd, All ought to be left desperate? We should shew very little Honesty, or Wisdom, to play the Tyrants with an Author's Text; to raze, alter, innovate, and overturn, at all Adventures, and to the utter Detriment of his Sense and Meaning: But to be so very reserved and cautious, as to interpose no Relief or Conjecture, where it manifestly labours and cries out for Assistance, seems, on the other hand, an indolent Absurdity.

As there are very few Pages in *Shakespeare*, upon which some Suspicions of Depravity do not reasonably arise; I have thought it my Duty, in the first place, by a diligent and laborious Collation to take in the Assistances of all the older Copies.

In his *Historical Plays*, whenever our *English* Chronicles, and in his Tragedies when *Greek* or *Roman* Story, could give any Light; no Pains have been omitted to set Passages right by comparing my Author with his Originals: for, as I have frequently observed, he was a close and accurate Copier where-ever his *Fable* was founded on *History*.

Where-ever the Author's Sense is clear and discoverable, (tho', perchance, low and trivial;) I have not by any Innovation tamper'd with his Text; out of an Ostentation of endeavouring to make him speak better than the old Copies have done.

Where, thro' all the former Editions, a Passage has labour'd under flat Nonsense and invincible Darkness, if, by the Addition or Alteration of a Letter or two, or a Transposition in the Pointing, I have restored to Him both *Sense* and *Sentiment*; such Corrections, I am persuaded, will need no Indulgence.

And whenever I have taken a greater Latitude and Liberty in amending, I have constantly endeavour'd to support my Corrections and Conjectures by parallel Passages and Authorities from himself, the surest Means of expounding any Author whatsoever. *Cette voïe d'interpreter un Autheur par lui-même est plus sure que tous les Commentaires*, says a very learned *French* Critick.

As to my *Notes*, (from which the common and learned Readers of our Author, I hope, will derive some Satisfaction;) I have endeavour'd to give them a Variety in some Proportion to their Number. Where-ever I have ventur'd at an Emendation, a *Note* is constantly subjoin'd to justify and assert the Reason of it. Where I only offer a Conjecture, and do not disturb the Text, I fairly set forth my Grounds for such Conjecture, and submit it to Judgment. Some Remarks are spent in explaining Passages, where the Wit or Satire depends on an obscure Point of History: Others, where Allusions are to Divinity, Philosophy, or other Branches of Science. Some are added to shew, where there is a Suspicion of our Author having borrow'd from the Ancients: Others, to shew where he is rallying his Contemporaries; or where He himself is rallied by them. And some are necessarily thrown in, to explain an obscure and obsolete *Term*, *Phrase*, or *Idea*. I once intended to have added a complete and copious *Glossary*; but as

I have been importun'd, and am prepar'd, to give a correct Edition of our Author's POEMS, (in which many Terms occur that are not to be met with in his *Plays*,) I thought a *Glossary* to all *Shakespeare*'s Works more proper to attend that Volume.

In reforming an infinite Number of Passages in the *Pointing*, where the Sense was before quite lost, I have frequently sub-join'd Notes to shew the *deprav'd*, and to prove the *reform'd*, Pointing: a Part of Labour in this Work which I could very willingly have spar'd myself. May it not be objected, why then have you burthen'd us with these Notes? The Answer is obvious, and, if I mistake not, very material. Without such Notes, these Passages in subsequent Editions would be liable, thro' the Ignor-ance of Printers and Correctors, to fall into the old Confusion: Whereas, a Note on every one hinders all possible Return to Depravity; and for ever secures them in a State of Purity and Integrity not to be lost or forfeited.

Again, as some Notes have been necessary to point out the Detection of the corrupted Text, and establish the Restoration of the genuine Readings; some others have been as necessary for the Explanation of Passages obscure and difficult. To under-stand the Necessity and Use of this Part of my Task, some Particulars of my Author's Character are previously to be explain'd. There are *Obscurities* in him, which are common to him with all Poets of the same Species; there are Others, the Issue of the Times he liv'd in; and there are Others, again, peculiar to himself. The Nature of Comic Poetry being entirely satirical, it busies itself more in exposing what we call Caprice and Humour, than Vices cognizable to the Laws. The *English*, from the Hap-piness of a free Constitution, and a Turn of Mind peculiarly speculative and inquisitive, are observ'd to produce more *Humourists* and a greater Variety of original *Characters*, than any other People whatsoever: And These owing their immediate Birth to the peculiar Genius of each Age, an infinite Number of Things alluded to, glanced at, and expos'd, must needs become obscure, as the *Characters* themselves are antiquated, and disused. An Editor therefore should be well vers'd in the History and

Manners of his Author's Age, if he aims at doing him a Service in this Respect.

Besides, *Wit* lying mostly in the Assemblage of *Ideas*, and in the putting Those together with Quickness and Variety, wherein can be found any Resemblance, or Congruity, to make up pleasant Pictures, and agreeable Visions in the Fancy; the Writer, who aims at Wit, must of course range far and wide for Materials. Now, the Age, in which *Shakespeare* liv'd, having, above all others, a wonderful Affection to appear Learned, They declined vulgar Images, such as are immediately fetch'd from Nature, and rang'd thro' the Circle of the Sciences to fetch their Ideas from thence. But as the Resemblances of such Ideas to the Subject must necessarily lie very much out of the common Way, and every Piece of Wit appear a Riddle to the Vulgar; This, that should have taught them the forced, quaint, unnatural Tract they were in, (and induce them to follow a more natural One,) was the very Thing that kept them attach'd to it. The ostentatious Affectation of abstruse Learning, peculiar to that Time, the Love that Men naturally have to every Thing that looks like Mystery, fixed them down to this Habit of Obscurity. Thus became the Poetry of DONNE (tho' the wittiest Man of that Age,) nothing but a continued Heap of Riddles. And our *Shakespeare*, with all his easy Nature about him, for want of the Knowledge of the true Rules of Art, falls frequently into this vicious Manner.

The third Species of *Obscurities*, which deform our Author, as the Effects of his own Genius and Character, are Those that proceed from his peculiar Manner of *Thinking*, and as peculiar a Manner of *cloathing* those *Thoughts*. With regard to his *Thinking*, it is certain, that he had a general Knowledge of all the Sciences: But his Acquaintance was rather That of a Traveller, than a Native. Nothing in Philosophy was unknown to him; but every Thing in it had the Grace and Force of Novelty. And as Novelty is one main Source of Admiration, we are not to wonder that He has perpetual Allusions to the most recondite Parts of the Sciences: and This was done not so much out of Affectation, as the Effect of Admiration begot by Novelty. Then, as to his *Style* and *Diction*, we may much more justly apply to SHAKESPEARE, what a celebrated Writer has said of MILTON; *Our Language sunk under him, and was unequal to that Greatness of Soul which furnish'd him with such glorious Conceptions.* He therefore frequently uses old Words, to give his Diction an Air of Solemnity; as he coins others, to express the Novelty and Variety of his Ideas.

Upon every distinct Species of these *Obscurities* I have thought it my Province to employ a Note, for the Service of my Author, and the Entertainment of my Readers. A few transient Remarks too I have not scrupled to intermix, upon the Poet's *Negligences* and *Omissions* in point of Art; but I have done it always in such a Manner, as will testify my Deference and Veneration for the Immortal Author. Some Censurers of *Shakespeare*, and particularly Mr. *Rymer*, have taught me to distinguish betwixt the *Railer* and *Critick*. The Outrage of his Quotations is so remarkably violent, so push'd beyond all Bounds of Decency and sober Reasoning, that it quite carries over the Mark at which it was levell'd. Extravagant Abuse throws off the Edge of the intended Disparagement, and turns the Madman's Weapon into his own Bosom. In short, as to *Rymer*, This is my Opinion of him from his *Criticisms* on the *Tragedies* of the Last Age. He writes with great Vivacity, and appears to have been a Scholar: but, as for his Knowledge of the Art of Poetry, I can't perceive it was any deeper than his Acquaintance with *Bossu* and *Dacier*, from whom he has transcrib'd many of his best Reflexions. The late Mr. *Gildon* was one attached to *Rymer* by a similar Way of Thinking and Studies. They were Both of that Species of Criticks, who are desirous of displaying their Powers rather in finding Faults, than in consulting the Improvement of the World: the *hypercritical* Part of the Science of *Criticism.*

I had not mentioned the modest Liberty I have here and there taken of animadverting on my Author, but that I was willing to obviate in time the splenetick Exaggerations of my Adversaries on this Head. From past Experiments I have reason to be conscious, in what Light this Attempt may be placed: and that what I call a *modest Liberty*, will, by a little of their Dexterity, be inverted into downright *Impudence*. From a hundred mean and dishonest Artifices employ'd to discredit this Edition, and to cry down its Editor, I have all the Grounds in Nature to beware of Attacks. But tho' the Malice of Wit, join'd to the Smoothness of Versification, may furnish some Ridicule; Fact, I hope, will be able to stand its Ground against Banter and Gaiety.

It has been my Fate, it seems, as I thought it my Duty, to discover some *Anachronisms* in our Author; which might have slept in Obscurity but for *this Restorer*, as Mr. *Pope* is pleas'd affectionately to stile me; as, for Instance, where *Aristotle* is mentioned by *Hector* in *Troilus* and *Cressida*: and *Galen*, *Cato*, and *Alexander* the Great, in *Coriolanus*. These, in Mr. *Pope*'s Opinion, are Blunders, which, the Illiteracy of the first Publishers of his Works has father'd upon the Poet's Memory: *it not being at all credible, that These could be the Errors of any Man who had the least Tincture of a School, or the least Conversation with Such as had.* But I have sufficiently proved, in the course of my *Notes*, that such *Anachronisms* were the Effect of Poetic Licence, rather than of Ignorance in our Poet. And if I may be permitted to ask a modest Question by the way, Why may not I restore an *Anachronism* really made by our Author, as well as Mr. *Pope* take the Privilege to fix others upon him, which he never had it in his Head to make; as I may venture to affirm He had not, in the Instance of Sir *Francis Drake*, to which I have spoke in the proper Place?

But who shall dare make any Words about this Freedom of Mr. *Pope*'s towards *Shakespeare*, if it can be prov'd, that, in his Fits of Criticism, he makes no more Ceremony with good *Homer* himself? To try, then, a Criticism of his own advancing; In the 8th Book of the *Odyssey*, where *Demodocus* sings the Episode of the Loves of *Mars* and *Venus*; and that, upon their being taken in the Net by *Vulcan*,

> — —'*The God of Arms*
> '*Must pay the Penalty for lawless Charms*;

Mr. *Pope* is so kind gravely to inform us, 'That *Homer* in This, as 'in many other Places, seems to allude to the Laws of *Athens*, 'where Death was the Punishment of Adultery.' But how is this significant Observation made out? Why, who can possibly object any Thing to the contrary?—*Does not* Pausanias *relate, that* Draco *the Lawgiver to the* Athenians *granted Impunity to any Person that took Revenge upon an Adulterer? And was it not also the Institution of* Solon, *that if Any One took an Adulterer in the Fact, he might use him as he pleas'd?* These Things are very true: and to see What a good Memory, and sound Judgment in Conjunction can atchieve! Tho' *Homer's* Date is not determin'd down to a single Year, yet 'tis pretty generally agreed that he liv'd above 300 Years before *Draco* and *Solon:* And That, it seems, has made him *seem* to allude to the very Laws, which these Two Legislators propounded above 300 Years after. If this Inference be not sometimes like an *Anachronism* or *Prolepsis*, I'll look once more into my Lexicons for the true Meaning of the Words. It appears to me, that somebody besides *Mars* and *Venus* has been caught in a Net by this Episode: and I could call in other Instances to confirm what treacherous Tackle this Net-work is, if not cautiously handled.

How just, notwithstanding, I have been in detecting the *Anachronisms* of my Author, and in defending him for the Use of them, Our late Editor seems to think, They should rather have slept in Obscurity: and the having discovered them is sneer'd at, as a sort of wrong-headed Sagacity.

The numerous Corrections, which I made of the Poet's Text in my SHAKESPEARE *Restor'd*, and which the Publick have been so kind to think well of, are, in the Appendix of Mr. *Pope's* last Edition, slightingly call'd *Various Readings, Guesses*, &c. He confesses to have inserted as many of them as he judg'd of any the least Advantage to the Poet; but says, that the Whole amounted to about 25 Words: and pretends to have annexed a compleat List of the Rest, which were not worth his embracing. Whoever has read my Book will at one Glance see, how in both these Points Veracity is strain'd, so an Injury might but be done. *Malus, etsi obesse non pote, tamen cogitat.*

Another Expedient, to make my Work appear of a trifling

Nature, has been an Attempt to depreciate *Literal Criticism*. To this end, and to pay a servile Compliment to Mr. *Pope*, an *Anonymous* Writer has, like a *Scotch* Pedlar in Wit, unbraced his Pack on the Subject. But, that his Virulence might not seem to be levelled singly at Me, he has done Me the Honour to join Dr. *Bentley* in the Libel. I was in hopes, We should have been Both abused with Smartness of Satire, at least; tho' not with Solidity of Argument: that it might have been worth some Reply in Defence of the Science attacked. But I may fairly say of this Author, as *Falstaffe* does of *Poins*;—*Hang him, Baboon! his Wit is as thick as* Tewksbury *Mustard; there is no more Conceit in him, than is in a* MALLET. If it be not Prophanation to set the Opinion of the divine *Longinus* against such a Scribler, he tells us expresly, 'That 'to make a Judgment upon *Words* (and *Writings*) is the most 'consummate Fruit of much Experience.' ἡ γὰρ τῶν λόγων κρί- σις πολλῆς ἐστὶ πείρας τελευταῖον ἐπιγέννημα. Whenever Words are depraved, the Sense of course must be corrupted; and thence the Readers betray'd into a false Meaning.

If the *Latin* and *Greek* Languages have receiv'd the greatest Advantages imaginable from the Labours of the Editors and Criticks of the two last Ages; by whose Aid and Assistance the Grammarians have been enabled to write infinitely better in that Art than even the preceding Grammarians, who wrote when those Tongues flourish'd as living Languages: I should account it a peculiar Happiness, that, by the faint Assay I have made in this Work, a Path might be chalk'd out, for abler Hands, by which to derive the same Advantages to our own Tongue: a Tongue, which, tho' it wants none of the fundamental Qualities of an universal Language, yet, as a *noble Writer* says, lisps and stammers as in its Cradle; and has produced little more towards its polishing than Complaints of its Barbarity.

Having now run thro' all those Points, which I intended should make any Part of this Dissertation, and having in my *former* Edition made publick Acknowledgments of the Assistances lent me, I shall conclude with a brief Account of the Methods taken in *This*.

It was thought proper, in order to reduce the Bulk and Price of the Impression, that the Notes, where-ever they would admit of it, might be abridg'd: for which Reason I have curtail'd a great Quantity of Such, in which Explanations were too prolix, or Authorities in Support of an Emendation too numerous: and Many I have entirely expung'd, which were judg'd rather Verbose and Declamatory, (and, so, Notes merely of Ostentation;) than necessary, or instructive.

The few literal Errors, which had escaped Notice, for want of Revisals, in the former Edition, are here reform'd: and the Pointing of innumerable Passages is regulated, with all the Accuracy I am capable of.

I shall decline making any farther Declaration of the Pains I have taken upon my Author, because it was my Duty, as his Editor, to publish him with my best Care and Judgment: and because, I am sensible, all such Declarations are construed to be laying a sort of a Debt on the Publick. As the former Edition has been received with much Indulgence, I ought to make my Acknowledgements to the Town for their favourable Opinion of it: and I shall always be proud to think That Encouragement the best Payment I can hope to receive from my poor Studies.

SIR THOMAS HANMER

Preface to 'The Works of Shakespear'

1744

WHAT the Publick is here to expect is a true and correct Edition of *Shakespear's* works cleared from the corruptions with which they have hitherto abounded. One of the great Admirers of this incomparable Author hath made it the amusement of his leisure hours for many years past to look over his writings with a careful eye, to note the obscurities and absurdities introduced into the text, and according to the best of his judgment to restore the genuine sense and purity of it. In this he proposed nothing to himself but his private satisfaction in making his own copy as perfect as he could: but as the emendations multiplied upon his hands, other Gentlemen equally fond of the Author desired to see them, and some were so kind as to give their assistance by communicating their observations and conjectures upon difficult passages which had occurred to them. Thus by degrees the work growing more considerable than was at first expected, they who had the opportunity of looking into it, too partial perhaps in their judgment, thought it worth being made publick; and he, who hath with difficulty yielded to their perswasions, is far from desiring to reflect upon the late Editors for the omissions and defects which they left to be supplied by others who should follow them in the same province. On the contrary, he thinks the world much obliged to them for the progress they made in weeding out so great a number of blunders and mistakes as they have done, and probably he who hath carried on the work might never have thought of such an undertaking if he had not found a considerable part so done to his hands.

From what causes it proceeded that the works of this Author

in the first publication of them were more injured and abused than perhaps any that ever pass'd the Press, hath been sufficiently explained in the Preface to Mr. *Pope's* Edition which is here subjoined, and there needs no more to be said upon that subject. This only the Reader is desired to bear in mind, that as the corruptions are more numerous and of a grosser kind than can well be conceived but by those who have looked nearly into them; so in the correcting them this rule hath been most strictly observed, not to give a loose to fancy, or indulge a licentious spirit of criticism, as if it were fit for any one to presume to judge what *Shakespear* ought to have written, instead of endeavouring to discover truly and retrieve what he did write: and so great caution hath been used in this respect, that no alterations have been made but what the sense necessarily required, what the measure of the verse often helped to point out, and what the similitude of words in the false reading and in the true, generally speaking, appeared very well to justify.

Most of those passages are here thrown to the bottom of the page and rejected as spurious, which were stigmatized as such in Mr. *Pope's* Edition; and it were to be wished that more had then undergone the same sentence. The promoter of the present Edition hath ventured to discard but few more upon his own judgment, the most considerable of which is that wretched piece of ribaldry in King *Henry V*. put into the mouths of the *French* Princess and an old Gentlewoman, improper enough as it is all in *French* and not intelligible to an *English* audience, and yet that perhaps is the best thing that can be said of it. There can be no doubt but a great deal more of that low stuff which disgraces the works of this great Author, was foisted in by the Players after his death, to please the vulgar audiences by which they subsisted: and though some of the poor witticisms and conceits must be supposed to have fallen from his pen, yet as he hath put them generally into the mouths of low and ignorant people, so it is to be remember'd that he wrote for the Stage, rude and unpolished as it then was; and the vicious taste of the age must stand condemned for them, since he hath left upon record a signal proof how much he despised them. In his Play of *The Merchant of Venice* a Clown is introduced quibbling in a miserable manner, upon which one who bears the character of a man of sense makes the following reflection: *How every fool can play upon a word! I think the best grace of wit will shortly turn into silence, and discourse grow commendable in none but parrots.* He could hardly have found stronger words to express his indignation at those false pretences to wit then in vogue; and therefore though such trash is frequently interspersed in his writings, it would be unjust to cast it as an imputation upon his taste and judgment and character as a Writer.

There being many words in *Shakespear* which are grown out of use and obsolete, and many borrowed from other languages which are not enough naturalized or known among us, a Glossary is added at the end of the work, for the explanation of all those terms which have hitherto been so many stumbling-blocks to the generality of Readers; and where there is any obscurity in the text not arising from the words but from a reference to some antiquated customs now forgotten, or other causes of that kind, a note is put at the bottom of the page to clear up the difficulty.

With these several helps if that rich vein of sense which runs through the works of this Author can be retrieved in every part and brought to appear in its true light, and if it may be hoped without presumption that this is here effected; they who love and admire him will receive a new pleasure, and all probably will be more ready to join in doing him justice, who does great honour to his country as a rare and perhaps a singular Genius: one who hath attained an high degree of perfection in those two great branches of Poetry, Tragedy and Comedy, different as they are in their natures from each other; and who may be said without partiality to have equalled, if not excelled, in both kinds, the best writers of any age or country who have thought it glory enough to distinguish themselves in either.

Since therefore other nations have taken care to dignify the works of their most celebrated Poets with the fairest impressions beautified with the ornaments of sculpture, well may our

Shakespear be thought to deserve no less consideration: and as a fresh acknowledgment hath lately been paid to his merit, and a high regard to his name and memory, by erecting his Statue at a publick expence; so it is desired that this new Edition of his works, which hath cost some attention and care, may be looked upon as another small monument designed and dedicated to his honour.

WILLIAM WARBURTON

Preface to 'The Works of Shakespear'

1747

IT hath been no unusual thing for Writers, when dissatisfied with the Patronage or Judgment of their own Times, to appeal to Posterity for a fair Hearing. Some have even thought fit to apply to it in the first Instance; and to decline Acquaintance with the Public till Envy and Prejudice had quite subsided. But, of all the Trusters to Futurity, commend me to the Author of the following Poems, who not only left it to Time to do him Justice as it would, but to find him out as it could. For, what between too great Attention to his Profit as a Player, and too little to his Reputation as a Poet, his Works, left to the Care of Door-keepers and Prompters, hardly escaped the common Fate of those Writings, how good soever, which are abandoned to their own Fortune, and unprotected by Party or Cabal. At length, indeed, they struggled into Light; but so disguised and travested, that no classic Author, after having run ten secular Stages thro' the blind Cloisters of Monks and Canons, ever came out in half so maimed and mangled a Condition. But for a full Account of his Disorders, I refer the Reader to the excellent Discourse which follows, and turn myself to consider the Remedies that have been applied to them.

Shakespear's Works, when they escaped the Players, did not fall into much better Hands when they came amongst Printers and Booksellers: who, to say the Truth, had, at first, but small Encouragement for putting him into a better Condition. The stubborn Nonsense, with which he was incrusted, occasioned his lying long neglected amongst the common Lumber of the Stage. And when that resistless Splendor, which now shoots all around him, had, by degrees, broke thro' the Shell of those Impurities, his dazzled Admirers became as suddenly insensible to the extraneous Scurf that still stuck upon him, as they had been before to the native Beauties that lay under it. So that, as then, he was thought not to deserve a Cure, he was now supposed not to need any.

His growing Eminence, however, required that he should be used with Ceremony: And he soon had his Appointment of an *Editor* in form. But the Bookseller, whose dealing was with Wits, having learnt of them, I know not what silly Maxim, that *none but a Poet should presume to meddle with a Poet*, engaged the ingenious Mr. *Rowe* to undertake this Employment. A Wit indeed he was; but so utterly unacquainted with the whole Business of Criticism, that he did not even collate or consult the first Editions of the Work he undertook to publish; but contented himself with giving us a meagre Account of the Author's Life, interlarded with some common-place Scraps from his Writings. The Truth is, *Shakespear's* Condition was yet but ill understood. The Nonsense, now, by consent, received for his own, was held in a kind of Reverence for its Age and Author: and thus it continued, till another great *Poet* broke the Charm; by shewing us, that the higher we went, the less of it was still to be found.

For the Proprietors, not discouraged by their first unsuccessful Effort, in due time, made a second; and, tho' they still stuck to their Poets, with infinitely more Success in their Choice of Mr. POPE. Who by the mere force of an uncommon Genius, without any particular Study or Profession of this Art, discharged the great Parts of it so well as to make his Edition the best Foundation for all further Improvements. He separated the genuine from the spurious Plays: And, with equal Judgment, tho' not always with the same Success, attempted to clear the genuine Plays from the interpolated Scenes: He then consulted the old Editions; and, by a careful Collation of them, rectified the faulty, and supplied the imperfect Reading, in a great number of Places: And lastly, in an admirable Preface, hath drawn a general, but very lively, Sketch of *Shakespear's* poetic Character; and, in the corrected

Text, marked out those peculiar Strokes of Genius which were most proper to support and illustrate that Character. Thus far Mr. POPE. And altho' much more was to be done before *Shakespear* could be restored to himself (such as amending the corrupted Text where the printed Books afford no Assistance; explaining his licentious Phraseology and obscure Allusions; and illustrating the Beauties of his Poetry;) yet, with great Modesty and Prudence, our illustrious Editor left this to the Critic by Profession.

But nothing will give the common Reader a better Idea of the Value of Mr. *Pope's* Edition, than the two Attempts which have been since made, by Mr. *Theobald* and Sir *Thomas Hanmer*, in Opposition to it. Who, altho' they concerned themselves only in the *first* of these three Parts of Criticism, the *restoring the Text*, (without any Conception of the *second*, or venturing even to touch upon the *third*) yet succeeded so very ill in it, that they left their Author in ten times a worse Condition than they found him. But, as it was my ill Fortune to have some accidental Connexions with these two *Gentlemen*, it will be incumbent on me to be a little more particular concerning them.

The One was recommended to me as a poor Man; the Other as a poor Critic: and to each of them, at different times, I communicated a great number of Observations, which they managed, as they saw fit, to the Relief of their several Distresses. As to Mr. *Theobald*, who wanted Money, I allowed him to print what I gave him for his own Advantage: and he allowed himself in the Liberty of taking one Part for his own, and sequestering another for the Benefit, as I supposed, of some future Edition. But, as to the *Oxford Editor*, who wanted nothing but what he might very well be without, the Reputation of a Critic, I could not so easily forgive him for trafficking with my Papers without my Knowledge; and, when that Project fail'd, for employing a number of my Conjectures in his Edition against my express Desire not to have that Honour done unto me.

Mr. *Theobald* was naturally turned to Industry and Labour. What he read he could transcribe: but, as what he thought, if

ever he did think, he could but ill express, so he read on; and by
that means got a Character of Learning, without risquing, to
every Observer, the Imputation of wanting a better Talent. By a
punctilious Collation of the old Books, he corrected what was
manifestly wrong in the *latter* Editions, by what was manifestly
right in the *earlier*. And this is his real merit; and the whole of it.
For where the Phrase was very obsolete or licentious in the
common Books, or only slightly corrupted in the *other*, he wanted
sufficient Knowledge of the Progress and various Stages of the
English Tongue, as well as Acquaintance with the Peculiarity of
Shakespear's Language, to understand what was right; nor had he
either common Judgment to see, or critical Sagacity to amend,
what was manifestly faulty. Hence he generally exerts his conjectural Talent in the wrong Place: He tampers with what is
sound in the *common* Books; and, in the *old* ones, omits all Notice
of *Variations* the Sense of which he did not understand.

How the *Oxford Editor* came to think himself qualified for this
Office, from which his whole Course of Life had been so remote,
is still more difficult to conceive. For whatever Parts he might
have either of Genius or Erudition, he was absolutely ignorant
of the Art of Criticism, as well as the Poetry of that Time, and
the Language of his Author: And so far from a Thought of
examining the *first* Editions, that he even neglected to compare
Mr. *Pope*'s, from which he printed his own, with Mr. *Theobald*'s;
whereby he lost the Advantage of many fine Lines which the
other had recovered from the old Quartos. Where he trusts to
his own Sagacity, in what affects the Sense, his Conjectures are
generally absurd and extravagant, and violating every Rule of
Criticism. Tho', in this Rage of Correcting, he was not absolutely
destitute of all *Art*. For, having a Number of my Conjectures
before him, he took as many of them as he saw fit, to work upon;
and by changing them to something, he thought, synonimous or
similar, he made them his own; and so became a Critic at a cheap
Expence. But how well he hath succeeded in this, as likewise in
his Conjectures which are properly his own, will be seen in the
course of my Remarks: Tho', as he hath declined to give the

Reasons for his Interpolations, he hath not afforded me so fair a hold of him as Mr. *Theobald* hath done, who was less cautious. But his principal Object was to reform his Author's Numbers; and this, which he hath done, on every Occasion, by the Insertion or Omission of a set of harmless unconcerning Expletives, makes up the gross Body of his innocent Corrections. And so, in spite of that extreme Negligence in Numbers, which distinguishes the first Dramatic Writers, he hath tricked up the old Bard, from Head to Foot, in all the finical Exactness of a modern Measurer of Syllables.

For the rest, all the Corrections which these two Editors have made on any *reasonable* Foundation, are here admitted into the Text; and carefully assigned to their respective Authors. A piece of Justice which the *Oxford Editor* never did; and which the *Other* was not always scrupulous in observing towards me. To conclude with them in a word, They separately possessed those two Qualities which, more than any other, have contributed to bring the Art of Criticism into disrepute, *Dulness of Apprehension*, and *Extravagance of Conjecture*.

I am now to give some Account of the present Undertaking. For as to all those Things which have been published under the titles of *Essays, Remarks, Observations*, &c. on *Shakespear*, (if you except some critical Notes on *Macbeth*, given as a Specimen of a projected Edition, and written, as appears, by a Man of Parts and Genius) the rest are absolutely below a serious Notice.

The whole a Critic can do for an Author who deserves his Service, is to correct the faulty Text; to remark the Peculiarities of Language; to illustrate the obscure Allusions; and to explain the Beauties and Defects of Sentiment or Composition. And surely, if ever Author had a Claim to this Service, it was our *Shakespear:* Who, widely excelling in the Knowledge of Human Nature, hath given to his infinitely varied Pictures of it, such Truth of Design, such Force of Drawing, such Beauty of Colouring, as was hardly ever equalled by any Writer, whether his Aim was the Use, or only the Entertainment of Mankind. The Notes in this Edition, therefore, take in the whole Compass of Criticism.

I. The first sort is employed in restoring the Poet's genuine Text; but in those Places only where it labours with inextricable Nonsense. In which, how much soever I may have given Scope to critical Conjecture, where the old Copies failed me, I have indulged nothing to Fancy or Imagination; but have religiously observed the severe Canons of literal Criticism; as may be seen from the Reasons accompanying every Alteration of the common Text. Nor would a different Conduct have become a Critic, whose greatest Attention, in this part, was to vindicate the established Reading from Interpolations occasioned by the fanciful Extravagancies of others. I once intended to have given the Reader a *body of Canons*, for literal Criticism, drawn out in form; as well such as concern the Art in general, as those that arise from the Nature and Circumstances of our Author's Works in particular. And this for two Reasons. First, To give the *unlearned Reader* a just Idea, and consequently a better Opinion of the Art of Criticism, now sunk very low in the popular Esteem, by the Attempts of some who would needs exercise it without either natural or acquired Talents; and by the ill Success of others, who seemed to have lost both, when they came to try them upon English Authors. Secondly, To deter the *unlearned Writer* from wantonly trifling with an Art he is a Stranger to, at the Expence of his own Reputation, and the Integrity of the Text of established Authors. But these Uses may be well supplied by what is occasionally said upon the Subject, in the Course of the following Remarks.

II. The second sort of Notes consists in an Explanation of the Author's Meaning, when, by one or more of these Causes, it becomes obscure; either from a *licentious Use of Terms;* or a *hard or ungrammatical Construction*; or lastly, from *far-fetch'd or quaint Allusions*.

1. This licentious Use of Words is almost peculiar to the Language of *Shakespear*. To common Terms he hath affixed Meanings of his own, unauthorised by Use, and not to be justified by Analogy. And this Liberty he hath taken with the noblest Parts of Speech, such as *Mixed-modes*; which, as they are

most susceptible of Abuse, so their Abuse most hurts the Clearness of the Discourse. The Critics (to whom *Shakespear's* Licence was still as much a Secret as his Meaning, which that Licence had obscured) fell into two contrary Mistakes; but equally injurious to his Reputation and his Writings. For some of them observing a Darkness, that pervaded his whole Expression, have censured him for Confusion of Ideas and Inaccuracy of reasoning. *In the Neighing of a Horse,* (says *Rymer*) *or in the Growling of a Mastiff, there is a Meaning, there is a lively Expression, and, may I say, more Humanity than many times in the tragical Flights of* Shakespear. The Ignorance of which Censure is of a Piece with its Brutality. The Truth is, no one thought clearer, or argued more closely than this immortal Bard. But his Superiority of Genius less needing the Intervention of Words in the Act of Thinking, when he came to draw out his Contemplations into Discourse, he took up (as he was hurried on by the Torrent of his Matter) with the first Words that lay in his Way; and if, amongst these, there were two *Mixed-modes* that had but a principal Idea in common, it was enough for him; he regarded them as synonimous, and would use the one for the other without Fear or Scruple.——— Again, there have been others, such as the two last Editors, who have fallen into a contrary Extreme, and regarded *Shakespear's* Anomalies (as we may call them) amongst the Corruptions of his Text; which, therefore, they have cashiered in great numbers, to make room for a Jargon of their own. This hath put me to additional Trouble; for I had not only their Interpolations to throw out again, but the genuine Text to replace, and establish in its stead; which, in many Cases, could not be done without shewing the peculiar Sense of the Terms, and explaining the Causes which led the Poet to so perverse an use of them. I had it once, indeed, in my Design, to give a general alphabetic *Glossary* of these Terms; but as each of them is explained in its proper Place, there seemed the less Occasion for such an Index.

2. The Poet's hard and unnatural Construction had a different Original. This was the Effect of mistaken Art and Design. The Public Taste was in its Infancy; and delighted (as it always does

during that State) in the high and turgid; which leads the Writer
to disguise a vulgar expression with hard and forced construction, whereby the Sentence frequently becomes cloudy and dark.
Here, his Critics shew their modesty, and leave him to himself.
For the arbitrary change of a Word doth little towards dispelling
an obscurity that ariseth, not from the licentious use of a single
Term, but from the unnatural arrangement of a whole Sentence.
And they risqued nothing by their silence. For *Shakespear* was
too clear in Fame to be suspected of a want of Meaning; and too
high in Fashion for any one to own he needed a Critic to find it
out. Not but, in his best works, we must allow, he is often so
natural and flowing, so pure and correct, that he is even a model
for stile and language.

3. As to his far-fetched and quaint Allusions, these are often a
cover to common thoughts; just as his hard construction is to
common expression. When they are not so, the Explanation of
them has this further advantage, that, in clearing the Obscurity,
you frequently discover some latent conceit not unworthy of his
Genius.

III. The third and last sort of Notes is concerned in a critical
explanation of the Author's Beauties and Defects; but chiefly of
his Beauties, whether in Stile, Thought, Sentiment, Character or
Composition. An odd humour of finding fault hath long prevailed amongst the Critics; as if nothing were worth *remarking* that
did not, at the same time, deserve to be reproved. Whereas the
public Judgment hath less need to be assisted in what it shall
reject, than in what it ought to prize; Men being generally more
ready at spying Faults than in discovering Beauties. Nor is the
value they set upon a Work, a certain proof that they understand
it. For 'tis ever seen, that half a dozen Voices of credit give the
lead: And if the Publick chance to be in good humour, or the
Author much in their favour, the People are sure to follow.
Hence it is that the true Critic hath so frequently attached himself to Works of established reputation; not to teach the World
to *admire*, which, in those circumstances, to say the truth, they
are apt enough to do of themselves; but to teach them how *with*

reason to admire: No easy matter, I will assure you, on the subject in question: For tho' it be very true, as Mr. *Pope* hath observed, that *Shakespear is the fairest and fullest subject for criticism,* yet it is not such a sort of criticism as may be raised mechanically on the Rules which *Dacier, Rapin* and *Bossu* have collected from Antiquity; and of which, such kind of Writers as *Rymer, Gildon, Dennis* and *Oldmixon,* have only gathered and chewed the Husks: nor on the other hand is it to be formed on the Plan of those crude and superficial Judgments, on books and things, with which a certain celebrated Paper so much abounds; too good indeed to be named with the Writers last mentioned, but being unluckily mistaken for a *Model,* because it was an *Original,* it hath given rise to a deluge of the worst sort of critical Jargon; I mean that which looks most like sense. But the kind of criticism here required is such as judgeth our Author by those only Laws and Principles on which he wrote, NATURE, and COMMON-SENSE.

Our Observations, therefore, being thus extensive, will, I presume, enable the Reader to form a right judgment of this favourite Poet, without drawing out his Character, as was once intended, in a continued discourse.

These, such as they are, were amongst my younger amusements, when, many years ago, I used to turn over these sort of Writers to unbend myself from more serious applications: And what, certainly, the Public, at this time of day, had never been troubled with, but for the conduct of the two last Editors, and the persuasions of dear Mr. POPE; whose memory and name,

> — — *semper acerbum,*
> *Semper honoratum (sic Di voluistis) habebo.*

He was desirous I should give a new Edition of this Poet, as he thought it might contribute to put a stop to a prevailing folly of altering the Text of celebrated Authors without Talents or Judgment. And he was willing that *his* Edition should be melted down into *mine,* as it would, he said, afford him (so great is the modesty of an ingenuous temper) a fit opportunity of confessing his Mistakes.* In memory of our Friendship, I have, therefore, made it our joint Edition. His admirable Preface is here added; all his Notes are given, with his name annexed; the Scenes are divided according to his regulation; and the most beautiful passages distinguished, as in his book, with inverted commas. In imitation of him, I have done the same by as many others as I thought most deserving of the Reader's attention, and have marked them with *double* commas.

If, from all this, *Shakespear* or good Letters have received any advantage, and the Public any benefit, or entertainment, the thanks are due to the *Proprietors*, who have been at the expence of procuring this Edition. And I should be unjust to several deserving Men of a reputable and useful Profession, if I did not, on this occasion, acknowledge the fair dealing I have always found amongst them; and profess my sense of the unjust Prejudice which lies against them; whereby they have been, hitherto, unable to procure that security for their Property, which they see the rest of their Fellow-Citizens enjoy: A prejudice in part arising from the frequent *Piracies* (as they are called) committed by Members of their own Body. But such kind of Members no Body is without. And it would be hard that this should be turned to the discredit of the honest part of the Profession, who suffer more from such Injuries than any other men. It hath, in part too, arisen from the clamours of profligate Scriblers, ever ready, for a piece of Money, to prostitute their bad sense for or against any Cause prophane or sacred; or in any Scandal public or private: These meeting with little encouragement from Men of account in the Trade, (who even in this enlightened Age are not the very worst Judges or Rewarders of merit) apply themselves to People of Condition; and support their importunities by false complaints against *Booksellers*.

But I should now, perhaps, rather think of my own Apology, than busy myself in the defence of others. I shall have some *Tartuffe* ready, on the first appearance of this Edition, to call out again, and tell me, that *I suffer myself to be wholly diverted from*

---

* See his Letters to me.

my purpose by these matters less suitable to my clerical Profession. 'Well,
but, says a Friend, why not take so candid an intimation in good
part? Withdraw yourself, again, as you are bid, into the clerical
Pale; examine the Records of sacred and prophane Antiquity; and,
on them, erect a Work to the confusion of Infidelity.' Why, I
have done all this, and more: And hear now what the same Men
have said to it. They tell me, *I have wrote to the wrong and injury of*
Religion, and furnished out more handles for Unbelievers. 'Oh now the
secret's out; and you may have your pardon, I find, upon easier
terms. 'Tis only, to write no more.'——Good Gentlemen! and
shall I not oblige them? They would gladly *obstruct* my way to
those things which every Man, who *endeavours well* in his Profession, must needs think he has some claim to, when he sees
them given to those who never did *endeavour*; at the same time
that they would *deter* me from taking those advantages which
Letters enable me to procure for myself. If then I am to write no
more; (tho' as much out of my Profession as they may please to
represent this Work, I suspect their modesty would not insist on
a scrutiny of our several applications of this prophane profit and
their purer gains) if, I say, I am to write no more, let me at least
give the Public, who have a better pretence to demand it of me,
some reason for my presenting them with these amusements.
Which, if I am not much mistaken, may be excused by the best
and fairest *Examples*; and, what is more, may be justified on the
surer *reason of things.*

The great Saint CHRYSOSTOM, a name consecrated to immortality by his Virtue and Eloquence, is known to have been so
fond of *Aristophanes* as to wake with him at his studies, and to
sleep with him under his pillow: and I never heard that this was
objected either to his Piety or his Preaching, not even in those
times of pure Zeal and primitive Religion. Yet, in respect of
Shakespear's great sense, *Aristophanes's* best wit is but buffoonry;
and, in comparison of *Aristophanes's* Freedoms, *Shakespear* writes
with the purity of a Vestal. But they will say, St. *Chrysostom*
contracted a fondness for the comic Poet *for the sake of his Greek.*
To this, indeed, I have nothing to reply. Far be it from me to

insinuate so unscholarlike a thing, as if We had the same Use for good *English* that a *Greek* had for his *Attic* elegance. Critic *Kuster*, in a taste and language peculiar to Grammarians of a certain order, hath decreed, that *the History and Chronology of* Greek *Words is the most SOLID entertainment of a Man of Letters.*

I fly, then, to a higher Example, much nearer home, and still more in point, The famous University of OXFORD. This illustrious Body, which hath long so justly held, and, with such equity, dispensed, the chief honours of the learned World, thought good Letters so much interested in correct Editions of the best *English* Writers, that they, very lately, in their public Capacity, undertook *one*, of this very Author, by subscription. And if the Editor hath not discharged his Task with suitable abilities for one so much honoured by them, this was not their fault but his, who thrust himself into the employment. After such an Example, it would be weakening any defence to seek further for Authorities. All that can be now decently urged is the *reason of the thing*; and this I shall do, more for the sake of that truly venerable Body than my own.

Of all the literary exercitations of speculative Men, whether designed for the use or entertainment of the World, there are none of so much importance, or what are more our immediate concern, than those which let us into the knowledge of our Nature. Others may exercise the Reason or amuse the Imagination; but these only can improve the Heart, and form the human Mind to Wisdom. Now, in this Science, our *Shakespear* is confessed to occupy the foremost place; whether we consider the amazing sagacity with which he investigates every hidden spring and wheel of human Action; or his happy manner of communicating this knowledge, in the just and living paintings which he has given us of all our Passions, Appetites and Pursuits. These afford a lesson which can never be too often repeated, or too constantly inculcated; And, to engage the Reader's due attention to it, hath been one of the principal objects of this Edition.

As this Science (whatever profound Philosophers may think)

is, to the rest, *in Things*; so, *in Words*, (whatever supercilious Pedants may talk) every one's mother tongue is to all other Languages. This hath still been the Sentiment of Nature and true Wisdom. Hence, the greatest men of Antiquity never thought themselves better employed than in cultivating their own country idiom. So *Lycurgus* did honour to *Sparta*, in giving the first compleat Edition of *Homer*; and *Cicero*, to *Rome*, in correcting the Works of *Lucretius*. Nor do we want Examples of the same good sense in modern Times, even amidst the cruel inrodes that Art and Fashion have made upon Nature and the simplicity of Wisdom. *Ménage*, the greatest name in *France* for all kinds of philologic Learning, prided himself in writing critical Notes on their best lyric Poet, *Malherbe:* And our greater *Selden*, when he thought it might reflect credit on his Country, did not disdain even to comment a very ordinary Poet, one *Michael Drayton*. But the *English* tongue, at this Juncture, deserves and demands our particular regard. It hath, by means of the many excellent Works of different kinds composed in it, engaged the notice, and become the study, of almost every curious and learned Foreigner, so as to be thought even a part of literary accomplishment. This must needs make it deserving of a critical attention: And its being yet destitute of a Test or Standard to apply to, in cases of doubt or difficulty, shews how much it wants that attention. For we have neither GRAMMAR nor DICTIONARY, neither Chart nor Compass, to guide us through this wide sea of Words. And indeed how should we? since both are to be composed and finished on the Authority of our best established Writers. But their Authority can be of little use till the Text hath been correctly settled, and the Phraseology critically examined. As, then, by these aids, a *Grammar* and *Dictionary*, planned upon the best rules of Logic and Philosophy, (and none but such will deserve the name) are to be procured; the forwarding of this will be a general concern: For, as *Quintilian* observes, 'Verborum *proprietas* ac *differentia* omnibus, qui sermonem curæ habent, debet esse communis.' By this way, the *Italians* have brought their tongue to a degree of Purity and Stability which no living Language ever attained unto before. It is with pleasure I observe, that these things now begin to be understood amongst ourselves; and that I can acquaint the Public, we may soon expect very elegant Editions of *Fletcher* and *Milton's Paradise Lost* from Gentlemen of distinguished Abilities and Learning. But this interval of good sense, as it may be short, is indeed but new. For I remember to have heard of a very learned Man, who, not long since, formed a design of giving a more correct Edition of *Spenser*; and, without doubt, would have performed it well; but he was dissuaded from his purpose by his Friends, as beneath the dignity of a Professor of the occult Sciences. Yet these very Friends, I suppose, would have thought it had added lustre to his high Station, to have new-furbished out some dull northern Chronicle, or dark Sibylline Ænigma. But let it not be thought that what is here said insinuates any thing to the discredit of *Greek* and *Latin* criticism. If the follies of particular Men were sufficient to bring any branch of Learning into disrepute, I don't know any that would stand in a worse situation than that for which I now apologize. For I hardly think there ever appeared, in any *learned* Language, so execrable a heap of nonsense, under the name of Commentaries, as hath been lately given us on a certain satiric Poet, of the last Age, by his Editor and Coadjutor.

I am sensible how unjustly the very best *classical* Critics have been treated. It is said, that our great Philosopher spoke with much contempt of the two finest Scholars of this Age, Dr. *Bentley* and Bishop *Hare*, for squabbling, as he expressed it, about an old Play-book; meaning, I suppose, *Terence's* Comedies. But this Story is unworthy of him; tho' well enough suiting the fanatic turn of the wild Writer that relates it; such censures are amongst the follies of men immoderately given over to one Science, and ignorantly undervaluing all the rest. Those learned Critics might, and perhaps did, laugh in their turn, (tho' still, sure, with the same indecency and indiscretion) at that incomparable Man, for wearing out a long Life in poring through a Telescope. Indeed, the weaknesses of Such are to be mentioned with reverence. But who can bear, without indignation, the fashionable cant of every trifling Writer, whose insipidity passes, with himself, for politeness, for pretending to be shocked, forsooth, with the rude and savage air of *vulgar* Critics; meaning such as *Muretus, Scaliger, Casaubon, Salmasius, Spanheim, Bentley*. When, had it not been for the deathless labours of such as these, the western World, at the revival of Letters, had soon faln back again into a state of ignorance and barbarity as deplorable as that from which Providence had just redeemed it.

To conclude with an observation of a fine Writer and great Philosopher of our own; which I would gladly bind, tho' with all honour, as a Phylactery, on the Brow of every awful Grammarian, to teach him at once, the *Use*, and *Limits* of his art: WORDS ARE THE MONEY OF FOOLS, AND THE COUNTERS OF WISE MEN.

SAMUEL JOHNSON

Preface to 'The Plays of William Shakespeare'

1765

THAT praises are without reason lavished on the dead, and that the honours due only to excellence are paid to antiquity, is a complaint likely to be always continued by those, who, being able to add nothing to truth, hope for eminence from the heresies of paradox; or those, who, being forced by disappointment upon consolatory expedients, are willing to hope from posterity what the present age refuses, and flatter themselves that the regard which is yet denied by envy, will be at last bestowed by time.

Antiquity, like every other quality that attracts the notice of mankind, has undoubtedly votaries that reverence it, not from reason, but from prejudice. Some seem to admire indiscriminately whatever has been long preserved, without considering that time has sometimes co-operated with chance; all perhaps are more willing to honour past than present excellence; and the mind contemplates genius through the shades of age, as the eye surveys the sun through artificial opacity. The great contention of criticism is to find the faults of the moderns, and the beauties of the ancients. While an authour is yet living we estimate his powers by his worst performance, and when he is dead we rate them by his best.

To works, however, of which the excellence is not absolute and definite, but gradual and comparative; to works not raised upon principles demonstrative and scientifick, but appealing wholly to observation and experience, no other test can be applied than length of duration and continuance of esteem. What mankind have long possessed they have often examined and compared, and if they persist to value the possession, it is because frequent comparisons have confirmed opinion in its favour. As

among the works of nature no man can properly call a river deep
or a mountain high, without the knowledge of many mountains
and many rivers; so in the productions of genius, nothing can
be stiled excellent till it has been compared with other works
of the same kind. Demonstration immediately displays its power,
and has nothing to hope or fear from the flux of years; but works
tentative and experimental must be estimated by their proportion to the general and collective ability of man, as it is discovered in a long succession of endeavours. Of the first building
that was raised, it might be with certainty determined that it
was round or square; but whether it was spacious or lofty must
have been referred to time. The Pythagorean scale of numbers
was at once discovered to be perfect; but the poems of *Homer* we
yet know not to transcend the common limits of human intelligence, but by remarking, that nation after nation, and century after century, has been able to do little more than transpose
his incidents, new-name his characters, and paraphrase his
sentiments.

The reverence due to writings that have long subsisted arises
therefore not from any credulous confidence in the superior
wisdom of past ages, or gloomy persuasion of the degeneracy of
mankind, but is the consequence of acknowledged and indubit-
able positions, that what has been longest known has been most
considered, and what is most considered is best understood.

The Poet, of whose works I have undertaken the revision,
may now begin to assume the dignity of an ancient, and claim
the privilege of established fame and prescriptive veneration. He
has long outlived his century, the term commonly fixed as the
test of literary merit. Whatever advantages he might once derive
from personal allusions, local customs, or temporary opinions,
have for many years been lost; and every topick of merriment
or motive of sorrow, which the modes of artificial life afforded
him, now only obscure the scenes which they once illuminated.
The effects of favour and competition are at an end; the tradition
of his friendships and his enmities has perished; his works support no opinion with arguments, nor supply any faction with

invectives; they can neither indulge vanity nor gratify malignity, but are read without any other reason than the desire of pleasure, and are therefore praised only as pleasure is obtained; yet, thus unassisted by interest or passion, they have past through variations of taste and changes of manners, and, as they devolved from one generation to another, have received new honours at every transmission.

But because human judgment, though it be gradually gaining upon certainty, never becomes infallible; and approbation, though long continued, may yet be only the approbation of prejudice or fashion; it is proper to inquire, by what peculiarities of excellence *Shakespeare* has gained and kept the favour of his countrymen.

Nothing can please many, and please long, but just representations of general nature. Particular manners can be known to few, and therefore few only can judge how nearly they are copied. The irregular combinations of fanciful invention may delight a-while, by that novelty of which the common satiety of life sends us all in quest; but the pleasures of sudden wonder are soon exhausted, and the mind can only repose on the stability of truth.

Shakespeare is above all writers, at least above all modern writers, the poet of nature; the poet that holds up to his readers a faithful mirrour of manners and of life. His characters are not modified by the customs of particular places, unpractised by the rest of the world; by the peculiarities of studies or professions, which can operate but upon small numbers; or by the accidents of transient fashions or temporary opinions: they are the genuine progeny of common humanity, such as the world will always supply, and observation will always find. His persons act and speak by the influence of those general passions and principles by which all minds are agitated, and the whole system of life is continued in motion. In the writings of other poets a character is too often an individual; in those of *Shakespeare* it is commonly a species.

It is from this wide extension of design that so much instruction is derived. It is this which fills the plays of *Shakespeare* with practical axioms and domestick wisdom. It was said of *Euripides*, that every verse was a precept; and it may be said of *Shakespeare*, that from his works may be collected a system of civil and oeconomical prudence. Yet his real power is not shewn in the splendour of particular passages, but by the progress of his fable, and the tenour of his dialogue; and he that tries to recommend him by select quotations, will succeed like the pedant in *Hierocles*, who, when he offered his house to sale, carried a brick in his pocket as a specimen.

It will not easily be imagined how much *Shakespeare* excells in accommodating his sentiments to real life, but by comparing him with other authours. It was observed of the ancient schools of declamation, that the more diligently they were frequented, the more was the student disqualified for the world, because he found nothing there which he should ever meet in any other place. The same remark may be applied to every stage but that of *Shakespeare*. The theatre, when it is under any other direction, is peopled by such characters as were never seen, conversing in a language which was never heard, upon topicks which will never arise in the commerce of mankind. But the dialogue of this authour is often so evidently determined by the incident which produces it, and is pursued with so much ease and simplicity, that it seems scarcely to claim the merit of fiction, but to have been gleaned by diligent selection out of common conversation, and common occurrences.

Upon every other stage the universal agent is love, by whose power all good and evil is distributed, and every action quickened or retarded. To bring a lover, a lady and a rival into the fable; to entangle them in contradictory obligations, perplex them with oppositions of interest, and harrass them with violence of desires inconsistent with each other; to make them meet in rapture and part in agony; to fill their mouths with hyperbolical joy and outrageous sorrow; to distress them as nothing human ever was distressed; to deliver them as nothing human ever was delivered, is the business of a modern dramatist. For this probability is violated, life is misrepresented, and language is depraved. But love is only one of many passions, and as it has no great influence upon the sum of life, it has little operation in the dramas of a poet, who caught his ideas from the living world, and exhibited only what he saw before him. He knew, that any other passion, as it was regular or exorbitant, was a cause of happiness or calamity.

Characters thus ample and general were not easily discriminated and preserved, yet perhaps no poet ever kept his personages more distinct from each other. I will not say with *Pope*, that every speech may be assigned to the proper speaker, because many speeches there are which have nothing characteristical; but perhaps, though some may be equally adapted to every person, it will be difficult to find, any that can be properly transferred from the present possessor to another claimant. The choice is right, when there is reason for choice.

Other dramatists can only gain attention by hyperbolical or aggravated characters, by fabulous and unexampled excellence or depravity, as the writers of barbarous romances invigorated the reader by a giant and a dwarf; and he that should form his expectations of human affairs from the play, or from the tale, would be equally deceived. *Shakespeare* has no heroes; his scenes are occupied only by men, who act and speak as the reader thinks that he should himself have spoken or acted on the same occasion: Even where the agency is supernatural the dialogue is level with life. Other writers disguise the most natural passions and most frequent incidents; so that he who contemplates them in the book will not know them in the world: *Shakespeare* approximates the remote, and familiarizes the wonderful; the event which he represents will not happen, but if it were possible, its effects would probably be such as he has assigned; and it may be said, that he has not only shewn human nature as it acts in real exigences, but as it would be found in trials, to which it cannot be exposed.

This therefore is the praise of *Shakespeare*, that his drama is the mirrour of life; that he who has mazed his imagination, in following the phantoms which other writers raise up before him, may here be cured of his delirious extasies, by reading human sentiments in human language; by scenes from which a hermit may estimate the transactions of the world, and a confessor predict the progress of the passions.

His adherence to general nature has exposed him to the censure of criticks, who form their judgments upon narrower principles. *Dennis* and *Rhymer* think his *Romans* not sufficiently *Roman*; and *Voltaire* censures his kings as not completely royal. *Dennis* is offended, that *Menenius*, a senator of *Rome*, should play the buffoon; and *Voltaire* perhaps thinks decency violated when the *Danish* Usurper is represented as a drunkard. But *Shakespeare* always makes nature predominate over accident; and if he preserves the essential character, is not very careful of distinctions superinduced and adventitious. His story requires Romans or kings, but he thinks only on men. He knew that *Rome*, like every other city, had men of all dispositions; and wanting a buffoon, he went into the senate-house for that which the senate-house would certainly have afforded him. He was inclined to shew an usurper and a murderer not only odious but despicable, he therefore added drunkenness to his other qualities, knowing that kings love wine like other men, and that wine exerts its natural power upon kings. These are the petty cavils of petty minds; a poet overlooks the casual distinction of country and condition, as a painter, satisfied with the figure, neglects the drapery.

The censure which he has incurred by mixing comick and tragick scenes, as it extends to all his works, deserves more consideration. Let the fact be first stated, and then examined.

Shakespeare's plays are not in the rigorous and critical sense either tragedies or comedies, but compositions of a distinct kind; exhibiting the real state of sublunary nature, which partakes of good and evil, joy and sorrow, mingled with endless variety of proportion and innumerable modes of combination; and expressing the course of the world, in which the loss of one is the gain of another; in which, at the same time, the reveller is hasting to his wine, and the mourner burying his friend; in which the malignity of one is sometimes defeated by the frolick of another;

and many mischiefs and many benefits are done and hindered without design.

Out of this chaos of mingled purposes and casualties the ancient poets, according to the laws which custom had prescribed, selected some the crimes of men, and some their absurdities; some the momentous vicissitudes of life, and some the lighter occurrences; some the terrours of distress, and some the gayeties of prosperity. Thus rose the two modes of imitation, known by the names of *tragedy* and *comedy*, compositions intended to promote different ends by contrary means, and considered as so little allied, that I do not recollect among the *Greeks* or *Romans* a single writer who attempted both.

Shakespeare has united the powers of exciting laughter and sorrow not only in one mind, but in one composition. Almost all his plays are divided between serious and ludicrous characters, and, in the successive evolutions of the design, sometimes produce seriousness and sorrow, and sometimes levity and laughter.

That this is a practice contrary to the rules of criticism will be readily allowed; but there is always an appeal open from criticism to nature. The end of writing is to instruct; the end of poetry is to instruct by pleasing. That the mingled drama may convey all the instruction of tragedy or comedy cannot be denied, because it includes both in its alternations of exhibition, and approaches nearer than either to the appearance of life, by shewing how great machinations and slender designs may promote or obviate one another, and the high and the low co-operate in the general system by unavoidable concatenation.

It is objected, that by this change of scenes the passions are interrupted in their progression, and that the principal event, being not advanced by a due gradation of preparatory incidents, wants at last the power to move, which constitutes the perfection of dramatick poetry. This reasoning is so specious, that it is received as true even by those who in daily experience feel it to be false. The interchanges of mingled scenes seldom fail to produce the intended vicissitudes of passion. Fiction cannot move so much, but that the attention may be easily transferred; and though it must be allowed that pleasing melancholy be sometimes interrupted by unwelcome levity, yet let it be considered likewise, that melancholy is often not pleasing, and that the disturbance of one man may be the relief of another; that different auditors have different habitudes; and that, upon the whole, all pleasure consists in variety.

The players, who in their edition divided our authour's works into comedies, histories, and tragedies, seem not to have distinguished the three kinds, by any very exact or definite ideas.

An action which ended happily to the principal persons, however serious or distressful through its intermediate incidents, in their opinion constituted a comedy. This idea of a comedy continued long amongst us, and plays were written, which, by changing the catastrophe, were tragedies to-day and comedies to-morrow.

Tragedy was not in those times a poem of more general dignity or elevation than comedy; it required only a calamitous conclusion, with which the common criticism of that age was satisfied, whatever lighter pleasure it afforded in its progress.

History was a series of actions, with no other than chronological succession, independent on each other, and without any tendency to introduce or regulate the conclusion. It is not always very nicely distinguished from tragedy. There is not much nearer approach to unity of action in the tragedy of *Antony and Cleopatra*, than in the history of *Richard the Second*. But a history might be continued through many plays; as it had no plan, it had no limits.

Through all these denominations of the drama, *Shakespeare's* mode of composition is the same; an interchange of seriousness and merriment, by which the mind is softened at one time, and exhilarated at another. But whatever be his purpose, whether to gladden or depress, or to conduct the story, without vehemence or emotion, through tracts of easy and familiar dialogue, he never fails to attain his purpose; as he commands us, we laugh or mourn, or sit silent with quiet expectation, in tranquillity without indifference.

When *Shakespeare's* plan is understood, most of the criticisms of *Rhymer* and *Voltaire* vanish away. The play of *Hamlet* is opened, without impropriety, by two sentinels; *Iago* bellows at *Brabantio's* window, without injury to the scheme of the play, though in terms which a modern audience would not easily endure; the character of *Polonius* is seasonable and useful; and the Gravediggers themselves may be heard with applause.

Shakespeare engaged in dramatick poetry with the world open before him; the rules of the ancients were yet known to few; the publick judgment was unformed; he had no example of such fame as might force him upon imitation, nor criticks of such authority as might restrain his extravagance: He therefore indulged his natural disposition, and his disposition, as *Rhymer* has remarked, led him to comedy. In tragedy he often writes with great appearance of toil and study, what is written at last with little felicity; but in his comick scenes, he seems to produce without labour, what no labour can improve. In tragedy he is always struggling after some occasion to be comick, but in comedy he seems to repose, or to luxuriate, as in a mode of thinking congenial to his nature. In his tragick scenes there is always something wanting, but his comedy often surpasses expectation or desire. His comedy pleases by the thoughts and the language, and his tragedy for the greater part by incident and action. His tragedy seems to be skill, his comedy to be instinct.

The force of his comick scenes has suffered little diminution from the changes made by a century and a half, in manners or in words. As his personages act upon principles arising from genuine passion, very little modified by particular forms, their pleasures and vexations are communicable to all times and to all places; they are natural, and therefore durable; the adventitious peculiarities of personal habits, are only superficial dies, bright and pleasing for a little while, yet soon fading to a dim tinct, without any remains of former lustre; but the discriminations of true passion are the colours of nature; they pervade the whole mass, and can only perish with the body that exhibits them. The accidental compositions of heterogeneous modes are dissolved by the chance which combined them; but the uniform simplicity of primitive qualities neither admits increase, nor suffers decay. The sand heaped by one flood is scattered by another, but the rock always continues in its place. The stream of time, which is continually washing the dissoluble fabricks of other poets, passes without injury by the adamant of *Shakespeare*.

If there be, what I believe there is, in every nation, a stile which never becomes obsolete, a certain mode of phraseology so consonant and congenial to the analogy and principles of its respective language as to remain settled and unaltered; this stile is probably to be sought in the common intercourse of life, among those who speak only to be understood, without ambition of elegance. The polite are always catching modish innovations, and the learned depart from established forms of speech, in hope of finding or making better; those who wish for distinction forsake the vulgar, when the vulgar is right; but there is a conversation above grossness and below refinement, where propriety resides, and where this poet seems to have gathered his comick dialogue. He is therefore more agreeable to the ears of the present age than any other authour equally remote, and among his other excellencies deserves to be studied as one of the original masters of our language.

These observations are to be considered not as unexceptionably constant, but as containing general and predominant truth. *Shakespeare*'s familiar dialogue is affirmed to be smooth and clear, yet not wholly without ruggedness or difficulty; as a country may be eminently fruitful, though it has spots unfit for cultivation: His characters are praised as natural, though their sentiments are sometimes forced, and their actions improbable; as the earth upon the whole is spherical, though its surface is varied with protuberances and cavities.

Shakespeare with his excellencies has likewise faults, and faults sufficient to obscure and overwhelm any other merit. I shall shew them in the proportion in which they appear to me, without

envious malignity or superstitious veneration. No question can
be more innocently discussed than a dead poet's pretensions
to renown; and little regard is due to that bigotry which sets
candour higher than truth.

His first defect is that to which may be imputed most of the
evil in books or in men. He sacrifices virtue to convenience, and
is so much more careful to please than to instruct, that he seems
to write without any moral purpose. From his writings indeed
a system of social duty may be selected, for he that thinks
reasonably must think morally; but his precepts and axioms
drop casually from him; he makes no just distribution of good
or evil, nor is always careful to shew in the virtuous a dis-
approbation of the wicked; he carries his persons indifferently
through right and wrong, and at the close dismisses them without further care, and leaves their examples to operate by chance.
This fault the barbarity of his age cannot extenuate; for it is
always a writer's duty to make the world better, and justice is a
virtue independant on time or place.

The plots are often so loosely formed, that a very slight consideration may improve them, and so carelessly pursued, that he
seems not always fully to comprehend his own design. He omits
opportunities of instructing or delighting which the train of his
story seems to force upon him, and apparently rejects those ex-
hibitions which would be more affecting, for the sake of those
which are more easy.

It may be observed, that in many of his plays the latter part is
evidently neglected. When he found himself near the end of his
work, and, in view of his reward, he shortened the labour, to
snatch the profit. He therefore remits his efforts where he should
most vigorously exert them, and his catastrophe is improbably
produced or imperfectly represented.

He had no regard to distinction of time or place, but gives to
one age or nation, without scruple, the customs, institutions,
and opinions of another, at the expence not only of likelihood,
but of possibility. These faults *Pope* has endeavoured, with more
zeal than judgment, to transfer to his imagined interpolators.

We need not wonder to find *Hector* quoting *Aristotle*, when we see the loves of *Theseus* and *Hippolyta* combined with the *Gothick* mythology of fairies. *Shakespeare*, indeed, was not the only violator of chronology, for in the same age *Sidney*, who wanted not the advantages of learning, has, in his *Arcadia*, confounded the pastoral with the feudal times, the days of innocence, quiet and security, with those of turbulence, violence and adventure.

In his comick scenes he is seldom very successful, when he engages his characters in reciprocations of smartness and contests of sarcasm; their jests are commonly gross, and their pleasantry licentious; neither his gentlemen nor his ladies have much delicacy, nor are sufficiently distinguished from his clowns by any appearance of refined manners. Whether he represented the real conversation of his time is not easy to determine; the reign of *Elizabeth* is commonly supposed to have been a time of stateliness, formality and reserve, yet perhaps the relaxations of that severity were not very elegant. There must, however, have been always some modes of gayety preferable to others, and a writer ought to chuse the best.

In tragedy his performance seems constantly to be worse, as his labour is more. The effusions of passion which exigence forces out are for the most part striking and energetick; but whenever he solicits his invention, or strains his faculties, the offspring of his throes is tumour, meanness, tediousness, and obscurity.

In narration he affects a disproportionate pomp of diction and a wearisome train of circumlocution, and tells the incident imperfectly in many words, which might have been more plainly delivered in few. Narration in dramatick poetry is naturally tedious, as it is unanimated and inactive, and obstructs the progress of the action; it should therefore always be rapid, and enlivened by frequent interruption. *Shakespeare* found it an encumbrance, and instead of lightening it by brevity, endeavoured to recommend it by dignity and splendour.

His declamations or set speeches are commonly cold and weak, for his power was the power of nature; when he endeavoured, like other tragick writers, to catch opportunities of amplification, and instead of inquiring what the occasion demanded, to show how much his stores of knowledge could supply, he seldom escapes without the pity or resentment of his reader.

It is incident to him to be now and then entangled with an unwieldy sentiment, which he cannot well express, and will not reject; he struggles with it a while, and if it continues stubborn, comprises it in words such as occur, and leaves it to be disentangled and evolved by those who have more leisure to bestow upon it.

Not that always where the language is intricate the thought is subtle, or the image always great where the line is bulky; the equality of words to things is very often neglected, and trivial sentiments and vulgar ideas disappoint the attention, to which they are recommended by sonorous epithets and swelling figures.

But the admirers of this great poet have most reason to complain when he approaches nearest to his highest excellence, and seems fully resolved to sink them in dejection, and mollify them with tender emotions by the fall of greatness, the danger of innocence, or the crosses of love. What he does best, he soon ceases to do. He is not long soft and pathetick without some idle conceit, or contemptible equivocation. He no sooner begins to move, than he counteracts himself; and terrour and pity, as they are rising in the mind, are checked and blasted by sudden frigidity.

A quibble is to *Shakespeare*, what luminous vapours are to the traveller; he follows it at all adventures, it is sure to lead him out of his way, and sure to engulf him in the mire. It has some malignant power over his mind, and its fascinations are irresistible. Whatever be the dignity or profundity of his disquisition, whether he be enlarging knowledge or exalting affection, whether he be amusing attention with incidents, or enchaining it in suspense, let but a quibble spring up before him, and he leaves his work unfinished. A quibble is the golden apple for which he will always turn aside from his career, or stoop from his elevation. A quibble, poor and barren as it is, gave him such delight, that he was content to purchase it, by the sacrifice of reason, propriety and truth. A quibble was to him the fatal *Cleopatra* for which he lost the world, and was content to lose it.

It will be thought strange, that, in enumerating the defects of this writer, I have not yet mentioned his neglect of the unities; his violation of those laws which have been instituted and established by the joint authority of poets and of criticks.

For his other deviations from the art of writing I resign him to critical justice, without making any other demand in his favour, than that which must be indulged to all human excellence; that his virtues be rated with his failings: But, from the censure which this irregularity may bring upon him, I shall, with due reverence to that learning which I must oppose, adventure to try how I can defend him.

His histories, being neither tragedies nor comedies, are not subject to any of their laws; nothing more is necessary to all the praise which they expect, than that the changes of action be so prepared as to be understood, that the incidents be various and affecting, and the characters consistent, natural and distinct. No other unity is intended, and therefore none is to be sought.

In his other works he has well enough preserved the unity of action. He has not, indeed, an intrigue regularly perplexed and regularly unravelled; he does not endeavour to hide his design only to discover it, for this is seldom the order of real events, and *Shakespeare* is the poet of nature: But his plan has commonly what *Aristotle* requires, a beginning, a middle, and an end; one event is concatenated with another, and the conclusion follows by easy consequence. There are perhaps some incidents that might be spared, as in other poets there is much talk that only fills up time upon the stage; but the general system makes gradual advances, and the end of the play is the end of expectation.

To the unities of time and place he has shewn no regard, and perhaps a nearer view of the principles on which they stand will diminish their value, and withdraw from them the veneration which, from the time of *Corneille*, they have very generally received, by discovering that they have given more trouble to the poet, than pleasure to the auditor.

The necessity of observing the unities of time and place arises from the supposed necessity of making the drama credible. The criticks hold it impossible, that an action of months or years can be possibly believed to pass in three hours; or that the spectator can suppose himself to sit in the theatre, while ambassadors go and return between distant kings, while armies are levied and towns besieged, while an exile wanders and returns, or till he whom they saw courting his mistress, shall lament the untimely fall of his son. The mind revolts from evident falsehood, and fiction loses its force when it departs from the resemblance of reality.

From the narrow limitation of time necessarily arises the contraction of place. The spectator, who knows that he saw the first act at *Alexandria*, cannot suppose that he sees the next at *Rome*, at a distance to which not the dragons of *Medea* could, in so short a time, have transported him; he knows with certainty that he has not changed his place; and he knows that place cannot change itself; that what was a house cannot become a plain; that what was *Thebes* can never be *Persepolis*.

Such is the triumphant language with which a critick exults over the misery of an irregular poet, and exults commonly without resistance or reply. It is time therefore to tell him, by the authority of *Shakespeare*, that he assumes, as an unquestionable principle, a position, which, while his breath is forming it into words, his understanding pronounces to be false. It is false, that any representation is mistaken for reality; that any dramatick fable in its materiality was ever credible, or, for a single moment, was ever credited.

The objection arising from the impossibility of passing the first hour at *Alexandria*, and the next at *Rome*, supposes, that when the play opens the spectator really imagines himself at *Alexandria*, and believes that his walk to the theatre has been a voyage to *Egypt*, and that he lives in the days of *Antony* and *Cleopatra*. Surely he that imagines this may imagine more. He that can take the stage at one time for the palace of the *Ptolemies*, may take it in half an hour for the promontory of *Actium*. Delusion, if delusion be admitted, has no certain limitation; if the spectator can be once persuaded, that his old acquaintance are *Alexander* and *Cæsar*, that a room illuminated with candles is the plain of *Pharsalia*, or the bank of *Granicus*, he is in a state of elevation above the reach of reason, or of truth, and from the heights of empyrean poetry, may despise the circumscriptions of terrestrial nature. There is no reason why a mind thus wandering in extasy should count the clock, or why an hour should not be a century in that calenture of the brains that can make the stage a field.

The truth is, that the spectators are always in their senses, and know, from the first act to the last, that the stage is only a stage, and that the players are only players. They come to hear a certain number of lines recited with just gesture and elegant modulation. The lines relate to some action, and an action must be in some place; but the different actions that compleat a story may be in places very remote from each other; and where is the absurdity of allowing that space to represent first *Athens*, and then *Sicily*, which was always known to be neither *Sicily* nor *Athens*, but a modern theatre.

By supposition, as place is introduced, time may be extended; the time required by the fable elapses for the most part between the acts; for, of so much of the action as is represented, the real and poetical duration is the same. If, in the first act, preparations for war against *Mithridates* are represented to be made in *Rome*, the event of the war may, without absurdity, be represented, in the catastrophe, as happening in *Pontus*; we know that there is neither war, nor preparation for war; we know that we are neither in *Rome* nor *Pontus*; that neither *Mithridates* nor *Lucullus* are before us. The drama exhibits successive imitations of successive actions, and why may not the second imitation represent an action that happened years after the first, if it be so connected with it, that nothing but time can be supposed to intervene. Time is, of all modes of existence, most obsequious to the imagination; a lapse of years is as easily conceived as a passage of hours. In contemplation we easily contract the time of real actions, and therefore willingly permit it to be contracted when we only see their imitation.

It will be asked, how the drama moves, if it is not credited. It is credited with all the credit due to a drama. It is credited, whenever it moves, as a just picture of a real original; as representing to the auditor what he would himself feel, if he were to do or suffer what is there feigned to be suffered or to be done. The reflection that strikes the heart is not, that the evils before us are real evils, but that they are evils to which we ourselves may be exposed. If there be any fallacy, it is not that we fancy the players, but that we fancy ourselves unhappy for a moment; but we rather lament the possibility than suppose the presence of misery, as a mother weeps over her babe, when she remembers that death may take it from her. The delight of tragedy proceeds from our consciousness of fiction; if we thought murders and treasons real, they would please no more.

Imitations produce pain or pleasure, not because they are mistaken for realities, but because they bring realities to mind. When the imagination is recreated by a painted landscape, the trees are not supposed capable to give us shade, or the fountains coolness; but we consider, how we should be pleased with such fountains playing beside us, and such woods waving over us. We are agitated in reading the history of *Henry* the Fifth, yet no man takes his book for the field of *Agencourt*. A dramatick exhibition is a book recited with concomitants that encrease or diminish its effect. Familiar comedy is often more powerful on the theatre, than in the page; imperial tragedy is always less. The humour of *Petruchio* may be heightened by grimace; but what voice or what gesture can hope to add dignity or force to the soliloquy of *Cato*.

A play read, affects the mind like a play acted. It is therefore evident, that the action is not supposed to be real, and it follows that between the acts a longer or shorter time may be allowed to pass, and that no more account of space or duration is to be taken by the auditor of a drama, than by the reader of a narrative, before whom may pass in an hour the life of a hero, or the revolutions of an empire.

Whether *Shakespeare* knew the unities, and rejected them by design, or deviated from them by happy ignorance, it is, I think, impossible to decide, and useless to enquire. We may reasonably suppose, that, when he rose to notice, he did not want the counsels and admonitions of scholars and criticks, and that he at last deliberately persisted in a practice, which he might have begun by chance. As nothing is essential to the fable, but unity of action, and as the unities of time and place arise evidently from false assumptions, and, by circumscribing the extent of the drama, lessen its variety, I cannot think it much to be lamented, that they were not known by him, or not observed: Nor, if such another poet could arise, should I very vehemently reproach him, that his first act passed at *Venice*, and his next in *Cyprus*. Such violations of rules merely positive, become the comprehensive genius of *Shakespeare*, and such censures are suitable to the minute and slender criticism of *Voltaire:*

> *Non usque adeo permiscuit imis*
> *Longus summa dies, ut non, si voce Metelli*
> *Serventur leges, malint a Cæsare tolli.*

Yet when I speak thus slightly of dramatick rules, I cannot but recollect how much wit and learning may be produced against me; before such authorities I am afraid to stand, not that I think the present question one of those that are to be decided by mere authority, but because it is to be suspected, that these precepts have not been so easily received but for better reasons than I have yet been able to find. The result of my enquiries, in which it would be ludicrous to boast of impartiality, is, that the unities of time and place are not essential to a just drama, that though they may sometimes conduce to pleasure, they are always to be sacrificed to the nobler beauties of variety and instruction; and that a play, written with nice observation of critical rules, is to be contemplated as an elaborate curiosity, as the product of superfluous and ostentatious art, by which is shewn, rather what is possible, than what is necessary.

He that, without diminution of any other excellence, shall preserve all the unities unbroken, deserves the like applause with the architect, who shall display all the orders of architecture in a citadel, without any deduction from its strength; but the principal beauty of a citadel is to exclude the enemy; and the greatest graces of a play, are to copy nature and instruct life.

Perhaps, what I have here not dogmatically but deliberatively written, may recal the principles of the drama to a new examination. I am almost frighted at my own temerity; and when I estimate the fame and the strength of those that maintain the contrary opinion, am ready to sink down in reverential silence; as *Æneas* withdrew from the defence of *Troy*, when he saw *Neptune* shaking the wall, and *Juno* heading the besiegers.

Those whom my arguments cannot persuade to give their approbation to the judgment of *Shakespeare*, will easily, if they consider the condition of his life, make some allowance for his ignorance.

Every man's performances, to be rightly estimated, must be compared with the state of the age in which he lived, and with his own particular opportunities; and though to the reader a book be not worse or better for the circumstances of the authour, yet as there is always a silent reference of human works to human abilities, and as the enquiry, how far man may extend his designs, or how high he may rate his native force, is of far greater dignity than in what rank we shall place any particular performance, curiosity is always busy to discover the instruments, as well as to survey the workmanship, to know how much is to be ascribed to original powers, and how much to casual and adventitious help. The palaces of *Peru* or *Mexico* were certainly mean and incommodious habitations, if compared to the houses of *European* monarchs; yet who could forbear to view them with astonishment, who remembered that they were built without the use of iron?

The *English* nation, in the time of *Shakespeare*, was yet struggling to emerge from barbarity. The philology of *Italy* had been transplanted hither in the reign of *Henry* the Eighth; and the learned languages had been successfully cultivated by *Lilly*, *Linacer*, and *More*; by *Pole*, *Cheke*, and *Gardiner*; and afterwards by *Smith*, *Clerk*, *Haddon*, and *Ascham*. Greek was now taught to boys in the principal schools; and those who united elegance with learning, read, with great diligence, the *Italian* and *Spanish* poets. But literature was yet confined to professed scholars, or to men and women of high rank. The publick was gross and dark; and to be able to read and write, was an accomplishment still valued for its rarity.

Nations, like individuals, have their infancy. A people newly awakened to literary curiosity, being yet unacquainted with the true state of things, knows not how to judge of that which is proposed as its resemblance. Whatever is remote from common appearances is always welcome to vulgar, as to childish credulity; and of a country unenlightened by learning, the whole people is the vulgar. The study of those who then aspired to plebeian learning was laid out upon adventures, giants, dragons, and enchantments. *The Death of Arthur* was the favourite volume.

The mind, which has feasted on the luxurious wonders of fiction, has no taste of the insipidity of truth. A play which imitated only the common occurrences of the world, would, upon the admirers of *Palmerin* and *Guy* of *Warwick*, have made little impression; he that wrote for such an audience was under the necessity of looking round for strange events and fabulous transactions, and that incredibility, by which maturer knowledge is offended, was the chief recommendation of writings, to unskilful curiosity.

Our authour's plots are generally borrowed from novels, and it is reasonable to suppose, that he chose the most popular, such as were read by many, and related by more; for his audience could not have followed him through the intricacies of the drama, had they not held the thread of the story in their hands.

The stories, which we now find only in remoter authours, were in his time accessible and familiar. The fable of *As you like it*, which is supposed to be copied from *Chaucer's* Gamelyn, was a little pamphlet of those times; and old Mr. *Cibber* remembered the tale of *Hamlet* in plain *English* prose, which the criticks have now to seek in *Saxo Grammaticus*.

His *English* histories he took from *English* chronicles and *English* ballads; and as the ancient writers were made known to his countrymen by versions, they supplied him with new subjects; he dilated some of *Plutarch's* lives into plays, when they had been translated by *North*.

His plots, whether historical or fabulous, are always crouded with incidents, by which the attention of a rude people was more easily caught than by sentiment or argumentation; and such is the power of the marvellous even over those who despise it, that every man finds his mind more strongly seized by the tragedies of *Shakespeare* than of any other writer; others please us by particular speeches, but he always makes us anxious for the event, and has perhaps excelled all but *Homer* in securing the first purpose of a writer, by exciting restless and unquenchable curiosity, and compelling him that reads his work to read it through.

The shows and bustle with which his plays abound have the same original. As knowledge advances, pleasure passes from the eye to the ear, but returns, as it declines, from the ear to the eye. Those to whom our authour's labours were exhibited had more skill in pomps or processions than in poetical language, and perhaps wanted some visible and discriminated events, as comments on the dialogue. He knew how he should most please; and whether his practice is more agreeable to nature, or whether his example has prejudiced the nation, we still find that on our stage something must be done as well as said, and inactive declamation is very coldly heard, however musical or elegant, passionate or sublime.

Voltaire expresses his wonder, that our authour's extravagances are endured by a nation, which has seen the tragedy of *Cato*. Let him be answered, that *Addison* speaks the language of poets, and *Shakespeare*, of men. We find in *Cato* innumerable beauties which enamour us of its authour, but we see nothing that acquaints us with human sentiments or human actions; we place it with the fairest and the noblest progeny which judgment propagates by conjunction with learning, but *Othello* is the vigorous and vivacious offspring of observation impregnated by genius. *Cato* affords a splendid exhibition of artificial and fictitious manners, and delivers just and noble sentiments, in diction easy, elevated and harmonious, but its hopes and fears communicate no vibration to the heart; the composition refers us only to the writer; we pronounce the name of *Cato*, but we think on *Addison*.

The work of a correct and regular writer is a garden accurately formed and diligently planted, varied with shades, and scented with flowers; the composition of *Shakespeare* is a forest, in which oaks extend their branches, and pines tower in the air, interspersed sometimes with weeds and brambles, and sometimes giving shelter to myrtles and to roses; filling the eye with awful pomp, and gratifying the mind with endless diversity. Other poets display cabinets of precious rarities, minutely finished, wrought into shape, and polished unto brightness. *Shakespeare* opens a mine which contains gold and diamonds in unexhaustible plenty, though clouded by incrustations, debased by impurities, and mingled with a mass of meaner minerals.

It has been much disputed, whether *Shakespeare* owed his excellence to his own native force, or whether he had the common helps of scholastick education, the precepts of critical science, and the examples of ancient authours.

There has always prevailed a tradition, that *Shakespeare* wanted learning, that he had no regular education, nor much skill in the dead languages. *Jonson*, his friend, affirms, that *he had small Latin, and less Greek*; who, besides that he had no imaginable temptation to falsehood, wrote at a time when the character and acquisitions of *Shakespeare* were known to multitudes. His evidence ought therefore to decide the controversy, unless some testimony of equal force could be opposed.

Some have imagined, that they have discovered deep learning in many imitations of old writers; but the examples which I have known urged, were drawn from books translated in his time; or were such easy coincidencies of thought, as will happen to all who consider the same subjects; or such remarks on life or axioms of morality as float in conversation, and are transmitted through the world in proverbial sentences.

I have found it remarked, that, in this important sentence, *Go before*, *I'll follow*, we read a translation of, *I prae*, *sequar*. I have been told, that when *Caliban*, after a pleasing dream, says, *I cry'd to sleep again*, the authour imitates *Anacreon*, who had, like every other man, the same wish on the same occasion.

There are a few passages which may pass for imitations, but so few, that the exception only confirms the rule; he obtained them from accidental quotations, or by oral communication, and as he used what he had, would have used more if he had obtained it.

The *Comedy of Errors* is confessedly taken from the *Menæchmi* of *Plautus*; from the only play of *Plautus* which was then in *English*. What can be more probable, than that he who copied that, would have copied more; but that those which were not translated were inaccessible?

Whether he knew the modern languages is uncertain. That his plays have some *French* scenes proves but little; he might easily procure them to be written, and probably, even though he had known the language in the common degree, he could not have written it without assistance. In the story of *Romeo* and *Juliet* he is observed to have followed the *English* translation, where it deviates from the *Italian*; but this on the other part proves nothing against his knowledge of the original. He was to copy, not what he knew himself, but what was known to his audience.

It is most likely that he had learned *Latin* sufficiently to make him acquainted with construction, but that he never advanced to an easy perusal of the *Roman* authours. Concerning his skill in modern languages, I can find no sufficient ground of determination; but as no imitations of *French* or *Italian* authours have been discovered, though the *Italian* poetry was then high in esteem, I am inclined to believe, that he read little more than *English*, and chose for his fables only such tales as he found translated.

That much knowledge is scattered over his works is very justly observed by *Pope*, but it is often such knowledge as books did not supply. He that will understand *Shakespeare*, must not be content to study him in the closet, he must look for his meaning sometimes among the sports of the field, and sometimes among the manufactures of the shop.

There is however proof enough that he was a very diligent reader, nor was our language then so indigent of books, but that he might very liberally indulge his curiosity without excursion into foreign literature. Many of the *Roman* authours were translated, and some of the *Greek*; the reformation had filled the kingdom with theological learning; most of the topicks of human disquisition had found *English* writers; and poetry had been cultivated, not only with diligence, but success. This was a stock of knowledge sufficient for a mind so capable of appropriating and improving it.

But the greater part of his excellence was the product of his own genius. He found the *English* stage in a state of the utmost rudeness; no essays either in tragedy or comedy had appeared, from which it could be discovered to what degree of delight either one or other might be carried. Neither character nor dialogue were yet understood. *Shakespeare* may be truly said to have introduced them both amongst us, and in some of his happier scenes to have carried them both to the utmost height.

By what gradations of improvement he proceeded, is not easily known; for the chronology of his works is yet unsettled. *Rowe* is of opinion, that *perhaps we are not to look for his beginning, like those of other writers, in his least perfect works; art had so little, and nature so large a share in what he did, that for ought I know*, says he, *the performances of his youth, as they were the most vigorous, were the best*. But the power of nature is only the power of using to any certain purpose the materials which diligence procures, or opportunity supplies. Nature gives no man knowledge, and when images are collected by study and experience, can only assist in combining or applying them. *Shakespeare*, however favoured by nature, could impart only what he had learned; and as he must increase his ideas, like other mortals, by gradual acquisition, he, like them, grew wiser as he grew older, could display life better, as he knew it more, and instruct with more efficacy, as he was himself more amply instructed.

There is a vigilance of observation and accuracy of distinction which books and precepts cannot confer; from this almost all original and native excellence proceeds. *Shakespeare* must have looked upon mankind with perspicacity, in the highest degree curious and attentive. Other writers borrow their characters from preceding writers, and diversify them only by the accidental appendages of present manners; the dress is a little varied, but the body is the same. Our authour had both matter and form to provide; for except the characters of *Chaucer*, to whom I think he is not much indebted, there were no writers in *English*, and perhaps not many in other modern languages, which shewed life in its native colours.

The contest about the original benevolence or malignity of man had not yet commenced. Speculation had not yet attempted to analyse the mind, to trace the passions to their sources, to unfold the seminal principles of vice and virtue, or sound the depths of the heart for the motives of action. All those enquiries, which from that time that human nature became the fashionable study, have been made sometimes with nice discernment, but often with idle subtilty, were yet unattempted. The tales, with which the infancy of learning was satisfied, exhibited only the superficial appearances of action, related the events but omitted the causes, and were formed for such as delighted in wonders rather than in truth. Mankind was not then to be studied in the closet; he that would know the world, was under the necessity of gleaning his own remarks, by mingling as he could in its business and amusements.

Boyle congratulated himself upon his high birth, because it favoured his curiosity, by facilitating his access. *Shakespeare* had no such advantage; he came to *London* a needy adventurer, and lived for a time by very mean employments. Many works of genius and learning have been performed in states of life, that appear very little favourable to thought or to enquiry; so many, that he who considers them is inclined to think that he sees enterprise and perseverance predominating over all external agency, and bidding help and hindrance vanish before them. The genius of *Shakespeare* was not to be depressed by the weight of poverty, nor limited by the narrow conversation to which men in want are inevitably condemned; the incumbrances of his fortune were shaken from his mind, *as dewdrops from a lion's mane*.

Though he had so many difficulties to encounter, and so little assistance to surmount them, he has been able to obtain an exact knowledge of many modes of life, and many casts of native dispositions; to vary them with great multiplicity; to mark them by nice distinctions; and to shew them in full view by proper combinations. In this part of his performances he had none to imitate, but has himself been imitated by all succeeding writers; and it may be doubted, whether from all his successors more maxims of theoretical knowledge, or more rules of practical prudence, can be collected, than he alone has given to his country.

Nor was his attention confined to the actions of men; he was an exact surveyor of the inanimate world; his descriptions have always some peculiarities, gathered by contemplating things as they really exist. It may be observed, that the oldest poets of many nations preserve their reputation, and that the following generations of wit, after a short celebrity, sink into oblivion. The first, whoever they be, must take their sentiments and descriptions immediately from knowledge; the resemblance is therefore just, their descriptions are verified by every eye, and their sentiments acknowledged by every breast. Those whom their fame invites to the same studies, copy partly them, and partly nature, till the books of one age gain such authority, as to stand in the place of nature to another, and imitation, always deviating a little, becomes at last capricious and casual. *Shakespeare*, whether life or nature be his subject, shews plainly, that he has seen with his own eyes; he gives the image which he receives, not weakened or distorted by the intervention of any other mind; the ignorant feel his representations to be just, and the learned see that they are compleat.

Perhaps it would not be easy to find any authour, except *Homer*, who invented so much as *Shakespeare*, who so much advanced the studies which he cultivated, or effused so much novelty upon his age or country. The form, the characters, the language, and the shows of the *English* drama are his. *He seems, says Dennis, to have been the very original of our* English *tragical harmony, that is, the harmony of blank verse, diversified often by dis-syllable and trissyllable terminations. For the diversity distinguishes it from heroick harmony, and by bringing it nearer to common use makes it more proper to gain attention, and more fit for action and dialogue. Such verse we make when we are writing prose; we make such verse in common conversation.*

I know not whether this praise is rigorously just. The dissyllable termination, which the critick rightly appropriates to the drama, is to be found, though, I think, not in *Gorboduc* which is confessedly before our authour; yet in *Hieronymo*, of which the date is not certain, but which there is reason to believe at least as old as his earliest plays. This however is certain, that he is the first who taught either tragedy or comedy to please, there being no theatrical piece of any older writer, of which the name is known, except to antiquaries and collectors of books, which are sought because they are scarce, and would not have been scarce, had they been much esteemed.

To him we must ascribe the praise, unless *Spenser* may divide it with him, of having first discovered to how much smoothness and harmony the *English* language could be softened. He has speeches, perhaps sometimes scenes, which have all the delicacy of *Rowe*, without his effeminacy. He endeavours indeed commonly to strike by the force and vigour of his dialogue, but he never executes his purpose better, than when he tries to sooth by softness.

Yet it must be at last confessed, that as we owe every thing to him, he owes something to us; that, if much of his praise is paid by perception and judgement, much is likewise given by custom and veneration. We fix our eyes upon his graces, and turn them from his deformities, and endure in him what we should in another loath or despise. If we endured without praising, respect for the father of our drama might excuse us; but I have seen, in the book of some modern critick, a collection of anomalies, which shew that he has corrupted language by every mode of depravation, but which his admirer has accumulated as a monument of honour.

He has scenes of undoubted and perpetual excellence, but perhaps not one play, which, if it were now exhibited as the work of a contemporary writer, would be heard to the conclusion. I am indeed far from thinking, that his works were wrought to his own ideas of perfection; when they were such as would satisfy the audience, they satisfied the writer. It is seldom that authours, though more studious of fame than *Shakespeare*, rise much above the standard of their own age; to add a little of what is best will always be sufficient for present praise, and those who find themselves exalted into fame, are willing to credit their encomiasts, and to spare the labour of contending with themselves.

It does not appear, that *Shakespeare* thought his works worthy of posterity, that he levied any ideal tribute upon future times, or had any further prospect, than of present popularity and present profit. When his plays had been acted, his hope was at an end; he solicited no addition of honour from the reader. He therefore made no scruple to repeat the same jests in many dialogues, or to entangle different plots by the same knot of perplexity, which may be at least forgiven him, by those who recollect, that of *Congreve*'s four comedies, two are concluded by a marriage in a mask, by a deception, which perhaps never happened, and which, whether likely or not, he did not invent.

So careless was this great poet of future fame, that, though he retired to ease and plenty, while he was yet little *declined into the vale of years*, before he could be disgusted with fatigue, or disabled by infirmity, he made no collection of his works, nor

desired to rescue those that had been already published from the
depravations that obscured them, or secure to the rest a better
destiny, by giving them to the world in their genuine state.

Of the plays which bear the name of *Shakespeare* in the late editions, the greater part were not published till about seven years
after his death, and the few which appeared in his life are apparently thrust into the world without the care of the authour,
and therefore probably without his knowledge.

Of all the publishers, clandestine or professed, their negligence
and unskilfulness has by the late revisers been sufficiently shown.
The faults of all are indeed numerous and gross, and have not
only corrupted many passages perhaps beyond recovery, but
have brought others into suspicion, which are only obscured
by obsolete phraseology, or by the writer's unskilfulness and
affectation. To alter is more easy than to explain, and temerity
is a more common quality than diligence. Those who saw that
they must employ conjecture to a certain degree, were willing
to indulge it a little further. Had the authour published his own
works, we should have sat quietly down to disentangle his intricacies, and clear his obscurities; but now we tear what we
cannot loose, and eject what we happen not to understand.

The faults are more than could have happened without the
concurrence of many causes. The stile of *Shakespeare* was in itself
ungrammatical, perplexed and obscure; his works were transcribed for the players by those who may be supposed to have
seldom understood them; they were transmitted by copiers
equally unskilful, who still multiplied errours; they were
perhaps sometimes mutilated by the actors, for the sake of
shortening the speeches; and were at last printed without
correction of the press.

In this state they remained, not as Dr. *Warburton* supposes,
because they were unregarded, but because the editor's art was
not yet applied to modern languages, and our ancestors were
accustomed to so much negligence of *English* printers, that they
could very patiently endure it. At last an edition was undertaken by *Rowe*; not because a poet was to be published by a

poet, for *Rowe* seems to have thought very little on correction or explanation, but that our authour's works might appear like those of his fraternity, with the appendages of a life and recommendatory preface. *Rowe* has been clamorously blamed for not performing what he did not undertake, and it is time that justice be done him, by confessing, that though he seems to have had no thought of corruption beyond the printer's errours, yet he has made many emendations, if they were not made before, which his successors have received without acknowledgement, and which, if they had produced them, would have filled pages and pages with censures of the stupidity by which the faults were committed, with displays of the absurdities which they involved, with ostentatious expositions of the new reading, and self congratulations on the happiness of discovering it.

As of the other editors, I have preserved the prefaces, I have likewise borrowed the author's life from Rowe, though not written with much elegance or spirit; it relates however what is now to be known, and therefore deserves to pass through all succeeding publications.

The nation had been for many years content enough with Mr. *Rowe*'s performance, when Mr. *Pope* made them acquainted with the true state of *Shakespeare*'s text, shewed that it was extremely corrupt, and gave reason to hope that there were means of reforming it. He collated the old copies, which none had thought to examine before, and restored many lines to their integrity; but, by a very compendious criticism, he rejected whatever he disliked, and thought more of amputation than of cure.

I know not why he is commended by Dr. *Warburton* for distinguishing the genuine from the spurious plays. In this choice he exerted no judgement of his own; the plays which he received, were given by *Hemings* and *Condel*, the first editors; and those which he rejected, though, according to the licentiousness of the press in those times, they were printed during *Shakespeare*'s life, with his name, had been omitted by his friends, and were never added to his works before the edition of 1664, from which they were copied by the later printers.

This was a work which *Pope* seems to have thought unworthy of his abilities, being not able to suppress his contempt of *the dull duty of an editor*. He understood but half his undertaking. The duty of a collator is indeed dull, yet, like other tedious tasks, is very necessary; but an emendatory critick would ill discharge his duty, without qualities very different from dulness. In perusing a corrupted piece, he must have before him all possibilities of meaning, with all possibilities of expression. Such must be his comprehension of thought, and such his copiousness of language. Out of many readings possible, he must be able to select that which best suits with the state, opinions, and modes of language prevailing in every age, and with his authour's particular cast of thought, and turn of expression. Such must be his knowledge, and such his taste. Conjectural criticism demands more than humanity possesses, and he that exercises it with most praise has very frequent need of indulgence. Let us now be told no more of the dull duty of an editor.

Confidence is the common consequence of success. They whose excellence of any kind has been loudly celebrated, are ready to conclude, that their powers are universal. *Pope*'s edition fell below his own expectations, and he was so much offended, when he was found to have left any thing for others to do, that he past the latter part of his life in a state of hostility with verbal criticism.

I have retained all his notes, that no fragment of so great a writer may be lost; his preface, valuable alike for elegance of composition and justness of remark, and containing a general criticism on his authour, so extensive that little can be added, and so exact, that little can be disputed, every editor has an interest to suppress, but that every reader would demand its insertion.

Pope was succeeded by *Theobald*, a man of narrow comprehension and small acquisitions, with no native and intrinsick splendour of genius, with little of the artificial light of learning, but zealous for minute accuracy, and not negligent in pursuing it. He collated the ancient copies, and rectified many errors. A man so anxiously scrupulous might have been expected to do more, but what little he did was commonly right.

In his reports of copies and editions he is not to be trusted, without examination. He speaks sometimes indefinitely of copies, when he has only one. In his enumeration of editions, he mentions the two first folios as of high, and the third folio as of middle authority; but the truth is, that the first is equivalent to all others, and that the rest only deviate from it by the printer's negligence. Whoever has any of the folios has all, excepting those diversities which mere reiteration of editions will produce. I collated them all at the beginning, but afterwards used only the first.

Of his notes I have generally retained those which he retained himself in his second edition, except when they were confuted by subsequent annotators, or were too minute to merit preservation. I have sometimes adopted his restoration of a comma, without inserting the panegyrick in which he celebrated himself for his atchievement. The exuberant excrescence of his diction I have often lopped, his triumphant exultations over *Pope* and *Rowe* I have sometimes suppressed, and his contemptible ostentation I have frequently concealed; but I have in some places shewn him, as he would have shewn himself, for the reader's diversion, that the inflated emptiness of some notes may justify or excuse the contraction of the rest.

Theobald, thus weak and ignorant, thus mean and faithless, thus petulant and ostentatious, by the good luck of having *Pope* for his enemy, has escaped, and escaped alone, with reputation, from this undertaking. So willingly does the world support those who solicite favour, against those who command reverence; and so easily is he praised, whom no man can envy.

Our authour fell then into the hands of Sir *Thomas Hanmer*, the *Oxford* editor, a man, in my opinion, eminently qualified by nature for such studies. He had, what is the first requisite to emendatory criticism, that intuition by which the poet's intention is immediately discovered, and that dexterity of intellect which despatches its work by the easiest means. He had undoubtedly read much; his acquaintance with customs, opinions, and traditions, seems to have been large; and he is often learned without shew. He seldom passes what he does not understand, without an attempt to find or to make a meaning, and sometimes hastily makes what a little more attention would have found. He is solicitous to reduce to grammar, what he could not be sure that his authour intended to be grammatical. *Shakespeare* regarded more the series of ideas, than of words; and his language, not being designed for the reader's desk, was all that he desired it to be, if it conveyed his meaning to the audience.

Hanmer's care of the metre has been too violently censured. He found the measure reformed in so many passages, by the silent labours of some editors, with the silent acquiescence of the rest, that he thought himself allowed to extend a little further the license, which had already been carried so far without reprehension; and of his corrections in general, it must be confessed, that they are often just, and made commonly with the least possible violation of the text.

But, by inserting his emendations, whether invented or borrowed, into the page, without any notice of varying copies, he has appropriated the labour of his predecessors, and made his own edition of little authority. His confidence indeed, both in himself and others, was too great; he supposes all to be right that was done by *Pope* and *Theobald*; he seems not to suspect a critick of fallibility, and it was but reasonable that he should claim what he so liberally granted.

As he never writes without careful enquiry and diligent consideration, I have received all his notes, and believe that every reader will wish for more.

Of the last editor it is more difficult to speak. Respect is due to high place, tenderness to living reputation, and veneration to genius and learning; but he cannot be justly offended at that liberty of which he has himself so frequently given an example, nor very solicitous what is thought of notes, which he ought never to have considered as part of his serious employments, and which, I suppose, since the ardour of composition is remitted, he no longer numbers among his happy effusions.

The original and predominant errour of his commentary, is acquiescence in his first thoughts; that precipitation which is produced by consciousness of quick discernment; and that confidence which presumes to do, by surveying the surface, what labour only can perform, by penetrating the bottom. His notes exhibit sometimes perverse interpretations, and sometimes improbable conjectures; he at one time gives the authour more profundity of meaning, than the sentence admits, and at another discovers absurdities, where the sense is plain to every other reader. But his emendations are likewise often happy and just; and his interpretation of obscure passages learned and sagacious.

Of his notes, I have commonly rejected those, against which the general voice of the publick has exclaimed, or which their own incongruity immediately condemns, and which, I suppose, the authour himself would desire to be forgotten. Of the rest, to part I have given the highest approbation, by inserting the offered reading in the text; part I have left to the judgment of the reader, as doubtful, though specious; and part I have censured without reserve, but I am sure without bitterness of malice, and, I hope, without wantonness of insult.

It is no pleasure to me, in revising my volumes, to observe how much paper is wasted in confutation. Whoever considers the revolutions of learning, and the various questions of greater or less importance, upon which wit and reason have exercised their powers, must lament the unsuccessfulness of enquiry, and the slow advances of truth, when he reflects, that great part of the labour of every writer is only the destruction of those that went before him. The first care of the builder of a new system, is to demolish the fabricks which are standing. The chief desire of him that comments an authour, is to shew how much other commentators have corrupted and obscured him. The opinions prevalent in one age, as truths above the reach of controversy, are confuted and rejected in another, and rise again to reception in remoter times. Thus the human mind is kept in motion without progress. Thus sometimes truth and errour, and sometimes contrarieties of errour, take each other's place by reciprocal invasion. The tide of seeming knowledge which is poured over one generation, retires and leaves another naked and barren; the sudden meteors of intelligence which for a while appear to shoot their beams into the regions of obscurity, on a sudden withdraw their lustre, and leave mortals again to grope their way.

These elevations and depressions of renown, and the contradictions to which all improvers of knowledge must for ever be exposed, since they are not escaped by the highest and brightest of mankind, may surely be endured with patience by criticks and annotators, who can rank themselves but as the satellites of their authours. How canst thou beg for life, says *Homer's* hero to his captive, when thou knowest that thou art now to suffer only what must another day be suffered by *Achilles?*

Dr. *Warburton* had a name sufficient to confer celebrity on those who could exalt themselves into antagonists, and his notes have raised a clamour too loud to be distinct. His chief assailants are the authours of *the Canons of criticism* and of the *Revisal of Shakespeare's text*; of whom one ridicules his errours with airy petulance, suitable enough to the levity of the controversy; the other attacks them with gloomy malignity, as if he were dragging to justice an assassin or incendiary. The one stings like a fly, sucks a little blood, takes a gay flutter, and returns for more; the other bites like a viper, and would be glad to leave inflammations and gangrene behind him. When I think on one, with his confederates, I remember the danger of *Coriolanus*, who was afraid that *girls with spits, and boys with stones, should slay him in puny battle*; when the other crosses my imagination, I remember the prodigy in *Macbeth*,

> *A falcon tow'ring in his pride of place,*
> *Was by a mousing owl hawk'd at and kill'd.*

Let me however do them justice. One is a wit, and one a scholar. They have both shown acuteness sufficient in the discovery of faults, and have both advanced some probable interpretations of obscure passages; but when they aspire to conjecture and emendation, it appears how falsely we all estimate our own abilities, and the little which they have been able to perform might have taught them more candour to the endeavours of others.

Before Dr. *Warburton's* edition, *Critical observations on* Shakespeare had been published by Mr. *Upton*, a man skilled in languages, and acquainted with books, but who seems to have had no great vigour of genius or nicety of taste. Many of his explanations are curious and useful, but he likewise, though he professed to oppose the licentious confidence of editors, and adhere to the old copies, is unable to restrain the rage of emendation, though his ardour is ill seconded by his skill. Every cold empirick, when his heart is expanded by a successful experiment, swells into a theorist, and the laborious collator at some unlucky moment frolicks in conjecture.

Critical, historical and explanatory notes have been likewise published upon *Shakespeare* by Dr. *Grey*, whose diligent perusal of the old *English* writers has enabled him to make some useful observations. What he undertook he has well enough performed, but as he neither attempts judicial nor emendatory criticism, he employs rather his memory than his sagacity. It were to be wished that all would endeavour to imitate his modesty who have not been able to surpass his knowledge.

I can say with great sincerity of all my predecessors, what I hope will hereafter be said of me, that not one has left *Shakespeare* without improvement, nor is there one to whom I have not been indebted for assistance and information. Whatever I have taken from them it was my intention to refer to its original authour, and it is certain, that what I have not given to another, I believed when I wrote it to be my own. In some perhaps I have been anticipated; but if I am ever found to encroach upon the remarks of any other commentator, I am willing that the honour, be it more or less, should be transferred to the first claimant, for his right, and his alone, stands above dispute; the second can prove his pretensions only to himself, nor can himself always distinguish invention, with sufficient certainty, from recollection.

They have all been treated by me with candour, which they have not been careful of observing to one another. It is not easy to discover from what cause the acrimony of a scholiast can naturally proceed. The subjects to be discussed by him are of very small importance; they involve neither property nor liberty; nor favour the interest of sect or party. The various readings of copies, and different interpretations of a passage, seem to be questions that might exercise the wit, without engaging the passions. But, whether it be, that *small things make mean men proud*, and vanity catches small occasions; or that all contrariety of opinion, even in those that can defend it no longer, makes proud men angry; there is often found in commentaries a spontaneous strain of invective and contempt, more eager and venomous than is vented by the most furious controvertist in politicks against those whom he is hired to defame.

Perhaps the lightness of the matter may conduce to the vehemence of the agency; when the truth to be investigated is so near to inexistence, as to escape attention, its bulk is to be enlarged by rage and exclamation: That to which all would be indifferent in its original state, may attract notice when the fate of a name is appended to it. A commentator has indeed great temptations to supply by turbulence what he wants of dignity, to beat his little gold to a spacious surface, to work that to foam which no art or diligence can exalt to spirit.

The notes which I have borrowed or written are either illustrative, by which difficulties are explained; or judicial, by which faults and beauties are remarked; or emendatory, by which depravations are corrected.

The explanations transcribed from others, if I do not subjoin any other interpretation, I suppose commonly to be right, at least I intend by acquiescence to confess, that I have nothing better to propose.

After the labours of all the editors, I found many passages which appeared to me likely to obstruct the greater number of readers, and thought it my duty to facilitate their passage. It is impossible for an expositor not to write too little for some, and too much for others. He can only judge what is necessary by his own experience; and how long soever he may deliberate, will at last explain many lines which the learned will think impossible to be mistaken, and omit many for which the ignorant will want his help. These are censures merely relative, and must be quietly endured. I have endeavoured to be neither superfluously copious, nor scrupulously reserved, and hope that I have made my authour's meaning accessible to many who before were frighted from perusing him, and contributed something to the publick, by diffusing innocent and rational pleasure.

The compleat explanation of an authour not systematick and consequential, but desultory and vagrant, abounding in casual allusions and light hints, is not to be expected from any single scholiast. All personal reflections, when names are suppressed, must be in a few years irrecoverably obliterated; and customs, too minute to attract the notice of law, such as modes of dress, formalities of conversation, rules of visits, disposition of furniture, and practices of ceremony, which naturally find places in familiar dialogue, are so fugitive and unsubstantial, that they are not easily retained or recovered. What can be known, will be collected by chance, from the recesses of obscure and obsolete papers, perused commonly with some other view. Of this knowledge every man has some, and none has much; but when an authour has engaged the publick attention, those who can add any thing to his illustration, communicate their discoveries, and time produces what had eluded diligence.

To time I have been obliged to resign many passages, which, though I did not understand them, will perhaps hereafter be explained, having, I hope, illustrated some, which others have neglected or mistaken, sometimes by short remarks, or marginal directions, such as every editor has added at his will, and often by comments more laborious than the matter will seem to deserve; but that which is most difficult is not always most important, and to an editor nothing is a trifle by which his authour is obscured.

The poetical beauties or defects I have not been very diligent to observe. Some plays have more, and some fewer judicial observations, not in proportion to their difference of merit, but because I gave this part of my design to chance and to caprice. The reader, I believe, is seldom pleased to find his opinion anticipated; it is natural to delight more in what we find or make, than in what we receive. Judgement, like other faculties, is improved by practice, and its advancement is hindered by submission to dictatorial decisions, as the memory grows torpid by the use of a table book. Some initiation is however necessary; of all skill, part is infused by precept, and part is obtained by habit; I have therefore shewn so much as may enable the candidate of criticism to discover the rest.

To the end of most plays, I have added short strictures, containing a general censure of faults, or praise of excellence; in which I know not how much I have concurred with the current opinion; but I have not, by any affectation of singularity, deviated from it. Nothing is minutely and particularly examined, and therefore it is to be supposed, that in the plays which are condemned there is much to be praised, and in these which are praised much to be condemned.

The part of criticism in which the whole succession of editors has laboured with the greatest diligence, which has occasioned the most arrogant ostentation, and excited the keenest acrimony, is the emendation of corrupted passages, to which the publick attention having been first drawn by the violence of the contention between *Pope* and *Theobald*, has been continued by the persecution, which, with a kind of conspiracy, has been since raised against all the publishers of *Shakespeare*.

That many passages have passed in a state of depravation through all the editions is indubitably certain; of these the restoration is only to be attempted by collation of copies or sagacity of conjecture. The collator's province is safe and easy, the conjecturer's perilous and difficult. Yet as the greater part of the plays are extant only in one copy, the peril must not be avoided, nor the difficulty refused.

Of the readings which this emulation of amendment has

hitherto produced, some from the labours of every publisher I have advanced into the text; those are to be considered as in my opinion sufficiently supported; some I have rejected without mention, as evidently erroneous; some I have left in the notes without censure or approbation, as resting in equipoise between objection and defence; and some, which seemed specious but not right, I have inserted with a subsequent animadversion.

Having classed the observations of others, I was at last to try what I could substitute for their mistakes, and how I could supply their omissions. I collated such copies as I could procure, and wished for more, but have not found the collectors of these rarities very communicative. Of the editions which chance or kindness put into my hands I have given an enumeration, that I may not be blamed for neglecting what I had not the power to do.

By examining the old copies, I soon found that the later publishers, with all their boasts of diligence, suffered many passages to stand unauthorised, and contented themselves with *Rowe's* regulation of the text, even where they knew it to be arbitrary, and with a little consideration might have found it to be wrong. Some of these alterations are only the ejection of a word for one that appeared to him more elegant or more intelligible. These corruptions I have often silently rectified; for the history of our language, and the true force of our words, can only be preserved, by keeping the text of authours free from adulteration. Others, and those very frequent, smoothed the cadence, or regulated the measure; on these I have not exercised the same rigour; if only a word was transposed, or a particle inserted or omitted, I have sometimes suffered the line to stand; for the inconstancy of the copies is such, as that some liberties may be easily permitted. But this practice I have not suffered to proceed far, having restored the primitive diction wherever it could for any reason be preferred.

The emendations, which comparison of copies supplied, I have inserted in the text; sometimes where the improvement was slight, without notice, and sometimes with an account of the reasons of the change.

Conjecture, though it be sometimes unavoidable, I have not wantonly nor licentiously indulged. It has been my settled principle, that the reading of the ancient books is probably true, and therefore is not to be disturbed for the sake of elegance, perspicuity, or mere improvement of the sense. For though much credit is not due to the fidelity, nor any to the judgement of the first publishers, yet they who had the copy before their eyes were more likely to read it right, than we who read it only by imagination. But it is evident that they have often made strange mistakes by ignorance or negligence, and that therefore something may be properly attempted by criticism, keeping the middle way between presumption and timidity.

Such criticism I have attempted to practise, and where any passage appeared inextricably perplexed, have endeavoured to discover how it may be recalled to sense, with least violence. But my first labour is, always to turn the old text on every side, and try if there be any interstice, through which light can find its way; nor would *Huetius* himself condemn me, as refusing the trouble of research, for the ambition of alteration. In this modest industry I have not been unsuccessful. I have rescued many lines from the violations of temerity, and secured many scenes from the inroads of correction. I have adopted the *Roman* sentiment, that it is more honourable to save a citizen, than to kill an enemy, and have been more careful to protect than to attack.

I have preserved the common distribution of the plays into acts, though I believe it to be in almost all the plays void of authority. Some of those which are divided in the later editions have no division in the first folio, and some that are divided in the folio have no division in the preceding copies. The settled mode of the theatre requires four intervals in the play, but few, if any, of our authour's compositions can be properly distributed in that manner. An act is so much of the drama as passes without intervention of time or change of place. A pause makes a new act. In every real, and therefore in every imitative action, the intervals may be more or fewer, the restriction of five acts being accidental and arbitrary. This *Shakespeare* knew, and this he

practised; his plays were written, and at first printed in one
unbroken continuity, and ought now to be exhibited with short
pauses, interposed as often as the scene is changed, or any considerable time is required to pass. This method would at once
quell a thousand absurdities.

In restoring the authour's works to their integrity, I have
considered the punctuation as wholly in my power; for what
could be their care of colons and commas, who corrupted words
and sentences. Whatever could be done by adjusting points is
therefore silently performed, in some plays with much diligence,
in others with less; it is hard to keep a busy eye steadily fixed
upon evanescent atoms, or a discursive mind upon evanescent
truth.

The same liberty has been taken with a few particles, or other
words of slight effect. I have sometimes inserted or omitted
them without notice. I have done that sometimes, which the
other editors have done always, and which indeed the state of
the text may sufficiently justify.

The greater part of readers, instead of blaming us for passing
trifles, will wonder that on mere trifles so much labour is expended, with such importance of debate, and such solemnity of
diction. To these I answer with confidence, that they are judging
of an art which they do not understand; yet cannot much reproach them with their ignorance, nor promise that they would
become in general, by learning criticism, more useful, happier or
wiser.

As I practised conjecture more, I learned to trust it less; and
after I had printed a few plays, resolved to insert none of my
own readings in the text. Upon this caution I now congratulate
myself, for every day encreases my doubt of my emendations.

Since I have confined my imagination to the margin, it must
not be considered as very reprehensible, if I have suffered it to
play some freaks in its own dominion. There is no danger in
conjecture, if it be proposed as conjecture; and while the text
remains uninjured, those changes may be safely offered, which are
not considered even by him that offers them as necessary or safe.

If my readings are of little value, they have not been ostentatiously displayed or importunately obtruded. I could have written longer notes, for the art of writing notes is not of difficult attainment. The work is performed, first by railing at the stupidity, negligence, ignorance, and asinine tastelessness of the former editors, and shewing, from all that goes before and all that follows, the inelegance and absurdity of the old reading; then by proposing something, which to superficial readers would seem specious, but which the editor rejects with indignation; then by producing the true reading, with a long paraphrase, and concluding with loud acclamations on the discovery, and a sober wish for the advancement and prosperity of genuine criticism.

All this may be done, and perhaps done sometimes without impropriety. But I have always suspected that the reading is right, which requires many words to prove it wrong; and the emendation wrong, that cannot without so much labour appear to be right. The justness of a happy restoration strikes at once, and the moral precept may be well applied to criticism, *quod dubitas ne feceris*.

To dread the shore which he sees spread with wrecks, is natural to the sailor. I had before my eye, so many critical adventures ended in miscarriage, that caution was forced upon me. I encountered in every page Wit struggling with its own sophistry, and Learning confused by the multiplicity of its views. I was forced to censure those whom I admired, and could not but reflect, while I was dispossessing their emendations, how soon the same fate might happen to my own, and how many of the readings which I have corrected may be by some other editor defended and established.

> *Criticks, I saw, that other's names efface,*
> *And fix their own, with labour, in the place;*
> *Their own, like others, soon their place resign'd,*
> *Or disappear'd, and left the first behind.*   POPE.

That a conjectural critick should often be mistaken, cannot be wonderful, either to others or himself, if it be considered, that in his art there is no system, no principal and axiomatical truth that regulates subordinate positions. His chance of errour is renewed at every attempt; an oblique view of the passage, a slight misapprehension of a phrase, a casual inattention to the parts connected, is sufficient to make him not only fail, but fail ridiculously; and when he succeeds best, he produces perhaps but one reading of many probable, and he that suggests another will always be able to dispute his claims.

It is an unhappy state, in which danger is hid under pleasure. The allurements of emendation are scarcely resistible. Conjecture has all the joy and all the pride of invention, and he that has once started a happy change, is too much delighted to consider what objections may rise against it.

Yet conjectural criticism has been of great use in the learned world; nor is it my intention to depreciate a study, that has exercised so many mighty minds, from the revival of learning to our own age, from the Bishop of *Aleria* to English *Bentley*. The criticks on ancient authours have, in the exercise of their sagacity, many assistances, which the editor of *Shakespeare* is condemned to want. They are employed upon grammatical and settled languages, whose construction contributes so much to perspicuity, that *Homer* has fewer passages unintelligible than *Chaucer*. The words have not only a known regimen, but invariable quantities, which direct and confine the choice. There are commonly more manuscripts than one; and they do not often conspire in the same mistakes. Yet *Scaliger* could confess to *Salmasius* how little satisfaction his emendations gave him. *Illudunt nobis conjecturæ nostræ, quarum nos pudet, posteaquam in meliores codices incidimus.* And *Lipsius* could complain, that criticks were making faults, by trying to remove them, *Ut olim vitiis, ita nunc remediis laboratur.* And indeed, where mere conjecture is to be used, the emendations of *Scaliger* and *Lipsius*, notwithstanding their wonderful sagacity and erudition, are often vague and disputable, like mine or *Theobald*'s.

Perhaps I may not be more censured for doing wrong, than for doing little; for raising in the publick expectations, which at last I have not answered. The expectation of ignorance is indefinite, and that of knowledge is often tyrannical. It is hard to satisfy those who know not what to demand, or those who demand by design what they think impossible to be done. I have indeed disappointed no opinion more than my own; yet I have endeavoured to perform my task with no slight solicitude. Not a single passage in the whole work has appeared to me corrupt, which I have not attempted to restore; or obscure, which I have not endeavoured to illustrate. In many I have failed like others; and from many, after all my efforts, I have retreated, and confessed the repulse. I have not passed over, with affected superiority, what is equally difficult to the reader and to myself, but where I could not instruct him, have owned my ignorance. I might easily have accumulated a mass of seeming learning upon easy scenes; but it ought not to be imputed to negligence, that, where nothing was necessary, nothing has been done, or that, where others have said enough, I have said no more.

Notes are often necessary, but they are necessary evils. Let him, that is yet unacquainted with the powers of *Shakespeare*, and who desires to feel the highest pleasure that the drama can give, read every play from the first scene to the last, with utter negligence of all his commentators. When his fancy is once on the wing, let it not stoop at correction or explanation. When his attention is strongly engaged, let it disdain alike to turn aside to the name of *Theobald* and of *Pope*. Let him read on through brightness and obscurity, through integrity and corruption; let him preserve his comprehension of the dialogue and his interest in the fable. And when the pleasures of novelty have ceased, let him attempt exactness, and read the commentators.

Particular passages are cleared by notes, but the general effect of the work is weakened. The mind is refrigerated by interruption; the thoughts are diverted from the principal subject; the reader is weary, he suspects not why; and at last throws away the book, which he has too diligently studied.

Parts are not to be examined till the whole has been surveyed;

there is a kind of intellectual remoteness necessary for the comprehension of any great work in its full design and in its true proportions; a close approach shews the smaller niceties, but the beauty of the whole is discerned no longer.

It is not very grateful to consider how little the succession of editors has added to this authour's power of pleasing. He was read, admired, studied, and imitated, while he was yet deformed with all the improprieties which ignorance and neglect could accumulate upon him; while the reading was yet not rectified, nor his allusions understood; yet then did *Dryden* pronounce 'that *Shakespeare* was the man, who, of all modern and perhaps ancient poets, had the largest and most comprehensive soul. All the images of nature were still present to him, and he drew them not laboriously, but luckily: When he describes any thing, you more than see it, you feel it too. Those who accuse him to have wanted learning, give him the greater commendation: he was naturally learned: he needed not the spectacles of books to read nature; he looked inwards, and found her there. I cannot say he is every where alike; were he so, I should do him injury to compare him with the greatest of mankind. He is many times flat and insipid; his comick wit degenerating into clenches, his serious swelling into bombast. But he is always great, when some great occasion is presented to him: No man can say, he ever had a fit subject for his wit, and did not then raise himself as high above the rest of poets,

Quantum lenta solent inter viburna cupressi.'

It is to be lamented, that such a writer should want a commentary; that his language should become obsolete, or his sentiments obscure. But it is vain to carry wishes beyond the condition of human things; that which must happen to all, has happened to *Shakespeare*, by accident and time; and more than has been suffered by any other writer since the use of types, has been suffered by him through his own negligence of fame, or perhaps by that superiority of mind, which despised its own performances, when it compared them with its powers, and judged those works unworthy to be preserved, which the criticks of following ages were to contend for the fame of restoring and explaining.

Among these candidates of inferiour fame, I am now to stand the judgment of the publick; and wish that I could confidently produce my commentary as equal to the encouragement which I have had the honour of receiving. Every work of this kind is by its nature deficient, and I should feel little solicitude about the sentence, were it to be pronounced only by the skilful and the learned.

RICHARD FARMER

An Essay on the Learning of Shakespeare:
Addressed to Joseph Cradock, Esq.

1767

PREFACE TO THE SECOND EDITION, 1767

THE AUTHOR of the following ESSAY was sollicitous only for
the honour of Shakespeare: he hath however, in *his own* capacity,
little reason to complain of *occasional* Criticks, or Criticks *by profession*. The very FEW, who have been pleased to controvert any
part of his Doctrine, have favoured him with better manners
than arguments; and claim his thanks for a further opportunity
of demonstrating the futility of *Theoretick* reasoning against
Matter of Fact. It is indeed strange that any *real* Friends of our
immortal POET should be still willing to force him into a situation which is not tenable: treat him as a *learned* Man, and what
shall excuse the most gross violations of History, Chronology,
and Geography?

Οὐ πείσεις οὐδ' ἢν πείσῃς is the Motto of every *Polemick*: like
his Brethren at the *Amphitheatre*, he holds it a merit to *die hard*;
and will not say, *Enough*, though the Battle be decided. 'Were
it shewn,' says some one, 'that the old Bard borrowed *all* his
allusions from *English* books then published, our *Essayist* might
have possibly established his System.'—In good time!—This
had scarcely been attempted by Peter Burman himself, with the
Library of Shakespeare before him.—'Truly,' as Mr. Dogberry
says, 'for *mine own* part, if I were as tedious as a King, I could
find in my heart to bestow it all on this Subject': but where

should I meet with a Reader?—When the main Pillars are taken away, the whole Building falls in course: Nothing hath been, or can be, pointed out, which is not easily removed; or rather, which was not *virtually* removed before: a very little *Analogy* will do the business. I shall therefore have no occasion to trouble myself any further; and may venture to call my Pamphlet, in the words of a pleasant Declaimer against *Sermons on the thirtieth of January*, 'an Answer to every thing that shall hereafter be written on the Subject.'

But 'this method of reasoning will prove any one ignorant of the Languages, who hath written when Translations were extant.'—Shade of Burgersdicius!—does it follow, because Shakespeare's early life was incompatible with a course of Education—whose Contemporaries, Friends and Foes, nay, and himself likewise, agree in his want of what is usually called *Literature*—whose mistakes from equivocal Translations, and even typographical Errors, cannot possibly be accounted for otherwise,—that Locke, to whom not one of these circumstances is applicable, understood no Greek?—I suspect, Rollin's Opinion of our Philosopher was not founded on this argument.

Shakespeare wanted not the Stilts of Languages to raise him above all other men. The quotation from Lilly in the *Taming of the Shrew*, if indeed it be his, strongly proves the extent of his reading: had he known Terence, he would not have quoted erroneously from his *Grammar*. Every one hath met with men in common life, who, according to the language of the *Water-poet*, 'got only from *Possum* to *Posset*,' and yet will throw out a line occasionally from their *Accidence* or their *Cato de Moribus* with tolerable propriety.—If, however, the old Editions be trusted in this passage, our Author's memory somewhat failed him in point of *Concord*.

The rage of *Parallelisms* is almost over, and in truth nothing can be more absurd. 'THIS was stolen from *one* Classick,—THAT from *another*';—and had I not stept in to his rescue, poor Shakespeare had been stript as naked of ornament, as when he first *held Horses* at the door of the Playhouse.

The late ingenious and modest Mr. Dodsley declared himself
Untutor'd in the lore of Greece or Rome:

Yet let us take a passage at a venture from any of his performances, and a thousand to one, it is stolen. Suppose it be his
celebrated Compliment to the *Ladies*, in one of his earliest pieces,
The Toy-shop: 'A good Wife makes the cares of the World sit
easy, and adds a sweetness to its pleasures; she is a Man's best
Companion in Prosperity, and his only Friend in Adversity; the
carefullest preserver of his Health, and the kindest Attendant
in his Sickness; a faithful Adviser in Distress, a Comforter in
Affliction, and a prudent Manager in all his domestic Affairs.'—
Plainly, from a fragment of Euripides preserved by Stobæus.

> Γυνὴ γὰρ ἐν κακοῖσι καὶ νόσοις πόσει
> "Ηδιστόν ἐστι, δώματ' ἦν οἰκῇ καλῶς,
> 'Οργήν τε πραΰνουσα, καὶ δυσθυμίας
> Ψυχὴν μεθιστᾶσ'!—*Par.* 4to. 1623.

Malvolio in the *Twelfth-Night* of Shakespeare hath some expressions very similar to Alnaschar in the *Arabian Tales*: which
perhaps may be sufficient for *some* Criticks to prove his acquaintance with Arabic!

It seems however, at last, that '*Taste* should determine the
matter.' This, as Bardolph expresses it, is a *word of exceeding
good command*: but I am willing that the Standard itself be somewhat better ascertained before it be opposed to demonstrative
Evidence.—Upon the whole, I may consider myself as the
Pioneer of the *Commentators*: I have removed a deal of *learned
Rubbish*, and pointed out to them Shakespeare's track in the ever-
pleasing *Paths of Nature*. This was necessarily a previous Inquiry; and I hope I may assume with some confidence, what one
of the first Criticks of the Age was pleased to declare on reading
the former Edition, that 'The Question is *now* for ever decided.'

 ⁎⁎⁎ I may just remark, lest they be mistaken for *Errata*, that the word *Catherine*
in the 47th page [p. 179] is written, according to the old Orthography, for
Catharine; and that the passage in the 51st page [p. 181] is copied from Upton,
who improperly calls Horatio and Marcellus in *Hamlet*, 'the *Centinels*.'

AN ESSAY ON THE LEARNING OF SHAKESPEARE:
ADDRESSED TO JOSEPH CRADOCK, ESQ.

'SHAKESPEARE,' says a Brother of the *Craft*, 'is a vast garden of criticism': and certainly no one can be favoured with more weeders *gratis*.

But how often, my dear Sir, are weeds and flowers torn up indiscriminately?—the ravaged spot is re-planted in a moment, and a profusion of critical thorns thrown over it for security.

'A prudent man, therefore, would not venture his fingers amongst them.'

Be, however, in little pain for your friend, who regards himself sufficiently to be cautious:—yet he asserts with confidence, that no improvement can be expected, whilst the natural soil is mistaken for a hot-bed, and the Natives of the banks of *Avon* are scientifically choked with the culture of exoticks.

Thus much for metaphor; it is contrary to the *Statute* to fly out so early: but who can tell, whether it may not be demonstrated by some critick or other, that a deviation from rule is peculiarly happy in an Essay of Shakespeare!

You have long known my opinion concerning the literary acquisitions of our immortal Dramatist; and remember how I congratulated myself on my coincidence with the last and best of his Editors. I told you, however, that his *small Latin and less Greek* would still be litigated, and you see very assuredly that I was not mistaken. The trumpet hath been sounded against 'the darling project of representing Shakespeare as one of the illiterate vulgar'; and indeed to so good purpose, that I would by all means recommend the performer to the army of the *braying Faction*, recorded by Cervantes. The testimony of his contemporaries is again disputed; constant tradition is opposed by flimsy arguments; and nothing is heard but confusion and nonsense. One could scarcely imagine this a topick very likely to inflame the passions: it is asserted by Dryden, that 'those who accuse him to have wanted learning, give him the greatest commendation'; yet an attack upon an article of faith hath been usually received with more temper and complacence, than the unfortunate opinion which I am about to defend.

But let us previously lament, with every lover of Shakespeare, that the Question was not fully discussed by Mr. Johnson himself: what he sees intuitively, others must arrive at by a series of proofs; and I have not time to *teach* with precision: be contented therefore with a few cursory observations, as they may happen to arise from the Chaos of Papers you have so often laughed at, 'a stock sufficient to set up an *Editor in form*.' I am convinced of the strength of my cause, and superior to any little advantage from sophistical arrangements.

General positions without proofs will probably have no great weight on either side, yet it may not seem fair to suppress them: take them therefore as their authors occur to me, and we will afterward proceed to particulars.

The testimony of Ben. stands foremost; and some have held it sufficient to decide the controversy: in the warmest Panegyrick that ever was written, he apologizes for what *he* supposed the only defect in his 'beloved friend,—

— Soul of the age!
Th' applause! delight! the wonder of our stage!—

whose memory he honoured almost to idolatry': and conscious of the worth of ancient literature, like any other man on the same occasion, he rather carries his acquirements *above* than *below* the truth. 'Jealousy!' cries Mr. Upton; 'People will allow others any qualities, but those upon which they highly value *themselves.*' Yes, where there *is* a competition, and the competitor formidable: but, I think, this Critick himself hath scarcely set in opposition the learning of Shakespeare and Jonson. When a superiority is universally granted, it by no means appears a man's literary interest to depress the reputation of his Antagonist.

In truth the received opinion of the pride and malignity of Jonson, at least in the earlier part of life, is absolutely groundless:

at this time scarce a play or a poem appeared without Ben's encomium, from the original Shakespeare to the translator of Du Bartas.

But Jonson is by no means our only authority. Drayton, the countryman and acquaintance of Shakespeare, determines his excellence to the *naturall Braine* only. Digges, a wit of the town before our Poet left the stage, is very strong to the purpose,

— Nature only helpt him, for looke thorow
This whole book, thou shalt find he doth not borow
One phrase from Greekes, nor Latines imitate,
Nor once from vulgar Languages translate.

Suckling opposes his *easier strain* to the *sweat of learned Jonson*. Denham assures us that all he had was from *old Mother-wit*. His *native wood-notes wild*, every one remembers to be celebrated by Milton. Dryden observes prettily enough, that 'he wanted not the spectacles of books to read Nature.' He came out of her hand, as some one else expresses it, like Pallas out of Jove's head, at full growth and mature.

The ever memorable Hales of Eton (who, notwithstanding his Epithet, is, I fear, almost forgotten) had too great a knowledge both of Shakespeare and the Ancients to allow much acquaintance between them: and urged very justly on the part of Genius in opposition to Pedantry, That 'if he had not *read* the Classicks, he had likewise not *stolen* from them; and if any Topick was produced from a Poet of antiquity, he would undertake to shew somewhat on the same subject, at least as well written by Shakespeare.'

Fuller, a diligent and equal searcher after truth and quibbles, declares positively that 'his learning was very little,—*Nature* was all the *Art* used upon him, as *he himself*, if alive, would confess.' And may we not say he did confess it, when he apologized for his *untutored lines* to his noble patron the Earl of Southampton? —this list of witnesses might be easily enlarged; but I flatter myself, I shall stand in no need of such evidence.

One of the first and most vehement assertors of the learning of

Shakespeare was the Editor of his Poems, the well-known Mr. Gildon; and his steps were most punctually taken by a subsequent labourer in the same department, Dr. Sewel.

Mr. Pope supposed 'little ground for the common opinion of his want of learning': once indeed he made a proper distinction between *learning* and *languages*, as I would be understood to do in my Title-page; but unfortunately he forgot it in the course of his disquisition, and endeavoured to persuade himself that Shakespeare's acquaintance with the Ancients might be actually proved by the same medium as Jonson's.

Mr. Theobald is 'very unwilling to allow him so poor a scholar as many have laboured to represent him'; and yet is 'cautious of declaring too positively on the other side the question.'

Dr. Warburton hath exposed the weakness of some arguments from *suspected* imitations; and yet offers others, which, I doubt not, he could as easily have refuted.

Mr. Upton wonders 'with what kind of reasoning any one could be so far imposed upon, as to imagine that Shakespeare had no learning'; and lashes with much zeal and satisfaction 'the pride and pertness of dunces, who, under such a name, would gladly shelter their own idleness and ignorance.'

He, like the learned Knight, at every anomaly in grammar or metre,

> Hath hard words ready to shew why,
> And tell what *Rule* he did it by.

How would the old Bard have been astonished to have found that he had very skilfully given the *trochaic dimeter brachycatalectic*, COMMONLY called the *ithyphallic* measure, to the Witches in *Macbeth!* and that now and then a halting Verse afforded a most beautiful instance of the *Pes proceleusmaticus!*

'But,' continues Mr. Upton, 'it was a learned age; Roger Ascham assures us that Queen Elizabeth read more Greek every day, than some *Dignitaries* of the Church did Latin in a whole week.' This appears very probable; and a pleasant proof it is of the general learning of the times, and of Shakespeare in particular. I wonder he did not corroborate it with an extract from her injunctions to her Clergy, that 'such as were but *mean Readers* should peruse over before, once or twice, the Chapters and Homilies, to the intent they might read to the better understanding of the people.'

Dr. Grey declares that Shakespeare's knowledge in the Greek and Latin tongues cannot *reasonably* be called in question. Dr. Dodd supposes it *proved*, that he was not such a novice in learning and antiquity as *some people* would pretend. And to close the whole, for I suspect you to be tired of quotation, Mr. Whalley, the ingenious Editor of Jonson, hath written a piece expressly on this side the question: perhaps from a very excusable partiality, he was willing to draw Shakespeare from the field of Nature to classick ground, where alone, he knew, his Author could possibly cope with him.

These criticks, and many others their coadjutors, have supposed themselves able to trace Shakespeare in the writings of the Ancients; and have sometimes persuaded us of their own learning, whatever became of their Author's. Plagiarisms have been discovered in every natural description and every moral sentiment. Indeed by the kind assistance of the various *Excerpta*, *Sententiæ*, and *Flores*, this business may be effected with very little expense of time or sagacity; as Addison hath demonstrated in his Comment on *Chevy-chace*, and Wagstaff on *Tom Thumb*: and I myself will engage to give you quotations from the elder *English* writers (for, to own the truth, I was once idle enough to collect such) which shall carry with them at least an equal degree of similarity. But there can be no occasion of wasting any future time in this department: the world is now in possession of the *Marks of Imitation*.

'Shakespeare, however, hath frequent allusions to the *facts* and *fables* of antiquity.' Granted:—and, as Mat. Prior says, to save the effusion of more Christian ink, I will endeavour to shew how they came to his acquaintance.

It is notorious that much of his *matter of fact* knowledge is deduced from Plutarch: but in what language he read him, hath yet been the question. Mr. Upton is pretty confident of his skill in the Original, and corrects accordingly the *Errors of his Copyists* by the Greek standard. Take a few instances, which will elucidate this matter sufficiently.

In the third act of *Anthony and Cleopatra*, Octavius represents to his Courtiers the imperial pomp of those illustrious lovers, and the arrangement of their dominion,

> — Unto her
> He gave the 'stablishment of Egypt, made her
> Of lower Syria, Cyprus, *Lydia*,
> Absolute Queen.

Read *Libya*, says the critick *authoritatively*, as is plain from Plutarch, Πρώτην μὲν ἀπέφηνε Κλεοπάτραν βασίλισσαν Αἰγύπτου καὶ Κύπρου καὶ ΛΙΒΥΗΣ, καὶ κοίλης Συρίας.

This is very true: Mr. Heath accedes to the correction, and Mr. Johnson admits it into the Text: but turn to the translation, from the French of Amyot, by Thomas North, in *Folio*, 1579; and you will at once see the origin of the mistake.

'First of all he did establish Cleopatra Queene of Ægypt, of Cyprus, of *Lydia*, and the lower Syria.'

Again in the Fourth Act,

> — My messenger
> He hath whipt with rods, dares me to personal combat,
> Cæsar to Anthony. Let th' old Ruffian know
> I have many other ways to die; mean time
> Laugh at his challenge.—

'What a reply is this?' cries Mr. Upton, ' 'tis acknowledging he should fall under the unequal combat. But if we read,

> —Let the old Ruffian know
> *He* hath many other ways to die; mean time
> *I* laugh at his challenge —

we have the poignancy and the very repartee of Cæsar in Plutarch.'

This correction was first made by Sir Thomas Hanmer, and Mr. Johnson hath received it. Most indisputably it is the sense of Plutarch, and given so in the modern translations: but Shakespeare was misled by the ambiguity of the old one, 'Antonius sent again to challenge Cæsar to fight him: Cæsar answered, That *he* had many other ways to die than so.'

In the Third Act of *Julius Cæsar*, Anthony in his well-known harangue to the people, repeats a part of the Emperor's will,

> — To every Roman citizen he gives,
> To every sev'ral man, seventy-five drachmas—
> Moreover he hath left you all his walks,
> His private arbours, and new-planted orchards,
> On *this* side Tyber.—

'Our Author certainly wrote,' says Mr. Theobald, 'On *that* side Tyber—

> *Trans* Tiberim—prope Cæsaris hortos.

And Plutarch, whom Shakespeare very diligently *studied*, expressly declares that he left the publick his gardens and walks, πέραν τοῦ Ποταμοῦ, *beyond* the *Tyber*.'

This emendation likewise hath been adopted by the subsequent Editors; but hear again the old Translation, where Shakespeare's *study* lay: 'He bequeathed unto every citizen of Rome seventy-five drachmas a man, and he left his gardens and arbours unto the people, which he had on *this* side of the river of Tyber.' I could furnish you with many more instances, but these are as good as a thousand.

Hence had our author his characteristick knowledge of Brutus and Anthony, upon which much argumentation for his learning hath been founded: and hence *literatim* the Epitaph on Timon, which, it was once presumed, he had corrected from the blunders of the Latin version, by his own superior knowledge of the Original.

I cannot, however, omit a passage of Mr. Pope. 'The *speeches* copy'd from Plutarch in *Coriolanus* may, I think, be as well made an instance of the learning of Shakespeare, as those copy'd from

Cicero in *Catiline*, of Ben. Jonson's.' Let us inquire into this matter, and transcribe a *speech* for a specimen. Take the famous one of Volumnia:

> Should we be silent and not speak, our raiment
> And state of bodies would bewray what life
> We've led since thy Exile. Think with thyself,
> How more unfortunate than all living women
> Are we come hither; since thy sight, which should
> Make our eyes flow with joy, hearts dance with comforts,
> Constrains them weep, and shake with fear and sorrow;
> Making the mother, wife, and child to see
> The son, the husband, and the father tearing
> His Country's bowels out: and to poor we
> Thy enmity's most capital; thou barr'st us
> Our prayers to the Gods, which is a comfort
> That all but we enjoy. For how can we,
> Alas! how can we, for our Country pray,
> Whereto we're bound, together with thy Victory,
> Whereto we're bound? Alack! or we must lose
> The Country, our dear nurse; or else thy Person,
> Our comfort in the Country. We must find
> An eminent calamity, though we had
> Our wish, which side shou'd win. For either thou
> Must, as a foreign Recreant, be led
> With manacles thorough our streets; or else
> Triumphantly tread on thy Country's ruin,
> And bear the palm, for having bravely shed
> Thy wife and children's blood. For myself, son,
> I purpose not to wait on Fortune, 'till
> These wars determine: if I can't persuade thee
> Rather to shew a noble grace to both parts,
> Than seek the end of one; thou shalt no sooner
> March to assault thy Country, than to tread
> (Trust to't, thou shalt not) on thy mother's womb,
> That brought thee to this world.

I will now give you the old Translation, which shall effectually confute Mr. Pope: for our Author hath done little more than throw the very words of North into blank verse.

'If we helde our peace (my sonne) and determined not to
speake, the state of our poore bodies, and present sight of our
rayment, would easely bewray to thee what life we haue led at
home, since thy exile and abode abroad. But thinke now with
thy selfe, howe much more unfortunately then all the women
liuinge we are come hether, considering that the sight which
should be most pleasaunt to all other to beholde, spitefull
fortune hath made most fearfull to us: making my selfe to see my
sonne, and my daughter here, her husband, besieging the walles
of his natiue countrie. So as that which is the only comfort to all
other in their adversitie and miserie, to pray unto the goddes, and
to call to them for aide, is the onely thinge which plongeth us into
most deepe perplexitie. For we cannot (alas) together pray,
both for victorie, for our countrie, and for safety of thy life also:
but a worlde of grievous curses, yea more then any mortall
enemie can heape uppon us, are forcibly wrapt up in our
prayers. For the bitter soppe of most harde choyce is offered thy
wife and children, to foregoe the one of the two: either to lose
the persone of thy selfe, or the nurse of their natiue contrie. For
my selfe (my sonne) I am determined not to tarrie, till fortune
in my life time doe make an ende of this warre. For if I cannot
persuade thee, rather to doe good unto both parties, then to
ouerthrowe and destroye the one, preferring loue and nature
before the malice and calamitie of warres: thou shalt see, my
sonne, and trust unto it, thou shalt no soner marche forward to
assault thy countrie, but thy foote shall tread upon thy mother's
wombe, that brought thee first into this world.'

The length of this quotation will be excused for it's curiosity;
and it happily wants not the assistance of a Comment. But
matters may not always be so easily managed:—a plagiarism
from Anacreon hath been detected:

> The Sun's a thief, and with his great attraction
> Robs the vast Sea. The Moon's an arrant thief,
> And her pale fire she snatches from the Sun.
> The Sea's a thief, whose liquid surge resolves
> The Moon into salt tears. The Earth's a thief,

That feeds and breeds by a composture stol'n
From gen'ral excrements: each thing's a thief.

'This,' says Dr. Dodd, 'is a good deal in the manner of the
celebrated *drinking Ode*, too well known to be inserted.' Yet it
may be alleged by those who imagine Shakespeare to have been
generally able to think for himself, that the topicks are obvious,
and their application is different.—But for argument's sake, let
the Parody be granted; and 'our Author,' says some one, 'may
be puzzled to prove that there was a Latin translation of
Anacreon at the time Shakespeare wrote his *Timon of Athens*.' This
challenge is peculiarly unhappy: for I do not at present recollect
any *other Classick* (if indeed, with great deference to Mynheer De
Pauw, Anacreon may be numbered amongst them) that was
originally published with *two* Latin translations.

But this is not all. Puttenham in his *Arte of English Poesie*, 1589,
quotes some one of a 'reasonable good facilitie in translation,
who finding *certaine* of Anacreon's Odes very well translated by
Ronsard the French poet—comes our Minion, and translates
the same out of French into English': and his strictures upon him
evince the publication. Now this identical Ode is to be met with
in Ronsard! and as his works are in few hands, I will take the
liberty of transcribing it:

> La terre les eaux va boivant,
> L'arbre la boit par sa racine,
> La mer salee boit le vent,
> Et le Soleil boit la marine.
> Le Soleil est beu de la Lune,
> Tout boit soit en haut ou en bas:
> Suivant ceste reigle commune,
> Pourquoy donc ne boirons-nous pas?
>
> Edit. Fol. p. 507.

I know not whether an observation or two relative to our
Author's acquaintance with Homer be worth our investigation.
The ingenious Mrs. Lenox observes on a passage of *Troilus and
Cressida*, where Achilles is roused to battle by the death of

Patroclus, that Shakespeare must *here* have had the *Iliad* in view, as 'the old Story, which in many places he hath faithfully copied, is absolutely silent with respect to this circumstance.'

And Mr. Upton is positive that the *sweet oblivious Antidote*, inquired after by Macbeth, could be nothing but the *Nepenthe* described in the *Odyssey*,

Νηπενθές τ' ἄχολόν τε, κακῶν ἐπίληθον ἁπάντων.

I will not insist upon the Translations by Chapman; as the first Editions are without date, and it may be difficult to ascertain the exact time of their publication. But the *former* circumstance might have been learned from Alexander Barclay; and the *latter* more fully from Spenser than from Homer himself.

'But Shakespeare,' persists Mr. Upton, 'hath some *Greek Expressions*.' Indeed!—'We have one in *Coriolanus*,

> — It is held
> That valour is the chiefest Virtue, and
> Most dignifies the *Haver*;—

and another in *Macbeth*, where Banquo addresses the *Weïrd-Sisters*,

> — My noble Partner
> You greet with present grace, and great prediction
> Of noble *Having*. —
> Gr. Ἔχεια,—and πρὸς τὸν Ἔχοντα, to the *Haver*.'

This was the common language of Shakespeare's time. 'Lye in a water-bearer's house!' says Master Mathew of Bobadil, 'a Gentleman of his *Havings*!'

Thus likewise John Davies in his *Pleasant Descant upon English Proverbs*, printed with his *Scourge of Folly*, about 1612:

> Do well and have well!—neyther so still:
> For some are good *Doers*, whose *Havings* are ill;

and Daniel the Historian uses it frequently. *Having* seems to be synonymous with *Behaviour* in Gawin Douglas and the elder Scotch writers.

Haver, in the sense of *Possessor*, is every where met with: tho'
unfortunately the πρὸς τὸν "Ἔχοντα of Sophocles, produced as
an authority for it, is suspected by Kuster, as good a critick in
these matters, to have absolutely a different meaning.

But what shall we say to the learning of the Clown in *Hamlet*,
'Ay, tell me that, and *unyoke*'? alluding to the Βουλυτὸς of the
Greeks: and Homer and his Scholiast are quoted accordingly!

If it be not sufficient to say, with Dr. Warburton, that the
phrase might be taken from Husbandry, without much depth of
reading; we may produce it from a *Dittie* of the workmen of
Dover, preserved in the additions to Holingshed, p. 1546.

> My bow is broke, I would *unyoke*,
> My foot is sore, I can worke no more.

An expression of my Dame Quickly is next fastened upon,
which you may look for in vain in the modern text; she calls
some of the pretended Fairies in the *Merry Wives of Windsor*,

> — *Orphan* Heirs of fixed Destiny;

'and how elegant is this!' quoth Mr. Upton, supposing the word
to be used, as a Grecian would have used it, 'ὀρφανὸς ab ὀρφνὸς
—acting in darkness and obscurity.'

Mr. Heath assures us that the bare mention of such an interpretation is a sufficient refutation of it: and his critical word
will be rather taken in Greek than in English: in the same hands
therefore I will venture to leave all our author's knowledge of
the *Old Comedy*, and his etymological learning in the word,
Desdemona.

Surely poor Mr. Upton was very little acquainted with
Fairies, notwithstanding his laborious study of Spenser. The last
authentick account of them is from our countryman William
Lilly; and it by no means agrees with the *learned* interpretation:
for the *angelical Creatures* appeared in his *Hurst* wood in a *most
illustrious Glory*,—'and indeed,' says the Sage, 'it is not given to
very many persons to endure their *glorious aspects*.'

The only use of transcribing these things is to shew what

absurdities men for ever run into, when they lay down an Hypothesis, and afterward seek for arguments in the support of it. What else could induce this man, by no means a bad scholar, to doubt whether *Truepenny* might not be derived from Τρύπανον; and quote upon us with much parade an old Scholiast on Aristophanes?—I will not stop to confute him: nor take any notice of two or three more Expressions, in which he was pleased to suppose some learned meaning or other; all which he might have found in every Writer of the time, or still more easily in the vulgar Translation of the Bible, by consulting the Concordance of Alexander Cruden.

But whence have we the Plot of *Timon*, except from the Greek of Lucian?—The Editors and Criticks have been never at a greater loss than in their inquiries of this sort; and the source of a Tale hath been often in vain sought abroad, which might easily have been found at home: My good friend, the very ingenious Editor of the *Reliques of ancient English Poetry*, hath shewn our Author to have been sometimes contented with a legendary *Ballad*.

The Story of the *Misanthrope* is told in almost every Collection of the time; and particularly in two books, with which Shakespeare was intimately acquainted; the *Palace of Pleasure*, and the *English Plutarch*. Indeed from a passage in an old Play, called *Jack Drum's Entertainment*, I conjecture that he had before made his appearance on the Stage.

Were this a proper place for such a disquisition, I could give you many cases of this kind. We are sent for instance to Cinthio for the Plot of *Measure for Measure*, and Shakespeare's judgement hath been attacked for some deviations from him in the conduct of it: when probably all he knew of the matter was from Madam Isabella in the *Heptameron* of Whetstone. Ariosto is continually quoted for the Fable of *Much ado about Nothing*; but I suspect our Poet to have been satisfied with the *Geneura* of Turberville. *As you like it* was *certainly borrowed*, if we believe Dr. Grey, and Mr. Upton, from the *Coke's Tale of Gamelyn*; which by the way was not *printed* 'till a century afterward: when in truth the old Bard, who was no hunter of MSS., contented himself solely with Lodge's *Rosalynd* or *Euphues' Golden Legacye*. 4to. 1590. The Story of *All's well that ends well*, or, as I suppose it to have been sometimes called, *Love's labour wonne*, is originally indeed the property of Boccace, but it came immediately to Shakespeare from Painter's *Giletta of Narbon*. Mr. Langbaine could not conceive whence the Story of *Pericles* could be taken, 'not meeting in History with any such *Prince of Tyre*'; yet his legend may be found at large in old Gower, under the name of *Appolynus*.

Pericles is one of the Plays omitted in the later Editions, as well as the early Folios, and not improperly; tho' it was published many years before the death of Shakespeare, with his name in the Title-page. Aulus Gellius informs us that some Plays are ascribed absolutely to Plautus, which he only *retouched* and *polished*; and this is undoubtedly the case with our Author likewise. The revival of this performance, which Ben Jonson calls *stale* and *mouldy*, was probably his earliest attempt in the Drama. I know that another of these discarded pieces, the *Yorkshire Tragedy*, hath been frequently called so; but most certainly it was not written by our Poet at all: nor indeed was it printed in his life-time. The Fact on which it is built was perpetrated no sooner than 1604: much too late for so mean a performance from the hand of Shakespeare.

Sometimes a very little matter detects a forgery. You may remember a Play called the *Double Falshood*, which Mr. Theobald was desirous of palming upon the world for a posthumous one of Shakespeare: and I see it is classed as such in the last Edition of the Bodleian Catalogue. Mr. Pope himself, after all the strictures of Scriblerus, in a Letter to Aaron Hill, supposes it of that age; but a mistaken accent determines it to have been written since the middle of the last century:

— This late example
Of base Henriquez, bleeding in me now,
From each good *Aspect* takes away my trust.

And in another place,

You have an *Aspect*, Sir, of wondrous wisdom.

The word *Aspect*, you perceive, is here accented on the *first* Syllable, which, I am confident, in *any* sense of it, was never the case in the time of Shakespeare; though it may sometimes appear to be so, when we do not observe a preceding *Elision*.

Some of the professed Imitators of our old Poets have not attended to this and many other *Minutiæ*: I could point out to you several performances in the respective Styles of Chaucer, Spenser, and Shakespeare, which the *imitated* Bard could not possibly have either read or construed.

This very accent hath troubled the Annotators on Milton. Dr. Bentley observes it to be 'a *tone* different from the present use.' Mr. Manwaring, in his *Treatise of Harmony and Numbers*, very solemnly informs us that 'this Verse is defective both in Accent and Quantity, B. 3. V. 266.

> His words here ended, but his meek *Aspéct*
> Silent yet spake.—

Here,' says he, 'a syllable is *acuted* and *long*, whereas it should be *short* and *graved*'!

And a still more extraordinary Gentleman, one Green, who published a Specimen of a *new Version* of the *Paradise Lost*, into BLANK verse, 'by which that amazing Work is brought somewhat nearer the Summit of Perfection,' begins with correcting a blunder in the fourth book, V. 540:

> — The setting Sun
> Slowly descended, and with right *Aspéct*—
> Levell'd his evening rays.—

Not so in the *New Version*:

> Meanwhile the setting Sun descending slow—
> Level'd with *áspect* right his ev'ning rays.

Enough of such Commentators.—The celebrated Dr. Dee had a *Spirit*, who would sometimes condescend to correct him, when peccant in *Quantity*: and it had been kind of him to have a little assisted the *Wights* above-mentioned.—Milton affected the *Antique*; but it may seem more extraordinary that the old Accent should be adopted in *Hudibras*.

After all, the *Double Falshood* is superior to Theobald. One passage, and one only in the whole Play, he pretended to have written:

> — Strike up, my Masters;
> But touch the Strings with a religious softness:
> Teach sound to languish thro' the Night's dull Ear,
> Till Melancholy start from her lazy Couch,
> And Carelessness grow Convert to Attention.

These lines were particularly admired; and his vanity could not resist the opportunity of claiming them: but his claim had been more easily allowed to *any other* part of the performance.

To whom then shall we ascribe it?—Somebody hath told us, who should seem to be a *Nostrum-monger* by his argument, that, let *Accents* be how they will, it is called *an original Play of William Shakespeare* in the *King's Patent*, prefixed to Mr. Theobald's Edition, 1728, and consequently there *could* be no fraud in the matter. Whilst, on the contrary, the *Irish* Laureat, Mr. Victor, remarks (and were it true, it would be certainly decisive) that the Plot is borrowed from a Novel of Cervantes, not published 'till the year after Shakespeare's death. But unluckily the same Novel appears in a part of *Don Quixote*, which was printed in Spanish, 1605, and in English by Shelton, 1612.—The same reasoning, however, which exculpated our Author from the *Yorkshire Tragedy*, may be applied on the present occasion.

But you want *my* opinion:—and from every mark of Style and Manner, I make no doubt of ascribing it to Shirley. Mr. Langbaine informs us that he left some Plays in MS.—These were written about the time of the *Restoration*, when the *Accent* in question was more generally altered.

Perhaps the mistake arose from an *abbreviation* of the name. Mr. Dodsley knew not that the Tragedy of *Andromana* was Shirley's, from the very same cause. Thus a whole stream of Biographers tell us that Marston's Plays were printed at

London, 1633, 'by the care of *William Shakespeare*, the famous
Comedian.'—Here again I suppose, in some Transcript, the real
Publisher's name, *William Sheares*, was *abbreviated*. No one hath
protracted the life of Shakespeare beyond 1616, except Mr.
Hume; who is pleased to add a year to it, in contradiction to all
manner of evidence.

Shirley is spoken of with contempt in *Mac Flecknoe*; but his
Imagination is sometimes fine to an extraordinary degree. I
recollect a passage in the fourth book of the *Paradise Lost*, which
hath been suspected of *Imitation*, as a *prettiness* below the Genius
of Milton: I mean, where *Uriel* glides *backward and forward* to
Heaven on a *Sun-beam*. Dr. Newton informs us that this might
possibly be hinted by a Picture of Annibal Caracci in the King of
France's Cabinet: but I am apt to believe that Milton had been
struck with a Portrait in Shirley. Fernando, in the Comedy of the
Brothers, 1652, describes Jacinta at *Vespers*:

> Her eye did seem to labour with a tear,
> Which suddenly took birth, but overweigh'd
> With it's own swelling, drop'd upon her bosome;
> Which, by reflexion of her light, appear'd
> As nature meant her sorrow for an ornament:
> After, her looks grew chearfull, and I saw
> A smile shoot gracefull upward from her eyes,
> As if they had gain'd a victory o'er grief,
> And with it many *beams* twisted themselves,
> Upon whose *golden threads* the *Angels* walk
> *To and again from Heaven.—*

You must not think me infected with the spirit of Lauder, if I
give you another of Milton's Imitations:

> — The Swan *with arched neck*
> Between her white wings mantling proudly, rows
> Her state with oary feet.—B. 7. V. 438, &c.

'The ancient Poets,' says Mr. Richardson, 'have not hit upon
this beauty; so lavish as they have been in their descriptions of

the *Swan*. Homer calls the Swan *long-necked*, δουλιχοδείρον; but how much more *pittoresque*, if he had *arched* this length of neck?'

For *this beauty*, however, Milton was beholden to Donne; whose name, I believe, at present is better known than his writings:

> —Like a Ship in her full trim,
> A *Swan*, so white that you may unto him
>   Compare all whitenesse, but himselfe to none,
> Glided along, and as he glided watch'd,
> And with his *arched neck* this poore fish catch'd.
>   *Progresse of the Soul*, St. 24.

Those highly finished Landscapes, the *Seasons*, are indeed copied from Nature: but Thomson sometimes recollected the hand of his Master:

> — The stately-sailing Swan
> Gives out his snowy plumage to the gale;
> *And, arching proud his neck, with oary feet,*
> Bears forward fierce, and guards his osier Isle,
> Protective of his young.—

But *to return*, as we say on other occasions. Perhaps the Advocates for Shakespeare's knowledge of the Latin language may be more successful. Mr. Gildon takes the Van. 'It is plain that He was acquainted with the Fables of antiquity very well: that some of the Arrows of Cupid are pointed with Lead, and others with Gold, he found in Ovid; and what he speaks of Dido, in Virgil: nor do I know any translation of these Poets so ancient as Shakespeare's time.' The passages on which these sagacious remarks are made occur in the *Midsummer Night's Dream*; and exhibit, we see, a clear proof of acquaintance with the Latin Classicks. But we are not answerable for Mr. Gildon's ignorance; he might have been told of Caxton and Douglas, of Surrey and Stanyhurst, of Phaer and Twyne, of Fleming and Golding, of Turberville and Churchyard! but these Fables were easily known without the help of either the originals or the translations. The Fate of Dido had been sung very early by Gower,

Chaucer, and Lydgate; Marloe had even already introduced her to the Stage: and Cupid's arrows appear with their characteristick differences in Surrey, in Sidney, in Spenser, and every Sonnetteer of the time. Nay, their very names were exhibited long before in the *Romaunt of the Rose*: a work you may venture to look into, notwithstanding Master Prynne hath so positively assured us, on the word of John Gerson, that the Author is most certainly damned, if he did not care for a serious repentance.

Mr. Whalley argues in the same manner, and with the same success. He thinks a passage in the *Tempest*,

— High Queen of State,
Great Juno comes; I know her by her *Gait*,

a remarkable instance of Shakespeare's knowledge of ancient Poetick story; and that the hint was furnished by the *Divum incedo Regina* of Virgil.

You know, honest John Taylor, the *Water-poet*, declares that *he never learned his Accidence*, and that *Latin and French* were to him *Heathen-Greek*; yet, by the help of Mr. Whalley's argument, I will prove him a *learned* Man, in spite of every thing he may say to the contrary: for thus he makes a *Gallant* address his *Lady*,

'Most inestimable Magazine of Beauty—in whom *the Port and Majesty of Juno*, the Wisdom of Jove's braine-bred Girle, and the Feature of Cytherea, have their domestical habitation.'

In the *Merchant of Venice*, we have an oath 'By *two-headed Janus*'; and here, says Dr. Warburton, Shakespeare shews his knowledge in the Antique: and so again does the *Water-poet*, who describes Fortune,

Like a *Janus* with a *double-face*.

But Shakespeare hath somewhere a *Latin Motto*, quoth Dr. Sewel; and so hath John Taylor, and a whole Poem upon it into the bargain.

You perceive, my dear Sir, how vague and indeterminate such arguments must be: for in fact this *sweet Swan of Thames*, as Mr. Pope calls him, hath more scraps of Latin, and allusions to antiquity, than are any where to be met with in the writings of Shakespeare. I am sorry to trouble you with trifles, yet what must be done, when grave men insist upon them?

It should seem to be the opinion of some modern criticks, that the personages of classick land began only to be known in England in the time of Shakespeare; or rather, that he particularly had the honour of introducing them to the notice of his countrymen.

For instance,—*Rumour painted full of tongues* gives us a Prologue to one of the parts of *Henry the fourth*; and, says Dr. Dodd, Shakespeare had doubtless a view to either Virgil or Ovid in their description of Fame.

But why so? Stephen Hawes, in his *Pastime of Pleasure*, had long before exhibited her in the same manner,

> A goodly Lady envyroned about
> With *tongues* of fyre;—

and so had Sir Thomas More in one of his *Pageants*,

> *Fame* I am called, mervayle you nothing
> Though with *tonges* I am compassed all rounde;

not to mention her elaborate Portrait by Chaucer, in the *Boke of Fame*; and by John Higgins, one of the Assistants in the *Mirour for Magistrates*, in his Legend of King Albanacte.

A very liberal Writer on the *Beauties of Poetry*, who hath been more conversant in the ancient Literature of other Countries than his own, 'cannot but wonder that a Poet, whose classical Images are composed of the finest parts, and breath the very spirit of ancient Mythology, should pass for being illiterate:

> See what a grace was seated on his brow!
> Hyperion's curls: the front of Jove himself:
> An eye like Mars to threaten and command:
> A station like the herald Mercury,
> New lighted on a heaven-kissing hill.   *Hamlet.*'

Illiterate is an ambiguous term: the question is, whether Poetick History could be only known by an Adept in *Languages*. It is no reflection on this ingenious Gentleman, when I say that I use on this occasion the words of a *better* Critick, who yet was not willing to carry the *illiteracy* of our Poet *too far*:—'They who are in such astonishment at the *learning* of Shakespeare, forget that the Pagan Imagery was familiar to all the Poets of his time; and that abundance of this sort of learning was to be picked up from almost every English book that he could take into his hands.' For not to insist upon Stephen Bateman's *Golden booke of the leaden Goddes*, 1577, and several other laborious compilations on the subject, all this and much more Mythology might as perfectly have been learned from the *Testament of Creseide*, and the *Fairy Queen*, as from a regular Pantheon, or Polymetis himself.

Mr. Upton, not contented with *Heathen* learning, when he finds it in the text, must necessarily superadd it, when it appears to be wanting; because Shakespeare most certainly hath lost it by accident!

In *Much ado about Nothing*, Don Pedro says of the insensible Benedict, 'He hath twice or thrice cut Cupid's bow-string, and the little *Hangman* dare not shoot at him.'

This mythology is not recollected in the Ancients, and therefore the critick hath no doubt but his Author wrote '*Henchman*, —*a Page, Pusio*: and *this* word seeming too hard for the Printer, he translated the little Urchin into a *Hangman*, a character no way belonging to him.'

But this character was not borrowed from the Ancients;—it came from the *Arcadia* of Sir Philip Sidney:

> Millions of yeares this old drivell Cupid lives;
> While still more wretch, more wicked he doth prove:
> Till now at length that Jove him office gives,
> (At Juno's suite who much did Argus love)
>   In this our world a *Hangman* for to be
>   Of all those fooles that will have all they see.
>   B. 2. Ch. 14.

I know it may be objected on the authority of such Biographers as Theophilus Cibber, and the Writer of the Life of Sir Philip,

prefixed to the modern Editions, that the *Arcadia* was not published before 1613, and consequently too late for this imitation:
but I have a Copy in my own possession, printed for W.
Ponsonbie, 1590, 4to. which hath escaped the notice of the
industrious Ames, and the rest of our typographical Antiquaries.

Thus likewise every word of antiquity is to be cut down to the
classical standard.

In a Note on the Prologue to *Troilus and Cressida* (which, by the
way, is not met with in the *Quarto*), Mr. Theobald informs us
that the very *names* of the gates of Troy have been barbarously
demolished by the Editors: and a deal of learned dust he makes
in setting them right again; much however to Mr. Heath's satisfaction. Indeed the learning is modestly withdrawn from the
later Editions, and we are quietly instructed to read,

> Dardan, and Thymbria, Ilia, Scæa, Troian,
> And Antenorides.

But had he looked into the *Troye boke* of Lydgate, instead of
puzzling himself with Dares Phrygius, he would have found the
horrid demolition to have been neither the work of Shakespeare
nor his Editors.

> Therto his cyte | compassed enuyrowne
> Hadde gates VI to entre into the towne:
> The firste of all | and strengest eke with all,
> Largest also | and moste pryncypall,
> Of myghty byldyng | alone pereless,
> Was by the kynge called | Dardanydes;
> And in storye | lyke as it is founde,
> Tymbria | was named the seconde;
> And the thyrde | called Helyas,
> The fourthe gate | hyghte also Cetheas;
> The fyfthe Trojana, | the syxth Anthonydes,
> Stronge and myghty | both in werre and pes.
> Lond. empr. by R. Pynson, 1513. Fol. B. 2. Ch. 11.

Our excellent friend Mr. Hurd hath born a noble testimony on
our side of the question. 'Shakespeare,' says this true Critick,

'owed the felicity of freedom from the bondage of classical superstition to the *want* of what is called the *advantage* of a learned
Education.—This, as well as a vast superiority to Genius, hath
contributed to lift this astonishing man to the glory of being
esteemed the most original *thinker* and *speaker*, since the times of
Homer.' And hence indisputably the amazing Variety of Style
and Manner, unknown to all other Writers: an argument of
itself sufficient to emancipate Shakespeare from the supposition
of a *Classical training*. Yet, to be honest, *one* Imitation is *fastened*
on our Poet: which hath been insisted upon likewise by Mr.
Upton and Mr. Whalley. You remember it in the famous Speech
of Claudio in *Measure for Measure*:

> Ay, but to die and go we know not where! &c.

Most certainly the Ideas of a 'Spirit bathing in fiery floods,'
of residing 'in thrilling regions of thick-ribbed ice,' or of being
'imprisoned in the viewless winds,' are not *original* in our Author;
but I am not sure that they came from the *Platonick Hell* of Virgil.
The Monks also had their hot and their cold Hell, 'The fyrste is
fyre that ever brenneth, and never gyveth lighte,' says an old
Homily:—'The seconde is passyng colde, that yf a grete hylle of
fyre were casten therin, it sholde torne to yce.' One of their
Legends, well remembered in the time of Shakespeare, gives us a
Dialogue between a Bishop and a Soul tormented in a piece of
ice, which was brought to cure *a grete brenning heate* in his foot:
take care you do not interpret this the *Gout*, for I remember M.
Menage quotes a *Canon* upon us,

Si quis dixerit Episcopum PODAGRA laborare, Anathema sit.

Another tells us of the Soul of a Monk fastened to a Rock,
which the winds were to blow about for a twelvemonth
and purge of it's Enormities. Indeed this doctrine was before
now introduced into poetick fiction, as you may see in a Poem,
'where the Lover declareth his pains to exceed far the pains
of Hell,' among the many miscellaneous ones subjoined to
the Works of Surrey. Nay, a very learned and inquisitive

Brother-Antiquary, our Greek Professor, hath observed to me on the authority of Blefkenius, that this was the ancient opinion of the inhabitants of Iceland; who were certainly very little read either in the *Poet* or the *Philosopher*.

After all, Shakespeare's curiosity might lead him to *Translations*. Gawin Douglas really changes the *Platonick Hell* into the 'punytion of Saulis in Purgatory': and it is observable that when the Ghost informs Hamlet of his Doom there,

> Till the foul crimes done in his days of nature
> Are *burnt and purg'd away*,—

the Expression is very similar to the Bishop's: I will give you his Version as concisely as I can; 'It is a nedeful thyng to suffer panis and torment—Sum in the wyndis, Sum under the watter, and in the fire uthir Sum:—thus the mony Vices—

> Contrakkit in the corpis be *done away*
> *And purgit.*'—
>
> $\qquad$ *Sixte Booke of Eneados.* Fol. p. 191.

It seems, however, 'that Shakespeare *himself* in the *Tempest* hath translated some expressions of *Virgil*: witness the *O Dea certe.*' I presume we are here directed to the passage where Ferdinand says of Miranda, after hearing the Songs of Ariel,

> — Most sure, the Goddess
> On whom these airs attend;

and so *very small Latin* is sufficient for this formidable translation, that if it be thought any honour to our Poet, I am loth to deprive him of it; but his honour is not built on such a sandy foundation. Let us turn to a *real Translator*, and examine whether the Idea might not be fully comprehended by an English reader; *supposing* it necessarily borrowed from Virgil. Hexameters in our own language are almost forgotten; we will quote therefore this time from Stanyhurst:

> O to thee, fayre Virgin, what terme may rightly be fitted?
> Thy tongue, thy visage no mortal frayltie resembleth.
> — *No doubt, a Godesse!* $\qquad$ Edit. 1583.

Gabriel Harvey desired only to be '*Epitaph'd*, the Inventor of the *English Hexameter*,' and for a while every one would be *halting on Roman feet*; but the ridicule of our Fellow-Collegian Hall, in one of his *Satires*, and the reasoning of Daniel, in his *Defence of Rhyme* against Campion, presently reduced us to our original Gothic.

But to come nearer the purpose, what will you say if I can shew you that Shakespeare, when, in the favourite phrase, he had a Latin Poet *in his Eye*, most assuredly made use of a Translation?

Prospero in the *Tempest* begins the Address to his attendant *Spirits*,

> Ye Elves of Hills, of standing Lakes, and Groves.

This speech Dr. Warburton rightly observes to be borrowed from Medea in Ovid: and 'it proves,' says Mr. Holt, 'beyond contradiction, that Shakespeare was perfectly acquainted with the Sentiments of the Ancients on the Subject of Inchantments.' The original lines are these,

> Auræque, & venti, montesque, amnesque, lacusque,
> Diique omnes nemorum, diique omnes noctis adeste.

It happens, however, that the translation by Arthur Golding is by no means literal, and Shakespeare hath closely followed it;

Ye Ayres and Winds; *Ye Elves of Hills*, of Brookes, of Woods alone, *Of standing Lakes*, and of the Night, approche ye everych one.

I think it is unnecessary to pursue this any further; especially as more powerful arguments await us.

In the *Merchant of Venice*, the Jew, as an apology for his cruelty to Anthonio, rehearses many *Sympathies* and *Antipathies* for which *no reason can be rendered*,

> Some love not a gaping Pig—
> And others when a *Bagpipe* sings i' th' nose
> Cannot contain their urine for *affection*.

This incident Dr. Warburton supposes to be taken from a passage in Scaliger's *Exercitations* against Cardan, 'Narrabo tibi jocosam Sympathiam Reguli Vasconis Equitis: Is dum viveret, audito *Phormingis* sono, urinam illico facere cogebatur.' 'And,' proceeds the Doctor, 'to make this jocular story still more ridiculous, Shakespeare, I suppose, translated *Phorminx* by *Bagpipes*.'

Here we seem fairly caught;—for Scaliger's work was never, as the term goes, *done into English*. But luckily in an old translation from the French of Peter le Loier, entitled, *A treatise of Specters, or straunge Sights, Visions and Apparitions appearing sensibly unto men*, we have this identical Story from Scaliger: and what is still more, a marginal Note gives us in all probability the very fact alluded to, as well as the word of Shakespeare, 'Another Gentleman of this quality liued of late in Deuon neere Excester, who could not endure the playing on a *Bagpipe*'.

We may just add, as some observation hath been made upon it, that *Affection* in the sense of *Sympathy* was formerly *technical*; and so used by Lord Bacon, Sir Kenelm Digby, and many other Writers.

A single word in Queen Catherine's Character of Wolsey, in *Henry the eighth*, is brought by the Doctor as another argument for the learning of Shakespeare:

> — He was a man
> Of an unbounded Stomach, ever ranking
> Himself with Princes; one that by *Suggestion*
> Ty'd all the kingdom. Simony was fair play.
> His own opinion was his law, i' th' presence
> He would say untruths, and be ever double
> Both in his words and meaning. He was never,
> But where he meant to ruin, pitiful.
> His promises were, as he then was, mighty;
> But his performance, as he now is, nothing.
> Of his own body he was ill, and gave
> The Clergy ill example.

'The word *Suggestion*,' says the Critick, 'is here used with great propriety, and *seeming* knowledge of the Latin tongue':

and he proceeds to settle the sense of it from *the late Roman writers and their glossers*. But Shakespeare's knowledge was from Holingshed, whom he follows *verbatim*:

'This Cardinal was of a great stomach, for he compted himself equal with princes, and by craftie *Suggestion* got into his hands innumerable treasure: he forced little on simonie, and was not pitifull, and stood affectionate in his own opinion: in open presence he would lie and saie untruth, and was double both in speech and meaning: he would promise much and performe little: he was vicious of his bodie, and gaue the clergie euil example.' Edit. 1587. p. 922.

Perhaps after this quotation you may not think that Sir Thomas Hanmer, who reads *Tyth'd* instead of *Ty'd all the kingdom*, deserves quite so much of Dr. Warburton's severity.— Indisputably the passage, like every other in the Speech, is intended to express the meaning of the parallel one in the Chronicle: it cannot therefore be credited that any man, when the *Original* was produced, should still chuse to defend a *cant* acceptation; and inform us, perhaps, *seriously*, that in *gaming* language, from I know not what practice, to *tye* is to *equal*! A sense of the word, as far as I have yet found, *unknown* to our old Writers; and, if *known*, would not surely have been used in *this* place by our Author.

But let us turn from conjecture to Shakespeare's authorities. Hall, from whom the above description is copied by Holingshed, is very explicit in the demands of the Cardinal: who, having insolently told the Lord Mayor and Aldermen, 'For sothe I thinke that *halfe* your substaunce were to litle,' assures them by way of comfort at the end of his harangue, that *upon an average* the *tythe* should be sufficient; 'Sers, speake not to breake that thyng that is concluded, for *some* shal not paie the *tenth* parte, and *some* more.'—And again; 'Thei saied, the Cardinall by Visitacions, makyng of Abbottes, probates of testamentes, graunting of faculties, licences, and other pollyngs in his Courtes legantines, had made his *threasore egall with the kynges*.' Edit. 1548. p. 138. and 143.

Skelton, in his *Why come ye not to Court*, gives us, after his rambling manner, a curious character of Wolsey:

> — By and by
> He will drynke us so dry
> And sucke us so nye
> That men shall scantly
> Haue penny or halpennye
> God saue hys noble grace
> And graunt him a place
> Endlesse to dwel
> With the deuill of hel
> For and he were there
> We nead neuer feare
> Of the feendes blacke
> For I undertake
> He wold so brag and crake
> That he wold than make
> The deuils to quake
> To shudder and to shake
> Lyke a fier drake
> And with a cole rake
> Bruse them on a brake
> And binde them to a stake
> And set hel on fyre
> At his owne desire
> He is such a grym syre!   Edit. 1568.

Mr. Upton and some other Criticks have thought it very *scholar-like* in Hamlet to swear the Centinels on a *Sword*: but this is for ever met with. For instance, in the *Passus primus* of *Pierce Plowman*,

> Dauid in his daies dubbed knightes,
> And did hem *swere on her sword* to serue truth euer.

And in *Hieronymo*, the common Butt of our Author, and the Wits of the time, says Lorenzo to Pedringano,

> Swear on this cross, that what thou sayst is true—
> But if I prove thee perjured and unjust,

> This very *sword*, whereon thou took'st thine oath,
> Shall be the worker of thy Tragedy!

We have therefore no occasion to go with Mr. Garrick as far as the French of Brantôme to illustrate this ceremony: a *Gentleman* who will be always allowed the *first Commentator* on Shakespeare, when he does not carry us beyond *himself*.

Mr. Upton, however, in the next place, produces a passage from *Henry the sixth*, whence he argues it to be very plain that our Author had not only *read* Cicero's *Offices*, but even more *critically* than many of the Editors:

> — This Villain here,
> Being Captain of a *Pinnace*, threatens more
> Than Bargulus, the strong Illyrian Pirate.

So the *Wight*, he observes with great exultation, is named by Cicero in the Editions of Shakespeare's time, 'Bargulus Illyrius latro'; tho' the modern Editors have chosen to call him Bardylis: —'and *thus* I found it in *two* MSS.'—And *thus* he might have found it in *two* Translations, before Shakespeare was born. Robert Whytinton, 1533, calls him, 'Bargulus a Pirate upon the see of Illiry'; and Nicholas Grimald, about twenty years afterward, 'Bargulus the Illyrian Robber.'

But it had been easy to have checked Mr. Upton's exultation, by observing that Bargulus does not appear in the *Quarto*.— Which also is the case with some fragments of Latin verses, in the different *Parts* of this *doubtful* performance.

It is scarcely worth mentioning that two or three more Latin passages, which are met with in our Author, are immediately transcribed from the Story or Chronicle before him. Thus in *Henry the fifth*, whose right to the kingdom of France is copiously demonstrated by the Archbishop:

> — There is no bar
> To make against your Highness' claim to France,
> But this which they produce from Pharamond:
> In terram Salicam mulieres ne succedant;

No Woman shall succeed in Salike land:
Which Salike land the French unjustly gloze
To be the realm of France, and Pharamond
The founder of this law and female bar.
Yet their own authors faithfully affirm
That the land Salike lies in Germany,
Between the floods of Sala and of Elve, &c.

Archbishop Chichelie, says Holingshed, 'did much inueie against the surmised and false fained law Salike, which the Frenchmen alledge euer against the kings of England in barre of their just title to the crowne of France. The very words of that supposed law are these, In terram Salicam mulieres ne succedant, that is to saie, Into the Salike land let not women succeed; which the French glossers expound to be the realm of France, and that this law was made by King Pharamond: whereas yet their owne authors affirme that the land Salike is in Germanie, between the rivers of Elbe and Sala,' &c. p. 545.

It hath lately been repeated from Mr. Guthrie's *Essay upon English Tragedy*, that the *Portrait* of Macbeth's *Wife* is copied from Buchanan, 'whose spirit, as well as words, is translated into the Play of Shakespeare: and it had signified nothing to have pored only on Holingshed for *Facts*.'—'Animus etiam, per se ferox, prope quotidianis conviciis uxoris (quæ omnium consiliorum ei erat conscia) stimulabatur.'—This is the whole that Buchanan says of the *Lady*; and truly I see no more *spirit* in the Scotch than in the English Chronicler. 'The wordes of the three weird Sisters also greatly encouraged him [to the Murder of Duncan], but specially his wife lay sore upon him to attempt the thing, as she that was very ambitious, brenning in unquenchable desire to beare the name of a Queene.' Edit. 1577. p. 244.

This part of Holingshed is an Abridgment of Johne Bellenden's translation of the *noble clerk*, Hector Boece, imprinted at *Edingburgh*, in Fol. 1541. I will give the passage as it is found there. 'His wyfe impacient of lang tary (*as all wemen ar*) specially quhare they ar desirus of ony purpos, gaif hym gret artation to pursew the thrid weird, that sche micht be ane quene, calland hym oft tymis febyl cowart and nocht desyrus of honouris, sen he durst not assailze the thing with manheid and curage, quhilk is offerit to hym be beniuolence of fortoun. Howbeit sindry otheris hes assailzeit sic thinges afore with maist terribyl jeopardyis, quhen they had not sic sickernes to succeid in the end of thair laubouris as he had.' p. 173.

But we can *demonstrate* that Shakespeare had not the Story from Buchanan. According to *him*, the Weïrd-Sisters salute Macbeth, 'Una Angusiæ Thamum, altera Moraviæ, tertia *Regem*.'—Thane of Angus, and of Murray, &c., but according to Holingshed, immediately from Bellenden, as it stands in Shakespeare: 'The first of them spake and sayde, All hayle Makbeth, Thane of Glammis,—the second of them said, Hayle Makbeth, Thane of Cawder; but the third sayde, All hayle Makbeth, that hereafter shall be *king of Scotland*.' p. 243.

1 *Witch*. All hail, Macbeth! Hail to thee, Thane of Glamis!
2 *Witch*. All hail, Macbeth! Hail to thee, Thane of Cawdor!
3 *Witch*. All hail, Macbeth! that shalt be King hereafter!

Here too our Poet found the equivocal Predictions, on which his Hero so fatally depended. 'He had learned of certain wysards, how that he ought to take heede of Macduffe;—and surely hereupon had he put Macduffe to death, but a certaine witch, whom he had in great trust, had tolde that he should neuer be slain with *man borne of any woman*, nor vanquished till the Wood of Bernane came to the Castell of Dunsinane.' p. 244. And the Scene between Malcolm and Macduff in the fourth act is almost literally taken from the Chronicle.

Macbeth was certainly one of Shakespeare's latest Productions, and it might possibly have been suggested to him by a little performance on the same subject at Oxford, before King James, 1605. I will transcribe my notice of it from Wake's *Rex Platonicus*: 'Fabulæ ansam dedit antiqua de Regia prosapia historiola apud Scoto-Britannos celebrata, quæ narrat tres olim Sibyllas occurrisse duobus Scotiæ proceribus, Macbetho & Banchoni, & illum prædixisse Regem futurum, sed Regem

nullum geniturum; hunc Regem non futurum, sed Reges geniturum multos. Vaticinii veritatem rerum eventus comprobavit.
Banchonis enim e stirpe Potentissimus Jacobus oriundus.' p. 29.

A stronger argument hath been brought from the Plot of
Hamlet. Dr. Grey and Mr. Whalley assure us that for *this* Shakespeare *must* have read *Saxo Grammaticus* in Latin, for no translation hath been made into any modern Language. But the truth is,
he did not take it from *Saxo* at all; a Novel called the *Hystorie of
Hamblet* was his original: a fragment of which, in *black Letter*, I
have been favoured with by a very curious and intelligent Gentleman, to whom the lovers of Shakespeare will some time or
other owe great obligations.

It hath indeed been said that, 'IF *such an history exists*, it is
almost impossible that any poet unacquainted with the Latin
language (supposing his perceptive faculties to have been ever
so acute) could have caught the characteristical madness of
Hamlet, described by *Saxo Grammaticus*, so happily as it is delineated by Shakespeare.'

Very luckily, our Fragment gives us a part of Hamlet's Speech
to his *Mother*, which sufficiently replies to this observation:—'It
was not without cause, and juste occasion, that my gestures,
countenances, and words seeme to proceed from a madman, and
that I desire to haue all men esteeme mee wholy depriued of
sence and reasonable understanding, bycause I am well assured
that he that hath made no conscience to kill his owne brother
(accustomed to murthers, and allured with desire of gouerne-
ment without controll in his treasons) will not spare to saue
himselfe with the like crueltie, in the blood and flesh of the loyns
of his brother, by him massacred: and therefore it is better for
me to fayne madnesse then to use my right sences as nature hath
bestowed them upon me. The bright shining clearnes therof I
am forced to hide vnder this shadow of dissimulation, as the sun
doth hir beams vnder some great cloud, when the wether in
summer time ouercasteth: the face of a mad man serueth to
couer my gallant countenance, and the gestures of a fool are fit
for me, to the end that, guiding my self wisely therin, I may

preserue my life for the Danes and the memory of my late deceased father, for that the desire of reuenging his death is so
ingrauen in my heart, that if I dye not shortly, I hope to take such
and so great vengeance, that these Countryes shall for euer
speake thereof. Neuerthelesse I must stay the time, meanes, and
occasion, lest by making ouer great hast I be now the cause of
mine owne sodaine ruine and ouerthrow, and by that meanes
end, before I beginne to effect my hearts desire: hee that hath
to doe with a wicked, disloyall, cruell, and discourteous man,
must vse craft, and politike inuentions, such as a fine witte can
best imagine, not to discouer his interprise: for seeing that by
force I cannot effect my desire, reason alloweth me by dissimulation, subtiltie, and secret practises to proceed therein.'

But to put the matter out of all question, my communicative
Friend above-mentioned, Mr. Capell (for why should I not give
myself the credit of his name?), hath been fortunate enough to
procure from the Collection of the Duke of Newcastle a *complete*
Copy of the *Hystorie of Hamblet*, which proves to be a translation
from the French of Belleforest; and he tells me that 'all the chief
incidents of the Play, and all the capital Characters, are there in
embryo, after a rude and barbarous manner: sentiments indeed
there are none that Shakespeare could borrow; nor any expression but *one*, which is, where Hamlet kills Polonius behind the
arras: in doing which he is made to cry out, as in the Play, "*a
rat, a rat!*" '—So much for *Saxo Grammaticus*!

It is scarcely conceivable how industriously the puritanical
Zeal of the last age exerted itself in destroying, amongst better
things, the innocent amusements of the former. Numberless
Tales and *Poems* are alluded to in old Books, which are now perhaps no where to be found. Mr. Capell informs me (and he is in
these matters the most able of all men to give information) that
our Author appears to have been beholden to some Novels which
he hath yet only seen in French or Italian: but he adds, 'to say
they are not in some English dress, prosaic or metrical, and perhaps with circumstances nearer to his stories, is what I will not
take upon me to do: nor indeed is it what I believe; but rather

the contrary, and that time and accident will bring some of them to light, if not all.'—

W. Painter, at the conclusion of the second *Tome* of his *Palace of Pleasure*, 1567, *advertises* the Reader, 'bicause sodaynly (contrary to expectation) this Volume is risen to greater heape of leaues, I doe omit for this present time *sundry Nouels* of mery deuise, reseruing the same to be joyned with the rest of an other part, wherein shall succeede the remnant of Bandello, specially sutch (suffrable) as the learned French man François de Belleforrest hath selected, and the choysest done in the Italian. Some also out of Erizzo, Ser Giouanni Florentino, Parabosco, Cynthio, Straparole, Sansouino, and the best liked out of the Queene of Nauarre, and other Authors. Take these in good part, with those that haue and shall come forth.'—But I am not able to find that a *third Tome* was ever published: and it is very probable that the Interest of his Booksellers, and more especially the prevailing Mode of the time, might lead him afterward to print his *sundry Novels* separately. If this were the case, it is no wonder that such *fugitive Pieces* are recovered with difficulty; when the *two Tomes*, which Tom. Rawlinson would have called *justa Volumina*, are almost annihilated. Mr. Ames, who searched after books of this sort with the utmost avidity, most certainly had not seen them when he published his *Typographical Antiquities*; as appears from his blunders about them: and possibly I myself might have remained in the same predicament, had I not been favoured with a Copy by my generous Friend, Mr. Lort.

Mr. Colman, in the Preface to his elegant Translation of Terence, hath offered some arguments for the Learning of Shakespeare, which have been retailed with much confidence, since the appearance of Mr. Johnson's Edition.

'Besides the resemblance of particular passages scattered up and down in different plays, it is well known that the *Comedy of Errors* is in great measure founded on the *Menæchmi* of Plautus; but I do not recollect ever to have seen it observed that the disguise of the *Pedant* in the *Taming of the Shrew*, and his assuming the name and character of *Vincentio*, seem to be evidently taken

from the disguise of the *Sycophanta* in the *Trinummus* of the said
Author; and there is a quotation from the *Eunuch* of Terence also,
so familiarly introduced into the Dialogue of the *Taming of the
Shrew*, that I think it puts the question of Shakespeare's having
read the Roman Comick Poets in the *original* language out of all
doubt,

> Redime te captum, quam queas, minimo.'

With respect to *resemblances*, I shall not trouble you any further.
—That the *Comedy of Errors* is founded on the *Menæchmi*, it is
notorious: nor is it less so, that a Translation of it by W. W.,
perhaps William Warner, the Author of *Albion's England*, was
extant in the time of Shakespeare; tho' Mr. Upton, and some
other advocates for his learning, have cautiously dropt the mention of it. Besides this (if indeed it were different), in the *Gesta
Grayorum*, the Christmas Revels of the Gray's-Inn Gentlemen,
1594, 'a *Comedy of Errors* like to Plautus his *Menechmus* was played
by the Players.' And the same hath been suspected to be the
Subject of the *goodlie Comedie of Plautus* acted at Greenwich before
the King and Queen in 1520; as we learn from Hall and Holingshed:—Riccoboni highly compliments the English on opening
their stage so well; but unfortunately Cavendish, in his *Life of
Wolsey*, calls it an *excellent Interlude in Latine*. About the same
time it was exhibited in German at Nuremburgh, by the celebrated Hanssach, the *Shoemaker*.

'But a character in the *Taming of the Shrew* is borrowed from
the *Trinummus*, and no translation of *that* was extant.'

Mr. Colman indeed hath been better employ'd: but if he had
met with an old Comedy, called *Supposes*, translated from Ariosto
by George Gascoigne, he certainly would not have appealed to
Plautus. Thence Shakespeare borrowed this part of the Plot (as
well as some of the phraseology), though Theobald pronounces
it his own invention: there likewise he found the quaint name of
Petruchio. My young Master and his Man exchange habits and
characters, and persuade a Scenæse, as he is called, to personate
the Father, exactly as in the *Taming of the Shrew*, by the pretended

danger of his coming from Sienna to Ferrara, contrary to the order of the government.

Still, Shakespeare quotes a line from the *Eunuch* of Terence: by memory too, and, what is more, 'purposely alters it, in order to bring the sense within the compass of one line.'—This remark was previous to Mr. Johnson's; or indisputably it would not have been made at all.—'Our Authour had this line from Lilly; which I mention that it may not be brought as an argument of his learning.'

But how, cries an unprovoked Antagonist, can you take upon you to say that he had it from Lilly, and not from Terence? I will answer for Mr. Johnson, who is above answering for himself.—Because it is quoted as it appears in the *Grammarian*, and not as it appears in the *Poet*.—And thus we have done with the *purposed* alteration. Udall likewise in his *Floures for Latine speakyng, gathered oute of Terence*, 1560, reduces the passage to a single line, and subjoins a Translation.

We have hitherto supposed Shakespeare the Author of the *Taming of the Shrew*, but his property in it is extremely disputable. I will give you my opinion, and the reasons on which it is founded. I suppose then the present Play not *originally* the work of Shakespeare, but restored by him to the Stage, with the whole *Induction* of the Tinker, and some other occasional improvements; especially in the Character of Petruchio. It is very obvious that the *Induction* and the *Play* were either the works of different hands, or written at a great interval of time: the former is in our Author's *best* manner, and the greater part of the *latter* in his *worst*, or even below it. Dr. Warburton declares it to be *certainly* spurious: and without doubt, *supposing* it to have been written by Shakespeare, it must have been one of his *earliest* productions; yet it is not mentioned in the List of his Works by Meres in 1598.

I have met with a facetious piece of Sir John Harrington, printed in 1596 (and possibly there may be an earlier Edition), called, *The Metamorphosis of Ajax*, where I suspect an allusion to the old Play: 'Read the *booke* of *Taming a Shrew*, which hath made a number of us so perfect, that *now* every one can rule a

Shrew in our Countrey, save he that hath hir.'—I am aware, a *modern* Linguist may object that the word *Book* does not at present seem *dramatick*, but it was once almost *technically* so: Gosson in his *Schoole of Abuse, contayning a pleasaunt inuective against Poets, Pipers, Players, Jesters, and such like Caterpillars of a Common-wealth,* 1579, mentions 'twoo prose *Bookes* plaied at the Belsauage'; and Hearne tells us, in a Note at the end of *William of Worcester,* that he had seen 'a MS. in the nature of a *Play* or *Interlude,* intitled, the *Booke* of Sir *Thomas Moore.'*

And in fact there is such an old *anonymous* Play in Mr. Pope's List: 'A pleasant conceited History, called, *The Taming of a Shrew*—sundry times acted by the Earl of Pembroke his Servants.' Which seems to have been republished by the Remains of that Company in 1607, when Shakespeare's copy appeared at the Black-Friars or the Globe.—Nor let this seem derogatory from the character of our Poet. There is no reason to believe that he wanted to claim the Play as his own; it was not even printed 'till some years after his death: but he merely revived it on his Stage as a *Manager.*—Ravenscroft assures us that this was really the case with *Titus Andronicus*; which, it may be observed, hath not Shakespeare's name on the Title-page of the only Edition published in his life-time. Indeed, from every internal mark, I have not the least doubt but this *horrible* Piece was originally written by the Author of the *Lines* thrown into the mouth of the *Player* in *Hamlet,* and of the Tragedy of *Locrine*: which likewise, from some assistance perhaps given to his Friend, hath been unjustly and ignorantly charged upon Shakespeare.

But the *sheet-anchor* holds fast: Shakespeare himself hath left some Translations from Ovid. The Epistles, says One, of *Paris* and *Helen* give a sufficient proof of his acquaintance with *that* poet; and it may be concluded, says Another, that he was a competent judge of *other* Authors who wrote in the same language.

This hath been the universal cry, from Mr. Pope himself to the Criticks of yesterday. Possibly, however, the Gentlemen will hesitate a moment, if we tell them that Shakespeare was *not* the Author of these Translations. Let them turn to a forgotten book, by Thomas Heywood, called *Britaines Troy*, printed by W. Jaggard in 1609, Fol. and they will find these identical Epistles, 'which being so pertinent to our Historie,' says Heywood, 'I thought necessarie to translate.'—How then came they ascribed to Shakespeare? We will tell them that likewise. The same voluminous Writer published an *Apology for Actors*, 4to. 1612, and in an Appendix directed to his new Printer, Nic. Okes, he accuses his old One, Jaggard, of 'taking the two Epistles of *Paris* to *Helen* and *Helen* to *Paris*, and printing them in a less volume and under the name of *Another*:—but *he* was much offended with Master Jaggard, that, altogether unknowne to him, he had presumed to make so bold with his Name.' In the same work of Heywood are all the other Translations which have been printed in the modern Editions of the Poems of Shakespeare.

You now hope for land: We have seen through little matters, but what must be done with a whole book?—In 1751 was reprinted 'A compendious or briefe examination of certayne ordinary complaints of diuers of our Countrymen in these our days: which although they are in some parte unjust and friuolous, yet are they all by way of Dialogue throughly debated and discussed by William Shakespeare, Gentleman.' 8vo.

This extraordinary piece was originally published in 4to. 1581, and dedicated by the Author, 'To the most vertuous and learned Lady, his most deare and soveraigne Princesse, Elizabeth; being inforced by her Majesties late and singular clemency in pardoning certayne his unduetifull misdemeanour.' And by the modern Editors, to the late King; as 'a Treatise composed by the most extensive and fertile Genius that ever any age or nation produced.'

Here we join issue with the Writers of that excellent tho' very unequal work, the *Biographia Britannica*: 'If,' say they, 'this piece could be written by our Poet, it would be absolutely decisive in the dispute about his learning; for many quotations appear in it from the Greek and Latin Classicks.'

The concurring circumstances of the *Name* and the *Misdemeanor*, which is supposed to be the old Story of *Deer-stealing*, seem fairly to challenge our Poet for the Author: but they hesitate. —His claim may appear to be confuted by the date 1581, when Shakespeare was only *Seventeen*, and the *long* experience which the Writer talks of.—But I will not keep you in suspense: the book was *not* written by Shakespeare.

Strype, in his *Annals*, calls the Author SOME *learned Man*, and this gave me the first suspicion. I knew very well that honest John (to use the language of Sir Thomas Bodley) did not waste his time with such *baggage books* as *Plays* and *Poems*; yet I must suppose that he had *heard* of the name of Shakespeare. After a while I met with the original Edition. Here in the Title-page, and at the end of the Dedication, appear only the Initials, W. S. Gent., and presently I was informed by Anthony Wood, that the book in question was written, not by William Shakespeare, but by William Stafford, Gentleman: which at once accounted for the *Misdemeanour* in the Dedication. For Stafford had been concerned at that time, and was indeed afterward, as Camden and the other Annalists inform us, with some of the conspirators against Elizabeth; which he properly calls his *unduetifull* behaviour.

I hope by this time that any One open to conviction may be nearly satisfied; and I will promise to give you on this head very little more trouble.

The justly celebrated Mr. Warton hath favoured us, in his *Life of Dr. Bathurst*, with some *hearsay* particulars concerning Shakespeare from the papers of Aubrey, which had been in the hands of Wood; and I ought not to suppress them, as the *last* seems to make against my doctrine. They came originally, I find, on consulting the MS., from one Mr. Beeston: and I am sure Mr. Warton, whom I have the honour to call my Friend, and an Associate in the question, will be in no pain about their credit.

'William Shakespeare's Father was a Butcher,—while he was a Boy he exercised his Father's trade, but when he killed a Calf, he would do it in a high stile, and make a speech. This William being inclined *naturally* to Poetry and Acting, came to London, I guess, about *eighteen*, and was an Actor in one of the Playhouses, and did act *exceedingly well*. He began *early* to make Essays in dramatique Poetry.—The humour of the Constable in the *Midsummer Night's Dream* he happened to take at Crendon in Bucks. —I think I have been told that he left near three hundred pounds to a *Sister*.—He *understood Latin pretty well*, FOR *he had been in his younger yeares a Schoolmaster in the Country.*'

I will be short in my animadversions; and take them in their order.

The account of the *Trade* of the Family is not only contrary to all other Tradition, but, as it may seem, to the instrument from the Herald's office, so frequently reprinted.—Shakespeare most certainly went to London, and commenced Actor thro' necessity, not natural inclination.—Nor have we any reason to suppose that he did act *exceedingly well*. Rowe tells us from the information of Betterton, who was inquisitive into this point, and had very early opportunities of Inquiry from Sir W. Davenant, that he was no *extraordinary Actor*; and that the top of his performance was the Ghost in his own *Hamlet*. Yet this *Chef d'Oeuvre* did not please: I will give you an original stroke at it. Dr. Lodge, who was for ever pestering the town with Pamphlets, published in the year 1596 *Wits miserie, and the Worlds madnesse, discovering the Devils incarnat of this Age.* 4to. One of these Devils is *Hate-virtue*, or *Sorrow for another mans good successe*, who, says the Doctor, is '*a foule lubber*, and looks as pale as the Visard of the Ghost, which cried so miserably at the Theatre, like an Oister-wife, *Hamlet revenge*.' Thus you see Mr. Holt's supposed *proof*, in the Appendix to the late Edition, that *Hamlet* was written after 1597, or perhaps 1602, will by no means hold good; whatever might be the case of the particular passage on which it is founded.

Nor does it appear that Shakespeare did begin *early* to make *Essays in Dramatique Poetry*: the *Arraignment of Paris*, 1584, which hath so often been ascribed to him on the credit of Kirkman and Winstanley, was written by George Peele; and Shakespeare is not met with, even as an Assistant, 'till at least seven years afterward.—Nash, in his Epistle to the Gentlemen Students of both Universities, prefixed to Greene's *Arcadia*, 4to. *black Letter*, recommends his friend, Peele, 'as the chiefe supporter of pleasance now living, the Atlas of Poetrie, and *primus Verborum Artifex*: whose first increase, the *Arraignment of Paris*, might plead to their opinions his pregnant dexteritie of wit, and manifold varietie of inuention.'

In the next place, unfortunately, there is neither such a Character as a Constable in the *Midsummer Night's Dream*: nor was the *three hundred pounds* Legacy to a Sister, but a Daughter.

And to close the whole, it is not possible, according to Aubrey himself, that Shakespeare could have been some *years a Schoolmaster in the Country*: on which circumstance only the supposition of his learning is professedly founded. He was not surely *very* young, when he was employed to *kill Calves*, and he commenced Player about *Eighteen*!—The truth is that he left his Father, for a Wife, a year sooner; and had at least two Children born at Stratford before he retired from thence to London. It is therefore sufficiently clear that poor Anthony had too much reason for his character of Aubrey: You will find it in his own Account of his Life, published by Hearne, which I would earnestly recommend to any Hypochondriack;

'A pretender to Antiquities, roving, magotie-headed, and sometimes little better than crased: and being exceedingly credulous, would stuff his many Letters sent to A. W. with *folliries* and misinformations.' p. 577.

Thus much for the Learning of Shakespeare with respect to the ancient languages: indulge me with an observation or two on his supposed knowledge of the modern ones, and I will promise to release you.

'It is *evident*,' we have been told, 'that he was not unacquainted with the Italian': but let us inquire into the *Evidence*.

Certainly some Italian words and phrases appear in the Works of Shakespeare; yet if we had nothing else to observe, their Orthography might lead us to suspect them to be not of the Writer's importation. But we can go further, and prove this.

When Pistol 'chears up himself with ends of verse,' he is only a copy of Hanniball Gonsaga, who ranted on yielding himself a Prisoner to an English Captain in the Low Countries, as you may read in an old Collection of Tales, called *Wits, Fits, and Fancies,*

> Si Fortuna me tormenta,
> Il speranza me contenta.

And Sir Richard Hawkins, in his Voyage to the South Sea, 1593, throws out the same jingling Distich on the loss of his Pinnace.

'Master Page, sit; good Master Page, sit; *Proface*. What you want in meat, we'll have in drink,' says Justice Shallow's *Fac totum*, Davy, in the 2d Part of *Henry the fourth*.

Proface, Sir Thomas Hanmer observes to be Italian, from *pro-faccia, much good may it do you*. Mr. Johnson rather thinks it a mistake for *perforce*. Sir Thomas however is right; yet it is no argument for his Author's Italian knowledge.

Old Heywood, the Epigrammatist, addressed his Readers long before,

> Readers, reade this thus: for Preface, *Proface*,
> Much good do it you, the poore repast here, &c.
> *Woorkes.* Lond. 4to. 1562.

And Dekker in his Play, *If it be not good, the Diuel is in it* (which is certainly true, for it is full of Devils), makes Shackle-soule, in the character of Friar Rush, tempt his Brethren with 'choice of dishes,'

> To which *proface*; with blythe lookes sit yee.

Nor hath it escaped the quibbling manner of the *Water-poet*, in the title of a Poem prefixed to his *Praise of Hempseed:* 'A Preamble, Preatrot, Preagallop, Preapace, or Preface; and *Proface*, my Masters, if your Stomacks serve.'

But the Editors are not contented without coining Italian .'*Rivo, says the Drunkard*,' is an Expression of the *madcap* Prince of Wales;

which Sir Thomas Hanmer corrects to *Ribi*, *Drink away*, or
again, as it should rather be translated. Dr. Warburton accedes
to this; and Mr. Johnson hath admitted it into his Text; but
with an observation, that *Rivo* might possibly be the cant of
English Taverns. And so indeed it was: it occurs frequently in
Marston. Take a quotation from his Comedy of *What you will*,
1607:

> Musicke, Tobacco, Sacke, and Sleepe,
> The Tide of Sorrow backward keep:
> If thou art sad at others fate,
> *Rivo*, drink deep, give care the mate.

In *Love's Labour Lost*, Boyet calls Don Armado,

> —A Spaniard that keeps here in Court,
> A Phantasme, a *Monarcho*.—

Here too Sir Thomas is willing to palm Italian upon us. We
should read, it seems, *Mammuccio*, a Mammet, or Puppet: Ital.
Mammuccia. But the allusion is to a fantastical *Character* of the
time.—'Popular applause,' says Meres, 'dooth nourish some,
neither do they gape after any other thing, but vaine praise and
glorie,—as in our age Peter Shakerlye of Paules, and MONARCHO
that liued about the Court.' p. 178.

I fancy you will be satisfied with one more instance.

'*Baccare*, You are marvellous forward,' quoth Gremio to
Petruchio in the *Taming of the Shrew*.

'But not so *forward*,' says Mr. Theobald, 'as our Editors are
indolent. This is a stupid corruption of the press, that none of them
have dived into. We must read *Baccalare*, as Mr. Warburton
acutely observed to me, by which the Italians mean, Thou
ignorant, presumptuous Man.'—'Properly indeed,' adds Mr.
Heath, 'a *graduated* Scholar, but ironically and sarcastically, a
pretender to Scholarship.'

This is admitted by the Editors and Criticks of every De-
nomination. Yet the word is neither wrong, nor Italian: it was
an old proverbial one, used frequently by John Heywood; who
hath made, what he pleases to call, *Epigrams* upon it.

Take two of them, such as they are,

> Backare, quoth Mortimer to his Sow:
> Went that Sow backe at that biddyng trowe you?

> Backare, quoth Mortimer to his sow: se
> Mortimers sow speakth as good latin as he.

Howel takes this from Heywood, in his Old Sawes and Adages:
and Philpot introduces it into the Proverbs collected by Camden.

We have but few observations concerning Shakespeare's
knowledge of the Spanish tongue. Dr. Grey indeed is willing to
suppose that the plot of Romeo and Juliet may be borrowed from
a COMEDY of Lopes de Vega. But the Spaniard, who was certainly acquainted with Bandello, hath not only changed the
Catastrophe, but the names of the Characters. Neither Romeo
nor Juliet, neither Montague nor Capulet, appears in this performance: and how came they to the knowledge of Shakespeare?
—Nothing is more certain than that he chiefly followed the
Translation by Painter from the French of Boisteau, and hence
arise the Deviations from Bandello's original Italian. It seems,
however, from a passage in Ames's Typographical Antiquities, that
Painter was not the only Translator of this popular Story: and it is
possible, therefore, that Shakespeare might have other assistance.

In the Induction to the Taming of the Shrew, the Tinker attempts to talk Spanish: and consequently the Author himself was
acquainted with it.

> Paucus pallabris, let the World slide, Sessa.

But this is a burlesque on Hieronymo; the piece of Bombast that
I have mentioned to you before:

> What new device have they devised, trow?
> Pocas pallabras, &c.—

Mr. Whalley tells us, 'the Author of this piece hath the happiness to be at this time unknown, the remembrance of him
having perished with himself': Philips and others ascribe it to

one William Smith: but I take this opportunity of informing him that it was written by Thomas Kyd; if he will accept the authority of his Contemporary, Heywood.

More hath been said concerning Shakespeare's acquaintance with the French language. In the Play of *Henry the fifth*, we have a whole Scene in it, and in other places it occurs familiarly in the Dialogue.

We may observe in general, that the early Editions have not half the quantity; and every sentence, or rather every word, most ridiculously blundered. These, for several reasons, could not possibly be published by the Author; and it is extremely probable that the French ribaldry was at first inserted by a different hand, as the many additions most certainly were after he had left the Stage.—Indeed, every friend to his memory will not easily believe that he was acquainted with the Scene between Catharine and the old Gentlewoman; or surely he would not have admitted such obscenity and nonsense.

Mr. Hawkins, in the Appendix to Mr. Johnson's Edition, hath an ingenious observation to prove that Shakespeare, supposing the French to be his, had very little knowledge of the language.

'Est-il impossible d'eschapper la force de ton *Bras*?' says a Frenchman.—'*Brass*, cur?' replies Pistol.

'Almost any one knows that the French word *Bras* is pronounced *Brau*; and what resemblance of sound does this bear to *Brass*?'

Mr. Johnson makes a doubt whether the pronunciation of the French language may not be changed since Shakespeare's time; 'if not,' says he, 'it may be suspected that some other man wrote the French scenes': but this does not appear to be the case, at least in this termination, from the rules of the Grammarians, or the practice of the Poets. I am certain of the former from the *French Alphabeth* of De la Mothe, and the *Orthoepia Gallica* of John Eliot; and of the latter from the Rhymes of Marot, Ronsard, and Du Bartas.—Connections of this kind were very common. Shakespeare himself assisted Ben. Jonson in his *Sejanus*, as it was originally written; and Fletcher in his *Two noble Kinsmen*.

But what if the French scene were occasionally introduced into every Play on this Subject? and perhaps there were more than one before our Poet's.—In *Pierce Penilesse his Supplication to the Diuell*, 4to. 1592 (which, it seems, from the Epistle to the Printer, was not the first Edition), the Author, Nash, exclaims, 'What a glorious thing it is to have *Henry the fifth* represented on the Stage leading the French King prisoner, and forcing both him and the Dolphin to sweare fealty!'—And it appears from the Jests of the famous Comedian, Tarlton, 4to. 1611, that he had been particularly celebrated in the Part of the Clown in *Henry the fifth*; but no such Character exists in the Play of Shakespeare. —*Henry the sixth* hath ever been doubted; and a passage in the above-quoted piece of Nash may give us reason to believe it was previous to our Author. 'How would it have joyed braue Talbot (the terror of the French) to thinke that after he had lyen two hundred yeare in his Toomb, he should triumph again on the Stage; and haue his bones new embalmed with the teares of ten thousand spectators at least (at seuerall times) who, in the Tragedian that represents his person, imagine they behold him fresh bleeding.'—I have no doubt but *Henry the sixth* had the same Author with *Edward the third*, which hath been recovered to the world in Mr. Capell's *Prolusions*.

It hath been observed that the Giant of Rabelais is sometimes alluded to by Shakespeare: and in *his* time no translation was extant.—But the Story was in every one's hand.

In a Letter by one Laneham, or Langham, for the name is written differently, concerning the Entertainment at Killing-woorth Castle, printed 1575, we have a list of the vulgar Romances of the age, 'King Arthurz book, Huon of Burdeaus, Friar Rous, Howleglass, and GARGANTUA.' Meres mentions him as equally hurtful to young minds with the *Four Sons of Aymon*, and the *Seven Champions*. And John Taylor hath him likewise in his catalogue of *Authors*, prefixed to Sir *Gregory Nonsence*.

But to come to a conclusion, I will give you an irrefragable argument that Shakespeare did *not* understand *two* very common words in the French and Latin languages.

According to the Articles of agreement between the Conqueror Henry and the King of France, the latter was to stile the former (in the corrected French of the modern Editions) 'Nostre *tres cher* filz Henry Roy d'Angleterre; and in Latin, *Præclarissimus* Filius, &c.' 'What,' says Dr. Warburton, 'is *tres cher* in French *præclarissimus* in Latin! we should read *præcarissimus*.'—This appears to be exceedingly true; but how came the blunder? It is a typographical one in Holingshed, which Shakespeare copied; but must indisputably have corrected, had he been acquainted with the languages.—'Our said Father, during his life, shall name, call, and write us in French in this maner: Nostre *tres chier* filz, Henry Roy d'Engleterre—and in Latine in this maner: *Præclarissimus* filius noster.' Edit. 1587, p. 574.

To corroborate this instance, let me observe to you, though it be nothing further to the purpose, that another error of the same kind hath been the source of a mistake in an historical passage of our Author; which hath ridiculously troubled the Criticks.

Richard the third harangues his army before the Battle of Bosworth:

> Remember whom ye are to cope withal,
> A sort of vagabonds, of rascals, runaways—
> And who doth lead them but a paltry fellow,
> Long kept in *Britaine* at *our Mother's* cost,
> A milksop, &c.—

'*Our* Mother', Mr. Theobald perceives to be wrong, and Henry was somewhere secreted on the *Continent*: he reads therefore, and all the Editors after him,

> Long kept in *Bretagne* at *his* mother's cost.

But give me leave to transcribe a few more lines from Holingshed, and you will find at once that Shakespeare had been there before me:—'Ye see further, how a companie of traitors, theeves, outlaws, and runnagates be aiders and partakers of his feat and enterprise.—And to begin with the erle of Richmond, captaine of this rebellion, he is a Welsh milksop—brought up by *my Moother's* meanes and mine, like a captive in a close cage, in the court of Francis duke of *Britaine.*' p. 756.

Holingshed copies this *verbatim* from his brother chronicler Hall, Edit. 1548, fol. 54; but his Printer hath given us by accident the word *Moother* instead of *Brother*; as it is in the Original, and ought to be in Shakespeare.

I hope, my good Friend, you have by this time acquitted our great Poet of all piratical depredations on the Ancients, and are ready to receive my *Conclusion.*—He remembered perhaps enough of his *school-boy* learning to put the *Hig, hag, hog,* into the mouth of Sir Hugh Evans; and might pick up in the Writers of the time, or the course of his conversation, a familiar phrase or two of French or Italian: but his *Studies* were most demonstratively confined to *Nature* and *his own Language.*

In the course of this disquisition, you have often smiled at 'all such reading as was never read': and possibly I may have indulged it too far: but it is the reading necessary for a Comment on Shakespeare. Those who apply solely to the Ancients for this purpose, may with equal wisdom study the TALMUD for an Exposition of TRISTRAM SHANDY. Nothing but an intimate acquaintance with the Writers of the time, who are frequently of no other value, can point out his allusions, and ascertain his Phraseology. The Reformers of his Text are for ever equally positive, and equally wrong. The Cant of the Age, a provincial Expression, an obscure Proverb, an obsolete Custom, a Hint at a Person or a Fact no longer remembered, hath continually defeated the best of our *Guessers*: You must not suppose me to speak at random, when I assure you that, from some forgotten book or other, I can demonstrate this to you in many hundred Places; and I almost wish that I had not been persuaded into a different Employment.

Tho' I have as much of the *Natale Solum* about me as any man whatsoever; yet, I own, the *Primrose Path* is still more pleasing than the *Fosse* or the *Watling Street*:

> Age cannot wither it, nor custom stale
> It's infinite variety.—

And when I am fairly rid of the Dust of topographical Antiquity, which hath continued much longer about me than I expected, you may very probably be troubled again with the ever fruitful Subject of SHAKESPEARE and his COMMENTATORS.

MAURICE MORGANN

An Essay on the Dramatic Character of Sir John Falstaff

1777

PREFACE

THE following sheets were written in consequence of a friendly conversation, turning by some chance upon the Character of FALSTAFF, wherein the Writer, maintaining, contrary to the general Opinion, that this Character was not intended to be shewn as a Coward, he was challenged to deliver and support that Opinion from the Press, with an engagement, now he fears forgotten, for it was three years ago, that he should be answered thro' the same channel: Thus stimulated, these papers were almost wholly written in a very short time, but not without those attentions, whether successful or not, which seemed necessary to carry them beyond the Press into the hands of the Public. From the influence of the foregoing circumstances it is, that the Writer has generally assumed rather the character and tone of an Advocate than of an Inquirer;—though if he had not first *inquired* and been *convinced*, he should never have attempted to have amused either himself or others with the subject.—The impulse of the occasion, however, being passed, the papers were thrown by, and almost forgotten: But having been looked into of late by some friends, who, observing that the Writer had not enlarged so far for the sake of FALSTAFF alone, but that the Argument was made subservient to Critical amusement, persuaded him to revise and convey it to the Press. This has been accordingly done, though he fears something too hastily, as he found it proper to add, while the papers were in the course of printing, some considerations on the *Whole* Character of FAL-STAFF; which ought to have been accompanied by a slight reform of a few preceding passages, which may seem, in consequence of this addition, to contain too favourable a representation of his Morals.

The vindication of FALSTAFF's Courage is truly no otherwise the object than some old fantastic Oak, or grotesque Rock, may be the object of a morning's ride; yet being proposed as such, may serve to limit the distance, and shape the course: The real object is Exercise, and the Delight which a rich, beautiful, picturesque, and perhaps unknown Country, may excite from every side. Such an Exercise may admit of some little excursion, keeping however the Road in view; but seems to exclude every appearance of labour and of toil.—Under the impression of such Feelings, the Writer has endeavoured to preserve to his Text a certain lightness of air, and chearfulness of tone; but is sensible, however, that the manner of discussion does not *every where*, particularly near the commencement, sufficiently correspond with his design.—If the Book shall be fortunate enough to obtain another Impression, a separation may be made; and such of the heavier parts as cannot be wholly dispensed with, sink to their more proper station,—a Note.

He is fearful likewise that he may have erred in the other extreme; and that having thought himself intitled, even in argument, to a certain degree of playful discussion, may have pushed it, in a few places, even to levity. This error might be yet more easily reformed than the other.—The Book is perhaps, as it stands, too bulky for the subject; but if the Reader knew how many pressing considerations, as it grew into size, the Author resisted, which yet seemed intitled to be heard, he would the more readily excuse him.

The whole is a mere Experiment, and the Writer considers it as such: It may have the advantages, but it is likewise attended with all the difficulties and dangers, of *Novelty*.

ON THE DRAMATIC CHARACTER OF
SIR JOHN FALSTAFF

THE ideas which I have formed concerning the Courage and
Military Character of the Dramatic Sir *John Falstaff* are so different from those which I find generally to prevail in the world,
that I shall take the liberty of stating my sentiments on the subject; in hope that some person, as unengaged as myself, will
either correct and reform my error in this respect; or, joining
himself to my opinion, redeem me from, what I may call, the
reproach of singularity.

I am to avow, then, that I do not clearly discern that Sir *John
Falstaff* deserves to bear the character so generally given him of
an absolute Coward; or, in other words, that I do not conceive
Shakespeare ever meant to make Cowardice an essential part of his
constitution.

I know how universally the contrary opinion prevails; and I
know what respect and deference are due to the public voice.
But if to the avowal of this singularity I add all the reasons that
have led me to it, and acknowledge myself to be wholly in the
judgment of the public, I shall hope to avoid the censure of too
much forwardness or indecorum.

It must, in the first place, be admitted that the appearances in
this case are singularly strong and striking; and so they had need
be, to become the ground of so general a censure. We see this
extraordinary Character, almost in the first moment of our
acquaintance with him, involved in circumstances of apparent
dishonour; and we hear him familiarly called *Coward* by his most
intimate companions. We see him, on occasion of the robbery at
Gads-Hill, in the very act of running away from the Prince and
Poins; and we behold him, on another of more honourable obligation, in open day light, in battle, and acting in his profession as a
Soldier, escaping from *Douglas* even out of the world as it were;
counterfeiting death, and deserting his very existence; and we
find him, on the former occasion, betrayed into those *lies* and
braggadocioes which are the usual concomitants of Cowardice in

Military men, and pretenders to valour. These are not only in themselves strong circumstances, but they are moreover thrust forward, prest upon our notice as the subject of our mirth, as the great business of the scene: No wonder, therefore, that the word should go forth that *Falstaff* is exhibited as a character of Cowardice and dishonour.

What there is to the contrary of this, it is my business to discover. Much, I think, will presently appear; but it lies so dispersed, is so latent, and so purposely obscured, that the reader must have some patience whilst I collect it into one body, and make it the object of a steady and regular contemplation.

But what have we to do, may my readers exclaim, with principles *so latent, so obscured*? In Dramatic composition the *Impression* is the *Fact*; and the Writer, who, meaning to impress one thing, has impressed another, is unworthy of observation.

It is a very unpleasant thing to have, in the first setting out, so many and so strong prejudices to contend with. All that one can do in such case, is, to pray the reader to have a little patience in the commencement; and to reserve his censure, if it must pass, for the conclusion. Under his gracious allowance, therefore, I presume to declare it as my opinion, that Cowardice *is not* the *Impression* which the *whole* character of *Falstaff* is calculated to make on the minds of an unprejudiced audience; tho' there be, I confess, a great deal of something in the *composition* likely enough to puzzle, and consequently to mislead the Understanding.— The reader will perceive that I distinguish between *mental Impressions* and the *Understanding*.—I wish to avoid every thing that looks like subtlety and refinement; but this is a distinction which we all comprehend.—There are none of us unconscious of certain feelings or sensations of mind which do not seem to have passed thro' the Understanding; the effects, I suppose, of some secret influences from without, acting upon a certain mental sense, and producing feelings and passions in just correspondence to the force and variety of those influences on the one hand, and to the quickness of our sensibility on the other. Be the cause, however, what it may, the fact is undoubtedly so; which is all I am concerned in. And it is equally a fact, which every man's experience may avouch, that the Understanding and those feelings are frequently at variance. The latter often arise from the most minute circumstances, and frequently from such as the Understanding cannot estimate, or even recognize; whereas the Understanding delights in abstraction, and in general propositions; which, however true considered as such, are very seldom, I had like to have said *never*, perfectly applicable to any particular case. And hence, among other causes, it is, that we often condemn or applaud characters and actions on the credit of some logical process, while our hearts revolt, and would fain lead us to a very different conclusion.

The Understanding seems for the most part to take cognizance of *actions* only, and from these to infer *motives* and *character*; but the sense we have been speaking of proceeds in a contrary course; and determines of *actions* from certain *first principles of character*, which seem wholly out of the reach of the Understanding. We cannot indeed do otherwise than admit that there must be distinct principles of character in every distinct individual: The manifest variety even in the minds of infants will oblige us to this. But what *are* these first principles of character? Not the objects, I am persuaded, of the Understanding; and yet we take as strong Impressions of them as if we could compare and assort them in a syllogism. We often love or hate at first sight; and indeed, in general, dislike or approve by some secret reference to these *principles*; and we judge even of conduct, not from any idea of abstract good or evil in the nature of actions, but by referring those actions to a supposed original character in the man himself. I do not mean that we *talk* thus; we could not indeed, if we would, explain ourselves in detail on this head; we can neither account for Impressions and passions, nor communicate them to others by *words*: Tones and looks will sometimes convey the *passion* strangely, but the *Impression* is incommunicable. The same causes may produce it indeed at the same time in many, but it is the separate possession of each, and not in its nature transferable: It is an imperfect sort of instinct, and proportionably dumb.—We might indeed, if we chose it, candidly confess to one another that we are greatly swayed by these feelings, and are by no means so *rational* in all points as we could wish; but this would be a betraying of the interests of that high faculty, the Understanding, which we so value ourselves upon, and which we more peculiarly call our own. This, we think, must not be; and so we huddle up the matter, concealing it as much as possible, both from ourselves and others. In Books indeed, wherein character, motive, and action, are all alike subjected to the Understanding, it is generally a very clear case; and we make decisions compounded of them all: And thus we are willing to approve of *Candide*, tho' he kills my Lord the Inquisitor, and runs thro' the body the Baron of *Thunder-ten-tronckh*, the son of his patron, and the brother of his beloved *Cunégonde*: But in real life, I believe, *my Lords the Judges* would be apt to inform the *Gentlemen of the Jury* that my *Lord the Inquisitor* was *ill killed*; as *Candide* did not proceed on the urgency of the moment, but on the speculation only of future evil. And indeed this clear perception, in Novels and Plays, of the union of character and action not seen in nature, is the principal defect of such compositions, and what renders them but ill pictures of human life, and wretched guides of conduct.

But if there was *one man* in the world who could make a more perfect draught of real nature, and steal such Impressions on his audience, without their special notice, as should keep their hold in spite of any error of their Understanding, and should thereupon venture to introduce an apparent incongruity of character and action, for ends which I shall presently endeavour to explain; such an imitation would be worth our nicest curiosity and attention. But in such a case as this, the reader might expect that he should find us all talking the language of the Understanding only; that is, censuring the action with very little conscientious investigation even of *that*; and transferring the censure, in every odious colour, to the actor himself; how much soever our hearts and affections might secretly revolt: For as to the *Impression*, we have already observed that it has no tongue; nor is its operation and influence likely to be made the subject of conference and communication.

It is not to the *Courage* only of *Falstaff* that we think these observations will apply: No part whatever of his character seems to be fully settled in our minds; at least there is something strangely incongruous in our discourse and affections concerning him. We all like *Old Jack*; yet, by some strange perverse fate, we all abuse him, and deny him the possession of any one single good or respectable quality. There is something extraordinary in this: It must be a strange art in *Shakespeare* which can draw our liking and good will towards so offensive an object. He has wit, it will be said; chearfulness and humour of the most characteristic and captivating sort. And is this enough? Is the humour and gaiety of vice so very captivating? Is the wit, characteristic of baseness and every ill quality, capable of attaching the heart and winning the affections? Or does not the apparency of such humour, and the flashes of such wit, by more strongly disclosing the deformity of character, but the more effectually excite our hatred and contempt of the man? And yet this is not our *feeling* of *Falstaff*'s character. When he has ceased to amuse us, we find no emotions of disgust; we can scarcely forgive the ingratitude of the Prince in the new-born virtue of the King, and we curse the severity of that poetic justice which consigns our old good-natured delightful companion to the custody of the *warden*, and the dishonours of the *Fleet*.

I am willing, however, to admit that if a Dramatic writer will but preserve to any character the qualities of a strong mind, particularly Courage and ability, that it will be afterwards no very difficult task (as I may have occasion to explain) to discharge that *disgust* which arises from vicious manners; and even to attach us (if such character should contain any quality productive of chearfulness and laughter) to the cause and subject of our mirth with some degree of affection.

But the question which I am to consider is of a very different nature: It is a question of fact, and concerning a quality which forms the basis of every respectable character; a quality which is the very essence of a Military man; and which is held up to us, in almost every Comic incident of the Play, as the subject of our observation. It is strange then that it should now be a question, whether *Falstaff* is or is not a man of Courage; and whether we do in fact contemn him for the want, or respect him for the possession of that quality: And yet I believe the reader will find that he has by no means decided this question, even for himself.— If then it should turn out that this difficulty has arisen out of the Art of *Shakespeare*, who has contrived to make secret Impressions upon us of Courage, and to preserve those Impressions in favour of a character which was to be held up for sport and laughter on account of actions of apparent Cowardice and dishonour, we shall have less occasion to wonder, as *Shakespeare* is a Name which contains All of Dramatic artifice and genius.

If in this place the reader shall peevishly and prematurely object that the observations and distinctions I have laboured to establish are wholly unapplicable; he being himself unconscious of ever having received any such Impression; what can be done in so nice a case, but to refer him to the following pages; by the number of which he may judge how very much I respect his objection, and by the variety of those proofs which I shall employ to induce him to part with it; and to recognize in its stead certain feelings, concealed and covered over perhaps, but not erazed, by time, reasoning, and authority?

In the mean while, it may not perhaps be easy for him to resolve how it comes about, that, whilst we look upon *Falstaff* as a character of the like nature with that of *Parolles* or of *Bobadil*, we should preserve for him a great degree of respect and good-will, and yet feel the highest disdain and contempt of the others, tho' they are all involved in similar situations. The reader, I believe, would wonder extremely to find either *Parolles* or *Bobadil* possess himself in danger: What then can be the cause that we are not at all surprized at the gaiety and ease of *Falstaff* under the most trying circumstances; and that we never think of charging *Shakespeare* with departing, on this account, from the truth and coherence of character? Perhaps, after all, the *real* character of *Falstaff* may be different from his *apparent* one; and possibly this difference between reality and appearance, whilst it accounts at once for our liking and our censure, may be the true point of humour in the character, and the source of all our laughter and delight. We may chance to find, if we will but examine a little into the nature of those circumstances which have accidentally involved him, that he was intended to be drawn as a character of much Natural courage and resolution; and be obliged thereupon to repeal those decisions which may have been made upon the credit of some general tho' unapplicable propositions; the common source of error in other and higher matters. A little reflection may perhaps bring us round again to the point of our departure, and unite our Understandings to our instinct.—Let us then for a moment *suspend* at least our decisions, and candidly and coolly inquire if Sir *John Falstaff* be, indeed, what he has so often been called by critic and commentator, male and female,—a *Constitutional Coward.*

It will scarcely be possible to consider the Courage of *Falstaff* as wholly detached from his other qualities: But I write not professedly of any part of his character, but what is included under the term, *Courage*; however, I may incidentally throw some lights on the whole.—The reader will not need to be told that this Inquiry will resolve itself of course into a Critique on the genius, the arts, and the conduct of *Shakespeare*: For what is *Falstaff*, what *Lear*, what *Hamlet*, or *Othello*, but different modifications of *Shakespeare*'s thought? It is true that this Inquiry is narrowed almost to a single point: But general criticism is as uninstructive as it is easy: *Shakespeare* deserves to be considered in detail;—a task hitherto unattempted.

It may be proper, in the first place, to take a short view of all the parts of *Falstaff*'s Character, and then proceed to discover, if we can, what *Impressions*, as to Courage or Cowardice, he had made on the persons of the Drama: After which we will examine, in course, such evidence, either of *persons* or *facts*, as are relative to the matter; and account as we may for those appearances which seem to have led to the opinion of his Constitutional Cowardice.

The scene of the robbery, and the disgraces attending it, which stand first in the Play, and introduce us to the knowledge of *Falstaff*, I shall beg leave (as I think this scene to have been the source of much unreasonable prejudice) to *reserve* till we are more fully acquainted with the whole character of *Falstaff*; and I shall therefore hope that the reader will not for a time advert to it, or to the jests of the Prince or of *Poins* in consequence of that unlucky adventure.

In drawing out the parts of *Falstaff*'s character, with which I shall begin this Inquiry, I shall take the liberty of putting Constitutional bravery into his composition; but the reader will be pleased to consider what I shall say in that respect as spoken hypothetically for the present, to be retained, or discharged out of it, as he shall finally determine.

To me then it appears that the leading quality in *Falstaff*'s character, and that from which all the rest take their colour, is a high degree of wit and humour, accompanied with great natural vigour and alacrity of mind. This quality, so accompanied, led him probably very early into life, and made him highly acceptable to society; so acceptable, as to make it seem unnecessary for him to acquire any other virtue. Hence, perhaps, his continued debaucheries and dissipations of every kind.—He seems, by nature, to have had a mind free of malice or any evil principle; but he never took the trouble of acquiring any good one. He found himself esteemed and beloved with all his faults; nay *for* his faults, which were all connected with humour, and for the most part grew out of it. As he had, possibly, no vices but such as he thought might be openly professed, so he appeared more dissolute thro' ostentation. To the character of wit and humour, to which all his other qualities seem to have conformed themselves, he appears to have added a very necessary support, *that* of the profession of a *Soldier*. He had from nature, as I presume to say, a spirit of boldness and enterprise; which in a Military age, tho' employment was only occasional, kept him always above contempt, secured him an honourable reception among the Great, and suited best both his particular mode of humour and

of vice. Thus living continually in society, nay even in Taverns,
and indulging himself, and being indulged by others, in every
debauchery; drinking, whoring, gluttony, and ease; assuming a
liberty of fiction, necessary perhaps to his wit, and often falling
into falsity and lies, he seems to have set, by degrees, all sober
reputation at defiance; and finding eternal resources in his wit,
he borrows, shifts, defrauds, and even robs, without dishonour.
—Laughter and approbation attend his greatest excesses; and
being governed visibly by no settled bad principle or ill design,
fun and humour account for and cover all. By degrees, however,
and thro' indulgence, he acquires bad habits, becomes an
humourist, grows enormously corpulent, and falls into the infirmities of age; yet never quits, all the time, one single levity or
vice of youth, or loses any of that chearfulness of mind which had
enabled him to pass thro' this course with ease to himself and
delight to others; and thus, at last, mixing youth and age, enterprize and corpulency, wit and folly, poverty and expence,
title and buffoonery, innocence as to purpose, and wickedness as
to practice; neither incurring hatred by bad principle, or contempt by Cowardice, yet involved in circumstances productive
of imputation in both; a butt and a wit, a humourist and a man
of humour, a touchstone and a laughing stock, a jester and a jest,
has Sir *John Falstaff*, taken at that period of his life in which we
see him, become the most perfect Comic character that perhaps
ever was exhibited.

It may not possibly be wholly amiss to remark in this place,
that if Sir *John Falstaff* had possessed any of that Cardinal quality,
Prudence, alike the guardian of virtue and the protector of vice;
that quality, from the possession or the absence of which, the
character and fate of men in this life take, I think, their colour,
and not from real vice or virtue; if he had considered his wit not
as *principal* but *accessary* only; as the instrument of power, and
not as power itself; if he had had much baseness to hide, if he
had had less of what may be called mellowness or good humour,
or less of health and spirit; if he had spurred and rode the world
with his wit, instead of suffering the world, boys and all, to ride

him;—he might, without any other essential change, have
been the admiration and not the jest of mankind:—Or if he had
lived in our day, and instead of attaching himself to one Prince,
had renounced *all* friendship and *all* attachment, and had let himself out as the ready instrument and Zany of every successive
Minister, he might possibly have acquired the high honour of
marking his shroud or decorating his coffin with the living rays of
an Irish at least, if not a British Coronet: Instead of which, tho'
enforcing laughter from every disposition, he appears, now, as
such a character which every wise man will pity and avoid,
every knave will censure, and every fool will fear: And accordingly *Shakespeare*, ever true to nature, has made *Harry* desert, and
Lancaster censure him:—He dies where he lived, in a Tavern,
broken-hearted, without a friend; and his final exit is given up to
the derision of fools. Nor has his misfortunes ended here; the
scandal arising from the misapplication of his wit and talents
seems immortal. He has met with as little justice or mercy from
his final judges the critics, as from his companions of the Drama.
With our cheeks still red with laughter, we ungratefully as unjustly censure him as a coward by nature, and a rascal upon
principle: Tho', if this were so, it might be hoped, for our own
credit, that we should behold him rather with disgust and disap-
probation than with pleasure and delight.

But to remember our question—*Is Falstaff a constitutional
coward?*

With respect to every infirmity, except that of Cowardice, we
must take him as at the period in which he is represented to us.
If we see him dissipated, fat,—it is enough;—we have nothing
to do with his youth, when he might perhaps have been modest,
chaste, '*and not an Eagle's talon in the waist*'. But *Constitutional
Courage* extends to a man's whole life, makes a part of his nature,
and is not to be taken up or deserted like a mere Moral quality.
It is true, there is a Courage founded upon *principle*, or rather a
principle independent of Courage, which will sometimes operate
in spite of nature; a principle which prefers death to shame, but
which always refers itself, in conformity to its own nature, to

the prevailing modes of honour, and the fashions of the age.—
But Natural courage is another thing: It is independent of
opinion; It adapts itself to occasions, preserves itself under
every shape, and can avail itself of flight as well as of action.—
In the last war, some Indians of America perceiving a line of
Highlanders to keep their station under every disadvantage, and
under a fire which they could not effectually return, were so
miserably mistaken in our points of honour as to conjecture,
from observation on the habit and stability of those troops, that
they were indeed the women of England, who wanted courage
to run away.—That Courage which is founded in nature and
constitution, *Falstaff*, as I presume to say, possessed;—but I am
ready to allow that the principle already mentioned, so far as it
refers to reputation only, began with every other Moral quality
to lose its hold on him in his old age; that is, at the time of life in
which he is represented to us; a period, as it should seem, approaching to *seventy*.—The truth is that he had drollery enough
to support himself in credit without the point of honour, and
had address enough to make even the preservation of his life a
point of drollery. The reader knows I allude, tho' something
prematurely, to his fictitious death in the battle of Shrewsbury.
This incident is generally construed to the disadvantage of
Falstaff: It is a transaction which bears the external marks of
Cowardice: It is also aggravated to the spectators by the idle
tricks of the Player, who practises on this occasion all the atti-
tudes and wild apprehensions of fear; more ambitious, as it
should seem, of representing a *Caliban* than a *Falstaff*; or indeed
rather a poor unwieldy miserable Tortoise than either.—The
painful Comedian lies spread out on his belly, and not only covers
himself all over with his robe as with a shell, but forms a kind of
round Tortoise-back by I know not what stuffing or contrivance;
in addition to which, he alternately lifts up, and depresses, and
dodges his head, and looks to the one side and to the other, so
much with the piteous aspect of that animal, that one would not
be sorry to see the ambitious imitator calipashed in his robe, and
served up for the entertainment of the gallery.—There is no

hint for this mummery in the Play: Whatever there may be of dishonour in *Falstaff*'s conduct, he neither does or says any thing on this occasion which indicates terror or disorder of mind: On the contrary, this very act is a proof of his having all his wits about him, and is a stratagem, such as it is, not improper for a buffoon, whose fate would be singularly hard, if he should not be allowed to avail himself of his Character when it might serve him in most stead. We must remember, in extenuation, that the executive, the destroying hand of *Douglas* was over him: '*It was 'time to counterfeit, or that hot termagant Scot had paid him scot and 'lot too.'* He had but one choice; he was obliged to pass thro' the ceremony of dying either in jest or in earnest; and we shall not be surprized at the event, when we remember his propensities to the former.—Life (and especially the life of *Falstaff*) might be a jest; but he could see no joke whatever in dying: To be chop-fallen was, with him, to lose both life and character together: He saw the point of honour, as well as every thing else, in ridiculous lights, and began to renounce its tyranny.

But I am too much in advance, and must retreat for more advantage. I should not forget how much opinion is against me, and that I am to make my way by the mere force and weight of evidence; without which I must not hope to possess myself of the reader: No address, no insinuation will avail. To this evidence, then, I now resort. The Courage of *Falstaff* is my Theme: And no passage will I spare from which any thing can be inferred as relative to this point. It would be as vain as injudicious to attempt concealment: How could I escape detection? The Play is in every one's memory, and a single passage remembered in detection would tell, in the mind of the partial observer, for fifty times its real weight. Indeed this argument would be void of all excuse if it declined any difficulty; if it did not meet, if it did not challenge opposition. Every passage then shall be produced from which, in my opinion, any inference, favourable or unfavourable, has or can be drawn;—but not methodically, not formally, as texts for comment, but as chance or convenience shall lead the way; but in what shape soever, they shall be always distinguishingly marked for notice. And so with that attention to truth and candour which ought to accompany even our lightest amusements I proceed to offer such proof as the case will admit, that *Courage* is a part of *Falstaff*'s *Character*, that it belonged to his constitution, and was manifest in the conduct and practice of his whole life.

Let us then examine, as a source of very authentic information, what Impressions *Sir John Falstaff* had made on the characters of the Drama; and in what estimation he is supposed to stand with mankind in general as to the point of Personal Courage. But the quotations we make for this or other purposes, must, it is confessed, be lightly touched, and no particular passage strongly relied on, either in his favour or against him. Every thing which he himself says, or is said of him, is so phantastically discoloured by humour, or folly, or jest, that we must for the most part look to the spirit rather than the letter of what is uttered, and rely at last only on a combination of the whole.

We will begin then, if the reader pleases, by inquiring what Impression the very Vulgar had taken of *Falstaff*. If it is not that of Cowardice, be it what else it may, that of a man of violence, or *a Ruffian in years*, as *Harry* calls him, or any thing else, it answers my purpose; how insignificant soever the characters or incidents to be first produced may otherwise appear;—for these Impressions must have been taken either from personal knowledge and observation; or, what will do better for my purpose, from common fame. Altho' I must admit some part of this evidence will appear so weak and trifling that it certainly ought not to be produced but in proof of *impression* only.

The *Hostess Quickly* employs two officers to arrest *Falstaff*: On the mention of his name, one of them immediately observes, '*that it may chance to cost some of them their lives, for that he will stab.*' —'*Alas a day,*' says the hostess, '*take heed of him, he cares not what* '*mischief he doth; if his weapon be out, he will foin like any devil; He will* '*spare neither man, woman, or child.*' Accordingly, we find that when they lay hold on him he resists to the utmost of his power, and calls upon *Bardolph*, whose arms are at liberty, to draw. '*Away,*

'*varlets, draw Bardolph, cut me off the villain's head, throw the quean in*
'*the kennel.*' The officers cry, *a rescue, a rescue!* But the Chief
Justice comes in and the scuffle ceases. In another scene, his
wench *Doll Tearsheet* asks him '*when he will leave fighting* * * * * * *
'*and patch up his old body for heaven.*' This is occasioned by his
drawing his rapier, on great provocation, and driving *Pistol*,
who is drawn likewise, down stairs, and hurting him in the
shoulder. To drive *Pistol* was no great feat; nor do I mention it as
such; but upon this occasion it was necessary. '*A Rascal bragging*
'*slave,*' says he, '*the rogue fled from me like quicksilver*': Expressions
which, as they remember the cowardice of *Pistol*, seem to prove
that *Falstaff* did not value himself on the adventure. Even something may be drawn from *Davy, Shallow's* serving man, who calls
Falstaff, in ignorant admiration, the *man of war.* I must observe
here, and I beg the reader will notice it, that there is not a single
expression dropt by these people, or either of *Falstaff's* followers,
from which may be inferred the least suspicion of Cowardice in
his character; and this is I think such an *implied negation* as
deserves considerable weight.

But to go a little higher, if, indeed, to consider *Shallow's*
opinion be to go *higher*: It is from him, however, that we get the
earliest account of *Falstaff*. He *remembers him a Page to Thomas
Mowbray, Duke of Norfolk:* '*He broke,*' says he, '*Schoggan's head at the*
'*Court-Gate when he was but a crack thus high.*' *Shallow*, throughout,
considers him as a great Leader and Soldier, and relates this fact
as an early indication only of his future Prowess. *Shallow*, it is
true, is a very ridiculous character; but he picked up these
Impressions somewhere; and he picked up none of a contrary
tendency.—I want at present only to prove that *Falstaff* stood
well in the report of common fame as to this point; and he was
now near seventy years of age, and had passed in a Military
line thro' the active part of his life. At this period common fame
may be well considered as the *seal* of his character; a seal which
ought not perhaps to be broke open on the evidence of any
future transaction.

But to proceed. *Lord Bardolph* was a man of the world, and of sense and observation. He informs *Northumberland*, erroneously indeed, that *Percy* had beaten the King at Shrewsbury. '*The* '*King*,' according to him, '*was wounded; the Prince of Wales and the* '*two Blunts slain, certain Nobles*, whom he names, *had escaped by* '*flight, and the Brawn Sir John Falstaff was taken prisoner.*' But how came *Falstaff* into this list? Common fame had put him there. He is singularly obliged to Common fame.—But if he had not been a Soldier of repute, if he had not been brave as well as fat, if he had been *mere brawn*, it would have been more germane to the matter if this lord had put him down among the baggage or the provender. The fact seems to be that there is a real consequence about Sir *John Falstaff* which is not brought forward: We see him only in his familiar hours; we enter the tavern with *Hal* and *Poins*; we join in the laugh and *take a pride to gird at him*: But there may be a great deal of truth in what he himself writes to the Prince, that tho' he be '*Jack Falstaff with his Familiars, he is* Sir John *with the rest of Europe.*' It has been remarked, and very truly I believe, that no man is a hero in the eye of his valet-de-chambre; and *thus* it is, we are witnesses only of *Falstaff*'s weakness and buffoonery; our acquaintance is with *Jack Falstaff, Plump Jack*, and *Sir John Paunch*; but if we would look for *Sir John Falstaff*, we must put on, as *Bunyan* would have expressed it, the spectacles of observation. With respect, for instance, to his Military command at Shrewsbury, nothing appears on the surface but the Prince's familiarly saying, in the tone usually assumed when speaking of *Falstaff*, '*I will procure this fat rogue a Charge of foot*'; and in another place, '*I will procure thee Jack a Charge of foot; meet* '*me to-morrow in the Temple Hall.*' Indeed we might venture to infer from this, that a Prince of so great ability, whose wildness was only external and assumed, would not have procured, in so nice and critical a conjuncture, a Charge of foot for a known Coward. But there was more it seems in the case: We now find from this report, to which *Lord Bardolph* had given full credit, that the world had its eye upon *Falstaff* as an officer of merit, whom it expected to find in the field, and whose fate in the battle was an object of Public concern: His life was, it seems, very material indeed; a thread of so much dependence, that *fiction*, weaving the fates of Princes, did not think it unworthy, how coarse soever, of being made a part of the tissue.

We shall next produce the evidence of the Chief Justice of England. He inquires of his attendant, '*if the man who was then* '*passing him was* Falstaff; *he who was in question for the robbery.*' The attendant answers affirmatively, but reminds his lord '*that he had* '*since done good service at Shrewsbury*'; and the Chief Justice, on this occasion, rating him for his debaucheries, tells him '*that his day's* '*service at Shrewsbury had gilded over his night's exploit at Gads Hill.*' This is surely more than Common fame: *The Chief Justice* must have known his whole character taken together, and must have received the most authentic information, and in the truest colours, of his behaviour in that action.

But, perhaps, after all, the Military men may be esteemed the best judges in points of this nature. Let us hear then *Coleville* of the dale, *a Soldier, in degree a Knight, a famous rebel, and* '*whose* '*betters, had they been ruled by him, would have sold themselves dearer*': A man who is of consequence enough to be guarded by *Blunt* and *led to present execution.* This man yields himself up even to the very Name and Reputation of *Falstaff.* '*I think,*' says he, '*you are* '*Sir John Falstaff, and in that thought yield me.*' But this is but one only among the men of the sword; they shall be produced then by *dozens*, if that will satisfy. Upon the return of the King and Prince Henry from Wales, the Prince seeks out and finds *Falstaff* debauching in a tavern; where *Peto* presently brings an account of ill news from the North; and adds, '*that as he came* '*along he met or overtook a dozen Captains, bare-headed, sweating,* '*knocking at the taverns, and asking every one for* Sir John Falstaff.' He is followed by *Bardolph*, who informs *Falstaff* that '*He must* '*away to the Court immediately; a dozen Captains stay at door for him.*' Here is Military evidence in abundance, and *Court evidence* too; for what are we to infer from *Falstaff*'s being sent for to Court on this ill news, but that his opinion was to be asked, as a Military man of skill and experience, concerning the defences necessary to be taken. Nor is *Shakespeare* content, here, with leaving us to gather up *Falstaff*'s *better character* from inference and deduction: He comments on the fact by making *Falstaff* observe that '*Men* '*of merit are sought after: The undeserver may sleep when the man of* '*action is called on.*' I do not wish to draw *Falstaff*'s character out of his own mouth; but this observation refers to the fact, and is founded in reason. Nor ought we to reject what in another place he says to the Chief Justice, as it is in the nature of an appeal to his knowledge. '*There is not a dangerous action,*' says he, '*can peep* '*out his head but I am thrust upon it.*' The Chief Justice seems by his answer to admit the fact. '*Well, be honest, be honest, and* '*heaven bless your expedition.*' But the whole passage may deserve transcribing.

Ch. Just. '*Well, the King has severed you and Prince Henry. I hear* '*you are going with Lord John of Lancaster against the Archbishop and* '*the Earl of Northumberland.*'

'Fals. *Yes, I thank your pretty sweet wit for it: but look you pray, all* '*you that kiss my lady peace at home, that our armies join not in a hot day;* '*for I take but two shirts out with me, and I mean not to sweat ex-* '*traordinarily: If it be a hot day, if I brandish any thing but a bottle,* '*would I might never spit white again. There is not a dangerous action* '*can peep out his head but I am thrust upon it. Well I cannot last for* '*ever.—But it was always the trick of our English nation, if they have a* '*good thing to make it too common. If you will needs say I am an old man* '*you should give me rest: I would to God my name were not so terrible to* '*the enemy as it is. I were better to be eaten to death with a rust than to be* '*scour'd to nothing with perpetual motion.*'

'Ch. Just. *Well be honest, be honest, and heaven bless your expedition.*'

Falstaff indulges himself here in humourous exaggeration;— these passages are not meant to be taken, nor are we to suppose that they were taken, literally;—but if there was not a ground of truth, if *Falstaff* had not had such a degree of Military reputation as was capable of being thus humourously amplified and ex- aggerated, the whole dialogue would have been highly prepos- terous and absurd, and the acquiescing answer of the *Lord Chief Justice* singularly improper.—But upon the supposition of *Fal-staff*'s being considered, upon the whole, as a good and gallant

Officer, the answer is just, and corresponds with the acknowledgment which had a little before been made, *'that his day's*
'service at Shrewsbury had gilded over his night's exploit at Gads Hill.—
'You may thank the unquiet time,' says the Chief Justice, *'for your*
'quiet o'erposting of that action'; agreeing with what *Falstaff* says in
another place;—*'Well, God be thanked for these Rebels, they offend*
'none but the virtuous; I laud them, I praise them.'—Whether this be
said in the true spirit of a Soldier or not, I do not determine; it is
surely not in that of a mere Coward and Poltroon.

It will be needless to shew, which might be done from a
variety of particulars, that *Falstaff* was known and had consideration at Court. *Shallow* cultivates him in the idea that *a friend at*
Court is better than a penny in purse: *Westmorland* speaks to him in
the tone of an equal: Upon *Falstaff*'s telling him that he thought
his lordship had been already at Shrewsbury, *Westmorland* replies,—*'Faith Sir John, 'tis more than time that I were there, and you*
'too; the King I can tell you looks for us all; we must away all to night.'
—*'Tut,'* says Falstaff, *'never fear me, I am as vigilant as a cat to steal*
'cream.'—He desires, in another place, of my lord John of Lancaster, *'that when he goes to Court, he may stand in his good report.'* His
intercourse and correspondence with both these lords seem easy
and familiar. *'Go,'* says he to the page, *'bear this to my Lord of*
'Lancaster, this to the Prince, this to the Earl of Westmorland, and this
'(for he extended himself on all sides) to old Mrs. Ursula,' whom,
it seems, the rogue ought to have married many years before.—
But these intimations are needless: We see him ourselves in the
Royal Presence; where, certainly, his buffooneries never brought
him; never was the Prince of a character to commit so high an
indecorum, as to thrust, upon a solemn occasion, a mere Tavern
companion into his father's Presence, especially in a moment
when he himself deserts his looser character, and takes up that of
a Prince indeed.—In a very important scene, where *Worcester* is
expected with proposals from *Percy*, and wherein he is received,
is treated with, and carries back offers of accommodation from
the King, the King's attendants upon the occasion are *the Prince*
of Wales, Lord John of Lancaster, the Earl of Westmorland, Sir

Walter Blunt, and Sir John Falstaff.—What shall be said to this? *Falstaff* is not surely introduced here in vicious indulgence to a mob audience;—he utters but one word, a buffoon one indeed, but aside, and to the Prince only. Nothing, it should seem, is wanting, if decorum would here have permitted, but that he should have spoken one sober sentence in the Presence (which yet we are to suppose him ready and able to do if occasion should have required; or his wit was given him to little purpose) and Sir *John Falstaff* might be allowed to pass for an established Courtier and counsellor of state. '*If I do grow great*', says he, '*I'll* '*grow less, purge and leave sack, and live as a nobleman should do.*' Nobility did not then appear to him at an unmeasurable distance; it was, it seems, in his idea, the very next link in the chain.

But to return. I would now demand what could bring *Falstaff* into the Royal Presence upon such an occasion, or justify the Prince's so public acknowledgment of him, but an established fame and reputation of Military merit? In short, just the like merit as brought Sir *Walter Blunt* into the same circumstances of honour.

But it may be objected that his introduction into this scene is a piece of indecorum in the author. But upon what ground are we to suppose this? Upon the ground of his being a notorious Coward? Why, this is the very point in question, and cannot be granted: Even the direct contrary I have affirmed, and am endeavouring to support. But if it be supposed upon any other ground, it does not concern me; I have nothing to do with *Shakespeare*'s indecorums in general. That there are indecorums in the Play I have no doubt: The indecent treatment of *Percy*'s dead body is the greatest;—the familiarity of the insignificant, rude, and even ill disposed *Poins* with the Prince, is another;—but the admission of *Falstaff* into the Royal Presence (supposing, which I have a right to suppose, that his Military character was unimpeached) does not seem to be in any respect among the number. In camps there is but one virtue and one vice; Military merit swallows up or covers all. But, after all, what have we to do with indecorums? Indecorums respect the propriety or impropriety of exhibiting certain actions;—not their *truth* or *falshood* when exhibited. *Shakespeare* stands to us in the place of *truth* and *nature*: If we desert this principle, we cut the turf from under us; I may then object to the robbery and other passages as indecorums, and as contrary to the truth of character. In short we may rend and tear the Play to pieces, and every man carry off what sentences he likes best.—But why this inveterate malice against poor *Falstaff*? He has faults enough in conscience without loading him with the infamy of Cowardice; a charge, which, if true, would, if I am not greatly mistaken, spoil all our mirth.—But of that hereafter.

It seems to me that, in our hasty judgment of some particular transactions, we forget the circumstances and condition of his whole life and character, which yet deserve our very particular attention. The author, it is true, has thrown the most advantageous of these circumstances into the *back ground*, as it were, and has brought nothing *out of the canvass* but his follies and buffoonery. We discover, however, that in a very early period of his life he was familiar with *John* of *Gaunt*; which could hardly be, unless he had possessed much personal gallantry and accomplishment, and had derived his birth from a distinguished at least, if not from a Noble family.

It may seem very extravagant to insist upon *Falstaff*'s birth as a ground from which, by any inference, Personal courage may be derived, especially after having acknowledged that he seemed to have deserted those points of honour which are more peculiarly the accompanyments of rank. But it may be observed that in the Feudal ages rank and wealth were not only connected with the point of honour, but with personal strength and natural courage. It is observable that Courage is a quality which is at least as transmissible to one's posterity as features and complexion. In these periods men acquired and maintained their rank and possessions by personal prowess and gallantry; and their marriage alliances were made, of course, in families of the same character: And from hence, and from the exercises of their youth, we must account for the distinguished force and bravery of our antient Barons. It is not therefore beside my purpose to inquire what hints of the origin and birth of *Falstaff*, *Shakespeare* may have dropped in different parts of the Play; for tho' we may be disposed to allow that *Falstaff* in his old age might, under particular influences, desert the point of honour, we cannot give up that unalienable possession of Courage, which might have been derived to him from a noble or distinguished stock.

But it may be said that *Falstaff* was in truth the child of invention only, and that a reference to the Feudal accidents of birth serves only to confound fiction with reality: Not altogether so. If the ideas of courage and *birth* were strongly associated in the days of *Shakespeare*, then would the assignment of high birth to *Falstaff* carry, and be intended to carry along with it, to the minds of the audience the associated idea of Courage, if nothing should be specially interposed to dissolve the connection;—and the question is as concerning this intention, and this effect.

I shall proceed yet farther to make a few very minute observations of the same nature: But if *Shakespeare* meant sometimes rather to *impress* than explain, no circumstances calculated to this end, either directly or by association, are too minute for notice. But however this may be, a more conciliating reason still remains: The argument itself, like the tales of our Novelists, is a *vehicle* only; *theirs*, as they profess, of moral instruction; and *mine* of critical amusement. The vindication of *Falstaff*'s Courage deserves not for its own sake the least sober discussion; *Falstaff* is the word only, *Shakespeare* is the *Theme*: And if thro' this channel I can furnish no irrational amusement, the reader will not, perhaps, every where expect from me the strict severity of logical investigation.

Falstaff, then, it may be observed, was introduced into the world,—(at least we are told so) by the name of *Oldcastle*.[1] This

[1] I believe the stage was in possession of some rude outline of *Falstaff* before the time of *Shakespeare*, under the name of *Sir John Oldcastle*; and I think it probable that this name was retained for a period in *Shakespeare*'s Hen. 4th. but changed to *Falstaff* before the play was printed. The expression of '*Old Lad of the Castle*,' used by the Prince, does not however decidedly prove this; as it might have been only some known and familiar appellation too carelessly transferred from the old Play.

was assigning him an origin of nobility; but the family of that name disclaiming any kindred with his vices, he was thereupon, as it is said, ingrafted into another stock¹ scarcely less distinguished, tho' fallen into indelible disgraces; and by this means he has been made, if the conjectures of certain critics are well founded, the Dramatic successor, tho', having respect to chronology, the natural *proavus* of another Sir *John*, who was no less than a Knight of the most noble order of the Garter, but a name for ever dishonoured by a frequent exposure in that Drum-and-trumpet Thing called *The first part of Henry* VI., written doubtless, or rather exhibited, long before *Shakespeare* was born,² tho' afterwards repaired, I think, and furbished up by him with here and there a little sentiment and diction. This family, if any branch

¹ I doubt if *Shakespeare* had Sir *John Fastolfe* in his memory when he called the character under consideration *Falstaff*. The title and name of *Sir John* were transferred from *Oldcastle* not *Fastolfe*, and there is no kind of similarity in the characters. If he had *Fastolfe* in his thought at all, it was that, while he approached the name, he might make such a departure from it as the difference of character seemed to require.

² It would be no difficult matter, I think, to prove that all those Plays taken from the English chronicle, which are ascribed to *Shakespeare*, were on the stage before his time, and that he was employed by the Players only to refit and repair; taking due care to retain the names of the characters and to preserve all those incidents which were the most popular. Some of these Plays, particularly the two parts of Hen. IV., have certainly received what may be called a *thorough repair*; that is, *Shakespeare* new-wrote them to the old names. In the latter part of Hen. V. some of the old materials remain; and in the Play which I have here censured (Hen. VI.) we see very little of the new. I should conceive it would not be very difficult to feel one's way thro' these Plays, and distinguish every where the metal from the clay. Of the two Plays of Hen. IV. there has been, I have admitted, a complete transmutation, preserving the old forms; but in the others, there is often no union or coalescence of parts, nor are any of them equal in merit to those Plays more peculiarly and emphatically *Shakespeare*'s *own*. The reader will be pleased to think that I do not reckon into the works of *Shakespeare* certain absurd productions which his editors have been so good as to compliment him with. I object, and strenuously too, even to *The Taming of the Shrew*; not that it wants merit, but that it does not bear the peculiar features and stamp of *Shakespeare*.

The rhyming parts of the Historic plays are all, I think, of an older date than the times of *Shakespeare*.—There was a Play, I believe, of *the Acts of King John*, of which the bastard *Falconbridge* seems to have been the hero and the fool: He appears to have spoken altogether in rhyme. *Shakespeare* shews him to us in the latter part of the second scene in the first act of *King John* in this condition; tho' he afterwards, in the course of the Play, thought fit to adopt him, to give him language and manners, and to make him his own.

of it remained in *Shakespeare's* time, might have been proud of their Dramatic ally, if indeed they could have any fair pretence to claim as such *him* whom *Shakespeare*, perhaps in contempt of Cowardice, wrote *Falstaff*, not *Fastolfe*, the true Historic name of the Gartered Craven.

In the age of Henry IV. a Family crest and arms were authentic proofs of gentility; and this proof, among others, *Shakespeare* has furnished us with: *Falstaff* always carried about him, it seems, *a Seal ring of his Grandfather's, worth*, as he says, *forty marks*: The Prince indeed affirms, but not seriously I think, that this ring was *copper*. As to the existence of the *bonds*, which were I suppose the negotiable securities or paper-money of the time, and which he pretended to have lost, I have nothing to say; but the ring, I believe, was really gold; tho' probably a little too much alloyed with baser metal. But this is not the point: The *arms* were doubtless genuine; they were borne by his Grandfather, and are proofs of an antient gentility; a gentility doubtless, in former periods, connected with wealth and possessions, tho' the gold of the family might have been transmuting by degrees, and perhaps, in the hands of *Falstaff*, converted into little better than copper. This observation is made on the supposition of *Falstaff*'s being considered as the head of the family, which I think however he ought not to be. It appears rather as if he ought to be taken in the light of a cadet or younger brother; which the familiar appellation of *John*, 'the only one (as he says) given him by his 'brothers and sisters,' seems to indicate. Be this as it may, we find he is able, in spite of dissipation, to keep up a certain *state* and *dignity* of appearance; retaining no less than four, if not five, followers or men servants in his train. He appears also to have had apartments in town, and, by his invitations of *Master Gower* to dinner and to supper, a regular table: And one may infer farther from the Prince's question, on his return from Wales, to *Bardolph*, '*Is your master* here *in London*,' that he had likewise a house in the country. Slight proofs it must be confessed, yet the inferences are so probable, so buoyant, in their own nature, that they may well rest on them. That he did not lodge at the Tavern is clear from the circumstances of the arrest. These various occasions of expence,—servants, taverns, houses, and whores,— necessarily imply that *Falstaff* must have had some funds which are not brought immediately under our notice. That these funds were not however adequate to his style of living is plain: Perhaps his train may be considered only as incumbrances, which the pride of family and the habit of former opulence might have brought upon his present poverty: I do not mean absolute poverty, but call it so as relative to his expence. To have *'but* *'seven groats and two-pence in his purse'* and a page to bear it, is truly ridiculous; and it is for that reason we become so familiar with its contents, *'He can find,'* he says, *'no remedy for this consumption of* *'the purse, borrowing does but linger and linger it out; but the disease is* *'incurable'*. It might well be deemed so in his course of dissipation: But I shall presently suggest one source at least of his supply much more constant and honourable than that of borrowing. But the condition of *Falstaff* as to opulence or poverty is not very material to my purpose: It is enough if his birth was distin- guished, and his youth noted for gallantry and accomplishments. To the first I have spoken, and as for the latter we shall not be at a loss when we remember that *'he was in his youth a page to Thomas* *'Mowbray, Duke of Norfolk'*; a situation at that time sought for by young men of the best families and first fortune. The house of every great noble was at that period a kind of Military school; and it is probable that *Falstaff* was singularly adroit at his exercises: *'He broke Schoggan's head,'* (some boisterous fencer I suppose) *'when he was but a crack thus high.'* *Shallow* remembers him as *notedly skilful at backsword*; and he was at that period, according to his own humourous account, *'scarcely an eagle's talon in the* *'waist, and could have crept thro' an alderman's thumb ring.'* Even at the age at which he is exhibited to us, we find him *foundering*, as he calls it, *nine score and odd miles*, with wonderful expedition, to join the army of Prince *John* of *Lancaster*; and declaring, after the surrender of *Coleville*, that *'had he but a belly of any indifferency, he* *'were simply the most active fellow in Europe'*. Nor ought we here to pass over his Knighthood without notice. It was, I grant, intended by the author as a dignity which, like his Courage and his wit, was to be debased; his knighthood by low situations, his Courage by circumstances and imputations of cowardice, and his wit by buffoonery. But how are we to suppose this honour was acquired? By that very Courage, it should seem, which we so obstinately deny him. It was not certainly given him, like a modern City Knighthood, for his wealth or gravity: It was in these days a Military honour, and an authentic badge of Military merit.

But *Falstaff* was not only a Military Knight, he possess'd an honourable *pension* into the bargain; the reward as well as retainer of service, and which seems (besides the favours perhaps of Mrs. *Ursula*) to be the principal and only solid support of his present expences. But let us refer to the passage. '*A pox of this 'gout, or a gout of this pox; for one or the other plays the rogue with my 'great toe: It is no matter if I do halt, I have the wars for my colour, 'and my pension shall seem the more reasonable.*' The mention *Falstaff* here makes of a pension, has I believe been generally construed to refer rather to *hope* than *possession*, yet I know not why: For the possessive MY, *my pension*, (not *a* pension) requires a different construction. Is it that we cannot enjoy a wit till we have stript him — of every worldly advantage, and reduced him below the level of our envy? It may be perhaps for this reason among others that *Shakespeare* has so obscured the better parts of *Falstaff* and stolen them secretly on our feelings, instead of opening them fairly to the notice of our understandings. How carelessly, and thro' what bye-paths, as it were, of casual inference, is this fact of a pension introduced! And how has he associated it with misfortune and infirmity! Yet I question, however, if, in this one place, the *Impression* which was intended be well and effectually made. It must be left to the reader to determine if, in that mass of things out of which *Falstaff* is compounded, he ever considered a pension as any part of the composition: A pension however he appears to have had, one that halting could only seem to make more reasonable, not more honourable. The inference arising from the fact, I shall leave to the reader. It is surely a circumstance highly advantageous to *Falstaff* (I speak of the pensions of former days), whether he be considered in the light of a soldier or a gentleman.

I cannot foresee the temper of the reader, nor whether he be content to go along with me in these kind of observations. Some of the incidents which I have drawn out of the Play may appear too minute, whilst yet they refer to principles which may seem too general. Many points require explanation; something should be said of the nature of *Shakespeare*'s Dramatic characters[1]; by

---

[1] The reader must be sensible of something in the composition of *Shakespeare*'s characters, which renders them essentially different from those drawn by other writers. The characters of every Drama must indeed be grouped; but in the groupes of other poets the parts which are not seen do not in fact exist. But there is a certain roundness and integrity in the forms of *Shakespeare*, which give them an independence as well as a relation, insomuch that we often meet with passages which, tho' perfectly felt, cannot be sufficiently explained in words, without unfolding the whole character of the speaker: And this I may be obliged to do in respect to that of *Lancaster*, in order to account for some words spoken by him in censure of *Falstaff*.—Something which may be thought too heavy for the *text*, I shall add *here*, as a conjecture concerning the composition of *Shakespeare*'s characters: Not that they were the effect, I believe, so much of a minute and laborious attention, as of a certain comprehensive energy of mind, involving within itself all the effects of system and of labour.

Bodies of all kinds, whether of metals, plants, or animals, are supposed to possess certain first principles of *being*, and to have an existence independent of the accidents which form their magnitude or growth: Those accidents are supposed to be drawn in from the surrounding elements, but not indiscriminately; each plant and each animal imbibes those things only which are proper to its own distinct nature, and which have besides such a secret relation to each other as to be capable of forming a perfect union and coalescence: But so variously are the surrounding elements mingled and disposed, that each particular body, even of those under the same species, has yet some *peculiar* of its own. *Shakespeare* appears to have considered the being and growth of the human mind as analogous to this system: There are certain qualities and capacities which he seems to have considered as first principles; the chief of which are certain energies of courage and activity, according to their degrees; together with different degrees and sorts of sensibilities, and a capacity, varying likewise in *degree*, of discernment and intelligence. The rest of the composition is drawn in from an atmosphere of surrounding things; that is, from the various influences of the different laws, religions and governments in the world; and from those of the different ranks and inequalities in society; and from the different professions of men, encouraging or repressing passions of particular sorts, and inducing different modes of thinking and habits of life; and he seems to have known intuitively what those influences in particular were which this or that original constitution would most freely imbibe and which would most easily associate and coalesce. But all these things being, in different situations, very differently disposed, and those differences exactly discerned by him, he found no difficulty in marking every individual,

what arts they were formed, and wherein they differ from those of other writers; something likewise more professedly of *Shakespeare* himself, and of the peculiar character of his genius. After such a review we may not perhaps think any consideration arising out of the Play, or out of general nature, either as too minute or too extensive.

Shakespeare is, in truth, an author whose mimic creation agrees in general so perfectly with that of nature, that it is not only wonderful in the great, but opens another scene of amazement to the discoveries of the microscope. We have been charged indeed by a Foreign writer with an overmuch admiring of this *Barbarian*: Whether we have admired with knowledge, or have blindly followed those feelings of affection which we could not resist, I cannot tell; but certain it is, that to the labours of his Editors he has not been overmuch obliged. They are however

even among characters of the same sort, with something peculiar and distinct.— Climate and complexion demand their influence; '*Be thus when thou art dead, and I will kill thee, and love thee after,*' is a sentiment characteristic of, and fit only to be uttered by a *Moor*.

But it was not enough for *Shakespeare* to have formed his characters with the most perfect truth and coherence; it was further necessary that he should possess a wonderful facility of compressing, as it were, his own spirit into these images, and of giving alternate animation to the forms. This was not to be done *from without*; he must have *felt* every varied situation, and have spoken thro' the organ he had formed. Such an intuitive comprehension of things and such a facility must unite to produce a *Shakespeare*. The reader will not now be surprised if I affirm that those characters in *Shakespeare*, which are seen only in part, are yet capable of being unfolded and understood in the whole; every part being in fact relative, and inferring all the rest. It is true that the point of action or sentiment, which we are most concerned in, is always held out for our special notice. But who does not perceive that there is a peculiarity about it, which conveys a relish of the whole? And very frequently, when no particular point presses, he boldly makes a character act and speak from those parts of the composition which are *inferred* only, and not distinctly shewn. This produces a wonderful effect; it seems to carry us beyond the poet to nature itself, and gives an integrity and truth to facts and character, which they could not otherwise obtain: And this is in reality that art in *Shakespeare* which, being withdrawn from our notice, we more emphatically call *nature*. A felt propriety and truth from causes unseen, I take to be the highest point of Poetic composition. If the characters of *Shakespeare* are thus *whole*, and as it were original, while those of almost all other writers are mere imitation, it may be fit to consider them rather as Historic than Dramatic beings; and, when occasion requires, to account for their conduct from the *whole* of character, from general principles, from latent motives, and from policies not avowed.

for the most part of the first rank in literary fame; but some of them had possessions of their own in Parnassus, of an extent too great and important to allow of a very diligent attention to the interests of others; and among those Critics more professionally so, the ablest and the best has unfortunately looked more to the praise of ingenious than of just conjecture. The character of his emendations are not so much that of *right* or *wrong*, as that, being in the extreme, they are always *Warburtonian*. Another has since undertaken the custody of our author, whom he seems to consider as a sort of wild Proteus or madman, and accordingly knocks him down with the butt-end of his critical staff, as often as he exceeds that line of sober discretion, which this learned Editor appears to have chalked out for him: Yet is this Editor notwithstanding 'a man, take him for all in all,' very highly respectable for his genius and his learning. What however may be chiefly complained of in these gentlemen is, that having erected themselves into the condition, as it were, of guardians and trustees of *Shakespeare*, they have never undertaken to discharge the disgraceful incumbrances of some wretched productions which have long hung heavy on his fame. Besides the evidence of taste, which indeed is not communicable, there are yet other and more general proofs that these incumbrances were not incurred by *Shakespeare*: The *Latin* sentences dispersed thro' the imputed trash is, I think, of itself a decisive one. *Love's Labour lost* contains a very conclusive one of another kind; tho' the very last Editor has, I believe, in his critical sagacity, suppressed the evidence, and withdrawn the record.

Yet whatever may be the neglect of some, or the censure of others, there are those who firmly believe that this wild, this uncultivated Barbarian has not yet obtained one half of his fame; and who trust that some new Stagyrite will arise, who instead of pecking at the surface of things will enter into the inward soul of his compositions, and expel, by the force of congenial feelings, those foreign impurities which have stained and disgraced his page. And as to those *spots* which will still remain, they may perhaps become invisible to those who shall seek them thro' the

medium of his beauties, instead of looking for those beauties, as
is too frequently done, thro' the smoke of some real or imputed
obscurity. When the hand of time shall have brushed off his
present Editors and Commentators, and when the very name of
Voltaire, and even the memory of the language in which he has
written, shall be no more, the *Apalachian* mountains, the banks
of the *Ohio*, and the plains of *Sciota* shall resound with the
accents of this Barbarian: In his native tongue he shall roll
the genuine passions of nature; nor shall the griefs of *Lear* be
alleviated, or the charms and wit of *Rosalind* be abated by time.
There is indeed nothing perishable about him, except that very
learning which he is said so much to want. He had not, it is true,
enough for the demands of the age in which he lived, but he had
perhaps too much for the reach of his genius, and the interest of
his fame. *Milton* and he will carry the decayed remnants and
fripperies of antient mythology into more distant ages than they
are by their own force intitled to extend; and the metamorphoses
of *Ovid*, upheld by them, lay in a new claim to unmerited
immortality.

Shakespeare is a name so interesting, that it is excusable to stop
a moment, nay it would be indecent to pass him without the
tribute of some admiration. He differs essentially from all other
writers: Him we may profess rather to feel than to understand;
and it is safer to say, on many occasions, that we are possessed
by him, than that we possess him. And no wonder;—He scatters
the seeds of things, the principles of character and action, with so
cunning a hand, yet with so careless an air, and, master of our
feelings, submits himself so little to our judgment, that every
thing seems superior. We discern not his course, we see no connection of cause and effect, we are rapt in ignorant admiration,
and claim no kindred with his abilities. All the incidents, all the
parts, look like chance, whilst we feel and are sensible that the
whole is design. His Characters not only act and speak in strict
conformity to nature, but in strict relation to us; just so much is
shewn as is requisite, just so much is impressed; he commands
every passage to our heads and to our hearts, and moulds us as

he pleases, and that with so much ease, that he never betrays his own exertions. We see these Characters act from the mingled motives of passion, reason, interest, habit, and complection, in all their proportions, when they are supposed to know it not themselves; and we are made to acknowledge that their actions and sentiments are, from those motives, the necessary result. He at once blends and distinguishes every thing;—every thing is complicated, every thing is plain. I restrain the further expressions of my admiration lest they should not seem applicable to man; but it is really astonishing that a mere human being, a part of humanity only, should so perfectly comprehend the whole; and that he should possess such exquisite art, that whilst every woman and every child shall feel the whole effect, his learned Editors and Commentators should yet so very frequently mistake or seem ignorant of the cause. A sceptre or a straw are in his hands of equal efficacy; he needs no selection; he converts every thing into excellence; nothing is too great, nothing is too base. Is a character efficient like *Richard*, it is every thing we can wish: Is it otherwise, like *Hamlet*, it is productive of equal admiration: Action produces one mode of excellence, and inaction another: The Chronicle, the Novel, or the Ballad; the king, or the beggar, the hero, the madman, the sot, or the fool; it is all one;— nothing is worse, nothing is better: The same genius pervades and is equally admirable in all. Or, is a character to be shewn in progressive change, and the events of years comprized within the hour;—with what a Magic hand does he prepare and scatter his spells! The Understanding must, in the first place, be subdued; and lo! how the rooted prejudices of the child spring up to confound the man! The Weird sisters rise, and order is extinguished. The laws of nature give way, and leave nothing in our minds but wildness and horror. No pause is allowed us for reflection: Horrid sentiment, furious guilt and compunction, air-drawn daggers, murders, ghosts, and inchantment, shake and *possess us wholly*. In the mean time the *process* is completed. *Macbeth* changes under our eye, *the milk of human kindness is converted to gall; he has supped full of horrors*, and his *May of life is*

fallen into the sear, the yellow leaf; whilst we, the fools of amazement, are insensible to the shifting of place and the lapse of time,
and, till the curtain drops, never once wake to the truth of things,
or recognize the laws of existence.—On such an occasion, a
fellow, like *Rymer,* waking from his trance, shall lift up his Constable's staff, and charge this great Magician, this daring *practicer
of arts inhibited,* in the name of *Aristotle,* to surrender; whilst
Aristotle himself, disowning his wretched Officer, would fall pros-
trate at his feet and acknowledge his supremacy.—O supreme
of Dramatic excellence! (*might he say*) not to me be imputed the
insolence of fools. The bards of *Greece* were confined within the
narrow circle of the Chorus, and hence they found themselves
constrained to practice, for the most part, the precision, and
copy the details of nature. I followed them, and knew not that a
larger circle might be drawn, and the Drama extended to the
whole reach of human genius. Convinced, I see that a more
compendious *nature* may be obtained; a nature of *effects* only, to
which neither the relations of place, or continuity of time, are
always essential. Nature, condescending to the faculties and
apprehensions of man, has drawn through human life a regular
chain of visible causes and effects: But Poetry delights in surprise,
conceals her steps, seizes at once upon the heart, and obtains the
Sublime of things without betraying the rounds of her ascent:
True Poesy is *magic,* not *nature*; an effect from causes hidden or
unknown. To the Magician I prescribed no laws; his law and his
power are one; his power is his law. Him, who neither imitates,
nor is within the reach of imitation, no precedent can or ought
to bind, no limits to contain. If his end is obtained, who shall
question his course? Means, whether apparent or hidden, are
justified in Poesy by success; but then most perfect and most
admirable when most concealed.[1]—But whither am I going! This

---

[1] These observations have brought me so near to the regions of Poetic *magic*
(using the word here in its strict and proper sense, and not loosely as in the *text*),
that, tho' they lie not directly in my course, I yet may be allowed in this place
to point the reader that way. A felt propriety, or truth of art, from an unseen,
tho' supposed adequate cause, we call *nature*. A like feeling of propriety and
truth, supposed without a cause, or as seeming to be derived from causes inadequate, fantastic, and absurd,—such as wands, circles, incantations, and so

copious and delightful topic has drawn me far beyond my design;
I hasten back to my subject, and am guarded, for a time at least,
against any further temptation to digress.

I was considering the dignity of *Falstaff* so far as it might
seem connected with or productive of military merit, and I
have assigned him *reputation* at least, if not *fame*, noble connection, birth, attendants, title, and an honourable pension; every

forth,—we call by the general name *magic*, including all the train of superstition,
witches, ghosts, fairies, and the rest.—*Reason* is confined to the line of visible
existence; our *passions* and our *fancy* extend far beyond into the *obscure*; but however lawless their operations may seem, the images they so wildly form have yet
a relation to truth, and are the shadows at least, however fantastic, of *reality*. I
am not investigating but passing this subject, and must therefore leave behind
me much curious speculation. Of Personifications however we should observe
that those which are made out of abstract ideas are the creatures of the Understanding only: Thus, of the mixed modes, virtue, beauty, wisdom and others,—
what are they but very obscure ideas of *qualities* considered as abstracted from
any *subject* whatever? The mind cannot steadily contemplate such an abstraction:
What then does it do?—Invent or imagine a subject in order to support these
qualities; and hence we get the Nymphs or Goddesses of virtue, of beauty, or of
wisdom; the very obscurity of the ideas being the cause of their conversion into
sensible objects, with precision both of feature and of form. But as reason has its
personifications, so has *passion*.—Every passion has its Object, tho' often distant
and obscure;—to be brought nearer then, and rendered more distinct, it is personified; and Fancy fantastically decks, or aggravates the *form*, and adds 'a
local habitation and a name.' But passion is the *dupe* of its own artifice and *realises*
the image it had formed. The Grecian theology was mixed of both these kinds
of personification. Of the images produced by passion it must be observed that
they are the images, for the most part, not of the passions themselves, but of
their remote effects. *Guilt* looks through the medium, and beholds a devil; *fear*,
spectres of every sort; *hope*, a smiling cherub; *malice* and *envy* see hags, and witches,
and inchanters dire; whilst the innocent and the young behold with fearful
delight the tripping fairy, whose shadowy form the moon gilds with its softest
beams.—Extravagant as all this appears, it has its laws so precise that we are
sensible both of a local and temporary and of an universal magic; the first derived
from the general nature of the human mind, influenced by particular habits,
institutions, and climate; and the latter from the same general nature abstracted
from those considerations: Of the first sort the *machinery* in *Macbeth* is a very
striking instance; a machinery, which, however exquisite at the time, has already lost more than half its force; and the Gallery now laughs in some places
where it ought to shudder:—But the magic of the *Tempest* is lasting and universal.
There is besides a species of writing for which we have no term of art, and
which holds a middle place between nature and magic; I mean where fancy
either alone, or mingled with reason, or reason assuming the appearance of
fancy, governs some real existence; but the whole of this art is pourtrayed in a
single Play; in the real madness of *Lear*, in the assumed wildness of *Edgar*, and
in the Professional *Fantasque* of the *Fool*, all operating to contrast and heighten
each other. There is yet another feat in this kind, which *Shakespeare* has performed;

one of them presumptive proofs of Military merit, and motives
of action. What deduction is to be made on these articles, and
why they are so much obscured may, perhaps, hereafter appear.

I have now gone through the examination of all the Persons of
the Drama from whose mouths any thing can be drawn relative
to the Courage of *Falstaff*, excepting the *Prince* and *Poins*, whose
evidence I have begged leave to *reserve*, and excepting a very
severe censure passed on him by Lord *John* of *Lancaster*, which I
shall presently consider: But I must first observe that, setting
aside the jests of the Prince and *Poins*, and this censure of *Lancaster*, there is not one expression uttered by any character in the
Drama that can be construed into any impeachment of *Falstaff*'s
Courage;—an observation made before as respecting some of the
Witnesses;—it is now extended to all: And though this silence
be a negative proof only, it cannot, in my opinion, under the
circumstances of the case, and whilst uncontradicted by facts, be
too much relied on. If *Falstaff* had been intended for the character
of a *Miles Gloriosus*, his behaviour ought and therefore would
have been commented upon by others. *Shakespeare* seldom trusts

—he has personified *malice* in his *Caliban*; a character kneaded up of three distinct
natures, the diabolical, the human, and the brute. The rest of his preternatural
beings are images of *effects* only, and cannot subsist but in a surrounding atmosphere of those passions from which they are derived. *Caliban* is the passion
itself, or rather a compound of malice, servility, and lust, *substantiated*; and therefore best shewn in contrast with the lightness of *Ariel* and the innocence of
Miranda.—*Witches* are sometimes substantial existences, supposed to be possessed by, or allyed to the unsubstantial: but the Witches in *Macbeth* are a gross
sort of shadows, 'bubbles of the earth,' as they are finely called by *Banquo*.—
Ghosts differ from other imaginary beings in this, that they belong to no element,
have no specific nature or character, and are effects, however harsh the expression,
supposed without a cause; the reason of which is that they are not the creation
of the poet, but the servile copies or transcripts of popular imagination, connected with supposed reality and religion. Should the poet assign the true cause,
and call them the mere painting or *coinage of the brain*, he would disappoint his
own end, and destroy the being he had raised. Should he assign fictitious causes,
and add a specific nature, and a local habitation, it would not be endured; or the
effect would be lost by the conversion of one being into another. The approach
to reality in this case defeats all the arts and managements of fiction.—The whole
play of the *Tempest* is of so high and superior a nature that *Dryden*, who had
attempted to imitate in vain, might well exclaim that
          '—*Shakespeare*'s *magic* could not copied be,
          'Within that circle none durst walk but *He*.'

to the apprehensions of his audience; his characters interpret for one another continually, and when we least suspect such artful and secret management: The conduct of *Shakespeare* in this respect is admirable, and I could point out a thousand passages which might put to shame the advocates of a formal Chorus, and prove that there is as little of necessity as grace in so mechanic a contrivance.[1] But I confine my censure of the Chorus to its supposed use of comment and interpretation only.

Falstaff is, indeed, so far from appearing to my eye in the light of a *Miles Gloriosus*, that, in the best of my taste and judgment, he does not discover, except in consequence of the robbery, the least *trait* of such a character. All his boasting speeches are humour, mere humour, and carefully spoken to persons who cannot misapprehend them, who cannot be imposed on: They contain indeed, for the most part, an unreasonable and imprudent ridicule of himself, the usual subject of his good humoured merriment; but in the company of ignorant people, such as the Justices, or his own followers, he is remarkably reserved, and does not hazard any thing, even in the way of humour, that may be subject to mistake: Indeed he no where seems to suspect that his character is open to censure on this side, or that he needs the arts of imposition.—'*Turk Gregory never did such deeds in arms as I have* '*done this day*' is spoken, whilst he breathes from action, to the Prince in a tone of jolly humour, and contains nothing but a light ridicule of his own inactivity: This is as far from real boasting as his saying before the battle, '*Wou'd it were bed-time*, Hal, *and all* '*were well*,' is from meanness or depression. This articulated wish is not the fearful outcry of a *Coward*, but the frank and honest breathing of a *generous fellow*, who does not expect to be seriously reproached with the character. Instead, indeed, of deserving the name of a vain glorious *Coward*, his modesty perhaps on this head, and whimsical ridicule of himself, have been a principal source of the imputation.

But to come to the very serious reproach thrown upon him by

---

[1] Ænobarbus, in Anthony and Cleopatra, is in effect the Chorus of the Play; as Menenius Agrippa is of Coriolanus.

that *cold blooded* boy, as he calls him, *Lancaster*.—*Lancaster* makes
a solemn treaty of peace with the *Archbishop of York, Mowbray,*
&c. upon the faith of which they disperse their troops; which is
no sooner done than *Lancaster* arrests the Principals, and pursues
the *scattered stray*: A transaction, by the bye, so singularly per-
fidious, that I wish *Shakespeare*, for his own credit, had not suffered
it to pass under his pen without marking it with the blackest
strokes of Infamy.—During this transaction, *Falstaff* arrives,
joins in the pursuit, and takes Sir *John Coleville* prisoner. Upon
being seen by *Lancaster* he is thus addressed:—

> '*Now, Falstaff, where have you been all this while?*
> '*When every thing is over, then you come:*
> '*These tardy tricks of yours will, on my life,*
> '*One time or other break some gallows' back.*'

This may appear to many a very formidable passage. It is
spoken, as we may say, in the hearing of the army, and by one
intitled as it were by his station to decide on military conduct;
and if no punishment immediately follows, the forbearance may
be imputed to a regard for the Prince of Wales, whose favour the
delinquent was known so unworthily to possess. But this reasoning will by no means apply to the real circumstances of the case.
The effect of this passage will depend on the credit we shall be
inclined to give to *Lancaster* for integrity and candour, and still
more upon the facts which are the ground of this censure, and
which are fairly offered by *Shakespeare* to our notice.

We will examine the evidence arising from both; and to this
end we must in the first place a little unfold the character of this
young Commander in chief;—from a review of which we may
more clearly discern the general impulses and secret motives of
his conduct: And this is a proceeding which I think the peculiar
character of *Shakespeare*'s Drama will very well justify.

We are already well prepared what to think of this young man:
—We have just seen a very pretty manœuvre of his in a matter of
the highest moment, and have therefore the less reason to be
surprized if we find him practising a more petty fraud with

suitable skill and address. He appears in truth to have been what *Falstaff* calls him, *a cold, reserved, sober-blooded boy*; a politician, as it should seem, by nature; bred up moreover in the school of *Bolingbroke* his father, and tutored to betray: With sufficient courage and ability perhaps, but with too much of the knave in his composition, and too little of enthusiasm, ever to be a great and superior character. That such a youth as this should, even from the propensities of character alone, take any plausible occasion to injure a frank unguarded man of wit and pleasure, will not appear unnatural. But he had other inducements. *Falstaff* had given very general scandal by his distinguished wit and noted poverty, insomuch that a little cruelty and injustice towards him was likely to pass, in the eye of the grave and prudent part of mankind, as a very creditable piece of fraud, and to be accounted to *Lancaster* for virtue and good service. But *Lancaster* had motives yet more prevailing; *Falstaff* was a Favourite, without the power which belongs to that character; and the tone of the Court was strongly against him, as the misleader and corrupter of the Prince; who was now at too great a distance to afford him immediate countenance and protection. A scratch then, between jest and earnest as it were, something that would not too much offend the prince, yet would leave behind a disgraceful scar upon *Falstaff*, was very suitable to the temper and situation of parties and affairs. With these observations in our thought, let us return to the passage: It is plainly intended for disgrace, but how artful, how cautious, how insidious is the manner! It may pass for sheer pleasantry and humour: *Lancaster* assumes the familiar phrase and *girding* tone of *Harry*; and the gallows, as he words it, appears to be in the most danger from an encounter with *Falstaff*.—With respect to the matter, 'tis a kind of *miching malicho*; it means mischief indeed, but there is not precision enough in it to intitle it to the appellation of a formal charge, or to give to *Falstaff* any certain and determined ground of defence. *Tardy tricks* may mean not Cowardice but neglect only, though the *manner* may seem to carry the imputation to both.—The reply of *Falstaff* is exactly suited to the qualities

of the speech;—for *Falstaff* never wants ability, but conduct
only. He answers the general effect of this speech by a feeling
and serious complaint of injustice; he then goes on to apply
his defence to the vindication both of his diligence and courage;
but he deserts by degrees his serious tone, and taking the handle
of pleasantry which *Lancaster* had held forth to him, he is
prudently content, as being sensible of *Lancaster*'s high rank and
station, to let the whole pass off in buffoonery and humour. But
the question is, however, not concerning the adroitness and
management of either party: Our business is, after putting the
credit of *Lancaster* out of the question, to discover what there
may be of truth and of fact either in the charge of the one, or
the defence of the other. From this only, we shall be able to draw
our inferences with fairness and with candour. The charge
against *Falstaff* is already in the possession of the reader: The
defence follows.—

Fals. '*I would be sorry, my lord, but it should be thus: I never knew*
'*yet but that rebuke and check were the reward of valour. Do you think*
'*me a swallow, an arrow, or a bullet? Have I in my poor and old motion*
'*the expedition of thought? I speeded hither within the very extremest inch*
'*of possibility. I have foundered ninescore and odd posts* (deserting by
degrees his serious tone, for *one* of more address and advantage),
'*and here, travel-tainted as I am, have I in my pure and immaculate*
'*valour taken Sir John Coleville of the dale, a most furious Knight and*
'*valorous enemy.*'

Falstaff's answer then is that he used all possible expedition to
join the army; the not doing of which, with an implication of
Cowardice as the cause, is the utmost extent of the charge against
him; and to take off this implication he refers to the evidence of
a fact present and manifest,—the surrender of *Coleville*; in whose
hearing he speaks, and to whom therefore he is supposed to
appeal. Nothing then remains but that we should inquire if
Falstaff's answer was really founded in truth; '*I speeded hither,*'
says he, '*within the extremest inch of possibility*': If it be so, he is
justified: But I am afraid, for we must not conceal any thing, that
Falstaff was really detained too long by his debaucheries in

London; at least, if we take the Chief Justice's words very strictly.

'Ch. Just. *How now, Sir John? What are you brawling here? Doth* 'this become your PLACE, *your* TIME, *your* BUSINESS? *You should* 'have been well on your way to York.'

Here then seems to be a delay worthy perhaps of rebuke; and if we could suppose *Lancaster* to mean nothing more by *tardy tricks* than idleness and debauch, I should not possibly think myself much concerned to vindicate *Falstaff* from the charge; but the words imply, to my apprehension, a designed and deliberate avoidance of danger. Yet to the contrary of this we are furnished with very full and complete evidence. *Falstaff,* the moment he quits London, discovers the utmost eagerness and impatience to join the army; he gives up his gluttony, his mirth, and his ease. We see him take up in his passage some recruits at *Shallow*'s house; and tho' he has pecuniary views upon *Shallow,* no inducement stops him; he takes no refreshment, he cannot *tarry dinner,* he hurries off; '*I will not*', says he to the Justices, 'use many words with you. Fare ye well, Gentlemen both; I thank ye, I 'must a dozen miles to night.'—He misuses, it is true, at this time the *King's Press damnably*; but that does not concern me, at least not for the present; it belongs to other parts of his character.—It appears then manifestly that *Shakespeare* meant to shew *Falstaff* as really using the utmost speed in his power; he arrives almost literally *within the extremest inch of possibility*; and if *Lancaster* had not accelerated the event by a stroke of perfidy much more subject to the imputation of Cowardice than the *Debauch* of *Falstaff,* he would have been time enough to have shared in the danger of a fair and honest decision. But great men have, it seems, a privilege; '*that in the* General's *but a choleric word, which* 'in the Soldier *were flat blasphemy.*' Yet after all, *Falstaff* did really come time enough, as it appears, to join in the villainous triumphs of the day, to take prisoner *Coleville of the dale, a most furious Knight and valorous enemy.*—Let us look to the fact. If this incident should be found to contain any striking proof of *Falstaff*'s Courage and Military fame, his defence against *Lancaster*

will be stronger than the reader has even a right to demand.
Falstaff encounters *Coleville* in the field, and, having demanded his
name, is ready to assail him; but *Coleville* asks him if he is not Sir
John Falstaff; thereby implying a purpose of surrender. *Falstaff*
will not so much as furnish him with a pretence, and answers
only, that *he is as good a man*. '*Do you yield Sir, or shall I sweat for*
'*you?*' '*I think,*' says Coleville, '*you are Sir John Falstaff, and in that*
'*thought yield me*'. This fact, and the incidents with which it is
accompanied, speak loudly; it seems to have been contrived by
the author on purpose to take off a rebuke so authoritatively
made by *Lancaster*. The fact is set before our eyes to confute the
censure: *Lancaster* himself seems to give up his charge, tho' not
his ill will; for upon *Falstaff*'s asking leave to pass through
Glostershire, and artfully desiring that, upon *Lancaster*'s return
to Court, *he might stand well in his report*, *Lancaster* seems in his
answer to mingle malice and acquittal. '*Far eye well*, Falstaff, *I in*
'*my condition shall better speak of you than you deserve.*' '*I would,*' says
Falstaff, who is left behind in the scene, '*You had but the wit;*
' '*twere better than your Dukedom.*' He continues on the stage some
time chewing the cud of dishonour, which, with all his facility,
he cannot well swallow. '*Good faith,*' says he, accounting to himself as well as he could for the injurious conduct of *Lancaster,*
'*this sober-blooded boy does not love me.*' This he might well believe.
'*A man,*' says he, '*cannot make him laugh; there's none of these demure*
'*boys come to any proof; but that's no marvel, they drink no sack.*'—
Falstaff then it seems knew no drinker of sack who was a Coward;
at least the instance was not home and familiar to him.—'*They*
'*all,*' says he, '*fall into a kind of Male green sickness, and are generally*
'*fools and Cowards.*' Anger has a privilege, and I think *Falstaff* has a
right to turn the tables upon *Lancaster* if he can; but *Lancaster*
was certainly no fool, and I think upon the whole no Coward;
yet the Male green sickness which *Falstaff* talks of seems to
have infected his manners and aspect, and taken from him all
external indication of gallantry and courage. He behaves in the
battle of Shrewsbury beyond the promise of his complexion and
deportment: '*By heaven thou hast deceived me Lancaster,*' says Harry,

'*I did not think thee Lord of such a spirit!*' Nor was his father less surprized '*at his holding Lord Percy at the point with lustier main-*'*tenance than he did look for from such an unripe warrior.*' But how well and unexpectedly soever he might have behaved upon that occasion, he does not seem to have been of a temper to trust fortune too much or too often with his safety; therefore it is that, in order to keep the event in his own hands, he loads the Die, in the present case, with villainy and deceit: The event however he piously ascribes, like a wise and prudent youth as he is, without paying that worship to himself which he so justly merits, to the special favour and interposition of Heaven.

> '*Strike up your drums, pursue the scattered stray.*
> '*Heaven, and not we, have safely fought to-day.*'

But the profane *Falstaff*, on the contrary, less informed and less studious of supernatural things, imputes the whole of this con- duct to thin potations, and the not drinking largely of good and excellent *sherris*; and so little doubt does he seem to entertain of the Cowardice and ill disposition of this youth, that he stands devising causes, and casting about for an hypothesis on which the whole may be physically explained and accounted for;—but I shall leave him and Doctor *Cadogan* to settle that point as they may.

The only serious charge against *Falstaff*'s Courage, we have now at large examined; it came from great authority, from the Commander in chief, and was meant as chastisement and rebuke; but it appears to have been founded in ill-will, in the particular character of *Lancaster*, and in the wantonness and insolence of power; and the author has placed near, and under our notice, full and ample proofs of its injustice.—And thus the deeper we look unto *Falstaff*'s character, the stronger is our conviction that he was not intended to be shewn as a Constitutional coward: Censure cannot lay sufficient hold on him,—and even malice turns away, and more than half pronounces his acquittal.

But as yet we have dealt principally in parole and circum- stantial evidence, and have referred to *Fact* only incidentally.

But *Facts* have a much more operative influence: They may be produced, not as arguments only, but Records; not to dispute alone, but to decide.—It is time then to behold *Falstaff* in actual service as a soldier, in danger, and in battle. We have already displayed one fact in his defence against the censure of *Lancaster*; a fact extremely unequivocal and decisive. But the reader knows I have others, and doubtless goes before me to the action at *Shrewsbury*. In the midst and in the heat of battle we see him come forwards;—what are his words? '*I have led my Rag-o-muffians where* '*they are peppered; there's not three of my hundred and fifty left alive.*' But to *whom* does he say this? To himself only; he speaks *in soliloquy*. There is no questioning the fact, *he had* led *them; they were peppered; there were not* three *left alive.* He was in luck, being in bulk equal to any two of them, to escape unhurt. Let the author answer for that, I have nothing to do with it: He was the Poetic maker of the whole *Corps*, and he might dispose of them as he pleased. Well might the Chief justice, as we now find, acknowledge *Falstaff*'s services in this day's battle; an acknowledgment which amply confirms the fact. A Modern officer, who had performed a feat of this kind, would expect, not only the praise of having done his duty, but the appellation of a hero. But poor *Falstaff* has too much wit to thrive: In spite of probability, in spite of inference, in spite of fact, he must be a Coward still. He happens unfortunately to have more Wit than Courage, and therefore we are maliciously determined that he shall have no Courage at all. But let us suppose that his modes of expression, even *in soliloquy*, will admit of some abatement;—how much shall we abate? Say that he brought off *fifty* instead of *three*; yet a Modern captain would be apt to look big after an action with two thirds of his men, as it were, in his belly. Surely *Shakespeare* never meant to exhibit this man as a Constitutional coward; if he did, his means were sadly destructive of his end. We see him, after he had expended his Rag-o-muffians, with sword and target in the midst of battle, in perfect possession of himself, and replete with humour and jocularity. He was, I presume, in some immediate personal danger, in danger also of a general defeat; too corpulent for flight; and to be led a prisoner was probably to be led to execution; yet we see him laughing and easy, offering a bottle of sack to the Prince instead of a pistol, punning, and telling him, *'there was that which would* sack *a city.'*—*'What, is it a* *'time,'* says the Prince *'to jest and dally now?'* No, a sober character would not jest on such an occasion, but a Coward could not; he would neither have the inclination, or the power. And what could support *Falstaff* in such a situation? Not principle; he is not suspected of the Point of honour; he seems indeed fairly to renounce it. *'Honour cannot set a leg or an arm; it has no skill in surgery:—What is* *'it? a word only; meer air. It is insensible to the dead; and detraction will* *'not let it live with the living.'* What then but a strong natural constitutional Courage, which nothing could extinguish or dismay? —In the following passages the true character of *Falstaff* as to Courage and Principle is finely touched, and the different colours at once nicely blended and distinguished. *'If Percy be alive, I'll* *'pierce him. If he do come in my way, so:—If he do not, if I come in his* *'willingly, let him make a Carbonado of me. I like not such grinning* *'honour as Sir Walter hath; give me life; which if I can save, so; if not,* *'honour comes unlook'd for, and there's an end.'* One cannot say which prevails most here, profligacy or courage; they are both tinged alike by the same humour, and mingled in one common mass; yet when we consider the superior force of *Percy*, as we must presently also that of *Douglas*, we shall be apt, I believe, in our secret heart, to forgive him. These passages are spoken in soliloquy and in battle: If every soliloquy made under similar circumstances were as audible as *Falstaff*'s, the imputation might perhaps be found too general for censure. These are among the passages that have impressed on the world an idea of Cowardice in *Falstaff*;—yet why? He is resolute to take his fate: If *Percy* do come in his way, *so*;—if not, he will not seek inevitable destruction; he is willing to save his life, but if that cannot be, why,— *'honour comes unlook'd for, and there's an end.'* This surely is not the language of Cowardice: It contains neither the Bounce or Whine of the character; he derides, it is true, and seems to renounce that grinning idol of Military zealots, *Honour*. But *Falstaff*

was a kind of Military free-thinker, and has accordingly incurred
the obloquy of his condition. He stands upon the ground of
natural Courage only and common sense, and has, it seems, too
much wit for a hero.—But let me be well understood;—I do not
justify *Falstaff* for renouncing the point of honour; it proceeded
doubtless from a general relaxation of mind, and profligacy of
temper. Honour is calculated to aid and strengthen natural
courage, and lift it up to heroism; but natural courage, which
can act as such without honour, is natural courage still; the very
quality I wish to maintain to *Falstaff*. And if, without the aid of
honour, he can act with firmness, his portion is only the more
eminent and distinguished. In such a character, it is to his actions, not his sentiments, that we are to look for conviction. But
it may be still further urged in behalf of *Falstaff*, that there may
be false honour as well as false religion. It is true; yet even in that
case candour obliges me to confess that the best men are most
disposed to conform, and most likely to become the dupes of
their own virtue. But it may however be more reasonably urged
that there are particular tenets both in honour and religion,
which it is the grossness of folly not to question. To seek out,
to court assured destruction, without leaving a single benefit
behind, may be well reckoned in the number: And this is precisely
the very folly which *Falstaff* seems to abjure;—nor are we, perhaps, intitled to say more, in the way of censure, than that he
had not virtue enough to become the dupe of honour, nor prudence enough to hold his tongue. I am willing however, if the
reader pleases, to compound this matter, and acknowledge, on
my part, that *Falstaff* was in all respects the *old soldier*; that he
had put himself under the sober discipline of discretion, and
renounced, in a great degree at least, what he might call the
Vanities and Superstitions of honour; if the reader will, on his
part, admit that this might well be, without his renouncing,
at the same time, the natural firmness and resolution he was
born to.

But there is a formidable objection behind. *Falstaff* counterfeits
basely on being attacked by *Douglas*; he assumes, in a cowardly

spirit, the appearance of death to avoid the reality. But there was no equality of force; not the least chance for victory, or life. And is it the duty then, *think we still*, of true Courage, to meet, without benefit to society, *certain death*? Or is it only the phantasy of honour?—But such a fiction is highly disgraceful;—true, and a man of nice honour might perhaps have *grinned* for it. But we must remember that *Falstaff* had a double character; he was a *wit* as well as a *soldier*; and his Courage, however eminent, was but the *accessary*; his wit was the *principal*; and the part, which, if they should come in competition, he had the greatest interest in maintaining. Vain indeed were the licentiousness of his principles, if he should seek death like a bigot, yet without the meed of honour; when he might live by wit, and encrease the reputation of that wit by living. But why do I labour this point? It has been already anticipated, and our improved acquaintance with *Falstaff* will now require no more than a short narrative of the fact.

Whilst in the battle of *Shrewsbury* he is exhorting and encouraging the Prince who is engaged with the *Spirit Percy*— '*Well said Hal, to him Hal,*'—he is himself attacked by the *Fiend Douglas*. There was no match; nothing remained but death or stratagem; grinning honour, or laughing life. But an expedient offers, a mirthful one,—Take your choice *Falstaff*, a point of honour, or a point of drollery.—It could not be a question;— *Falstaff* falls, *Douglas* is cheated, and the world laughs. But does he fall like a Coward? No, like a buffoon only; the superior principle prevails, and *Falstaff* lives by a stratagem growing out of his character, to prove himself *no counterfeit*, to jest, to be employed, and to fight again. That *Falstaff* valued himself, and expected to be valued by others, upon this piece of saving wit, is plain. It was a stratagem, it is true; it argued presence of mind; but it was moreover, what he most liked, a very laughable joke; and as such he considers it; for he continues to counterfeit after the danger is over, that he may also deceive the Prince, and improve the event into more laughter. He might, for ought that appears, have concealed the transaction; the Prince was too earnestly engaged for observation; he might have formed a thousand excuses for his fall; but he lies still and listens to the pronouncing of his epitaph by the Prince with all the waggish glee and levity of his character. The circumstance of his wounding *Percy* in the thigh, and carrying the dead body on his back like luggage, is *indecent* but not cowardly. The declaring, though in jest, that he killed *Percy*, seems to me *idle*, but it is not meant or calculated for *imposition*; it is spoken to the *Prince himself*, the man in the world who could not be, or be supposed to be, imposed on. But we must hear, whether to the purpose or not, what it is that *Harry* has to say over the remains of his old friend.

> *P. Hen.* What, old acquaintance! could not all this flesh
> Keep in a little life? Poor *Jack*, farewell!
> I could have better spared a better man.
> Oh! I shou'd have a heavy miss of thee,
> If I were much in love with vanity.
> Death hath not struck so fat a *deer* to-day,
> Tho' many a *dearer* in this bloody fray;
> Imbowelled will I see thee by and by;
> Till then, in blood by noble *Percy* lye.

This is wonderfully proper for the occasion; it is affectionate, it is pathetic, yet it remembers his vanities, and, with a faint gleam of recollected mirth, even his plumpness and corpulency; but it is a pleasantry softned and rendered even vapid by tenderness, and it goes off in the sickly effort of a miserable pun.[1]— But to our immediate purpose,—why is not his Cowardice remembered too? what, no surprize that *Falstaff* should lye by the

---

[1] The censure commonly passed on *Shakespeare's puns*, is, I think, not well founded. I remember but very few, which are undoubtedly his, that may not be justifyed; and if *so*, a greater instance cannot be given of the art which he so peculiarly possessed of converting base things into excellence.
> 'For if the Jew doth cut but deep enough,
> 'I'll pay the forfeiture *with all my heart*.'
A play upon words is the most that can be expected from one who affects gaiety under the pressure of severe misfortunes; but so imperfect, so broken a gleam, can only serve more plainly to disclose the gloom and darkness of the mind; it is an effort of fortitude, which, failing in its operation, becomes the truest, because the most unaffected *pathos*; and a skilful actor, well managing his tone and action, might with this miserable pun steep a whole audience suddenly in tears.

side of the noble *Percy* in the bed of honour! No reflection that flight, though unfettered by disease, could not avail; that fear could not find a subterfuge from death? Shall his corpulency and his vanities be recorded, and his more characteristic quality of Cowardice, even in the moment that it particularly demanded notice and reflection, be forgotten? If by sparing a better man be here meant a *better soldier*, there is no doubt but there were better Soldiers in the army, more active, more young, more principled, more knowing; but none, it seems, taken for all in all, more acceptable. The comparative *better* used here leaves to *Falstaff* the praise at least of *good*; and to be a good soldier, is to be a great way from Coward. But *Falstaff*'s goodness, in this sort, appears to have been not only enough to redeem him from disgrace, but to mark him with reputation; if I was to add with *eminence* and *distinction*, the funeral honours which are intended his obsequies, and his being bid, till then, *to lye in blood by the noble Percy*, would fairly bear me out.

Upon the whole of the passages yet before us, why may I not reasonably hope that the good natured reader (and I write to no other), not offended at the levity of this exercise, may join with me in thinking that the character of *Falstaff*, as to valour, may be fairly and honestly summed up in the very words which he himself uses to *Harry*; and which seem, as to this point, to be intended by *Shakespeare* as a *Compendium* of his character. '*What*,' says the Prince, '*a Coward, Sir John Paunch!*' *Falstaff* replies, '*Indeed I am not* John of Gaunt *your grandfather, but yet* no Coward, '*Hal.*'

The robbery at *Gads-Hill* comes now to be considered. But *here*, after such long argumentation, we may be allowed to breath a little.

I know not what Impression has been made on the reader; a good deal of evidence has been produced, and much more remains to be offered. But how many sorts of men are there whom no evidence can persuade! How many, who, ignorant of *Shakespeare*, or forgetful of the text, may as well read heathen Greek, or the laws of the land, as this unfortunate Commentary? How

many, who, proud and pedantic, hate all novelty, and damn it
without mercy under one compendious word, Paradox? How
many more, who, not deriving their opinions immediately from
the sovereignty of reason, hold at the will of some superior
lord, to whom accident or inclination has attached them, and
who, true to their vassalage, are resolute not to surrender, without express permission, their base and ill-gotten possessions.
These, however habited, are the mob of mankind, who hoot and
holla, hiss or huzza, just as their various leaders may direct. I
challenge the whole Pannel as not holding by free tenure, and
therefore not competent to the purpose either of condemnation
or acquittal. But to the men of very nice honour what shall be
said? I speak not of your men of good service, but such as Mr.
* * * * '*Souls made of fire*, and *children of the sun.*' These gentlemen,
I am sadly afraid, cannot in honour or prudence admit of any
composition in the very nice article of Courage; *suspicion* is *disgrace*, and they cannot stay to parley with dishonour. The misfortune in cases of this kind is that it is not easy to obtain a fair
and impartial Jury: When we censure others with an eye to our
own applause, we are as seldom sparing of reproach, as inquisitive
into circumstance; and bold is the man who, tenacious of justice,
shall venture to weigh circumstances, or draw lines of distinction
between Cowardice and any apparently similar or neighbour
quality: As well may a lady, virgin or matron, of immaculate
honour, presume to pity or palliate the soft failing of some
unguarded friend, and thereby confess, as it were, those sym-
pathetic feelings which it behoves her to conceal under the most
contemptuous disdain; a disdain, always proportioned, I believe,
to a certain consciousness which we must not explain. I am afraid
that poor *Falstaff* has suffered not a little, and may yet suffer by
this fastidiousness of temper. But though we may find these
classes of men rather unfavourable to our wishes, the Ladies, one
may hope, whose smiles are most worth our ambition, may be
found more propitious; yet they too, through a generous conformity to the *brave*, are apt to take up the high tone of honour.
Heroism is an idea perfectly conformable to the natural delicacy

and elevation of their minds. Should we be fortunate enough therefore to redeem *Falstaff* from the imputations of Cowardice, yet plain Courage, I am afraid, will not serve the turn: Even their heroes, I think, must be for the most part in the bloom of youth, or *just where youth ends, in manhood's freshest prime*; but to be '*Old, cold,* '*and of intolerable entrails; to be fat and greasy; as poor as Job, and as* '*slanderous as Satan*';—Take him away, he merits not a fair trial; he is too offensive to be turned, too odious to be touched. I grant, indeed, that the subject of our lecture is not without his infirmity; '*He cuts three inches on the ribs, he was short-winded*,' and his breath possibly not of the sweetest. '*He had the gout*,' or something worse, '*which played the rogue with his great toe*.'—But these considerations are not to the point; we shall conceal, as much as may be, these offences; our business is with his *heart* only, which, as we shall endeavour to demonstrate, lies in the right place, and is firm and sound, notwithstanding a few indications to the contrary.—As for you, Mrs. MONTAGUE, I am grieved to find that *you* have been involved in a popular error; so much you must allow me to say;—for the rest, I bow to your genius and your virtues: You have given to the world a very elegant composition; and I am told your manners and your mind are yet more pure, more elegant than your book. *Falstaff* was too gross, too infirm, for your inspection; but if you durst have looked nearer, you would not have found Cowardice in the number of his infirmities.—We will try if we cannot redeem him from this universal censure.—Let the venal corporation of authors duck *to the golden fool*, let them shape their sordid quills to the mercenary ends of unmerited praise, or of baser detraction;—*old Jack*, though deserted by princes, though censured by an ungrateful world, and persecuted from age to age by Critic and Commentator, and though never rich enough to hire one literary prostitute, shall find a Voluntary defender; and that too at a time when the whole body of the *Nabobry* demands and requires defence; whilst their ill-gotten and almost untold gold feels loose in their unassured grasp, and whilst they are ready to shake off portions of the enormous heap, that they may the more securely clasp the remainder.—But not to digress without end,—to the candid, to the chearful, to the elegant reader we appeal; our exercise is much too light for the sour eye of strict severity; it professes amusement only, but we hope of a kind more rational than the History of Miss *Betsy*, eked out with the Story of Miss *Lucy*, and the Tale of Mr. *Twankum*: And so, in a leisure hour, and with the good natured reader, it may be hoped, to friend, we return, with an air as busy and important as if we were engaged in the grave office of measuring the *Pyramids*, or settling the antiquity of *Stonehenge*, to converse with this jovial, this fat, this roguish, this frail, but, I think, *not cowardly* companion.

Though the robbery at *Gads-Hill*, and the supposed Cowardice of *Falstaff* on that occasion, are next to be considered, yet I must previously declare, that I think the discussion of this matter to be *now* unessential to the re-establishment of *Falstaff*'s reputation as a man of Courage. For suppose we should grant, in form, that *Falstaff* was surprized with fear in this single instance, that he was off his guard, and even acted like a Coward; what will follow, but that *Falstaff*, like greater heroes, had his weak moment, and was not exempted from panic and surprize? If a single exception can destroy a general character, *Hector* was a *Coward*, and *Anthony* a *Poltroon*. But for these seeming contradictions of Character we shall seldom be at a loss to account, if we carefully refer to circumstance and situation.—In the present instance, *Falstaff* had done an illegal act; the exertion was over; and he had unbent his mind in security. The spirit of enterprize, and the animating principle of hope, were withdrawn:—In this situation, he is unexpectedly attacked; he has no time to recall his thoughts, or bend his mind to action. He is not now acting in the Profession and in the Habits of a Soldier; he is associated with known Cowards; his assailants are vigorous, sudden, and bold; he is conscious of guilt; he has dangers to dread of every form, present and future; prisons and gibbets, as well as sword and fire; he is surrounded with darkness, and the Sheriff, the Hangman, and the whole *Posse Commitatus* may be at his heels:—

Without a moment for reflection, is it wonderful that, under these circumstances, '*he should run and roar, and carry his guts* '*away with as much dexterity as possible*'?

But though I might well rest the question on this ground, yet as there remains many good topics of vindication, and as I think a more minute inquiry into this matter will only bring out more evidence in support of *Falstaff*'s constitutional Courage, I will not decline the discussion. I beg permission therefore to state fully, as well as fairly, the whole of this obnoxious transaction, this unfortunate robbery at *Gads-Hill*.

In the scene wherein we become first acquainted with *Falstaff*, his character is opened in a manner worthy of *Shakespeare*: We see him in a green old age, mellow, frank, gay, easy, corpulent, loose, unprincipled, and luxurious; a *Robber*, as he says, *by his vocation*; yet not altogether so:—There was much, it seems, of mirth and *recreation* in the case: '*The poor abuses of the times*,' he wantonly and humourously tells the Prince, '*want countenance;* '*and he hates to see resolution fobbed off, as it is, by the rusty curb of old* '*father antic, the law.*'—When he quits the scene, we are acquaint-ed that he is only passing to the Tavern: '*Farewell*,' says he, with an air of careless jollity and gay content, '*You will find me in* '*East-Cheap.*' '*Farewell*,' says the Prince, '*thou latter spring; farewell,* '*all-hallown summer.*' But though all this is excellent for *Shakespeare*'s purposes, we find, as yet at least, no hint of *Falstaff*'s Cowardice, no appearance of Braggadocio, or any preparation whatever for laughter under this head.—The instant *Falstaff* is withdrawn, *Poins* opens to the Prince his meditated scheme of a double rob-bery; and here then we may reasonably expect to be let into these parts of *Falstaff*'s character.—We shall see.

Poins. '*Now my good sweet lord, ride with us tomorrow; I have a jest* '*to execute that I cannot manage alone.* Falstaff, Bardolph, Peto, *and* '*Gadshill shall rob those men that we have already waylaid; yourself* '*and I will not be there; and when they have the booty, if you and I do* '*not rob them, cut this head from off my shoulders.*'

This is giving strong surety for his words; perhaps he thought the case required it: '*But how*,' says the Prince, '*shall we part*

'*with them in setting forth?*' *Poins* is ready with his answer; he had
matured the thought, and could solve every difficulty:—'*They*
'*could set out before, or after; their horses might be tied in the wood;*
'*they could change their visors; and he had already procured cases of*
'buckram *to inmask their outward garments.*' This was going far;
it was doing business in good earnest. But if we look into the
Play we shall be better able to account for this activity; we shall
find that there was at least as much malice as jest in *Poins*'s intention. The rival situations of *Poins* and *Falstaff* had produced
on both sides much jealousy and ill will, which occasionally
appears, in *Shakespeare*'s manner, by side lights, without con-
founding the main action; and by the little we see of this *Poins*,
he appears to be an unamiable, if not a very brutish and bad,
character.—But to pass this;—the Prince next says, with a
deliberate and wholesome caution, '*I doubt they will be too hard*
'*for us.*' *Poins*'s reply is remarkable; '*Well, for two of them, I know*
'*them to be as true bred Cowards as ever turned back; and for the* third,
'*if he fights longer than he sees cause, I will forswear arms.*' There is in
this reply a great deal of management: There were *four* persons
in all, as *Poins* well knew, and he had himself, but a little before,
named them,—*Falstaff, Bardolph, Peto,* and *Gadshill*; but now he
omits one of the number, which must be either *Falstaff,* as not
subject to any imputation in point of Courage; and in that case
Peto will be the *third*;—or, as I rather think, in order to diminish
the force of the Prince's objection, he artfully drops *Gadshill*, who
was then out of town, and might therefore be supposed to be
less in the Prince's notice; and upon this supposition *Falstaff* will
be the *third, who will not fight longer than he sees reason.* But on either
supposition, what evidence is there of a pre-supposed Cowardice
in *Falstaff?* On the contrary, what stronger evidence can we
require that the Courage of *Falstaff* had to this hour, through
various trials, stood wholly unimpeached, than that *Poins*, the
ill-disposed *Poins*, who ventures, for his own purposes, to steal,
as it were, *one* of the *four* from the notice and memory of the
Prince, and who shews himself, from worse motives, as skilfull
in *diminishing* as *Falstaff* appears afterwards to be in *increasing* of

numbers, than that this very *Poins* should not venture to put down *Falstaff* in the list of Cowards; though the occasion so strongly required that he should be degraded. What *Poins* dares do however in this sort, he *does*. '*As to the third*,' for so he describes *Falstaff* (as if the name of this Veteran would have excited too strongly the ideas of Courage and resistance), '*if he fights longer than he sees reason, I will forswear arms.*' This is the old trick of cautious and artful malice: The turn of expression, or the tone of voice does all; for as to the words themselves, simply considered, they might be now truly spoken of almost any man who ever lived, except the iron-headed hero of *Sweden.*—But *Poins* however adds something, which may appear more decisive; '*The virtue of this jest will be the incomprehensible lyes which this fat* '*rogue will tell when we meet at supper; how thirty at least he fought* '*with; and what wards, what blows, what extremities, he endured: And* '*in the reproof of this lies the jest*':—Yes, and the *malice* too.—This prediction was unfortunately fulfilled, even beyond the letter of it; a completion more incident, perhaps, to the predictions of malice than of affection. But we shall presently see how far either the prediction, or the event, will go to the impeachment of *Falstaff*'s Courage.—The Prince, who is never duped, comprehends the whole of *Poins*'s views. But let that pass.

In the next scene we behold all the parties at *Gads-Hill* in preparation for the robbery. Let us carefully examine if it contains any intimation of Cowardice in *Falstaff*. He is shewn under a very ridiculous vexation about his horse, which is hid from him; but this is nothing to the purpose, or only proves that *Falstaff* knew no terror equal to that of walking *eight yards of uneven ground.* But on occasion of *Gadshill*'s being asked concerning the number of the travellers, and having reported that they were eight or ten, *Falstaff* exclaims, '*Zounds! will they not rob us!*' If he had said more seriously, '*I doubt they will be too hard for us*,' —he would then have only used the Prince's own words upon a less alarming occasion. This cannot need defence. But the Prince, in his usual stile of mirth, replies, '*What a Coward, Sir* '*John Paunch!*' To this one would naturally expect from *Falstaff*

some light answer; but we are surprized with a very serious one;
—'*I am not indeed* John of Gaunt *your grandfather, but yet no*
'Coward, Hal.' This is singular: It contains, I think, the true
character of *Falstaff*; and it seems to be thrown out *here*, at a very
critical conjuncture, as a caution to the audience not to take too
sadly what was intended only (to use the Prince's words) '*as*
'*argument for a week, laughter for a month, and a good jest for ever*
'*after.*' The whole of *Falstaff*'s past life could not, it should seem,
furnish the Prince with a reply, and he is, therefore, obliged to
draw upon the coming hope. '*Well,*' says he, *mysteriously,* '*let the*
'*event try*'; meaning the event of the concerted attack on *Falstaff*;
an event so probable, that he might indeed venture to rely on it.
—But the travellers approach: The Prince hastily proposes a
division of strength; that he with *Poins* should take a station
separate from the rest, so that if the travellers should escape one
party, they might light on the other: *Falstaff* does not object,
though he supposes the travellers to be eight or ten in number.
We next see *Falstaff* attack these travellers with alacrity, using
the accustomed words of threat and terror;—they make no
resistance, and he binds and robs them.

Hitherto I think there has not appeared the least *trait* either
of boast or fear in *Falstaff.* But now comes on the concerted
transaction, which has been the source of so much dishonour.
As they are sharing the booty (says the stage direction) *the Prince
and* Poins *set upon them, they all run away; and* Falstaff *after a blow or
two runs away too, leaving the booty behind them.*—'*Got with much*
'*ease,*' says the Prince, as an event beyond expectation, '*Now*
'*merrily to horse.*'—Poins adds, as they are going off, '*How the*
'*rogue roared!*' This observation is afterwards remembered by the
Prince, who, urging the jest to *Falstaff,* says, doubtless with all
the licence of exaggeration,—'*And you,* Falstaff, *carried your guts*
'*away as nimbly, with as quick dexterity, and roared for mercy, and still*
'*ran and roared, as I ever heard bull-calf.*' If he did roar for mercy, it
must have been a very inarticulate sort of roaring; for there is
not a single word set down for *Falstaff* from which this roaring
may be inferred, or any stage direction to the actor for that

purpose: But, in the spirit of mirth and derision, the lightest exclamation might be easily converted into the roar of a bull-calf.

We have now gone through this transaction considered simply on its own circumstances, and without reference to any future boast or imputation. It is upon these circumstances the case must be tried, and every colour subsequently thrown on it, either by wit or folly, ought to be discharged. Take it, then, as it stands hitherto, with reference only to its own preceding and concomitant circumstances, and to the unbounded ability of *Shakespeare* to obtain his own ends, and we must, I think, be compelled to confess that this transaction was never intended by *Shakespeare* to detect and expose the false pretences of a real Coward; but, on the contrary, to involve a man of allowed Courage, though in other respects of a very peculiar character, in such circumstances and suspicions of Cowardice as might, by the operation of those peculiarities, produce afterwards much temporary mirth among his familiar and intimate companions: Of this we cannot require a stronger proof than the great attention which is paid to the decorum and truth of character in the stage direction already quoted: It appears, from thence, that it was not thought *decent* that *Falstaff* should run at all, until he had been deserted by his companions, and had even afterwards exchanged blows with his assailants;—and thus, a just distinction is kept up between the natural Cowardice of the three associates and the accidental Terror of *Falstaff*.

Hitherto, then, I think it is very clear that no laughter either is, or is intended to be, raised upon the score of *Falstaff*'s Cowardice. For after all, it is not singularly ridiculous that an old inactive man of no boast, as far as appears, or extraordinary pretensions to valour, should endeavour to save himself by flight from the assault of two bold and vigorous assailants. The very Players, who are, I think, the very worst judges of *Shakespeare*, have been made sensible, I suppose from long experience, that there is nothing in this transaction to excite any extraordinary laughter; but this they take to be a defect in the management of their author, and therefore I imagine it is, that they hold themselves obliged to supply the vacancy, and fill it up with some low buffoonery of their own. Instead of the dispatch necessary on this occasion, they bring *Falstaff*, *stuffing and all*, to the very front of the stage; where, with much mummery and grimace, he seats himself down, with a canvas money-bag in his hand, to divide the spoil. In this situation he is attacked by the *Prince* and *Poins*, whose tin swords hang idly in the air and delay to strike till the *Player Falstaff*, who seems more troubled with flatulence than fear, is able to rise: which is not till after some ineffectual efforts, and with the assistance (to the best of my memory) of one of the thieves, who lingers behind, in spite of terror, for this friendly purpose; after which, without any resistance on his part, he is goaded off the stage like a fat ox for slaughter by these *stony-hearted* drivers in *buckram*. I think he does not *roar*;—perhaps the player had never perfected himself in the tones of a bull-calf. This whole transaction should be shewn between the interstices of a back scene: The less we see in such cases, the better we conceive. Something of resistance and afterwards of celerity in flight we should be made witnesses of; the *roar* we should take on the credit of *Poins*. Nor is there any occasion for all that bolstering with which they fill up the figure of *Falstaff*; they do not distinguish betwixt humourous exaggeration and necessary truth. The Prince is called *starveling, dried neat's tongue, stockfish*, and other names of the same nature. They might with almost as good reason search the glass-houses for some exhausted stoker to furnish out a Prince of *Wales* of sufficient correspondence to this picture.

We next come to the scene of *Falstaff*'s braggadocioes. I have already wandered too much into details; yet I must, however, bring *Falstaff* forward to this last scene of trial in all his proper colouring and proportions. The progressive discovery of *Falstaff*'s character is excellently managed.—In the first scene we become acquainted with his figure, which we must in some degree consider as a part of his character; we hear of his gluttony and his debaucheries, and become witnesses of that indistinguishable mixture of humour and licentiousness which runs through his whole character; but what we are principally struck with, is the ease of his manners and deportment, and the unaffected freedom and wonderful pregnancy of his wit and humour. We see him, in the next scene, agitated with vexation: His horse is concealed from him, and he gives on this occasion so striking a description of his distress, and his words so labour and are so loaded with heat and vapour, that, but for laughing, we should pity him; laugh, however, we must at the extreme incongruity of a man, at once corpulent and old, associating with youth in an enterprize demanding the utmost extravagance of spirit, and all the wildness of activity: And this it is which makes his complaints so truly ridiculous. '*Give me my horse!*' says he, in another spirit than that of *Richard*; '*Eight yards of uneven ground,*' adds this *Forrester of Diana*, this *enterprizing gentleman of the shade*, '*is threescore and ten miles* a-foot *with me.*'—In the heat and agitation of the robbery, out comes more and more extravagant instances of incongruity. Though he is most probably older and much fatter than either of the travellers, yet he calls them, *Bacons*, *Bacon-fed, and gorbellied knaves*: '*Hang them,*' says he, '*fat chuffs, they* '*hate us youth: What! young men, must live:—You are grand Jurors,* '*are ye? We'll jure ye, i' faith.*' But, as yet, we do not see the whole length and breadth of him: This is reserved for the braggadocio scene. We expect entertainment, but we don't well know of what kind. *Poins*, by his prediction, has given us a hint: But we do not see or feel *Falstaff* to be a Coward, much less a boaster; without which even Cowardice is not sufficiently ridiculous; and therefore it is, that on the stage we find them always connected. In this uncertainty on our part, he is, with much artful preparation, produced.—His entrance is delayed to stimulate our expectation; and, at last, to take off the dullness of anticipation, and to add surprize to pleasure, he is called in, as if for another purpose of mirth than what we are furnished with: We now behold him, fluctuating with fiction, and labouring with dissembled passion and chagrin: Too full for utterance, *Poins* provokes him by a few simple words, containing a fine contrast of affected ease,— '*Welcome,* Jack, *where hast thou been?*' But when we hear him burst forth, '*A plague on all Cowards! Give me a cup of sack. Is there no 'virtue extant!*'—We are at once in possession of the whole man, and are ready to hug him, guts, lyes and all, as an inexhaustible fund of pleasantry and humour. *Cowardice*, I apprehend, is out of our thought; it does not, I think, mingle in our mirth. As to this point, I have presumed to say already, and I repeat it, that we are, in my opinion, the dupes of our own wisdom, of systematic reasoning, of second thought, and after reflection. The first spectators, I believe, thought of nothing but the laughable scrape which so singular a character was falling into, and were delighted to see a humourous and unprincipled wit so happily taken in his own inventions, precluded from all rational defence, and driven to the necessity of crying out, after a few ludicrous evasions, '*No more of that*, Hal, *if thou lov'st me.*'

I do not conceive myself obliged to enter into a consideration of *Falstaff's* lyes concerning the transaction at *Gad's-Hill*. I have considered his conduct as independent of those lyes; I have examined the whole of it apart, and found it free of Cowardice or fear, except in one instance, which I have endeavoured to account for and excuse. I have therefore a right to infer that those lyes are to be derived, not from Cowardice, but from some other part of his character, which it does not concern me to examine: But I have not contented myself hitherto with this sort of negative defence; and the reader I believe is aware that I am resolute (though I confess not untired) to carry this fat rogue out of the reach of every imputation which affects, or may seem to affect, his natural Courage.

The first observation then which strikes us, as to his braggadocioes, is, that they are braggadocioes *after the fact*. In other cases we see the Coward of the Play bluster and boast for a time, talk of distant wars, and private duels, out of the reach of knowledge and of evidence; of storms and stratagems, and of falling in upon the enemy pell-mell and putting thousands to the sword; till, at length, on the proof of some present and apparent fact, he is brought to open and *lasting* shame; to shame I mean as a *Coward*; for as to what there is of *lyar* in the case, it is considered only as accessory, and scarcely reckoned into the account of dis-honour.—But in the instance before us, every thing is reversed: The Play opens with the *Fact*; a Fact, from its circumstances as well as from the age and inactivity of the man, very excusable and capable of much apology, if not of defence. This Fact is preceded by no bluster or pretence whatever;—the lyes and braggadocioes follow; but they are not *general*; they are confined and have reference to this one Fact only; the detection is *immediate*; and after some accompanying mirth and laughter, the shame of that detection ends; it has no *duration*, as in other cases; and, for the rest of the Play, the character stands just where it did before, *without any punishment or degradation whatever*.

To account for all this, let us only suppose that *Falstaff* was a man of natural Courage, though in all respects unprincipled; but that he was surprized in one single instance into an act of real terror; which, instead of excusing upon circumstances, he endeavours to cover by lyes and braggadocio; and that these lyes become thereupon the subject, in this place, of detection. Upon these suppositions the whole difficulty will vanish at once, and every thing be natural, common, and plain. The *Fact* itself will be of course *excusable*; that is, it will arise out of a combination of such circumstances as, being applicable to one case only, will not destroy the general character: It will not be *preceded* by any braggadocio, containing any fair indication of Cowardice; as real Cowardice is not supposed to exist in the character. But the first act of real or apparent Cowardice would naturally throw a vain unprincipled man into the use of lyes and braggadocio; but these would have reference only to the *Fact in question*, and not apply to other cases or infect his general character, which is not supposed to stand in need of imposition. Again,—the detection of Cowardice as such, is more diverting after a long and various course of Pretence, where the lye of character is preserved, as it were, whole, and brought into sufficient magnitude for a burst of discovery; yet, mere occasional lyes, such as *Falstaff* is hereby supposed to utter, are, for the purpose of sport, best detected in the telling; because, indeed, they cannot be preserved for a

future time; the exigence and the humour will be past: But the
shame arising to *Falstaff* from the detection of *mere lyes* would be
temporary only; his character as to this point, being already known,
and *tolerated for the humour*. Nothing, therefore, could follow but
mirth and laughter, and the temporary triumph of baffling a wit
at his own weapons, and reducing him to an absolute surrender:
After which, we ought not to be surprized if we see him rise
again, like a boy from play, and run another race with as little
dishonour as before.

What then can we say, but that it is clearly the lyes only, not
the *Cowardice*, of *Falstaff* which are here detected: *Lyes*, to which
what there may be of Cowardice is incidental only, improving
indeed the Jest, but by no means the real Business of the scene.—
And now also we may more clearly discern the true force and
meaning of *Poins*'s prediction. '*The Jest will be*,' says he, '*the*
'*incomprehensible Lyes that this fat rogue will tell us: How thirty at*
'*least he fought with:—and in the reproof of this lyes the jest*'; That is,
in the detection of these lyes *simply*; for as to *Courage*, he had never
ventured to insinuate more than that *Falstaff* would not fight
longer than he saw cause: *Poins* was in expectation indeed that
Falstaff would fall into some dishonour on this occasion; an event
highly probable: But this was not, it seems, to be the principal
ground of their mirth, but the detection of those *incomprehensible
lyes*, which he boldly predicts, upon his knowledge of *Falstaff*'s
character, this *fat rogue*, not *Coward*, would tell them. This
prediction therefore, and the completion of it, go only to the
impeachment of *Falstaff*'s *veracity*, and not of his *Courage*. '*These*
'*lyes*,' says the Prince, '*are like the father of them, gross as a mountain,*
'*open, palpable.—Why, thou clay-brained gutts, thou knotty-pated*
'*fool; how couldst thou know these men in Kendal Green, when it was so*
'*dark thou couldst not see thy hand? Come, tell us your reason.*'
    '*Poins. Come, your reason*, Jack, *your reason.*'
    Again, says the Prince, '*Hear how a plain Tale shall put you down—*
'*What trick, what device, what starting hole canst thou now find out to*
'*hide thee from this open and apparent shame?*'
    '*Poins. Come, let's hear*, Jack, *what trick hast thou now?*'

All this clearly refers to *Falstaff*'s lyes only *as such*; and the objection seems to be, that he had not told them well, and with sufficient skill and probability. Indeed nothing seems to have been required of *Falstaff* at any period of time but a good evasion. The truth is, that there is so much mirth, and so little of malice or imposition in his fictions, that they may for the most part be considered as mere strains of humour and exercises of wit, impeachable only for defect, when that happens, of the quality from which they are principally derived. Upon this occasion *Falstaff*'s evasions fail him; he is at the end of his invention; and it seems fair that, in defect of wit, the law should pass upon him, and that he should undergo the temporary censure of that Cowardice which he could not pass off by any evasion whatever. The best he could think of, was *instinct*: He was indeed a *Coward upon instinct*; in that respect *like a valiant lion, who would not touch the true Prince*. It would have been a vain attempt, the reader will easily perceive, in *Falstaff*, to have gone upon other ground, and to have aimed at justifying his Courage by a serious vindication: This would have been to have mistaken the true point of argument: It was his *lyes*, not his *Courage*, which was really in question. There was besides no getting out of the toils in which he had entangled himself: If he was not, he ought at least, by his own shewing, to have *been at half-sword with a dozen of them two hours together*; whereas, it unfortunately appears, and that too evidently to be evaded, that he had run with singular celerity from *two*, after the exchange of *a few blows* only. This precluded *Falstaff* from all rational defence in his own person;—but it has not precluded me, who am not the advocate of his *lyes*, but of his *Courage*.

But there are other singularities in *Falstaff*'s lyes, which go more directly to his vindication.—That they are confined to one scene and one occasion only, we are not *now* at a loss to account for;—but what shall we say to their extravagance? The lyes of *Parolles* and *Bobadill* are brought into some shape; but the fictions of *Falstaff* are so preposterous and *incomprehensible*, that one may fairly doubt if they ever were intended for credit; and therefore, if they ought to be called *lyes*, and not rather *humour*; or, to compound the matter, *humourous rhodomontades*. Certain it is, that they destroy their own purpose, and are clearly not the effect, in this respect, of a regulated practice, and a habit of imposition. The real truth seems to be, that had *Falstaff*, loose and unprincipled as he is, been born a Coward and bred a Soldier, he must, naturally, have been a great *Braggadocio*, a true *miles gloriosus*. But in such case he should have been exhibited active and young; for it is plain that age and corpulency are an excuse for Cowardice, which ought not to be afforded him. In the present case, wherein he was not only involved in suspicious circumstances, but wherein he seems to have felt some conscious touch of infirmity, and having no candid construction to expect from his laughing companions, he bursts at once, and with all his might, into the most unweighed and preposterous fictions, determined to put to proof on this occasion his boasted talent of *swearing truth out of England*. He tried it here, to its utmost extent, and was unfortunately routed on his own ground; which indeed, with such a mine beneath his feet, could not be otherwise. But without this, he had mingled in his deceits so much whimsical humour and fantastic exaggeration that he must have been detected; and herein appears the admirable address of *Shakespeare*, who can shew us *Falstaff* in the various light, not only of what he is, but what he would have been under one single variation of character,—the want of natural Courage; whilst with an art not enough understood, he most effectually preserves the real character of *Falstaff* even in the moment he seems to depart from it, by making his lyes too extravagant for practised imposition; by grounding them more upon humour than deceit; and turning them, as we shall next see, into a fair and honest proof of general Courage, by appropriating them to the concealment only of a single exception. And hence it is, that we see him draw so deeply and so confidently upon his former credit for Courage and atchievment: '*I never dealt better in my life,—thou know'st* '*my old ward, Hal,*' are expressions which clearly refer to some known feats and defences of his former life. His exclamations against Cowardice, his reference to his own manhood, '*Die when* '*thou wilt, old* Jack, *if manhood, good manhood, be not forgot upon the* '*face of the earth, then am I a shotten herring*': These, and various expressions such as these, would be absurdities not impositions, Farce not Comedy, if not calculated to conceal some defect supposed unknown to the hearers; and these hearers were, in the present case, his constant companions, and the daily witnesses of his conduct. If before this period he had been a known and detected Coward, and was conscious that he had no credit to lose, I see no reason why he should fly so violently from a familiar ignominy which had often before attacked him; or why falshoods, seemingly in such a case neither calculated for or expecting credit, should be censured, or detected, as lyes or imposition.

That the whole transaction was considered as a mere jest, and as carrying with it no serious imputation on the Courage of *Falstaff*, is manifest, not only from his being allowed, when the laugh was past, to call himself, without contradiction in the personated character of *Hal* himself, 'valiant *Jack Falstaff, and the* '*more* valiant *being, as he is,* old Jack Falstaff,' but from various other particulars, and, above all, from the declaration, which the Prince makes on that very night, of his intention of procuring this *fat rogue a Charge of foot*;—a circumstance, doubtless, contrived by *Shakespeare* to wipe off the seeming dishonour of the day: And from this time forward we hear of no imputation arising from this transaction; it is born and dies in a convivial hour; it leaves no trace behind, nor do we see any longer in the character of *Falstaff* the boasting or braggadocio of a Coward.

Tho' I have considered *Falstaff*'s character as relative only to one single quality, yet so much has been said, that it cannot escape the reader's notice that he is a character made up by *Shakespeare* wholly of incongruities;—a man at once young and old, enterprizing and fat, a dupe and a wit, harmless and wicked, weak in principle and resolute by constitution, cowardly in appearance and brave in reality; a knave without malice, a lyar without deceit; and a knight, a gentleman, and a soldier, without either dignity, decency, or honour: This is a character, which, though it may be de-compounded, could not, I believe, have been formed, nor the ingredients of it duly mingled, upon any receipt whatever: It required the hand of *Shakespeare* himself to give to every particular part a relish of the whole, and of the whole to every particular part;—alike the same incongruous, identical *Falstaff*, whether to the grave Chief Justice he vainly talks of his youth, and offers to *caper for a thousand*; or cries to Mrs. *Doll*, 'I am old, I am old,' though she is seated on his lap, and he is courting her for busses. How *Shakespeare* could furnish out sentiment of so extraordinary a composition, and supply it with such appropriated and characteristic language, humour and wit, I cannot tell; but I may, however, venture to infer, and that confidently, that he who so well understood the uses of incongruity, and that laughter was to be raised by the opposition of qualities in the same man, and not by their agreement or conformity, would never have attempted to raise mirth by shewing us Cowardice in a Coward unattended by Pretence, and softened by every excuse of age, corpulence, and infirmity: And of this we cannot have a more striking proof than his furnishing this very character, on one instance of real terror, however excusable, with boast, braggadocio, and pretence, exceeding that of all other stage Cowards the whole length of his superior wit, humour, and invention.

What then upon the whole shall be said but that *Shakespeare* has made certain Impressions, or produced certain effects, of which he has thought fit to conceal or obscure the cause? How he has done this, and for what special ends, we shall now presume to guess.—Before the period in which *Shakespeare* wrote, the fools and Zanys of the stage were drawn out of the coarsest and cheapest materials: Some essential folly, with a dash of knave and coxcomb, did the feat. But *Shakespeare*, who delighted in difficulties, was resolved to furnish a richer repast, and to give to one eminent buffoon the high relish of wit, humour, birth, dignity, and Courage. But this was a process which required the nicest hand, and the utmost management and address: These enumerated qualities are, in their own nature, productive of

respect; an Impression the most opposite to laughter that can be.
This Impression then, it was, at all adventures, necessary to with-
hold; which could not perhaps well be without dressing up these
qualities in fantastic forms, and colours not their own; and thereby cheating the eye with shews of baseness and of folly, whilst he
stole as it were upon the palate a richer and a fuller *goût*. To this
end, what arts, what contrivances, has he not practised! How
has he steeped this singular character in bad habits for fifty years
together, and brought him forth saturated with every folly and
with every vice not destructive of his essential character, or incompatible with his own primary design! For this end, he has
deprived *Falstaff* of every good principle; and for another, which
will be presently mentioned, he has concealed every bad one. He
has given him also every infirmity of body that is not likely to
awaken our compassion, and which is most proper to render both
his better qualities and his vices ridiculous: he has associated
levity and debauch with *age*, corpulence and inactivity with
courage, and has roguishly coupled the gout with *Military
honours*, and a *pension* with the *pox*. He has likewise involved this
character in situations, out of which neither wit nor Courage
can extricate him with honour. The surprize at *Gads-Hill* might
have betrayed a hero into flight, and the encounter with
Douglas left him no choice but death or stratagem. If he plays an
after-game, and endeavours to redeem his ill fortune by lyes and
braggadocio, his ground fails him; no wit, no evasion will avail:
Or is he likely to appear respectable in his person, rank, and
demeanor, how is that respect abated or discharged! *Shakespeare*
has given him a kind of state indeed; but of what is it composed?
Of that fustian cowardly rascal *Pistol*, and his yoke-fellow of few
words, the equally deedless *Nym*; of his cup-bearer the fiery
Trigon, whose zeal burns in his nose, *Bardolph*; and of the boy,
who bears the purse with *seven groats and two-pence*;—a boy who
was given him on purpose to set him off, and whom he walks
before, according to his own description, '*like a sow that had over-
'whelmed all her litter but one.*'

But it was not enough to render *Falstaff* ridiculous in his

figure, situations, and equipage; *still* his respectable qualities
would have come forth, at least occasionally, to spoil our mirth;
or they might have burst the intervention of such slight im-
pediments, and have every where shone through: It was necessary then to go farther, and throw on him that substantial
ridicule, which only the incongruities of real vice can furnish;
of vice, which was to be so mixed and blended with his frame as
to give a durable character and colour to the whole.

But it may here be necessary to detain the reader a moment in
order to apprize him of my further intention; without which,
I might hazard that good understanding, which I hope has
hitherto been preserved between us.

I have 'till now looked only to the Courage of *Falstaff*, a
quality which, having been denied, in terms, to belong to his
constitution, I have endeavoured to vindicate to the Understandings of my readers; the Impression on their Feelings (in
which all Dramatic truth consists) being already, as I have supposed, in favour of the character. In the pursuit of this subject I
have taken the general Impression of the whole character pretty
much, I suppose, like other men; and, when occasion has required, have so transmitted it to the reader; joining in the
common Feeling of *Falstaff*'s pleasantry, his apparent freedom
from ill principle, and his companionable wit and good humour:
With a stage character, in the article of exhibition, we have
nothing more to do; for in fact what is it but an Impression; an
appearance, which we are to consider as a reality, and which we
may venture to applaud or condemn as such, without further
inquiry or investigation? But if we would account for our Impressions, or for certain sentiments or actions in a character, not
derived from its apparent principles, yet appearing, we know
not why, natural, we are then compelled to look farther, and
examine if there be not something more in the character than is
shewn; something inferred, which is not brought under our special
notice: In short, we must look to the art of the writer, and to the
principles of human nature, to discover the hidden causes of
such effects.—Now this is a very different matter.—The former

considerations respected the Impression only, without regard to the Understanding; but this question relates to the Understanding alone. It is true that there are but few Dramatic characters which will bear this kind of investigation, as not being drawn in exact conformity to those principles of general nature to which we must refer. But this is not the case with regard to the characters of *Shakespeare*; they are struck out *whole*, by some happy art which I cannot clearly comprehend, out of the general mass of things, from the block as it were of nature: And it is, I think, an easier thing to give a just draught of man from these Theatric forms, which I cannot help considering as originals, than by drawing from real life, amidst so much intricacy, obliquity, and disguise. If therefore, for further proofs of *Falstaff*'s Courage, or for the sake of curious speculation, or for both, I change my position, and look to causes instead of effects, the reader must not be surprized if he finds the former *Falstaff* vanish like a dream, and another, of more disgustful form, presented to his view; one whose final punishment we shall be so far from regretting, that we ourselves shall be ready to consign him to a severer doom.

The reader will very easily apprehend that a character, which we might wholly disapprove of, considered as existing in human life, may yet be thrown on the stage into certain peculiar situations, and be compressed by external influences into such temporary appearances, as may render such character for a time highly acceptable and entertaining, and even more distinguished for qualities, which on this supposition would be accidents only, than another character really possessing those qualities, but which, under the pressure of the same situation and influences, would be distorted into a different form, or totally lost in timidity and weakness. If therefore the character before us will admit of this kind of investigation, our Inquiry will not be without some dignity, considered as extending to the principles of human nature, and to the genius and arts of Him, who has best caught every various form of the human mind, and transmitted them with the greatest happiness and fidelity.

To return then to the vices of *Falstaff*.—We have frequently

referred to them under the name of ill habits;—but perhaps the
reader is not fully aware how very vicious he indeed is;—he is a
robber, a glutton, a cheat, a drunkard, and a lyar; lascivious, vain,
insolent, profligate, and profane:—A fine infusion this, and such
as without very excellent cookery must have thrown into the
dish a great deal too much of the *fumet*. It was a nice operation;—
these vices were not only to be of a particular sort, but it was
also necessary to guard them at both ends; on the *one*, from all
appearance of malicious motive, and indeed from the manifesta-
tion of any ill principle whatever, which must have produced
disgust,—a sensation no less opposite to laughter than is *respect*;—
and, on the *other*, from the notice, or even apprehension, in the
spectators, of *pernicious effect*; which produces *grief* and *terror*, and
is the proper province of Tragedy alone.

Actions cannot with strict propriety be said to be either
virtuous or vicious. These qualities, or attributes, belong to
agents only; and are derived, even in respect to *them*, from intention alone. The abstracting of qualities, and considering them
as independent of any *subject*, and the applying of them afterwards to actions independent of the agent, is a double operation
which I do not pretend, thro' any part of it, to understand. All
actions may most properly, in their own nature, I think, be
called *neutral*; tho' in common discourse, and in writing where
perfection is not requisite, we often term them *vicious*, transferring on these occasions the attributive from the *agent* to the
action; and sometimes we call them *evil*, or of pernicious effect, by
transferring, in like manner, the injuries incidentally arising
from certain actions to the life, happiness, or interest of human
beings, to the natural operation, whether moral or physical, of
the *actions* themselves: *One* is a colour thrown on them by the
intention, in which I think consists all moral turpitude, and the
other by effect: If therefore a Dramatic writer will use certain
managements to keep vicious intention as much as possible
from our notice, and make us sensible that no evil effect follows,
he may pass off actions of very vicious motive, without much ill
impression, as mere *incongruities*, and the effect of *humour* only;—

words these, which, as applied to human conduct, are employed, I believe, to cover a great deal of what may deserve much harder appellation.

The *difference* between suffering an evil effect to take place, and of preventing such effect, from actions precisely of the same nature, is so great, that it is often *all the difference* between Tragedy and Comedy. The Fine gentleman of the Comic scene, who so promptly draws his sword, and wounds, without killing, some other gentleman of the same sort; and *He* of Tragedy, whose stabs are mortal, differ very frequently in no other point whatever. If our *Falstaff* had really *peppered* (as he calls it) *two rogues in buckram suits*, we must have looked for a very different conclusion, and have expected to have found *Falstaff*'s Essential prose converted into blank verse, and to have seen him move off, in slow and measured paces, like the City Prentice to the tolling of a Passing bell;—'*he would have become a cart as well as another*, '*or a plague on his bringing up.*'

Every incongruity in a rational being is a source of laughter, whether it respects manners, sentiments, conduct, or even dress, or situation;—but the greatest of all possible incongruity is vice, whether in the intention itself, or as transferred to, and becoming more manifest in action;—it is inconsistent with moral agency, nay, with rationality itself, and all the ends and purposes of our being.—Our author describes the natural ridicule of vice in his MEASURE *for* MEASURE in the strongest terms, where, after having made the angels weep over the vices of men, he adds, that *with* our spleens *they might laugh themselves quite mortal*. Indeed if we had a perfect discernment of the ends of this life only, and could preserve ourselves from sympathy, disgust, and terror, the vices of mankind would be a source of perpetual entertainment. The great difference between *Heraclitus* and *Democritus* lay, it seems, in their spleen only;—for a wise and good man must either laugh or cry without ceasing. Nor indeed is it easy to conceive (to instance in one case only) a more laughable, or a more melancholy object, than a human being, his nature and duration considered, earnestly and anxiously exchanging peace of mind and conscious integrity for gold; and for gold too, which he has often no occasion for, or dares not employ:—But *Voltaire* has by one Publication rendered all *arguments* superfluous: He has told us, in his *Candide*, the merriest and most diverting tale of frauds, murders, massacres, rapes, rapine, desolation, and destruction, that I think it possible on any other plan to invent; and he has given us *motive* and *effect*, with every possible aggravation, to improve the sport. One would think it difficult to preserve the point of ridicule, in such a case, unabated by contrary emotions; but now that the feat is performed it appears of easy imitation, and I am amazed that our race of imitators have made no efforts in this sort: It would answer I should think in the way of profit, not to mention the moral uses to which it might be applied. The managements of *Voltaire* consists in this, that he assumes a gay, easy, and light tone himself; that he never excites the reflections of his readers by making any of his own; that he hurries us on with such a rapidity of narration as prevents our emotions from resting on any particular point; and to gain this end, he has interwoven the conclusion of one fact so into the commencement of another, that we find ourselves engaged in new matter before we are sensible that we had finished the old; he has likewise made his crimes so enormous, that we do not sadden on any sympathy, or find ourselves partakers in the guilt.—But what is truly singular as to this book, is, that it does not appear to have been written for any moral purpose, but for That only (if I do not err) of satyrising Providence itself; a design so enormously profane, that it may well pass for the most ridiculous part of the whole composition.

But if vice, divested of disgust and terror, is thus in its own nature ridiculous, we ought not to be surprised if the very same vices which spread horror and desolation thro' the Tragic scene should yet furnish the Comic with its highest laughter and delight, and that tears, and mirth, and even humour and wit itself, should grow from the same root of incongruity: For what is humour in the humourist, but incongruity, whether of sentiment, conduct, or manners? What in the man of humour, but a quick discernment and keen sensibility of these incongruities? And what is wit itself, without presuming however to give a complete definition where so many have failed, but a talent, for the most part, of marking with force and vivacity unexpected points of likeness in things supposed incongruous, and points of incongruity in things supposed alike: And hence it is that wit and humour, tho' always distinguished, are so often coupled together; it being very possible, I suppose, to be a man of humour without wit; but I think not a man of wit without humour.

But I have here raised so much new matter, that the reader may be out of hope of seeing this argument, any more than the tale of *Tristram*, brought to a conclusion: He may suppose me now prepared to turn my pen to a moral, or to a dramatic Essay, or ready to draw the line between vice and virtue, or Comedy and Tragedy, as fancy shall lead the way;—But he is happily mistaken; I am pressing earnestly, and not without some impatience, to a conclusion. The principles I have now opened are necessary to be considered for the purpose of estimating the character of *Falstaff*, considered as relatively to human nature: I shall then reduce him with all possible dispatch to his Theatric condition, and restore him, I hope, without injury, to the stage.

There is indeed a vein or two of argument running through the matter that now surrounds me, which I might open for my own more peculiar purposes; but which, having resisted much greater temptations, I shall wholly desert. It ought not, however, to be forgotten, that if *Shakespeare* has used arts to abate our respect of *Falstaff*, it should follow by just inference, that, without such arts, his character would have grown into a *respect* inconsistent with laughter; and that yet, without Courage, he could not have been respectable at all;—that it required nothing less than the union of ability and Courage to support his other more accidental qualities with any tolerable coherence. Courage and Ability are first principles of Character, and not to be destroyed whilst the united frame of body and mind continues whole and unimpaired; they are the pillars on which he stands firm in spight of all his vices and disgraces;—but if we should take

Courage away, and reckon Cowardice among his other defects, all the intelligence and wit in the world could not support him through a single Play.

The effect of taking away the influence of this quality upon the manners of a character, tho' the quality and the influence be assumed only, is evident in the cases of *Parolles* and *Bobadil*. *Parolles*, at least, did not seem to want wit; but both these characters are reduced almost to non-entity, and, after their disgraces, walk only thro' a scene or two, the mere mockery of their former existence. *Parolles* was so changed, that neither the *fool*, nor the old lord *Le-feu*, could readily recollect his person; and his wit seemed to be annihilated with his Courage.

Let it not be here objected that *Falstaff* is universally considered as a Coward;—we do indeed call him so; but that is nothing, if the character itself does not act from any consciousness of this kind, and if our Feelings take his part, and revolt against our understanding.

As to the arts by which *Shakespeare* has contrived to obscure the vices of *Falstaff*, they are such as, being subservient only to the mirth of the Play, I do not feel myself obliged to detail.

But it may be well worth our curiosity to inquire into the composition of *Falstaff*'s character.—Every man we may observe has two characters; that is, every man may be seen externally, and from without;—or a section may be made of him, and he may be illuminated from within.

Of the external character of *Falstaff*, we can scarcely be said to have any steady view. *Jack Falstaff* we are familiar with, but *Sir John* was better known, it seems, *to the rest of Europe*, than to his intimate companions; yet we have so many glimpses of him, and he is opened to us occasionally in such various points of view, that we cannot be mistaken in describing him as a man of birth and fashion, bred up in all the learning and accomplishments of the times;—of ability and Courage equal to any situation, and capable by nature of the highest affairs; trained to arms, and possessing the tone, the deportment, and the manners of a gentleman;—but yet these accomplishments and advantages

276 MAURICE MORGANN

seem to hang loose on him, and to be worn with a slovenly carelessness and inattention: A too great indulgence of the qualities
of humour and wit seems to draw him too much one way, and
to destroy the grace and orderly arrangement of his other accomplishments;—and hence he becomes strongly marked for
one advantage, to the injury, and almost forgetfulness in the
beholder, of all the rest. Some of his vices likewise strike through,
and stain his Exterior;—his modes of speech betray a certain
licentiousness of mind; and that high Aristocratic tone which
belonged to his situation was pushed on, and aggravated into
unfeeling insolence and oppression. '*It is not a confirmed brow*,' says
the Chief Justice, '*nor the throng of words that come with such more
'than impudent sauciness from you, can thrust me from a level considera-
'tion*': '*My lord*,' answers *Falstaff*, '*you call honourable boldness
'impudent sauciness. If a man will court'sie and say nothing, he is
'virtuous: No, my lord, my humble duty remembered, I will not be your
'suitor. I say to you I desire deliverance from these officers, being upon
'hasty employment in the King's affairs.*' '*You speak*,' replies the Chief
Justice, '*as having power to do wrong.*'—His whole behaviour to the
Chief Justice, whom he despairs of winning by flattery, is singularly insolent; and the reader will remember many instances of
his insolence to others: Nor are his manners always free from the
taint of vulgar society;—'*This is the right fencing grace, my lord,*'
says he to the Chief Justice, with great impropriety of manners,
'*tap for tap, and so part fair*': '*Now the lord lighten thee,*' is the reflection of the Chief Justice, '*thou art a very great fool.*'—Such a
character as I have here described, strengthened with that vigour,
force, and alacrity of mind, of which he is possessed, must have
spread terror and dismay thro' the ignorant, the timid, the
modest, and the weak: Yet is he however, when occasion requires, capable of much accommodation and flattery;—and in
order to obtain the protection and patronage of the great, so
convenient to his vices and his poverty, he was put under the
daily necessity of practising and improving these arts; a baseness which he compensates to himself, like other unprincipled
men, by an increase of insolence towards his inferiors.—There is

also a natural activity about *Falstaff* which, for want of proper employment, shews itself in a kind of swell or bustle, which seems to correspond with his bulk, as if his mind had inflated his body, and demanded a habitation of no less circumference: Thus conditioned he rolls (in the language of *Ossian*) like a *Whale of Ocean*, scattering the smaller fry; but affording, in his turn, noble contention to *Hal* and *Poins*; who, to keep up the allusion, I may be allowed on this occasion to compare to the Thresher and the Sword-fish.

To this part of *Falstaff*'s character, many things which he does and says, and which appear unaccountably natural, are to be referred.

We are next to see him *from within*: And here we shall behold him most villainously unprincipled and debauched; possessing indeed the same Courage and ability, yet stained with numerous vices, unsuited not only to his primary qualities, but to his age, corpulency, rank, and profession;—reduced by these vices to a state of dependence, yet resolutely bent to indulge them at any price. These vices have been already enumerated; they are many, and become still more intolerable by an excess of unfeeling insolence on one hand, and of base accommodation on the other.

But what then, after all, is become of *old Jack?* Is this the jovial delightful companion—*Falstaff*, the favourite and the boast of the Stage?—by no means. But it is, I think however, the *Falstaff* of Nature; the very stuff out of which the *Stage Falstaff* is composed; nor was it possible, I believe, out of any other materials he could have been formed. From this disagreeable draught we shall be able, I trust, by a proper disposition of light and shade, and from the influence of compression of external things, to produce *plump Jack*, the life of humour, the spirit of pleasantry, and the soul of mirth.

To this end, *Falstaff* must no longer be considered as a single independent character, but grouped, as we find him shewn to us in the Play;—his ability must be disgraced by buffoonery, and his Courage by circumstances of imputation; and those qualities be thereupon reduced into subjects of mirth and laughter:—His vices must be concealed at each end from vicious design and evil effect, and must thereupon be turned into incongruities, and assume the name of humour only;—his insolence must be re- pressed by the superior tone of *Hal* and *Poins*, and take the softer name of spirit only, or alacrity of mind;—his state of dependence, his temper of accommodation, and his activity, must fall in precisely with the indulgence of his humours; that is, he must thrive best and flatter most, by being extravagantly incon- gruous; and his own tendency, impelled by so much activity, will carry him with perfect ease and freedom to all the necessary excesses. But why, it may be asked, should incongruities recom- mend *Falstaff* to the favour of the Prince?—Because the Prince is supposed to possess a high relish of humour and to have a temper and a force about him, which, whatever was his pursuit, delight- ed in excess. This, *Falstaff* is supposed perfectly to comprehend; and thereupon not only to indulge himself in all kinds of in- congruity, but to lend out his own superior wit and humour against himself, and to heighten the ridicule by all the tricks and arts of buffoonery for which his corpulence, his age, and situation, furnish such excellent materials. This compleats the Dramatic character of *Falstaff*, and gives him that appearance of perfect good-nature, pleasantry, mellowness, and hilarity of mind, for which we admire and almost love him, tho' we feel certain reserves which forbid our going that length; the true reason of which is, that there will be always found a difference between mere appearances and reality: Nor are we, nor can we be, in- sensible that whenever the action of external influence upon him is in whole or in part relaxed, the character restores itself pro- portionably to its more unpleasing condition.

A character really possessing the qualities which are on the stage imputed to *Falstaff*, would be best shewn by its own natural energy; the least compression would disorder it, and make us feel for it all the pain of sympathy: It is the artificial condition of *Falstaff* which is the source of our delight; we enjoy his distresses, we *gird at him* ourselves, and urge the sport without the least alloy of compassion; and we give him, when the laugh is over, undeserved credit for the pleasure we enjoyed. If any one thinks that these observations are the effect of too much refinement, and that there was in truth more of chance in the case than of management or design, let him try his own luck;—perhaps he may draw out of the wheel of fortune a *Macbeth*, an *Othello*, a *Benedict*, or a *Falstaff*.

Such, I think, is the true character of this extraordinary buffoon; and from hence we may discern for what special purposes *Shakespeare* has given him talents and qualities, which were to be afterwards obscured, and perverted to ends opposite to their nature; it was clearly to furnish out a Stage buffoon of a peculiar sort; a kind of Game-bull which would stand the baiting thro' a hundred Plays, and produce equal sport, whether he is pinned down occasionally by *Hal* or *Poins*, or tosses such mongrils as *Bardolph*, or the Justices, sprawling in the air. There is in truth no such thing as totally demolishing *Falstaff*; he has so much of the invulnerable in his frame that no ridicule can destroy him; he is safe even in defeat, and seems to rise, like another *Antæus*, with recruited vigour from every fall; in this, as in every other respect, unlike *Parolles* or *Bobadil*: They fall by the first shaft of ridicule, but *Falstaff* is a butt on which we may empty the whole quiver, whilst the substance of his character remains unimpaired. His ill habits, and the accidents of age and corpulence, are no part of his essential constitution; they come forward indeed on our eye, and solicit our notice, but they are second natures, not *first*; mere shadows, we pursue them in vain; *Falstaff* himself has a distinct and separate subsistence; he laughs at the chace, and when the sport is over, gathers them with unruffled feather under his wing: And hence it is that he is made to undergo not one detection only, but a series of detections; that he is not formed for one Play only, but was intended originally at least for two; and the author, we are told, was doubtful if he should not extend him yet farther, and engage him in the wars with *France*. This he might well have done, for there is nothing perishable in the nature of *Falstaff*: He might have involved him, by the vicious part of his character, in new difficulties and unlucky situations, and have enabled him, by the better part, to have scrambled through, abiding and retorting the jests and laughter of every beholder.

But whatever we may be told concerning the intention of *Shakespeare* to extend this character farther, there is a manifest preparation near the end of the second part of Henry IV. for his disgrace: The disguise is taken off, and he begins openly to pander to the excesses of the Prince, intitling himself to the character afterwards given him of being *the tutor and the feeder of his riots.* '*I will fetch off,*' says he, '*these Justices.—I will devise matter* '*enough out of this* Shallow *to keep the Prince in continual laughter the* '*wearing out of six fashions.—If the young* dace *be a bait for the old* 'pike,' (speaking with reference to his own designs upon *Shallow*) '*I see no reason in the law of nature but I may snap at him.*'—This is shewing himself abominably dissolute: The laborious arts of fraud, which he practises on *Shallow* to induce the loan of a thousand pound, create *disgust*; and the more, as we are sensible this money was never likely to be *paid back,* as we are told that *was,* of which the travellers had been robbed. It is true we feel no pain for *Shallow,* he being a very bad character, as would fully appear, if he were unfolded; but *Falstaff*'s deliberation in fraud is not on that account more excusable.—The event of the old King's death draws him out almost into detestation.—'*Master* 'Robert Shallow, *chuse what office thou wilt in the land,—'tis thine.—I* '*am fortune's steward.—Let us take any man's horses.—The laws of* '*England are at my commandment.—Happy are they who have been my* '*friends;—and woe to my* Lord Chief Justice.'—After this we ought not to complain if we see Poetic justice duly executed upon him, and that he is finally given up to shame and dishonour.

But it is remarkable that, during this process, we are not acquainted with the success of *Falstaff*'s designs upon *Shallow* 'till the moment of his disgrace. '*If I had had time,*' says he to *Shallow,* as the King is approaching, '*to have made new liveries, I would have* '*bestowed the thousand pounds I borrowed of you*';—and the first word he utters after this period is, '*Master* Shallow, *I owe you a thousand*

'*pounds*': We may from hence very reasonably presume, that
Shakespeare meant to connect this fraud with the punishment of
Falstaff, as a more avowed ground of censure and dishonour: Nor
ought the consideration that this passage contains the most exquisite comic humour and propriety in another view, to diminish
the truth of this observation.

But however just it might be to demolish *Falstaff* in this way,
by opening to us his bad principles, it was by no means *convenient*.
If we had been to have seen a single representation of him only,
it might have been proper enough; but as he was to be shewn
from night to night, and from age to age, the disgust arising
from the *close* would by degrees have spread itself over the whole
character; reference would be had throughout to his bad principles, and he would have become less acceptable as he was more
known: And yet it was necessary to bring him, like all other
stage characters, to some conclusion. Every play must be wound
up by some event, which may shut in the characters and the
action. If some *hero* obtains a crown, or a mistress, involving
therein the fortune of others, we are satisfied;—we do not desire
to be afterwards admitted of his council, or his bed-chamber: Or
if through jealousy, causeless or well founded, *another* kills a beloved wife, and himself after,—there is no more to be said;—they
are dead, and there an end; Or if in the scenes of Comedy, parties
are engaged, and plots formed, for the furthering or preventing
the completion of that great article Cuckoldom, we expect to be
satisfied in the point as far as the nature of so nice a case will permit, or at least to see such a manifest *disposition* as will leave us in
no doubt of the event. By the bye, I cannot but think that the
Comic writers of the last age treated this matter as of more importance, and made more bustle about it, than the temper of the
present times will well bear; and it is therefore to be hoped that
the Dramatic authors of the present day, some of whom, to the
best of my judgment, are deserving of great praise, will consider
and treat this business, rather as a common and natural incident
arising out of modern manners, than as worthy to be held forth
as the great object and sole end of the Play.

But whatever be the question, or whatever the character, the
curtain must not only be dropt before the eyes, but over the
minds of the spectators, and nothing left for further examination
and curiosity.—But how was this to be done in regard to *Falstaff*?
He was not involved in the fortune of the Play; he was engaged
in no action which, as to him, was to be compleated; he had reference to no system, he was attracted to no center; he passes
thro' the Play as a lawless meteor, and we wish to know what
course he is afterwards likely to take: He is detected and disgraced, it is true; but he lives by detection, and thrives on disgrace; and we are desirous to see him detected and disgraced
again. The *Fleet* might be no bad scene of further amusement;—
he carries *all* within him, *and what matter* where, *if he be still the
same*, possessing the same force of mind, the same wit, and the
same incongruity. This, *Shakespeare* was fully sensible of, and knew
that this character could not be compleatly dismissed but by
death.—'Our author,' says the Epilogue to the Second Part of
Henry IV., 'will continue the story with Sir *John* in it, and make
'you merry with fair *Catherine* of *France*; where, for any thing I
'know, *Falstaff* shall dye of a sweat, unless already he be killed
'with your hard opinions.' If it had been prudent in *Shakespeare* to
have killed *Falstaff* with *hard opinion*, he had the means in his
hand to effect it;—but dye, it seems, he must, in one form or
another, and a *sweat* would have been no unsuitable catastrophe.
However we have reason to be satisfied as it is;—his death was
worthy of his birth and of his life: '*He was born*,' he says, '*about
'three o'clock in the afternoon, with a white head, and something a round
'belly.*' But if he came into the world in the evening with these
marks of age, he departs out of it in the morning in all the follies
and vanities of youth;—'*He was shaked*' (we are told) '*of a burning
'quotidian tertian;—the young King had run bad humours on the knight;
'—his heart was fracted and corroborate; and a' parted just between
'twelve and one, even at the turning of the tide, yielding the crow a
'pudding, and passing directly into* Arthur's bosom, *if ever man went
'into the bosom of* Arthur.'—So ended this singular buffoon; and
with him ends an Essay, on which the reader is left to bestow

what character he pleases: An Essay professing to treat of the Courage of *Falstaff*, but extending itself to his Whole character; to the arts and genius of his Poetic-Maker, SHAKESPEARE; and thro' him sometimes, with ambitious aim, even to the principles of human nature itself.

NOTES

NICHOLAS ROWE

2–3. *Some Latin without question... written wholly in it.* This passage, down to the reference to the scene in *Henry V*, is omitted by Pope. *Love's Labour's Lost*, IV. ii. 95; *Titus Andronicus*, IV. ii. 20; *Henry V*, III. iv.

3. *Deer-stealing.* This tradition—which was first recorded in print by Rowe—has often been doubted. See, however, Halliwell-Phillipps's *Outlines of the Life of Shakespeare*, 1887, ii, p. 71, and E. K. Chambers, *William Shakespeare*, 1930, i, pp. 18–21.

4. *the first Play he wrote.* Pope inserted here the following footnote: 'The highest date of any I can yet find is *Romeo and Juliet* in 1597, when the author was 33 years old, and *Richard the 2d* and *3d* in the next year, viz. the 34th of his age.' The two last had been printed in 1597.

Mr. Dryden seems to think that Pericles ... the last Act. This sentence was omitted by Pope. See Dryden's *Miscellany Poems*, 1684, 'An Epilogue', p. 292, '*Shakespear's* own Muse her *Pericles* first bore'.

5. *the best Conversations, &c.* Rowe here controverts the opinion expressed by Dryden in his *Essay on the Dramatic Poetry of the Last Age*: 'I cannot find that any of them had been conversant in courts, except Ben Johnson; and his genius lay not so much that way as to make an improvement by it. Greatness was not then so easy of access, nor conversation so free, as now it is' (*Essays*, ed. W. P. Ker, i, p. 175).

A fair Vestal. *Midsummer Night's Dream*, II. i. 158. In the original Rowe adds to his quotations from Shakespeare the page references to his own edition.

The Merry Wives. The tradition that the *Merry Wives* was written at the command of Elizabeth had been recorded by Dennis in the preface to his version of the play, *The Comical Gallant, or the Amours of Sir John Falstaffe* (1702): 'This Comedy was written at her command, and by her direction, and she was so eager to see it acted, that she commanded it to be finished in fourteen days; and was afterwards, as Tradition tells us, very well pleas'd at the Representation.' Cf. Dennis's *Defence of a Regulated Stage*: 'she not only commanded Shakespear to write the comedy of the *Merry Wives*, and to write it in ten day's time', &c. (*Original Letters*, 1721, i, p. 232).

5. *this Part of Falstaff.* Rowe is here indebted apparently to the account of John Fastolfe in Fuller's *Worthies of England* (1662). But neither in it, nor in the similar passage on Oldcastle in the *Church History of Britain* (1655, bk. iv, cent. xv, p. 168), does Fuller say that the name was altered at the command of the queen, on objection being made by Oldcastle's descendants. This may have been a tradition at Rowe's time, as there was then apparently no printed authority for it, but, as Halliwell-Phillipps showed in his *Character of Sir John Falstaff*, 1841, and in his *Outlines of the Life of Shakespeare*, 1887, ii, pp. 351, &c., it is partially confirmed. See also E. K. Chambers, *Shakespeare*, 1930, ii, pp. 241–2.

Name of Oldcastle. Pope added in a footnote, '*See the Epilogue to* Henry 4th'.

Venus and Adonis. The portion of the sentence following this title was omitted by Pope because it is inaccurate. *The Rape of Lucrece* also was dedicated to the Earl of Southampton. The error is alluded to in Sewell's preface to the seventh volume of Pope's Shakespeare, 1725.

6. *Eunuchs.* Pope reads 'Singers'.

6–7. *Amongst these . . . what is here said of him.* This passage dealing with Spenser was omitted by Pope. But it is interesting to know Dryden's opinion, even though it is probably erroneous. 'Dr. Ethel Seaton plausibly identifies Spenser's "pleasant Willy" with Richard Wills or Willey. See her edition (1950) of Abraham Fraunce's *Arcadian Rhetorike* (1588). Educated at Winchester and New College, Wills was admitted to the Society of Jesus in 1565, but had returned to England and to protestantism by 1573. He had a reputation for learning, Latin poetry, and travel. His prose discourse *De Re Poetica* of 1573, edited by A. D. S. Fowler (1958), is believed to be the first formal defence of poetry published in England. He died in or about the year 1579.' (F. P. W.)

7. *After this they were profess'd Friends.* This description of Ben Jonson, down to the words 'with infinite Labour and Study could but hardly attain to', was omitted by Pope, for reasons which appear in his Preface. See pp. 50, 51.

Ben was naturally Proud and Insolent. Rowe here paraphrases and expands Dryden's description in his *Discourse concerning Satire* of Jonson's verses to the memory of Shakespeare, 'an insolent, sparing, and invidious panegyric' (ed. W. P. Ker, ii, p. 18).

8. *In a Conversation,* &c. The authority for this conversation is Dryden, who had recorded it as early as 1668 in his *Essay of Dramatic Poesy*, at the conclusion of the magnificent eulogy of Shakespeare. He had also spoken of it to Charles Gildon, who, in his *Reflections on Mr. Rymer's Short View of Tragedy* (1694), had given it with greater fullness of detail. Each of the three accounts contains certain particulars lacking in the other two, but they have unmistakably a common source. Dryden probably told the

story to Rowe, as he had already told it to Gildon. The chief difficulty is the source, not of Rowe's information, but of Dryden's. If Jonson was present at the discussion, it must have taken place by 1637. It is such a discussion as prompted Suckling's *Session of the Poets* (1637), wherein Hales and Falkland figure. It cannot be dated 'before 1633' (as in Ingleby's *Centurie of Prayse*, pp. 198–9). The Lord Falkland mentioned in Gildon's account is undoubtedly the *second* lord, who succeeded in 1633, and died in 1643. Dryden may have got his information from Davenant. Pope condensed the passage thus: 'Mr. *Hales*, who had sat still for some time, told 'em, That if *Shakespear* had not read the Ancients, he had likewise not stollen anything from 'em; and that if he would produce', &c.

8. *Johnson did indeed take a large liberty.* The concluding portion of this paragraph from these words is omitted by Pope.

The *Menaechmi* was translated by 'W. W.', possibly William Warner. It was licensed in June 1594 and published in 1595, but, as the preface states, it had been circulated in manuscript before it was printed. The *Comedy of Errors*, which was acted by 1594, may have been founded on the *Historie of Error*, which was given at Hampton Court in 1576–7, and probably also at Windsor in 1582–3. See Farmer's *Essay*, p. 188.

The following passage dealing with Rymer is omitted by Pope. He retains of this paragraph the first two lines (. . . 'Shakespear's Works') and the last three ('so I will only take', &c.).

Thomas Rymer, the editor of the *Fœdera*, published his *Short View of Tragedy* in 1693. The criticism of *Othello* and *Julius Caesar* contained therein he had promised as early as 1678 in his *Tragedies of the Last Age*. His 'sample of Tragedy', *Edgar or the British Monarch*, appeared in 1678.

10. *Falstaff's Billet-doux . . . expressions of love in their way,* omitted by Pope.

11. *The Merchant of Venice* was turned into a comedy, with the title the *Jew of Venice*, by George Granville, Pope's 'Granville the polite', afterwards Lord Lansdowne. It was acted at Lincoln's Inn Fields in 1701. The part of the Jew was performed by Dogget. Betterton played Bassanio. See Genest's *English Stage*, ii. 243, &c.

is a little too much (line 22). Pope reads *is too much*.

Difficile est . . . Horace, *Ars poetica*, 128.

All the World's a Stage . . . As you like it, II. vii. 139.

12. *She never told her Love,* &c. *Twelfth Night*, II. iv. 113–18: line 116, 'And with a green and yellow melancholy', is omitted.

Pope omits *a passage or two in* (line 9).

13. *Ornament to the Sermons.* Cf. Addison, *Spectator*, No. 61: 'The greatest Authors, in their most serious Works, made frequent use of Punns. The

Sermons of Bishop Andrews, and the Tragedies of Shakespear, are full of
them.'

13. *the former publishers.* Pope omits *former* (line 21).

Caliban. Cf. Dryden's Preface to *Troilus and Cressida* (ed. W. P. Ker, i,
p. 219) and the *Spectator*, Nos. 279 and 419. Johnson criticized the remark
in his notes on the *Tempest* (ed. 1765, i, p. 21).

14. Note. *Ld. Falkland*, Lucius Cary (1610–43), second Viscount Falkland;
Ld. C. J. Vaughan, Sir John Vaughan (1603–74), Lord Chief Justice of the
Common Pleas; *John Selden* (1584–1654), the jurist.

Among the particular Beauties. . . . This passage, to the end of the quotation
from Dryden's Prologue, is omitted by Pope.

16. *Dorastus and Faunia*, the alternative title of Robert Greene's *Pandosto,
or the Triumph of Time*, 1588.

17. Pope omits *tyrannical, cruel, and* (line 11).

Plutarch. Rowe's statement that Shakespeare 'copy'd' his Roman
characters from Plutarch is—as it stands—inconsistent with the previous
argument as to his want of learning. His use of North's translation was not
established till the days of Johnson and Farmer.

18. *André Dacier* (1651–1722) was best known in England by his *Essay on
Satire*, which was included in his edition of Horace (1681, &c.), and by his
edition of the *Poetics* of Aristotle (1692). The former was used by Dryden
in his *Discourse concerning Satire*, and appeared in English in 1692 and 1695;
the latter was translated in 1705. In 1692 he brought out a prose translation, 'with remarks', of the *Oedipus* and *Electra* of Sophocles. Rowe's reference is to Dacier's preface to the latter play, pp. 253, 254. Cf. his *Poetics*,
notes to ch. xv, and the *Spectator*, No. 44.

But howsoever. . . . *Hamlet*, I. v. 84.

19. *Betterton's* contemporaries unite in praise of his performance of
Hamlet. John Downes tells in his *Roscius Anglicanus* (1708, p. 21) how
Betterton benefited by Shakespeare's coaching: Joseph Taylor 'of the
Black-Fryars Company' was 'instructed by the Author Mr. Shakespear'
and was seen by Sir William Davenant who 'taught Mr. Betterton in
every particle of it; which by his exact Performance of it gain'd him esteem
and reputation superlative to all other plays'. Cf. *The Rise and Progress of the
English Theatre*, appended to Colley Cibber's *Apology*, 1750, p. 516.

The epilogue for Betterton's 'benefit' on 7 April 1709 was written by
Rowe. Betterton died in 1710.

19–20. *Since I had at first resolv'd . . . said of him made good.* This second
criticism of Rymer is also omitted by Pope.

20. *Ten in the Hundred,* &c. Reed, Steevens, and Malone have proved conclusively, if somewhat laboriously, that these verses are not by Shakespeare. See also Halliwell-Phillipps's *Outlines,* i, p. 326. See E. K. Chambers, *Shakespeare,* 1930, ii, pp. 138–41.

21. *as engrav'd in the Plate.* A poor full-page engraving of the Stratford monument faces this statement in Rowe's edition.

He had three Daughters. Shakespeare had two daughters, and a son named Hamnet. Susannah was the *elder* daughter.

Pope omits *tho' as I* . . . *Friendship* and *venture to* (lines 17–18).

22. *Cæsar did never Wrong,* &c. Cf. *Julius Cæsar,* III. i. 47, 48, where the lines read:

> Know, Caesar doth not wrong, nor without cause
> Will he be satisfied.

Gerard Langbaine in his *Account of the English Dramatick Poets* (1691) ascribes to Shakespeare 'about forty-six plays, all which except three are bound in one volume in Fol., printed London, 1685' (p. 454). The three plays not printed in the fourth folio are the *Birth of Merlin, or the Child has lost his Father,* a tragi-comedy, said by Langbaine to be by Shakespeare and Rowley; *John King of England his troublesome Reign*; and the *Death of King John at Swinstead Abbey.* Langbaine thinks that the last two 'were first writ by our Author, and afterwards revised and reduced into one Play by him: that in the Folio being far the better'. He mentions also the *Arraignment of Paris,* but does not ascribe it to Shakespeare, as he has not seen it.

a late Collection of Poems,—*Poems on Affairs of State, from the year* 1620 *to the year* 1707, vol. iv.

Natura sublimis, &c. Horace, *Epistles,* ii. 1. 165.
The concluding paragraph is omitted by Pope.

JOHN DENNIS

23. *Shakespear* . . . *Tragick Stage.* Contrast Rymer's *Short View,* p. 156: 'Shakespear's genius lay for Comedy and Humour. In Tragedy he appears quite out of his element.' Cf. Dennis's later statement, p. 38.

24. *the very Original of our English Tragical Harmony.* Cf. Dryden, Epistle Dedicatory of the *Rival Ladies,* ed. W. P. Ker, i, p. 6, and Bysshe, *Art of English Poetry,* 1702, p. 36. See Johnson's criticism of this passage, Preface, p. 130.

Such Verse we make. Dennis makes these two lines illustrate themselves.

25. *Jack-Pudding.* See the *Spectator*, No. 47. The term was common at this time for a 'merry wag'. It had also the more special sense of 'one attending on a mountebank', as in Etherege's *Comical Revenge*, III. iv.

Coriolanus. Contrast Dennis's opinion of *Coriolanus* in his letter to Steele of 26 March 1719: 'Mr. Dryden has more than once declar'd to me, that there was something in this very Tragedy of *Coriolanus* as it was writ by Shakespear, that is truly great and truly Roman; and I more than once answer'd him, that it had always been my own Opinion.'

28. *Poetical Justice.* The phrase had been first used by Rymer in his *Tragedies of the Last Age* (1678) and was adopted by Dryden in the preface to his *Troilus and Cressida* (1679). Dennis defended the doctrine of poetical justice in the first of the two additional letters published with the letters on Shakespeare. Addison had examined this 'ridiculous doctrine in modern criticism' in the *Spectator*, No. 40 (16 April 1711).

Natura fieret. Horace, *Ars poetica*, 408.

29. *a circular Poet*, i.e. a cyclic poet. This is the only example of this sense of *circular* in the *Oxford English Dictionary*.

30. *Hector speaking of Aristotle*—*Troilus and Cressida*, II. ii. 166; *Milo*, id. II• iii. 258; *Alexander*, *Coriolanus*, V. iv. 23.

31. *Plutarch.* Dennis is right in his conjecture that Shakespeare used a translation of Plutarch, probably the second edition of North's translation, 1595. He is in error about Livy. Philemon Holland's translation had appeared in 1600.

Offenduntur enim. Ars poetica, 248.

32. *Cæsar.* Cf. the criticism of *Julius Cæsar* in Sewell's preface to the seventh volume of Pope's Shakespeare, 1725.

34. *Haec igitur.* Cicero, *Pro M. Marcello*, ix.

36. *Julius Cæsar.* Dennis alludes to the version of *Julius Cæsar* by John Sheffield, Duke of Buckinghamshire, published in 1722. In the altered form a chorus is introduced between the acts, and the 'play begins the day before Cæsar's death, and ends within an hour after it'. Buckinghamshire wrote also *The Tragedy of Marcus Brutus*.

Dryden, Preface to the Translation of Ovid's *Epistles* (1680) *ad fin.*: 'That of *Œnone* to *Paris* is in Mr. *Cowley's* way of Imitation only. I was desir'd to say that the Authour who is of the Fair Sex, understood not *Latin*. But if she does not, I am afraid she has given us occasion to be asham'd who do.' The author was Mrs. Behn.

37. *Hudibras*, i. I, 661. But *Hudibras* has it slightly differently—'Though out of Languages in which.'

37. *a Version of two Epistles of Ovid.* The poems in the seventh volume of Rowe's edition of Shakespeare include Thomas Heywood's *Amorous Epistle of Paris to Helen* and *Helen to Paris.* They were attributed to Shakespeare, till Farmer proved their authorship (pp. 190–1). Cf. Gildon, *Essay on the Stage,* 1710, p. vi.

Scriptor. Ars poetica, 120.

38. *Menechmi of Plautus.* Dennis's 'vehement suspicion' is justified. See above, note on p. 8.

38–39. *the Testimony of . . . Ben Johnson*—'small Latin and less Greek' (*Verses to the Memory of Shakespeare*).

39. *Milton,—L'Allegro,* 133: 'Or sweetest Shakespeare, Fancy's child'. The same misquotation occurs in Sewell's preface, 1725.

Dryden, Essay of Dramatic Poesy: 'Those who accuse him to have wanted learning give him the greater commendation' (ed. W. P. Ker, i, p. 80).

Colchus. Ars poetica, 118.

40. *Si quid tamen.* Id. 386. The form *Mæci* was restored about this time by Bentley.

we are told by Ben Johnson. See p. 21. But Heminge and Condell tell us so themselves in the preface to the Folio: 'His mind and hand went together: And what he thought, he uttered with that easinesse, that wee have scarse received from him a blot in his papers.'

Vos, O. Ars poetica, 291.

41. *Poets lose half the Praise,* &c. These lines are not by the Earl of Roscommon, but by Edmund Waller. They occur in Waller's prefatory verses to Roscommon's translation of Horace's *Ars poetica.*

Dennis's criticism of Jonson may have been inspired by Rymer's remarks on *Catiline* (*Short View,* pp. 159–63). 'In short,' says Rymer, 'it is strange that *Ben,* who understood the turn of Comedy so well, and had found the success, should thus grope in the dark, and jumble things together without head or tail, without any rule or proportion, without any reason or design.'

Vir bonus. Horace, *Ars poetica,* 445.

42. *ad Populum Phalerae.* Persius, iii. 30.

Milton. See Milton's prefatory note to *Samson Agonistes.*

43. *Veneration for Shakespear.* Cf. Dennis's letter to Steele, 26 March 1719: 'Ever since I was capable of reading *Shakespear,* I have always had and have always exprest that Veneration for him which is justly his due; of which

I believe no one can doubt, who has read the Essay which I publish'd some years ago upon his Genius and Writings.'

43. *Italian Ballad*. Cf. Dennis's *Essay on the Operas after the Italian Manner*, 1706.

ALEXANDER POPE

45. *His Characters*. The same idea had been expressed by Gildon in his *Essay on the Stage*, 1710, p. li: 'He has not only distinguish'd his principal persons, but there is scarce a messenger comes in but is visibly different from all the rest of the persons in the play. So that you need not to mention the name of the person that speaks, when you read the play, the manners of the persons will sufficiently inform you who it is speaks.' Cf. also Addison's criticism of Homer, *Spectator*, No. 273: 'There is scarce a speech or action in the *Iliad*, which the reader may not ascribe to the person that speaks or acts, without seeing his name at the head of it.'

47. *To judge...of Shakespear by Aristotle's rules*. This comparison had appeared in Farquhar's *Discourse upon Comedy*: 'The rules of English Comedy don't lie in the compass of Aristotle, or his followers, but in the Pit, Box, and Galleries. And to examine into the humour of an English audience, let us see by what means our own English poets have succeeded in this point. To determine a suit at law we don't look into the archives of Greece or Rome, but inspect the reports of our own lawyers, and the acts and statutes of our Parliaments; and by the same rule we have nothing to do with the models of Menander or Plautus, but must consult Shakespear, Johnson, Fletcher, and others, who by methods much different from the Ancients have supported the English Stage, and made themselves famous to posterity.' Cf. also Rowe, p. 15: 'it would be hard to judge him by a law he knew nothing of.' Is it unnecessary to point out that there are no 'rules' in Aristotle? The term 'Aristotle's rules' was commonly used to denote the 'rules of the classical drama', which, though based on the *Poetics*, were formulated by Italian and French critics of the sixteenth and seventeenth centuries.

The Dates of his plays. Pope here controverts Rowe's statement, p. 4.

48. *blotted a line*. See note, p. 40. Though Pope here controverts the traditional opinion, he found it to his purpose to accept it in the *Epistle to Augustus*, ll. 279–81:

> And fluent Shakespear scarce effac'd a line.
> Ev'n copious Dryden wanted, or forgot,
> The last and greatest art, the art to blot.

'Pope is referring to the following editions, all in quarto except *The True Tragedy*, which is in octavo: *The Merry Wives* (1602), *Henry V* (1600), *Hamlet* (1603), *The First part of the Contention between the Houses of York and Lancaster* (1594), and *The True Tragedy of Richard Duke of York* (1595). The two last plays, which correspond to 2 and 3 *Henry VI*, were reprinted in 1619 with the joint title *The Whole Contention*. The orthodox view is that these five texts, as also *Romeo and Juliet* (1597), are not first drafts of which revised texts were printed in the First Folio but imperfect memorial reconstructions of plays substantially in agreement with the Folio texts.'

On these early imperfect editions see W. W. Greg, *The Shakespeare First Folio*, 1955. (F. P. W.)

49. *Coriolanus and Julius Caesar.* Pope replies tacitly to Dennis's criticism of these plays.

50. *those Poems which pass for his.* The seventh or supplementary volume of Rowe's and Pope's editions contained, in addition to some poems by Marlowe, translations of Ovid by Thomas Heywood. Like Rowe, Pope has some doubt as to the authorship of the poems, but on the score of the dedications he attributes to him *Venus and Adonis* and the *Rape of Lucrece*. Both editors ignored the Sonnets.

Plautus. Cf. Rowe, p. 8. Gildon had claimed for Shakespeare greater acquaintance with the Ancients than Rowe had admitted, and Pope had both opinions in view when he wrote the present passage. 'I think there are many arguments to prove', says Gildon, 'that he knew at least some of the Latin poets, particularly Ovid; two of his Epistles being translated by him: His motto to *Venus and Adonis* is another proof. But that he had read Plautus himself, is plain from his *Comedy of Errors*, which is taken visibly from the *Menæchmi* of that poet. . . . The characters he has in his plays drawn of the Romans is a proof that he was acquainted with their historians. . . . I contend not here to prove that he was a perfect master of either the Latin or Greek authors; but all that I aim at, is to shew that as he was capable of reading some of the Romans, so he had actually read Ovid and Plautus, without spoiling or confining his fancy or genius' (1710, p. vi).

Dares Phrygius. The reference is to the prologue of *Troilus and Cressida*. See the note in Theobald's edition, and Farmer, p. 175.

Chaucer. See Gildon's remarks on *Troilus and Cressida*, 1710, p. 358.

our Author than some. Ed. 2 has 'our Author's worse sort than some'.

Ben Johnson. Pope is here indebted to Betterton. Cf. his remark as recorded by Spence, *Anecdotes*, ed. Singer, 1820, p. 5. 'It was a general opinion that Ben Jonson and Shakespeare lived in enmity against one another. Betterton has assured me often that there was nothing in it; and that such a supposition was founded only on the two parties, which in their lifetime listed under one, and endeavoured to lessen the character of the other mutually. Dryden used to think that the verses Jonson made on Shakespeare's death had something of satire at the bottom; for my part, I can't discover any thing like it in them.'

51. *Pessimum genus*, &c. Tacitus, *Agricola*, 41.

   Si ultra placitum, &c. Virgil, *Eclogues*, vii. 27, 28.

   Dryden. *Discourse concerning Satire, ad init.* (ed. W. P. Ker, ii, p. 18).

52. *Enter three Witche solus.* 'This blunder appears to be of Mr. Pope's own invention. It is not to be found in any one of the four folio copies of *Macbeth*, and there is no quarto edition of it extant' (Steevens).

   Hector's quoting Aristotle. Troilus and Cressida, II. ii. 166.

53. *those who play the Clowns.* 'Act iii, Sc. 4' in Pope's edition, but Act iii, Sc. 2 in modern editions.

54. *Procrustes.* Cf. *Spectator*, No. 58.

   Note 2. In the edition of 1728, Pope added to this note 'which last words are not in the first quarto edition'.

55. *led into the Buttery by the Steward.* 'Mr. Pope probably recollected the following lines in *The Taming of the Shrew*, spoken by a Lord, who is giving directions to his servant concerning some players:

> Go, Sirrah, take them to the *buttery*,
> And give them friendly welcome every one.

But he seems not to have observed that the players here introduced were *strollers*; and there is no reason to suppose that our author, Heminge, Burbage, Lowin, etc., who were licensed by King James, were treated in this manner' (Malone).

56. *London Prodigal.* After these seven plays Pope added in the edition of 1728 'and a thing call'd the *Double Falshood*' (see Introduction, p. xlv). He also inserted *Comedy of Errors* between *The Winter's Tale* and *Titus Andronicus*, and omitted 'eight'.

   tho' they were then printed in his name. His name was given on the title-pages of *Pericles*, *Sir John Oldcastle*, the *Yorkshire Tragedy*, and the *London Prodigal*.

LEWIS THEOBALD

60. *above the Direction of their Tailors.* Cf. Pope, p. 48. The succeeding remarks on the individuality of Shakespeare's characters also appear to have been suggested by Pope.

61. *wanted a Comment.* Contrast Rowe, p. 1.

62. *Judith* was Shakespeare's younger daughter (cf. Rowe, p. 21). It is now known that Shakespeare was married at the end of 1582. See E. K. Chambers, *Shakespeare*, i, p. 17.

64. *Spenser's Thalia.* Cf. Rowe, pp. 6–7 and note. The original editions read 'Tears of his Muses.'

Rymer's Fœdera, vol. xvi, p. 505. *Fletcher*, i.e. Lawrence Fletcher.

the Bermuda Islands. Cf. Theobald's note on 'the still-vext Bermoothes', vol. i, p. 13 (1733). Though Shakespeare is probably indebted to the account of Sir George Somers's shipwreck on the Bermudas, Theobald is wrong, as Farmer pointed out, in saying that the Bermudas were not discovered till 1609. A description of the islands by Henry May, who was shipwrecked on them in 1593, is given in Hakluyt, 1600, iii, pp. 573–4.

65. *Mr. Pope, or his Graver.* So the quotation appears in the full-page illustration facing p. xxxi of Rowe's Account in Pope's edition; but the illustration was not included in all the copies. The quotation appears correctly in the engraving in Rowe's edition.

66–67. *New-place.* Queen Henrietta Maria's visit was from 11 to 13 July 1643. Theobald's 'three weeks' should read 'three days'. See Halliwell-Phillipps, *Outlines*, 1887, ii, p. 108.

67. *We have been told . . . in print*, in *An Answer to Mr. Pope's Preface to Shakespear. . . . By a Stroling Player* [John Roberts], 1729, p. 45.

68. *Nullum sine Venia.* Seneca, *Epistles*, 114. 12.

Complaisance . . . to a bad Taste. Cf. Rowe, p. 6, Dennis p. 43, and Theobald's dedication to *Shakespeare Restored*; yet Theobald himself had complied to the bad taste in several pantomimes.

69. *Speret idem.* Horace, *Ars Poetica*, 241.

Indeed to point out, &c. In the first edition of the Preface, Theobald had given 'explanations of those beauties that are less obvious to common readers'. He has unadvisedly retained the remark that such explanations 'should deservedly have a share in a general critic upon the author'. The 'explanations' were omitted probably because they were inspired by Warburton.

70. *And therefore the Passages . . . from the Classics.* Cf. the following passage with Theobald's letter to Warburton of 17 March 1729–30 (see Nichols, *Illustrations*, ii, pp. 564, &c.). The letter throws strong light on Theobald's indecision on the question of Shakespeare's learning.

'The very learned critic of our nation' is Warburton himself. See his letter to Concanen of 2 January 1726 (Malone's *Shakespeare*, 1821, xii,

p. 158). Cf. Theobald's Preface to *Richard II*, 1720, and Whalley's *Enquiry*, 1748, p. 51.

71. *Effusion of Latin Words.* Theobald has omitted a striking passage in the original preface. It was shown that Shakespeare's writings, in contrast with Milton's, contain few or no Latin phrases, though they have many Latin words made English; and this fact was advanced as the truest criterion of his knowledge of Latin.

The passage is referred to by Hurd in his *Letter to Mr. Mason on the Marks of Imitation* (1757, p. 74). Hurd thinks that the observation is too good to have come from Theobald. His opinion is confirmed by the entire omission of the passage in the second edition. Warburton himself claimed it as his own. Though the passage was condensed by Theobald, Warburton's claim is still represented by the passage from *For I shall find* (p. 70, last line) to *Royal Taste* (p. 71, l. 24).

72. *Shakespeare . . . astonishing Force and Splendor.* Cf. Pope, p. 47.

Had Homer, &c. Cf. Pope, p. 52.

Indulging his private sense. See p. 57.

73. *Lipsius—Satyra Menippæa* (*Opera*, 1611, p. 640).

Sive homo, &c. Quintus Serenus, *De Medicina*, xlvi, 'Hominis ac simiae morsui.'

75. *Nature of any Distemper . . . corrupt Classic.* Cf. *Shakespeare Restored*, pp. iv, v.

Bentley's edition of *Paradise Lost* had appeared in 1732.

76. *the true Duty of an Editor.* A hit at Pope's 'dull duty of an editor', Preface, p. 57.

as I have formerly observ'd, in the Introduction to *Shakespeare Restored*, pp. ii and iv. The paragraph is quoted almost verbatim.

77. *labour'd under flat Nonsense.* Here again Theobald incorporates a passage from the Introduction to *Shakespeare Restored*, p. vi.

Corrections and Conjectures. Yet another passage appropriated from his earlier work. The French quotation, however, is new.

78. *Edition of our Author's Poems.* Theobald did not carry out his intention of editing the *Poems*. References to the proposed edition will be found in Warburton's letters to him of 17 May and 14 October 1734 (see Nichols, *Illustrations*, ii, pp. 634, 654).

The only attempt as yet towards a Shakespearian Glossary is to be found in the supplementary volumes of Rowe's and Pope's editions. It is far from 'copious and complete'.

78. *The English . . . are observ'd to produce more Humourists.* See Congreve's letter to Dennis *Concerning Humour in Comedy*, 1695.

79. *Wit lying mostly in the Assemblage of Ideas*, &c. So Locke, *Essay concerning the Human Understanding*, book ii, ch. xi, § 2. The passage had been popularized by Addison, *Spectator*, No. 62.

Donne. Cf. Dryden's criticism of Donne.

80. *a celebrated Writer.* Addison, *Spectator*, No. 297.

Bossu. René le Bossu (1631–80), author of the *Traité du poème épique* (1675). An English translation by 'W. J.' was printed in 1695, and again in 1719.

Dacier. See note, p. 18.

Gildon showed himself to be of the same school as Rymer in his *Essay on the Art, Rise, and Progress of the Stage* (1710) and his *Art of Poetry* (1718); yet his earliest piece of criticism was a vigorous attack on Rymer. The title reads curiously in the light of his later pronouncements: *Some Reflections on Mr. Rymer's Short View of Tragedy, and an Attempt at a Vindication of Shakespear.* It was printed in a volume of *Miscellaneous Letters and Essays* (1694).

81. *Anachronisms.* The passage referred to occurs on pp. 134, 135 of *Shakespeare Restored.*

this Restorer. See the *Dunciad* (1729), i. 106, note.

it not being at all credible. See p. 52.

Sir Francis Drake. Pope had suggested in a note that the imperfect line in *1 Henry VI*, I. i. 56, might have been completed with the words 'Francis Drake'. He had not, however, incorporated the words in the text. 'I can't guess', he says, 'the occasion of the Hemystic, and imperfect sense, in this place; 'tis not impossible it might have been fill'd up with—Francis Drake—tho' that were a terrible Anachronism (as bad as Hector's quoting Aristotle in Troil. and Cress.); yet perhaps, at the time that brave Englishman was in his glory, to an English-hearted audience, and pronounced by some favourite Actor, the thing might be popular, though not judicious; and therefore by some Critick, in favour of the author, afterwards struck out. But this is a meer slight conjecture.' Theobald has a lengthy note on this in his edition. He does not allude to the suggestion which he had submitted to Warburton. See Introduction, p. xlv.

Odyssey. This passage, to the end of the paragraph, appears in Theobald's letter to Warburton of 17 March 1729–30 (Nichols, ii, p. 566). In the same letter he had expressed his doubts as to whether he should include this passage in his proposed pamphlet against Pope, as the notes to the *Odyssey* were written by Broome. He had cast aside these scruples now

The preface does not bear out his profession to Warburton that he was indifferent to Pope's treatment.

82. *Malus . . . cogitat.* Publilius Syrus M 39 (Meyer).

83. David Mallet had just brought out his poem *Of Verbal Criticism* (1733) anonymously. It is a paraphrase and expansion of Pope's statements. 'As the design of the following poem is to rally the abuse of *Verbal Criticism*, the author could not, without manifest partiality, overlook the Editor of Milton and the Restorer of Shakespear' (introductory note).

Boswell attributed this 'contemptuous mention of Mallet' to Warburton (Boswell's *Malone*, 1821, i, p. 42, n). But it was not claimed by Warburton, and there is nothing, except perhaps the vigour of the passage, to support Boswell's contention. In the same note Boswell points out that the comparison of Shakespeare and Jonson in Theobald's Preface reappears in Warburton's note on *Love's Labour's Lost*, Act i, Sc. 1.

Hang him, Baboon, &c. 2 *Henry IV*, II. iv. 261.

Longinus, On the Sublime, vi.

noble Writer, the Earl of Shaftesbury, in his *Characteristicks*: 'The British Muses, in this Dinn of Arms, may well lie abject and obscure; especially being as yet in their mere Infant-State. They have hitherto scarce arriv'd to any thing of Shapeliness or Person. They lisp as in their Cradles: and their stammering Tongues, which nothing but their Youth and Rawness can excuse, have hitherto spoken in wretched Pun and Quibble' (1711, i, p. 217).

Complaints of its Barbarity, as in Dryden's *Discourse concerning Satire, ad fin.* (ed. W. P. Ker, ii, pp. 110, 113).

SIR THOMAS HANMER

85. The 'other Gentlemen' who communicated their observations to Hanmer include Warburton (see Introduction), the 'reverend Mr. Smith of Harleston in Norfolk' (see Zachary Grey, *Notes on Shakespeare*, Preface), and probably Thomas Cooke, editor of Plautus, &c. (see *Correspondence of Hanmer*, ed. Bunbury, 1838, p. 228).

much obliged to them. Amid the quarrels of Pope, Theobald, and Warburton, it is pleasant to find an editor admitting some merit in his predecessors.

86. *what Shakespear ought to have written.* Cf. the following passage in the *Remarks on the Tragedy of Hamlet* attributed to Hanmer: 'The former [Theobald] endeavours to give us an author as he is: the latter [Pope], by the correctness and excellency of his own genius, is often tempted to give us an author as he thinks he ought to be.' Theobald, it is said, is 'generally thought to have understood our author best' (p. 4).

86. *Henry V*, III. iv.

87. *Merchant of Venice*, III. v. 48.

Hanmer's Glossary, given at the end of vol. vi, shows a distinct advance in every way on the earlier glossary in the supplementary volume to Rowe's and to Pope's edition. It is fuller, though it runs only to a dozen pages, and more scholarly.

fairest impressions, &c. The edition is indeed a beautiful piece of printing. Each play is preceded by a full-page plate engraved by Gravelot from designs by Francis Hayman, or, as in vol. iv, by himself. (See *Correspondence of Hanmer*, pp. 83–84.)

88. *his Statue*. The statue in the Poet's Corner in Westminster Abbey, erected by public subscription in 1741. See the *Gentleman's Magazine* for February 1741, p. 105: 'A fine Monument is erected in *Westminster-Abbey* to the Memory of *Shakespear*, by the Direction of the Earl of *Burlington*, Dr. *Mead*, Mr. *Pope*, and Mr. *Martin*. Mr. *Fleetwood*, Master of *Drury-Lane* Theatre, and Mr. *Rich*, of that of *Covent-Garden*, gave each a Benefit, arising from one of his own Plays towards it, and the Dean and Chapter made a present of the Ground. The Design, by Mr. *Kent*, was executed by Mr. *Scheemaker*.'

WILLIAM WARBURTON

89. *the excellent Discourse which follows*, i.e. Pope's Preface, which was reprinted by Warburton along with Rowe's Account of Shakespeare.

93. *Essays, Remarks, Observations*, &c. Warburton apparently refers to the following works:

Some Remarks on the Tragedy of Hamlet, Prince of Denmark, written by Mr. William Shakespeare. London, 1736. Perhaps by Sir Thomas Hanmer.

An Essay towards fixing the True Standards of Wit, Humour, Raillery, Satire, and Ridicule. To which is added, an Analysis of the Characters of an Humourist, Sir John Falstaff, Sir Roger de Coverly, and Don Quixote. London, 1744. By Corbyn Morris, who signs the Dedication.

Miscellaneous Observations on the Tragedy of Macbeth: with Remarks on Sir Thomas Hanmer's Edition of Shakespeare. To which is affixed Proposals for a new Edition of Shakespear, with a Specimen. London, 1745. By Samuel Johnson, but anonymous.

Critical Observations on Shakespeare. By John Upton, Prebendary of Rochester. London, 1746. Second edition, with a preface replying to Warburton, 1748.

An Essay upon English Tragedy. With Remarks upon the Abbé de Blanc's Observations on the English Stage. By William Guthrie, Esq. [1747.]

The last of these appeared, however, about the same time as Warburton's edition.

93. Johnson is said by Boswell to have ever entertained a grateful remembrance of this allusion to him 'at a time when praise was of value'. But though the criticism is merited, is it too sinister a suggestion that it was prompted partly by the reference in Johnson's pamphlet to 'the learned Mr. Warburton'? When Johnson's edition appeared in 1765, Warburton expressed a very different opinion (see note on pp. 136–7).

whole Compass of Criticism. Cf. Theobald's account of the 'Science of Criticism', p. 76, &c., which Warburton appears to have suggested.

94. *Canons of literal Criticism.* This phrase suggested the title of the ablest and most damaging attack on Warburton's edition—*The Canons of Criticism, and Glossary being a Supplement to Mr. Warburton's Edition of Shakespear.* The author was Thomas Edwards (1699–1757), a 'gentleman of Lincoln's Inn', who accordingly figures in the notes to the *Dunciad*, iv. 568. When the book first appeared in 1748 it was called *A Supplement to Mr. Warburton's Edition of Shakespear. Being the Canons of Criticism.* It reached a seventh edition in 1765.

95. Rymer, *Short View of Tragedy* (1693), pp. 95, 96.

97. *as Mr. Pope hath observed.* Preface, p. 44.

Dacier, Bossu. See notes, pp. 18 and 80.

René Rapin (1621–87). His fame as a critic rests on his *Réflexions sur la Poétique d'Aristote et sur les Ouvrages des Poètes anciens et modernes* (1674), which was Englished by Rymer immediately on its publication. His treatise *De Carmine Pastorali*, of which a translation is included in Creech's *Idylliums of Theocritus* (1684), was used by Pope for the preface to his *Pastorals.* An edition of *The Whole Critical Works of Monsieur Rapin* . . . *newly translated into English by several Hands*, 2 vols., appeared in 1706; it is not, however, complete.

John Oldmixon (1673–1742), who, like Dennis and Gildon, has a place in the *Dunciad*, was the author of *An Essay on Criticism, as it regards Design, Thought, and Expression in Prose and Verse* (1728) and *The Arts of Logick and Rhetorick, illustrated by examples taken out of the best authors* (1728). The latter is based on the *Manière de bien penser* of Bouhours.

A certain celebrated Paper—The Spectator.

semper acerbum, &c. Virgil, *Aeneid*, v. 49.

98. *Note*, 'See his Letters to me'. These letters are not extant.

99. *Saint Chrysostom . . . Aristophanes*. This had been a commonplace in the discussions at the end of the seventeenth century, in England and France, on the morality of the drama.

100. *Ludolf Kuster* (1670–1716) appears also in the *Dunciad*, iv, l. 237. His edition of Suidas was published, through Bentley's influence, by the University of Cambridge in 1705. He also edited Aristophanes (1710), and wrote *De vero usu Verborum Mediorum apud Graecos*. Cf. Farmer's *Essay*, p. 165.

who thrust himself into the employment. Hanmer's letters to the University of Oxford do not bear out Warburton's statement.

101. Gilles Ménage (1613–92). *Les Poésies de M. de Malherbe avec les Observations de M. Ménage* appeared in 1666.

Selden's 'Illustrations' or notes appeared with the first part of *Polyolbion* in 1612. This allusion was suggested by a passage in a letter from Pope of 27 November 1742: 'I have a particular reason to make you Interest your self in Me and My Writings. It will cause both them and me to make the better figure to posterity. A very mediocre Poet, one Drayton, is yet taken some notice of, because Selden writ a very few notes on one of his Poems' (ed. Sherburn, iv, p. 425).

Verborum proprietas, &c. Quintilian, *Institut. Orat.*, Prooem. 16.

102. Warburton alludes to the edition of Beaumont and Fletcher 'by the late Mr. Theobald, Mr. Seward of Eyam in Derbyshire, and Mr. Sympson of Gainsborough', which appeared in ten volumes in 1750. The long and interesting preface is by Seward. Warburton's reference would not have been so favourable could he have known Seward's opinion of his Shakespeare. See the letter printed in the *Correspondence of Hanmer*, ed. Bunbury, pp. 352, &c.

The edition of *Paradise Lost* is that by Thomas Newton (1704–82), afterwards Bishop of Bristol. It appeared in 1749, and a second volume containing the other poems was added in 1752. In the preface Newton gratefully acknowledges this recommendation, and alludes with pride to the assistance he had received from Warburton, who had proved himself to be 'the best editor of Shakespeare'.

Some dull northern Chronicle, &c. Cf. the *Dunciad*, iii. 185–94.

a certain satiric Poet. The reference is to Zachary Grey's edition of *Hudibras* (1744). Yet Warburton had contributed to it. In the preface 'the Rev. and learned Mr. William Warburton' is thanked for his 'curious and critical observations'.

Grey's 'coadjutor' was 'the reverend Mr. Smith of Harleston in Nor-folk', as Grey explains in the preface to the *Notes on Shakespeare*. In his preface to *Hudibras*, Grey had given Smith no prominence in his long list of helpers. Smith had also assisted Hanmer.

In 1754 Grey brought out his *Critical, Historical, and Explanatory Notes on Shakespeare*, and in 1755 retaliated on Warburton in his *Remarks upon a late edition of Shakespear . . . to which is prefixed a defence of the late Sir Thomas Hanmer*. Grey appears to be the author also of *A word or two of advice to William Warburton, a dealer in many words*, 1746.

102. *our great Philosopher*, Sir Isaac Newton. His remark is recorded by William Whiston in the *Historical Memoirs of the Life of Dr. Samuel Clarke* (1730), p. 143: 'To observe such laymen as *Grotius*, and *Newton*, and *Lock*, laying out their noblest Talents in sacred Studies; while such Clergymen as Dr. *Bentley* and Bishop *Hare*, to name no others at present, have been, in the Words of Sir *Isaac Newton*, fighting with one another *about a Play-book* [*Terence*]: This is a Reproach upon them, their holy Religion, and holy Function plainly intolerable.' Warburton's defence of himself in the previous pages must have been inspired partly by the 'fanatical turn' of this 'wild writer'. Whiston would hardly excuse Clarke for editing Homer till he 'perceived that the pains he had taken about Homer were when he was much younger, and the notes rather transcrib'd than made new'; and Warburton is careful to state that his Shakespearian studies were amongst his 'younger amusements'.

Francis Hare (1671–1740), successively Dean of Worcester, Dean of St. Paul's, Bishop of St. Asaph, and Bishop of Chichester. For his quarrel with Bentley, see Monk's *Life of Bentley*, ii, pp. 217, &c. Hare is referred to favourably in the *Dunciad* (iii. 204), and was a friend of Warburton.

103. *Words are the money*, &c. Hobbes, *Leviathan*, part i, ch. iv: 'For words are wise men's counters, they do but reckon by them; but they are the money of fools'.

SAMUEL JOHNSON

105. *the poems of Homer*. Cf. Johnson's remark recorded in the *Diary of the Right Hon. William Windham*, August 1784 (ed. 1866, p. 17): 'The source of everything in or out of nature that can serve the purpose of poetry to be found in Homer.'

his century. Cf. Horace, *Epistles*, ii. 1. 39, and Pope, *Epistle to Augustus*, 55, 56.

106. *Nothing can please many*, &c. This had been the theme of the 59th number of the *Idler*.

107. *Hierocles.* See the *Asteia* attributed to Hierocles, No. 9 (*Hierocliis Commentarius in Aurea Carmina*, ed. Needham, 1709, p. 462).

108. *Pope.* Preface, p. 45.

109. *Dennis.* See p. 24. 'Has not Mr. Johnson here made too liberal a concession to Dennis? and on an examination of the play of Coriolanus, would it not appear that the character of Menenius, though marked with the peculiarities of an hearty old gentleman, is by no means that of a buffoon? Many have defended Polonius, who is much less respectable than Menenius.' (George Colman, *The St. James's Chronicle*, 10 October 1765; *Prose on Several Occasions*, 1787, vol. ii, p. 63.)

Rhymer. See *Short View of Tragedy*, chap. viii, 'Reflections on the *Julius Cæsar*'. Johnson consistently misspells Rymer's name in the Preface, and the error remained till corrected by Isaac Reed in ed. 1785, vol. i. But Johnson has 'Rymer' in the *Lives of the Poets* ('Dryden' first published 1779).

Voltaire. In replying to Voltaire, Johnson has in view, throughout the whole Preface, the essay *Du Théâtre anglais, par Jerome Carré*, 1761 (*Œuvres*, 1785, vol. 61). He apparently ignores the earlier *Discours sur la tragédie à Milord Bolingbroke*, 1730, and *Lettres philosophiques* (dix-huitième lettre, 'Sur la tragédie') 1734. Voltaire replied thus to Johnson in the passage 'Du Théâtre anglais' in the *Dictionnaire philosophique*: 'J'ai jeté les yeux sur une édition de Shakespeare, donnée par le sieur Samuel Johnson. J'y ai vu qu'on y traite de *petits esprits* les étrangers qui sont étonnés que, dans les pièces de ce grand Shakespeare, "un senateur romain fasse le bouffon, et qu'un roi paraisse sur le théâtre en ivrogne." Je ne veux point soupçonner le sieur Johnson d'être un mauvais plaisant, et d'aimer trop le vin; mais je trouve un peu extraordinaire qu'il compte la bouffonnerie et l'ivrognerie parmi les beautés du théâtre tragique; la raison qu'il en donne n'est pas moins singulière. "Le poète, dit il, dédaigne ces distinctions accidentelles de conditions et de pays, comme un peintre qui, content d'avoir peint la figure, néglige la draperie.' La comparaison serait plus juste s'il parlait d'un peintre qui, dans un sujet noble, introduirait des grotesques ridicules, peindrait dans la bataille d'Arbelles Alexandre-le-Grand monté sur un âne, et la femme de Darius buvant avec des goujats dans un cabaret', &c. (1785, vol. 48, p. 205). On Voltaire's attitude to Shakespeare, see Jusserand, *Shakespeare en France*, 1898, and Lounsbury, *Shakespeare and Voltaire*, 1902.

comick and tragick scenes. The ensuing passage gives stronger expression to what Johnson had said in *The Rambler*, No. 156.

110. *I do not recollect.* Johnson forgets the *Cyclops* of Euripides. Cf. Dryden's Essay *Of Dramatick Poesie*: 'Aristophanes, Plautus, Terence, never any of them writ a Tragedy; Æschylus, Euripides, Sophocles and Seneca, never medled with Comedy: the Sock and Buskin were not worn by the same Poet.' (Ker, i. 50.)

110. *instruct by pleasing.* Cf. Horace, *Ars poetica*, 343–4.

alternations. All editions published in Johnson's lifetime have *alterations.* The correction was made by Isaac Reed, ed. 1785, i. 10.

111. *tragedies to-day, and comedies to-morrow.* As the *Aglaura* of Sir John Suckling and the *Vestal-Virgin* of Sir Robert Howard, which have a double fifth act. Downes records in his *Roscius Anglicanus*, 1708, p. 22, in his account of Sir William Davenant's company from 1662 to 1665, that *Romeo and Juliet* was made into a comedy by James Howard, 'he preserving Romeo and Juliet alive; so that when the Tragedy was reviv'd again, 'twas play'd alternately, tragical one day and tragicomical another; for several days together'.

112. *Rhymer and Voltaire.* See *Short View*, pp. 96, &c., and *Du Théâtre anglais*, *passim*.

as Rhymer has remarked. See *Short View*, p. 156: 'Shakespears genius lay for Comedy and Humour. In Tragedy he appears quite out of his Element; his Brains are turn'd, he raves and rambles, without any coherence, any spark of reason, or any rule to controul him, or set bounds to his phrenzy.'

'This opinion in which Mr. J. concurs with the Arch Zoilus of our author, is however very disputable; and we cannot help thinking that what is said in this place, as well as what is afterwards thrown out on this head, in speaking of the faults, is infinitely too strong' (Colman, *The St. James's Chronicle*, 10 Oct. 1765, *Prose* ii. 65). Cf. Courthope, *History of English Poetry* (1903), iv, 474: 'it is a question whether Shakespeare's comic style does not afford proof of more original genius than even his tragic inventions.'

113. *Shakespeare . . . has likewise faults.* Cf. Johnson's letter of 16 October 1765, to Charles Burney: 'We must confess the faults of our favourite, to gain credit to our praise of his excellencies. He that claims either for himself or for another the honours of perfection, will surely injure the reputation which he designs to assist.' (*Letters*, ed. Chapman, i. 178.)

114. *Pope.* Preface, p. 52.

115. *In tragedy, &c.* Cf. Pope in Spence's *Anecdotes*, ed. Singer, 1820, p. 173: 'Shakespeare generally used to stiffen his style with high words and metaphors for the speeches of his kings and great men: he mistook it for a mark of greatness.'

116. *But the admirers of this great poet.* The beginning of this paragraph originally ran thus: 'But the admirers of this great poet have never less reason to indulge their hopes of supreme excellence, than when he seems fully resolved . . . crosses of love. He is not long soft and pathetick. . . .' The alteration was first made in the edition of 1778. There can be no doubt about who was the author of the inserted sentence: 'What he does best, he soon ceases to do.'

117. *his neglect of the unities.* Johnson's discussion of the three unities is perhaps the most famous passage in the whole Preface. Cf. *The Rambler*, No. 156; Farquhar, *A Discourse upon Comedy* (1702); *Some Remarks on the Tragedy of Hamlet* (1736); Upton, *Critical Observations on Shakespeare* (1746, 1748), i, sect. ix; Fielding, *Tom Jones*, prefatory chapter of book v; Kames, *Elements of Criticism* (1762), iii, ch. xxiii, 'The Three Unities'. 'Attic' Hurd had defended Gothic 'unity of design' in his *Letters on Chivalry and Romance* (1762), Letter viii.

the time of Corneille. His *Discours dramatiques*, the second of which deals with the three unities, was published in 1660; but he had observed the unities since the publication of the *Sentiments de l'Académie sur le Cid* (1638).

121. *Venice . . . Cyprus.* See Voltaire, *Du Théâtre anglais*, vol. 61, p. 377 (ed. 1785), and Rymer, *Short View*, chap. vii.

Non usque. Lucan, *Pharsalia*, iii. 138–40.

122. *deliberatively written.* The later edition of 1765 has *deliberately written*, and this reading was copied in subsequent editions.

Every man's performances. Cf. Johnson, *Lives of the Poets*, Dryden (1779): 'To judge rightly of an author we must transport ourselves to his time, and examine what were the wants of his contemporaries, and what were his means of supplying them' (ed. G. B. Hill, 1905; i. 411; also iii. 238). And cf. Pope, *Essay on Criticism*, 118–23, 233–4.

123. *Nations, like individuals, have their infancy.* Cf. Johnson's Dedication to Mrs. Lennox's *Shakespear Illustrated*, 1753, viii, ix. See note on Mrs. Lennox, p. 163.

The Death of Arthur. Johnson means a volume, perhaps only a chapbook, in which the death of Arthur is described; he does not refer to a volume with that title.

As you like it. Theobald, Upton, and Zachary Grey thought that *As You Like It* was founded on 'the *Coke's Tale of Gamelyn in Chaucer*'. Johnson shares the common error when he says 'Chaucer's *Gamelyn*', but he knows that the immediate source of the play is Thomas Lodge's *Rosalynde, Euphues Golden Legacie*, 1590. The inclusion of the Tale of Gamelyn in several manuscripts of the *Canterbury Tales* accounted for its erroneous ascription to Chaucer. It was still in manuscript in Shakespeare's days. See Farmer's *Essay*, p. 166.

124. *old Mr. Cibber*—Colley Cibber (1671–1757), actor and poet-laureate.

English ballads. Johnson has in mind the ballad of *King Leire and his Three Daughters*, but it is of later date than the play. He included all but six of its twenty-three stanzas at the end of his notes on *King Lear*, believing that 'the play was posteriour to the ballad rather than the ballad to the play'. His attention had been drawn to it by Mrs. Lennox's *Shakespear Illustrated*, iii. 303–8, where it is taken from *A Collection of old Ballads*, 1723, ii. 12–17. It is first found in *The Golden Garland of princely pleasures and delicate delights . . . the third time imprinted, enlarged and corrected by Rich. Johnson*, 1620. (See Halliwell-Phillipps, *Outlines*, No. 216, ed. 1887, ii. 338, and Walter Perrett, *The Story of King Lear*, Palaestra xxxv, Berlin, 1904, pp. 129–42.) It continued to be printed in the big editions of Shakespeare by Steevens and Malone, but in the edition of 1793 Steevens added this note by Ritson: 'This ballad by no means deserves a place in any edition of Shakespeare . . . I much doubt whether any common ballad can be produced anterior to a play upon the same subject, unless in the case of some very recent event.' Percy had printed it from *The Golden Garland* in his *Reliques* some months before the publication of the *Shakespeare*, but showed his doubts if it was earlier than the play. See *Reliques*, 1765, i. 211, and letter to Farmer, 9 October 1763, *Correspondence of Percy and Farmer*, ed. Cleanth Brooks, 1946, p. 56.

Voltaire . . . Cato. See *Du Théâtre anglais*, vol. 61, p. 366 (ed. 1785), and cf. *Lettres philosophiques*, 'Sur la Tragédie', *ad fin.*, and *Le Siècle de Louis XIV*, ch. xxxiv.

Similar remarks on *Cato* occur in William Guthrie's *Essay upon English Tragedy* (1747) and Edward Young's *Conjectures on Original Composition* (1759). The former may owe something to Johnson's conversation.

125. *a correct and regular writer.* Cf. the comparison of Dryden and Pope in Johnson's life of the latter: 'Dryden's page is a natural field, rising into inequalities, and diversified by the varied exuberance of abundant vegetation; Pope's is a velvet lawn, shaven by the scythe, and levelled by the roller.' The 'garden-and-forest' comparison had already appeared, in a versified form, in *The Connoisseur*, No. 125, 17 June 1756 (not in the original number but in the revised collected edition, 1757, iv. 164). Cf. also Mrs. Piozzi's *Anecdotes of Johnson*, 1786, p. 59: 'Corneille is to Shakespeare (replied Mr. Johnson) as a clipped hedge is to a forest.'

Jonson—substituted for 'Johnson' in ed. 1778.

Small Latin, and less Greek—Ben Jonson's poem 'To the Memory of . . . Mr. William Shakespeare' prefixed to the First Folio, 1623, l. 31. The

editions of 1765 read '*no Greek*'. The error was corrected in the edition
of 1773; it had been at once pointed out by Colman in *The St. James's
Chronicle*. Cf. Kenrick's *Review of Johnson's new edition of Shakespeare*, 1765,
p. 106, and the *London Magazine*, October 1765, p. 536. See Farmer's
Essay, p. 154 and note.

126. *Go before, I'll follow.* This remark was made by Zachary Grey in his
Notes upon Shakespeare, vol. ii, p. 53. He says that 'Go you before, and I will
follow you' (*Richard III*), I. i. 144, is 'in imitation of *Terence*, I præ, sequar.
Terentii Andr. I, l. 177.'

The Menæchmi of Plautus. See note on p. 8, and cf. Farmer, p. 188.

confessedly taken—an unexpected use of 'confessedly'.

127. *Pope.* Pp. 49, 50.
   Rowe. P. 4.

128. *Chaucer.* Johnson has probably his eye on Pope's statement, p. 50.
   Boyle. See Birch's *Life of Robert Boyle*, 1744, pp. 18, 19.

   dewdrops from a lion's mane. Troilus and Cressida, III. iii. 224.

130. *Dennis.* P. 24.

   Hieronymo, ed. 1778; earlier editions have *Hieronnymo*. See Farmer's
Essay, p. 197.

   there being no theatrical piece,—'Dr. Johnson said of these writers generally
that "they were sought after because they were scarce, and would not
have been scarce had they been much esteemed.' His decision is neither
true history nor sound criticism. They were esteemed, and they deserved
to be so' (Hazlitt, *Lectures on the Age of Elizabeth*, i).

131. *the book of some modern critick.* Upton's *Critical Observations on Shakespeare*, book iii (ed. 1748, pp. 294-365).

   present profit. Cf. Pope, *Epistle to Augustus*, 69-73.

   declined into the vale of years. Othello, III. iii. 265.

132. *as Dr. Warburton supposes.* P. 89.

   Not because a poet was to be published by a poet, as Warburton had said. P. 90.

133. *As of the other editors.* In the original editions of the Preface, this
sentence began thus: 'Of *Rowe*, as of all the editors, I have preserved the
preface, and have likewise retained the authour's life, though not written
with much elegance or spirit.' The alteration was made in the edition of
1773.

The 'spurious' plays were added to the third Folio (1663) when it
was reissued in 1664.

134. *This was a work*—'is' ed. 1778.

134. *the dull duty of an editor.* P. 57. Cf. the condensed criticism of Pope's edition in the *Life of Pope.*

134, l. 11. The 1925 edition of *Johnson on Shakespeare* (O.U.P.) reads 'the state of opinions, and modes of language', but this conjecture need not be adopted.

136, l. 11. *He found the measure*—'measures' before 1773.

Johnson's appreciation of Hanmer was shared by Zachary Grey. 'Sir Thomas Hanmer', says Grey, 'has certainly done more towards the emendation of the text than any one, and as a fine gentleman, good scholar and (what was best of all) a good Christian, who has treated every editor with decency, I think his memory should have been exempt from ill treatment of every kind, after his death' (*Notes on Shakespeare,* 1754, Preface). Johnson's earliest criticism of Hanmer's edition was unfavourable.

136–7. Warburton was incensed by this passage and the many criticisms throughout the edition, but Johnson's prediction that 'he'll not come out, he'll only growl in his den' proved correct. He was content to show his annoyance in private letters. See Nichols, *Anecdotes,* v. 595.

138. *Homer's hero,* substituted for *Achilles* in ed. 1773. *Iliad,* xxi. 111–13.

the Canons of criticism. See note, p. 94. Cf. Johnson's criticism of Edwards as recorded by Boswell: 'Nay (said Johnson) he has given him some smart hits to be sure; but there is no proportion between the two men; they must not be named together. A fly, Sir, may sting a stately horse and make him wince; but one is but an insect, and the other is a horse still' (ed. Birkbeck Hill, i. 263).

A Revisal of Shakespear's text was published anonymously by Benjamin Heath (1704–66) in 1765. According to the preface it had been written about 1759 and was intended as 'a kind of supplement to the *Canons of Criticism*'. The announcement of Johnson's edition induced Heath to publish it: 'Notwithstanding the very high opinion the author had ever, and very deservedly, entertained of the understanding, genius, and very extensive knowledge of this distinguished writer, he thought he saw sufficient reason to collect, from the specimen already given on Macbeth, that their critical sentiments on the text of Shakespear would very frequently, and very widely, differ.' The original editions of Johnson's Preface have *Review* instead of *Revisal*; the correction was made in ed. 1778. See note, p. 159.

girls with spits. Coriolanus, iv. iv. 5 (iv. iii. 5 in Johnson's own edition): 'lest that thy wives with spits, and boys with stones, In puny battle slay me.'

A falcon tow'ring. Macbeth, ii. iv. 12. The original editions have 'An eagle tow'ring'; the correction was made in ed. 1773.

140. *small things make mean men proud.* 2 *Henry VI*, IV. i. 106 ('mean' is Johnson's adaptation of 'base').

143. *collectors of these rarities.* This passage is said to have been aimed specially at Garrick. At least Garrick took offence at it. On 22 January 1766 Joseph Warton writes to his brother that 'Garrick is intirely off from Johnson, and cannot, he says, forgive him his insinuating that he withheld his old editions, which always were open to him' (Wooll's *Biographical Memoirs of Joseph Warton*, 1806, p. 313). Cf. the *London Magazine*, October 1765, p. 538.

144. *Huetius.* Pierre Daniel Huet (1630–1721), Bishop of Avranches, author of *De Interpretatione libri duo: quorum prior est de optimo genere interpretandi, alter de claris interpretibus*, 1661. The best known of his French works is the *Traité de l'origine de romans*. See *Huetiana*, 1722, and *Memoirs of Huet*, translated by John Aikin, 1810.

four intervals in the play. Cf. *Rambler*, No. 156.

146. *by railing at the stupidity*, &c. Johnson has Warburton in his mind here, though the description is applicable to others.

Criticks, I saw, &c. Pope, *Temple of Fame*, 37–40.

147. *the Bishop of Aleria.* Giovanni Antonio Andrea (Joannes Andreas), 1417–*c*. 1480, successively Bishop of Accia and Aleria, librarian and secretary to Pope Sixtus IV, and editor of Herodotus, Livy, Lucan, Ovid, Quintilian, &c.

Illudunt nobis. See letter of J. J. Scaliger to Salmasius, 14 July 1608, *Iosephi Scaligeri Epistolae*, 1627, p. 534.

149. *and in its true proportions*, ed. 1778.

Dryden, in the *Essay of Dramatic Poesy*. In the *Life of Dryden* Johnson refers to this passage as a 'perpetual model of encomiastic criticism', adding that the editors and admirers of Shakespeare, in all their emulation of reverence, cannot 'boast of much more than of having diffused and paraphrased this epitome of excellence'.

should want a commentary. Contrast Rowe, Account, *ad init*. In the editions of 1773 and 1778 Johnson ended the Preface with the following paragraph: 'Of what has been performed in this revisal, an account is given in the following pages by Mr. Steevens, who might have spoken both of his own diligence and sagacity, in terms of greater self-approbation, without deviating from modesty or truth.'

RICHARD FARMER

151. *Joseph Cradock* (1742–1826) had been a student at Emmanuel College, Cambridge. He left the University without a degree, but in 1765 was granted the honorary degree of M.A. by the Chancellor, the Duke of Newcastle. His *Literary and Miscellaneous Memoirs* appeared in 1828.

Were it shewn,' says some one. See the review of Farmer's *Essay* in the *Critical Review* of January 1767 (vol. xxiii, p. 50).

Peter Burman (1668–1741), Professor at Utrecht and at Leyden; editor of Horace, Ovid, Lucan, Quintilian, and other Latin classics.

'Truly,' as Mr. *Dogberry* says. *Much Ado*, III. v. 22.

152. *Burgersdicius.* Franco Burgersdijck (1590–1629), Dutch logician, Professor at Leyden. His *Institutionum logicarum libri duo* was for long a standard textbook. Cf. Goldsmith, *Life of Parnell, ad init.*: 'His progress through the college course of study was probably marked with but little splendour; his imagination might have been too warm to relish the cold logic of Burgersdicius.' See also the *Dunciad*, iv. 198.

Locke. This paragraph is a reply to an argument in the *Critical Review* (xxiii, pp. 47, 48).

Quotation from Lilly. See p. 189.

the Water-poet, John Taylor (1580–1653); cf. Farmer's note, p. 329. The quotation is from *Taylor's Motto* (Spenser Society Reprint of Folio of 1630, p. 217):

> I was well entred (forty Winters since)
> As far as *possum* in my *Accidence*;
> And reading but from *possum* to *posset*,
> There I was mir'd, and could no further get.

In his *Thief* he says 'all my schollership is schullership' (id., p. 282).

held Horses at the door of the Playhouse. This anecdote was given in Theophilus Cibber's *Lives of the Poets*, 1753, i, p. 130. Johnson appended it, in his edition, to Rowe's *Account of Shakespeare* (ed. 1765, p. clii), and it was printed in the same year in the *Gentleman's Magazine* (xxxv, p. 475). The story was told to Pope by Rowe, who got it from Betterton, who in turn had heard it from Davenant; but Rowe wisely doubted its authenticity and did not insert it in his *Account* (see the Variorum edition of 1803, i, pp. 120–2). Farmer makes fun of it here, and uses it to vary the *Critical* reviewer's description—'as naked with respect to all literary merit as he was when he first went under the ferula' (*Crit. Rev.* xxiii, p. 50).

153. *Dodsley*, Robert (1703–64), publisher and author, declared himself

'Untutored by the love of Greece or Rome' in his blank verse poem *Agriculture*, 1753, canto ii, line 319. His *Toy-Shop, a Dramatick Satire*, was acted and printed in 1735. The quotation is not verbally accurate; see the *New British Theatre*, 1787, xvii, p. 48.

153. *A word of exceeding good command.* 2 *Henry IV*, III. ii. 84.

learned Rubbish. Cf. Pope, *Essay on Criticism*, line 613.

Paths of Nature. Cf. Prior, *Charity*, line 25.

one of the first Criticks of the Age. Dr. Johnson: see Introduction, p. xxvii.

154. *a brother of the craft.* 'Mr. Seward, in his Preface to *Beaumont and Fletcher*, 10 vols. 8vo, 1750' (Farmer). Cf. Theobald, Introduction to *Shakespeare Restored*: 'Shakespeare's works have always appear'd to me like what he makes his Hamlet compare the world to, an *unweeded Garden grown to Seed*.'

contrary to the Statute. See Horace, *Ars Poetica*, 136, &c.

Small Latin and less Greek. 'This passage of Ben. Jonson, so often quoted, is given us in the admirable preface to the late edition, with a various reading, "small Latin and *no* Greek"; which hath been held up to the publick for a modern sophistication: yet whether an error or not, it was adopted above a century ago by W. Towers, in a panegyrick on Cartwright. His eulogy, with more than fifty others, on this now forgotten poet, was prefixed to the edit. 1651' (Farmer). Johnson corrected the error in subsequent editions. See note, p. 125.

'*darling project*', &c. Kenrick, *Review of Dr. Johnson's New Edition of Shakespeare*, 1765, p. 106: 'Your darling project ... of invidiously representing him as a *varlet*, one of the illiterate vulgar.'

braying faction. See *Don Quixote*, ii. 25 and 27.

those who accuse him, &c. Dryden, *Essay of Dramatic Poesy*: cf. p. 149. 'Greatest commendation' should read 'greater commendation'.

editor in form. See Warburton, p. 90.

sufficient to decide the controversy. See Johnson, p. 125.

155. *whose memory he honoured.* Farmer has added to the quotation from Jonson's Poem 'To the Memory of my Beloved Mr. William Shakespeare' a phrase from the passage 'De Shakespeare Nostrati' in Jonson's *Discoveries*: 'I loved the man, and do honour his memory on this side idolatry as much as any.'

'*Jealousy*,' *cries Mr. Upton.* In his *Critical Observations*, 1748, p. 5.

156. *Drayton*, 'In his Elegie on Poets and Poesie, p. 206. Fol., 1627' (Farmer).

Digges, Leonard (1588–1635). 'From his Poem "upon Master William Shakespeare,' intended to have been prefixed, with the other of his

FARMER

311

composition, to the folio of 1623: and afterward printed in several miscellaneous collections: particularly the spurious edition of Shakespeare's *Poems*, 1640. Some account of him may be met with in Wood's *Athenae* (Farmer).

156. *Suckling. Fragmenta Aurea*, 1646, p. 35:
> The sweat of learned *Johnson's* brain
> And gentle *Shakespear's* easier strain.

Denham. 'On Mr. Abraham Cowley', *Poems*, 1671, p. 90:
> Old Mother Wit and Nature gave
> *Shakespear* and *Fletcher* all they have.

Milton. L'Allegro, 134.

Dryden. Essay of Dramatic Poesy: see p. 149.

some one else. Edward Young, the author of *Night Thoughts*, in his first *Conjectures on Original Composition*, 1759, p. 31.

Hales of Eton. See p. 8.

Fuller,—Worthies of England, 1662, 'Warwickshire', p. 126: 'Indeed his Learning was very little, so that as *Cornish diamonds* are not polished by any Lapidary, but are pointed and smoothed even as they are taken out of the Earth, so *nature* it self was all the *art* which was used upon him. The concluding phrase of Farmer's quotation is taken from an earlier portion of Fuller's description: 'William Shakespeare . . . in whom three eminent Poets may seem in some sort to be compounded, 1. *Martial* . . . 2. *Ovid* . . . 3. *Plautus*, who was an exact comædian, yet never any Scholar, as our *Shake-speare* (if alive) would confess himself.'

untutored lines. Dedication of the *Rape of Lucrece*.

157. *Mr. Gildon.* 'Hence perhaps the *ill-starr'd rage* between this critick and his elder brother, John Dennis, so pathetically lamented in the *Dunciad*. Whilst the former was persuaded that "the man who doubts of the learning of Shakespeare hath none of his own," the latter, above regarding the attack in his *private* capacity, declares with great patriotick vehemence that "he who allows Shakespeare had learning, and a familiar acquaintance with the Ancients, ought to be looked upon as a detractor from the glory of Great Britain." Dennis was expelled his college for attempting to stab a man in the dark: Pope would have been glad of this anecdote' (Farmer). Farmer supplied the details in a letter to Isaac Reed dated 28 January 1794: see the *European Magazine*, June 1794, pp. 412–13.

Sewell, in the preface to the seventh volume of Pope's Shakespear, 1725.

Pope. See p. 49.

Theobald. See p. 70.

Warburton, in his notes to Shakespeare, *passim*.

157. *Upton*, in his *Critical Observations*, 1748, pp. 3 and 5.

'*Hath hard words*', &c. *Hudibras*, I. i. 85–86.

trochaic dimeter, &c. See Upton, *Critical Observations*, p. 366, &c.

'*it was a learned age*', &c. Id., p. 5. Cf. Hurd's *Marks of Imitation*, 1757, p. 24.

158. *Grey*, in his *Notes on Shakespeare*, 1754, vol. i, p. vii.

Dodd, William (1729–77), the forger, editor of the *Beauties of Shakespeare*, 1752.

Whalley. Farmer is here unfair to Whalley. The *Enquiry into the Learning of Shakespeare* shows plainly that Whalley preferred Shakespeare to Jonson. Further, his *Enquiry* was earlier than his edition of Jonson. In it Whalley expresses the hope 'that some Gentleman of Learning would oblige the Public with a correct Edition' (p. 23).

Addison . . . Chevy–Chace. See the *Spectator*, Nos. 70 and 74 (May 1711).

Wagstaff, William (1685–1725), ridiculed Addison's papers on *Chevy Chase* in *A Comment upon the History of Tom Thumb*, 1711.

Marks of Imitation. Hurd's *Letter to Mr. Mason, on the Marks of Imitation* was printed in 1757. It was added to his edition of Horace's Epistles to the Pisos and Augustus.

as Mat. Prior says—Alma, i. 241: 'And save much Christian ink's effusion.'

159. *Read Libya*. Upton, *Critical Observations*, p. 255.

Heath. 'It is extraordinary that this Gentleman should attempt so voluminous a work as the *Revisal of Shakespeare's Text*, when, he tells us in his Preface, "he was not so fortunate as to be furnished with either of the Folio editions, much less any of the ancient Quartos": and even "Sir Thomas Hanmer's performance was known to him only by Mr. Warburton's representation" ' (Farmer).

Thomas North. 'I find the character of this work pretty early delineated:

" 'Twas Greek at first, that Greek was Latin made,
That Latin French, that French to English straid:
Thus 'twixt one Plutarch there's more difference,
Than i' th' same Englishman return'd from France." ' (Farmer).

'*What a reply is this?*' Upton, *Critical Observations*, p. 249.

160. '*Our author certainly wrote*', &c. Theobald, ed. 1733, vi, p. 178.

Epitaph on Timon. 'See Theobald's Preface to *K. Richard 2d*. 8vo, 1720' (Farmer).

160. *I cannot however omit,* &c. The following passage, down to 'from Homer himself' (p. 164, l. 12) was added in the second edition.

'*The speeches copy'd from Plutarch*', &c. See Pope's Preface, p. 49.

161. *Should we be silent. Coriolanus,* V. iii. 94, &c.

162. *The Sun's a thief. Timon of Athens,* IV. iii. 439, &c.

163. *Dodd.* See the *Beauties of Shakespeare,* 1752, iii. 285, n. The remark was omitted in the edition of 1780.

'*our Author,*' *says some one.* This quotation is from the criticism of Farmer's *Essay* in the *Critical Review* of January 1767 (vol. xxiii, p. 50; cf. vol. xxi, p. 21).

Mynheer De Pauw. See *Anacreontis Odae et Fragmenta, Graece et Latine . . . cum notis Joannis Cornelii de Pauw,* Utrecht, 1732.

two Latin translations. 'By Henry Stephens and Elias Andreas, Paris, 1554, 4to, ten years before the birth of Shakspeare. The former version hath been ascribed without reason to John Dorat. Many other translators appeared before the end of the century: and particularly the Ode in question was made popular by Buchanan, whose pieces were soon to be met with in almost every modern language' (Farmer).

Puttenham. Arte of English Poesie, iii, ch. xxii (Arber, p. 259; *Elizabethan Critical Essays,* ed. Gregory Smith, ii, p. 171). The 'some one of a reasonable good facilitie in translation' is John Southern, whose *Musyque of the Beautie of his Mistresse Diana,* containing translations from Ronsard, appeared in 1584.

Mrs. Lennox, Charlotte Ramsay or Lennox (1720–1804), author of *Shakespear Illustrated: or the Novels and Histories on which the Plays of Shakespear are founded, collected and translated from the original Authors, with critical Remarks,* 3 vols., 1753–4, iii. 100. She is better known by her *Female Quixote,* 1752.

164. *the old story.* 'It was originally *drawn into Englishe* by Caxton under the name of the *Recuyel of the Historyes of Troy,* etc. . . . Wynken de Worde printed an edit. Fol. 1503, and there have been several subsequent ones' (Farmer).

sweet oblivious antidote. Upton, p. 42, n.

Νηπενθές. *Odyssey,* iv. 221.

Chapman's seven books of the *Iliad* appeared in 1598. The translation of the *Iliad* was completed in 1611 and that of the *Odyssey* in 1614.

Barclay. ' "Who list thistory of Patroclus to reade," etc. *Ship of Fooles,* 1570, p. 21' (Farmer).

Spenser. Farmer quotes in a note from the *Faerie Queene,* IV. iii. 43.

Greek expressions. Upton, p. 321.

164. *'Lye in a water-bearer's house'*, *Every Man in his Humour*, Act i, Sc. 3.

Daniel the Historian, i.e. Samuel Daniel the poet (1562–1619), whose *Collection of the Historie of England* appeared in 1612 and 1618. Cf. p. 178.

165. *Kuster.* See note on p. 100. 'Aristophanis Comoediae undecim. Gr. and Lat. Amst. 1710. Fol., p. 596' (Farmer).

unyoke (*Hamlet*, v. i. 59). See Upton, pp. 321, 322.

Orphan heirs (*Merry Wives*, v. v. 43), id., p. 322. 'Dr. Warburton corrects *orphan* to *ouphen*; and not without plausibility, as the word *ouphes* occurs both before and afterward. But I fancy, in acquiescence to the vulgar doctrine, the address in this line is to a part of the *Troop*, as Mortals by birth, but adopted by the Fairies: *Orphans* with respect to their *real* Parents, and now only dependant on *Destiny* herself. A few lines from Spenser will sufficiently illustrate the passage' (Farmer). Farmer then quotes from the *Faerie Queene*, III. iii. 26.

Heath. '*Revisal*, pp. 75, 323, and 561' (Farmer).

Upton. His edition of the *Faerie Queene* appeared in 1758.

William Lilly (1602–81), astrologer. '*History of his Life and Times*, p. 102, preserved by his dupe, Mr. Ashmole' (Farmer). *Elias Ashmole* (1617–92), who bequeathed his museum and library to the University of Oxford.

166. *Truepenny.* Upton, p. 26.

a legendary Ballad. The reference is to *King Lear.* But the ballad to *King Leire and his Three Daughters* is of later date than the play. This error in Percy's *Reliques* was for long repeated by editors and critics.

The Palace of Pleasure, 'beautified, adorned, and well furnished with pleasaunt Histories and excellent Nouelles, selected out of diuers good and commendable authors by William Painter, Clarke of the Ordinaunce and Armarie', appeared in two volumes in 1566–7; reprinted by Haslewood in 1813 and by Joseph Jacobs in 1890.

English Plutarch. See above.

Jacke Drums Entertainment: or the Comedie of Pasquill and Katherine, 4to, London, 1601; reprinted 1616 (another issue, 1618). It is now attributed to John Marston.

We are sent . . . to Cinthio, in Mrs. Lennox's *Shakespear Illustrated*, 1753, vol. i, pp. 21–37.

Heptameron of Whetstone. 'Lond., 4to, 1582. She *reports*, in the fourth dayes exercise, the rare *Historie of Promos and Cassandra.* A marginal note informs us that Whetstone was the author of the *Commedie* on that subject; which likewise had probably fallen into the hands of Shakespeare' (Farmer).

Geneura of Turberville. '"The tale is a pretie comicall matter, and hath bin written in English verse some few years past, learnedly and with good grace, by M. George Turberuil." Harrington's *Ariosto*, Fol. 1591, p. 39' (Farmer).

166. *Coke's Tale of Gamelyn.* Cf. Johnson's Preface, p. 124.

167. *Love's Labour Wonne.* 'See Meres's *Wits Treasury*, 1598, p. 282' (Farmer). Cf. the allusion to it in Tyrwhitt's *Observations and Conjectures*, 1766, p. 16. *Love's Labour Wonne* has been identified also with the *Taming of the Shrew*, *Much Ado*, *Midsummer Night's Dream*, the *Tempest*, and *Love's Labour's Lost*.

Boccace. 'Our ancient poets are under greater obligations to Boccace than is generally imagined. Who would suspect that Chaucer hath borrowed from an Italian the facetious tale of the *Miller of Trumpington*?' &c. (Farmer).

Painter's Giletta of Narbon. 'In the first vol. of the *Palace of Pleasure*, 4to, 1566' (Farmer).

Langbaine. *Account of the English Dramatick Poets*, 1691, p. 462.

Appolynus. 'Confessio Amantis, printed by T. Berthelet, Fol. 1532, p. 175, etc.' (Farmer). See G. C. Macaulay's edition of Gower, Oxford, 1901, iii. 396 (bk. viii, ll. 375, &c.).

Pericles. On Farmer's suggestion, Malone included *Pericles* in his edition of Shakespeare, and it has appeared in all subsequent editions except Keightley's. See *Cambridge Shakespeare*, vol. ix, p. ix.

Aulus Gellius, Noct. Attic. iii. 3. 6.

Ben. Jonson. 'Ode on the *New Inn*', stanza 3.

The Yorkshire Tragedy. ' "William Caluerley, of Caluerley in Yorkshire, Esquire, murdered two of his owne children in his owne house, then stabde his wife into the body with full intent to haue killed her, and then instantlie with like fury went from his house to haue slaine his yongest childe at nurse, but was preuented. Hee was prest to death in Yorke the 5 of August, 1604." *Edm. Howes' Continuation of John Stowe's Summarie*, 8vo, 1607, p. 574. The story appeared before in a 4to pamphlet, 1605. It is omitted in the Folio chronicle, 1631' (Farmer).

the strictures of Scriblerus. 'These, however, he assures Mr. Hill, were the property of Dr. Arbuthnot' (Farmer). See Pope's *Works*, ed. Elwin & Courthope, x, p. 53.

This late example. Double Falshood, II. iv. 6–8.

You have an aspect. Id. IV. i. 46.

168. *a preceding elision.* 'Thus a line in Hamlet's description of the Player should be printed as in the old Folios:

"Tears in his eyes, distraction in's aspéct,"
agreeably to the accent in a hundred other places' (Farmer).

168. *This very accent*, &c. This passage, down to the end of the quotation from Thomson (p. 171, l. 19), was added in the second edition.

Bentley. Preface to his edition of *Paradise Lost*, 1732.

Manwaring, Edward. See his treatise *Of Harmony and Numbers in Latin and English Prose, and in English Poetry* (1744), p. 49.

Green. Madan and others (see *N. & Q.*, 6th ser. xi. 318) attribute to George Smith Green, the Oxford watchmaker, poet, and playwright, *A New Version of the Paradise Lost: or, Milton Paraphrased, in which the Measure and Versification are corrected and harmonized*, &c. By a Gentleman of Oxford, Printed by W. Jackson, 1756. It was advertised as published 'this Day' in *Jackson's Oxford Journal*, 4 December 1756; and the Bodl. copy happens to be bound in a vol. which also contains one of G. S. Green's poems. Nevertheless, he usually describes himself as 'A Tradesman of Oxford'. Might the author be Edward Burnaby Greene, known for translations of the classics, and *Poetical Essays*, 1772?

Dee, John (1527–1608), astrologer.

169. *Strike up, my masters.* *Double Falshood*, Act i, Sc. 3.

Victor, Benjamin (died 1778), was made Poet Laureate of Ireland in 1755. He produced in 1761, in two volumes, the *History of the Theatres of London and Dublin, from the year 1730 to the present time*. A third volume brought the history of the theatre down to 1771. Farmer refers to vol. ii, p. 107: 'Double Falshood, a Tragedy, by Mr. *Theobald*, said by him to be written by *Shakespear*, which no one credited; and on Enquiry, the following Contradiction appeared; the Story of the *Double Falshood* is taken from the *Spanish* of *Cervantes*, who printed it in the year after *Shakespear* died. This Play was performed twelve Nights.'

Langbaine informs us. English Dramatick Poets, p. 475.

Andromana. 'This play hath the letters J. S. in the title page, and was printed in the year 1660, but who was its author I have not been able to learn', Dodsley, *Collection of Old Plays*, 1744, vol. xi, p. 172. In the second edition (ed. Isaac Reed, 1780) the concluding words are replaced by a reference to the prologue written in 1671, which says that ''Twas Shirley's muse that labour'd for its birth.' But there appears to be no further evidence that the play was by Shirley.

170. *Hume.* See the account of Shakespeare in David Hume's *History*, reign of James I, *ad fin.*, 1754: 'He died in 1617, aged 53 years.' The date of his death, but not his age, was corrected in the edition of 1770.

Mac Flecknoe, line 102.

170. *Newton informs us,* in the note on *Paradise Lost,* iv. 556 (ed. 1757, i, p. 202). See note on p. 102.

Her eye did seem to labour. The Brothers, Act i, Sc. 1. 'Middleton, in an obscure play, called *A Game at Chesse,* hath some very pleasing lines on a similar occasion:

> Upon those lips, the sweete fresh buds of youth,
> The holy dew of prayer lies like pearle,
> Dropt from the opening eye-lids of the morne
> Upon the bashfull Rose' (Farmer).

Lauder, William (died 1771), author of *An Essay on Milton's use and imitation of the Moderns in his Paradise Lost,* 1750.

Richardson, Jonathan (1665–1745), portrait painter, joint author with his son of *Explanatory Notes and Remarks on Milton's Paradise Lost,* 1734. The quotation is taken from p. 338.

171. *The stately sailing Swan.* Thomson, *Spring,* 778–82.

Gildon. See Pope's Shakespeare, vol. vii, p. 358.

172. *Master Prynne.* 'Had our zealous Puritan been acquainted with the real crime of De Mehun, he would not have joined in the clamour against him. Poor Jehan, it seems, had raised the expectations of a monastery in France, by the legacy of a great chest, and the weighty contents of it; but it proved to be filled with nothing better than *vetches.* The friars, enraged at the ridicule and disappointment, would not suffer him to have Christian burial. See the Hon. Mr. Barrington's very learned and curious *Observations on the Statutes,* 4to, 1766, p. 24. From the *Annales d'Acquytayne,* Paris, 1537.—Our author had his full share in distressing the spirit of this restless man. "Some Play-books are grown from *Quarto* into *Folio;* which yet bear so good a price and sale, that I cannot but with griefe relate it.—*Shack-speer's Plaies* are printed in the best Crowne-paper, far better than most *Bibles!*" ' (Farmer).

Whalley. Enquiry, pp. 54–55; *Tempest,* IV. i. 101; *Aeneid,* i. 46. Farmer added the following note in the second edition: 'Others would give up this passage for the *Vera incessu patuit Dea;* but I am not able to see any improvement in the matter: even supposing the poet had been speaking of Juno, and no previous translation were extant.' See the *Critical Review,* xxiii, p. 52.

John Taylor. See notes, pp. 152 and 199.

'*Most inestimable Magazine*', &c. From *A Whore,* Spenser Society Reprint of Folio of 1630, p. 272.

By two-headed Janus. Merchant of Venice, I. i. 50.

172. *Like a Janus with a double-face—Taylor's Motto*, Spenser Society Reprint, p. 206.

Sewel. Apparently a mistake for 'Gildon', whose *Essay on the Stage* is preceded immediately, in the edition of 1725, by Sewell's preface. 'His motto to *Venus and Adonis* is another proof', says Gildon, p. iv.

Taylor . . . a whole Poem,—Taylor's Motto, 'Et habeo, et careo, et curo', Spenser Soc. Reprint, pp. 204, &c.

sweet Swan of Thames. Pope, *Dunciad*, iii. 20:

> Taylor, their better Charon, lends an oar
> (Once Swan of Thames, tho' now he sings no more).

173. *Dodd. Beauties of Shakespeare*, iii, p. 18 (ed. 1780).

Pastime of Pleasure. 'Cap. i, 4to, 1555' (Farmer).

Pageants. 'Amongst "the things which Mayster More wrote in his youth for his pastime" prefixed to his *Workes*, 1557, Fol.' (Farmer).

a very liberal Writer. See Daniel Webb's *Remarks on the Beauties of Poetry*, 1762, pp. 120, 121.

This passage, to 'classical standard' (p. 175, l. 7), was added in the second edition.

See, what a grace. Hamlet, III. iv. 55.

174. *the words of a better Critick.* Hurd, *Marks of Imitation*, 1757, p. 24.

Testament of Creseide. 'Printed amongst the works of Chaucer, but reay written by *Robert Henderson*' (Farmer). It was never *ascribed* to Chaucer, not even in Thynne's edition.

Fairy Queen. 'It is observable that *Hyperion* is used by Spenser with the same error in quantity' (Farmer).

Upton. Critical Observations, pp. 230, 231. *Much Ado*, III. ii. 11.

Theophilus Cibber (1703–58), the actor, put his name on the title-page of the *Lives of the Poets* (five vols., 1753), which was mainly the work of Robert Shiels (died 1753); see Johnson's *Life of Hammond, ad init.*, and Boswell, ed. Birkbeck Hill, iii. 29–31. For the reference to the *Arcadia*, see 'Cibber's' *Lives*, i. 83.

175. *Ames,* Joseph (1689–1759), author of *Typographical Antiquities*, 1749.

Lydgate. Farmer has a long note here on the versification of Lydgate and Chaucer. 'Let me here', he says, 'make an observation for the benefit of the next editor of Chaucer. Mr. Urry, probably misled by his predecessor Speght, was determined, Procrustes-like, to *force* every line in the *Canterbury Tales* to the same standard; but a precise number of syllables was not the object of our old poets', &c.

175. *Hurd.* This quotation, which Farmer added in the second edition, is from Hurd's Notes to Horace's *Epistolae ad Pisones et Augustum*, 1757, vol. i, p. 214. Cf. also his *Discourse on Poetical Imitation*, pp. 125 and 132, and the *Marks of Imitation*, p. 74. The passage in which the 'one imitation is fastened on our Poet' occurs in the *Marks of Imitation*, pp. 19, 20. Cf. note on p. 158.

176. *Upton. Critical Observations*, p. 217.

Whalley. Enquiry, pp. 55, 56.

Measure for Measure, III. i. 118.

Platonick Hell of Virgil. Farmer quotes in a note *Aeneid*, vi. 740–2.

an old Homily. 'At the ende of the *Festyuall*, drawen oute of *Legenda aurea*, 4to, 1508. It was first printed by Caxton, 1483, "in helpe of such Clerkes who excuse theym for defaute of bokes, and also by symplenes of connynge" ' (Farmer).

brenning heate. 'On all soules daye, p. 152' (Farmer).

Menage. Cf. p. 101.

177. *our Greek Professor.* Michael Lort (1725–90), Regius Professor in Cambridge University from 1759 to 1771.

Blefkenius—Dithmar Blefken, who visited Iceland in 1563 and wrote the first account of the island. '*Islandiae Descript.* Lugd. Bat. 1607, p. 46' (Farmer).

After all, Shakespeare's curiosity, &c. . . . *original Gothic* (top of p. 178), added in second edition.

Douglas. Farmer has used the 1710 Folio of Gavin Douglas's *Aeneid*.

Till the foul crimes. Hamlet, I. v. 12.

'*Shakespeare himself in the Tempest.*' Quotedf rom the *Critical Review*, xxiii, p. 50; cf. also xix, p. 165.

Most sure, the Goddess. Tempest, I. ii. 421.

178. *Epitaphed, the inventor of the English hexameter.* Gabriel Harvey's *Four Letters* (Third Letter). See *Elizabethan Critical Essays*, ed. Gregory Smith, ii. 230.

halting on Roman feet. Pope, *Epistle to Augustus*, 98: 'And Sidney's verse halts ill on Roman feet.'

Hall. Satire i. 6.

Daniel's *Defence of Rhyme*, in answer to Campion's *Observations on the Art of English Poesie*, appeared in 1603.

in his eye. Cf. Theobald, Preface to *Richard II*, p. 5, and Whalley, *Enquiry*, p. 54.

178. *Ye elves of hills. Tempest*, v. i. 33.

Holt. 'In some remarks on the *Tempest*, published under the quaint title of *An Attempte to rescue that aunciente English Poet and Play-wrighte, Maister Williaume Shakespeare, from the many Errours faulsely charged upon him by certaine new-fangled Wittes.* Lond. 8vo, 1749, p. 81' (Farmer). On the title-page Holt signs himself 'a gentleman formerly of Gray's Inn'. He issued proposals in 1750 for an edition of Shakespeare. Cf. p. 193.

Auraeque, &c. Ovid, *Met.* vii. 197–8.

Golding. 'His work is dedicated to the Earl of Leicester in a long epistle in verse, from Berwicke, April 20, 1567' (Farmer). The translation of the first four books had appeared in 1565.

Some love not a gaping Pig. Merchant of Venice, IV. i. 47.

179. *Peter le Loier.* 'M. Bayle hath delineated the singular character of our *fantastical* author. His work was originally translated by one Zacharie Jones. My edit. is in 4to, 1605, with an anonymous Dedication to the King: the Devonshire story was therefore well known in the time of Shakespeare.—The passage from Scaliger is likewise to be met with in *The Optick Glasse of Humors*, written, I believe, by T. Wombwell; and in several other places' (Farmer). Reed quotes a manuscript note by Farmer on the statement that it was written by Wombwell: 'So I imagined from a note of Mr. Baker's, but I have since seen a copy in the library of Canterbury Cathedral, printed 1607, and ascribed to T. Walkington of St. John's, Cambridge.'

He was a man, etc. *Henry VIII*, IV. ii. 33.

180. *Holingshed.* Farmer's quotations from Holinshed are not *literatim*.

Indisputably the passage, &c. (to the end of the quotation from Skelton)—added in the second edition.

Hall's *Union of the Two Noble and Illustre Famelies of Lancastre and Yorke* (1548) was freely used by Holinshed, but there is a passage in *Henry VIII* which shows that the dramatist knew Hall's chronicle at first hand.

181. *Skelton.* 'His Poems are printed with the title of *Pithy, Pleasaunt, and Profitable Workes of Maister Skelton, Poete Laureate*', &c. Farmer then explains with his usual learning Skelton's title of 'poet laureate'.

Upton. Critical Observations, p. 47, n.

Pierce Plowman. This reference was added in the second edition. On the other hand, the following reference, which was given in the first edition after the quotation from *Hieronymo*, was omitted: 'And in Dekker's *Satiro-Mastix, or the Untrussing of the humourous Poet*, Sir Rees ap Vaughan swears in the same manner.'

181. *Hieronymo*, II. ii. 87, 91–93 (*Works of Thomas Kyd*, ed. Boas, p. 24).

182. *Garrick.* 'Mr. Johnson's edit., vol. viii, p. 171' (Farmer). The following three pages, from '*a Gentleman*' (top of p. 182) to the end of the Latin quotation at the top of p. 185, were added in the second edition.

Upton. Critical Observations, p. 300.

This villain here. 2 *Henry VI*, IV. i. 106.

Grimald's 'Three Bookes of Duties, tourned out of Latin into English' appeared in 1555. 'I have met with a writer who tells us that a translation of the *Offices* was printed by Caxton in the year 1481: but such a book never existed. It is a mistake for *Tullius of Old Age*, by John Tiptoft, Earl of Worcester' (Farmer).

There is no bar. Henry V, I. ii. 35.

183. *It hath lately been repeated*, &c. In the *Critical Review*, xxiii, p. 50; cf. xxi, p. 21.

Guthrie, William (1708–70), whose reports to the *Gentleman's Magazine* were revised by Johnson. He wrote histories of *England* (4 vols., 1744, &c.), the *World* (12 vols., 1764, &c.), and *Scotland* (10 vols., 1767). His *Essay upon English Tragedy* had appeared in 1747. See note, p. 93.

184. *All hail, Macbeth*, I. iii. 48–50.

Macbeth. The probable date of *Macbeth* is 1606.

Wake, Sir Isaac (1580–1632). The *Rex Platonicus*, celebrating the visit of James I to Oxford in 1605, appeared in 1607.

185. *Grey. Notes on Shakespeare*, p. vii; cf. vol. ii, p. 289, &c.

Whalley. Enquiry, p. v.

a very curious and intelligent gentleman. Capell: see below, p. 186.

It hath indeed been said, &c. In the *Critical Review*, xxiii, p. 50. Accordingly the following passage (to 'Mr. Lort', near the foot of p. 187) was added in the second edition.

Saxo Grammaticus. ' "Falsitatis enim (Hamlethus) alienus haberi cupidus, ita astutiam veriloquio permiscebat, ut nec dictis veracitas deesset, nec acuminis modus verorum judicio proderetur." This is quoted, as it had been before, in Mr. Guthrie's *Essay on Tragedy*, with a *small* variation from the *Original*. See edit. fol. 1644, p. 50' (Farmer). The quotation was given in the *Critical Review*, xxiii, p. 50.

186. *The Hystorie of Hamblet.* It is now believed that Shakespeare's 'original' was the early play of Hamlet, written *c.* 1587–90, possibly by Thomas Kyd.

Though Farmer disproves Shakespeare's use of *Saxo Grammaticus*, he errs in the importance he gives to the *Hystorie of Hamblet*. No English 'translation from the French of Belleforest' appears to have been issued before 1608. The words '*a rat, a rat!*' were probably taken from Shakespeare's play.

186. *Duke of Newcastle*, Thomas Pelham-Holles (1693–1768), First Lord of the Treasury, 1754, Lord Privy Seal, 1765–6, Chancellor of Cambridge University from 1748.

187. *Painter*. See above, p. 166.

Tom Rawlinson (1681–1725), satirized as 'Tom Folio' by Addison in the *Tatler*, No. 158.

Colman, George, the elder (1732–94), brought out the *Comedies of Terence translated into familiar blank verse* in 1765. He replied to Farmer's *Essay*, the merit of which he admitted, in the appendix to a later edition. Farmer's answer is given in the letter which Steevens printed as an appendix to his edition of Johnson's Shakespeare, 1773, viii, App. ii, note on *Love's Labour's Lost*, IV. ii. In a long footnote in the *Essay*, Farmer replies also to an argument advanced by Bonnell Thornton (1724–68), Colman's associate in the *Connoisseur*, in his translation of the *Trinummus*, 1767.

188. *Redime te captum. Eunuchus*, I. i. 29; *Taming of the Shrew*, I. i. 167.

translation of the Menaechmi. 'It was published in 4to, 1595. The printer of Langbaine, p. 524, hath accidently given the date 1515, which hath been copied implicitly by Gildon, Theobald, Cooke, and several others. Warner is now almost forgotten, yet the old criticks esteemed him one of "our chiefe heroical *makers*." Meres informs us that he had "heard him termed of the best wits of both our Universities, our *English Homer*"' (Farmer). See note on p. 8.

Riccoboni, Luigi (1674–1753). See his *Réflexions historiques sur les differens théâtres de l'Europe*, 1738, English translation, 1741, p. 163: 'If really that good comedy Plautus was the first that appeared, we must yield to the English the merit of having opened their stage with a good prophane piece, whilst the other nations in Europe began theirs with the most wretched farces.'

Hanssach, Hans Sachs (1494–1576).

Gascoigne. 'His works were first collected under the singular title of "A hundreth sundrie Flowres bounde up in one small Poesie. Gathered partly (by translation) in the fyne outlandish Gardins of *Euripides, Ouid, Petrarke, Ariosto*, and others: and partly by inuention, out of our owne fruitefull Orchardes in Englande: yelding sundrie sweete sauours of tragical, comical, and morall discourses, bothe pleasaunt and profitable to the well smellyng noses of learned Readers." *Black letter*, 4to, no date' (Farmer). It was published in 1573.

189. '*Our authour had this line from Lilly.*' Johnson, edition of 1765, vol. iii, p. 20.

an unprovoked antagonist. 'W. Kenrick's Review of Dr. Johnson's edit. of Shakespeare, 1765, 8vo, p. 105' (Farmer).

We have hitherto supposed. The next three paragraphs were added in the second edition.

190. *Gosson.* See Arber's reprint, p. 40.

Hearne, Thomas (1678–1735), edited William of Worcester's *Annales Rerum Anglicarum* in 1728. 'I know indeed there is extant a very old poem, in *black letter*, to which it might have been supposed Sir John Harrington alluded, had he not spoken of the discovery as a *new* one, and recommended it as worthy the notice of his countrymen: I am persuaded the method in the old bard will not be thought *either*. At the end of the sixth volume of Leland's *Itinerary*, we are *favoured* by Mr. Hearne with a Macaronic poem on a battle at Oxford between the scholars and the townsmen: on a line of which, "Invadunt aulas *bycheson cum forth* geminantes," our commentator very wisely and gravely remarks: "*Bycheson*, id est, *son* of a *byche*, ut e codice Rawlinsoniano edidi. Eo nempe modo quo et olim *whorson* dixerunt pro *son of a whore*. Exempla habemus cum alibi tum in libello quodam lepido & antiquo (inter codices Seldenianos in Bibl. Bodl.) qui inscribitur: *The Wife lapped in Morels Skyn: or the Taming of a Shrew*"' (Farmer). Farmer then gives Hearne's quotation of two verses from it, pp. 36 and 42.

Pope's list. At the end of vol. vi of his edition.

Ravenscroft, Edward, in his *Titus Andronicus, or the Rape of Lavinia*, 1687, 'To the Reader'; see *Shakespeare Allusion Book*, ed. E. K. Chambers, ii, 319.

The Epistles, says one, of Paris and Helen. Sewell, Preface to Pope's Shakespeare, vol. vii, 1725, p. 10.

it may be concluded, says another. Whalley, *Enquiry*, p. 79.

191. *Jaggard.* 'It may seem little matter of wonder that the name of Shakespeare should be borrowed for the benefit of the bookseller; and by the way, as probably for a *play* as a *poem*: but modern criticks may be surprised perhaps at the complaint of John Hall, that "certayne chapters of the *Proverbes*, translated by him into English metre, 1550, had before been untruely *entituled* to be the doyngs of Mayster Thomas Sternhold"' (Farmer).

Biographia Britannica, 1763, vol. vi. Farmer has a note at this passage correcting a remark in the life of Spenser and showing by a quotation from Browne's *Britannia's Pastorals* that the *Faerie Queene* was left unfinished—not that part of it had been lost.

192. *Anthony Wood.* 'Fasti, 2d Edit., v. I. 208.—It will be seen on turning to the former edition, that the latter part of the paragraph belongs to another *Stafford*.—I have since observed that Wood is not the first who hath given us the true author of the pamphlet' (Farmer). *Fasti*, ed. Bliss, i. 378. But Stafford's authorship of this pamphlet has now been disproved: see the *English Historical Review*, vi. 284–305.

Warton, Thomas. *Life of Ralph Bathurst*, 2 vols., 1761.

Aubrey. See *Brief Lives*, ed. Andrew Clark, 1898, vol. ii, pp. 225–7. For *Beeston*, see vol. i, pp. 96–97.

193. *Crendon*. 'It was observed in the former edition that this place is not met with in Spelman's *Villare*, or in Adams's *Index*; nor, it might have been added, in the *first* and the *last* performance of this sort, Speed's *Tables* and Whatley's *Gazetteer*: perhaps, however, it may be meant under the name of *Crandon*; but the inquiry is of no importance. It should, I think, be written *Credendon*; tho' better antiquaries than Aubrey have acquiesced in the vulgar corruption' (Farmer). But *Crendon* is only a misprint for *Grendon*.

Rowe tells us. See p. 3.

'It is now held that Lodge's reference to *Hamlet*—and others in Nashe (1589), Henslowe's Diary (1594), *A Warning for Fair Women* (1599), and Dekker (1601)—are to an early pre-Shakespearian *Hamlet*, possibly by Thomas Kyd. Shakespeare's Ghost never cries "Hamlet, Revenge"' (F. P. W.)

Holt. See above, p. 178. Johnson's edition of Shakespeare, vol. viii, Appendix, note on viii. 194.

Kirkman, Francis, bookseller, published his *Exact Catalogue of all the English Stage Plays* in 1671.

Winstanley, William (1628–98), compiler of *Lives of the most famous English Poets*, 1687. 'These people, who were the Curls of the last age, ascribe likewise to our author those miserable performances, *Mucidorus* and the *Merry Devil of Edmonton*' (Farmer).

seven years afterward. 'Mr. Pope asserts "The troublesome Raigne of King John," in two parts, 1611, to have been written by Shakespeare and Rowley: which edition is a mere copy of another in black letter, 1591. But I find his assertion is somewhat to be doubted: for the old edition hath no name of *author* at all; and that of 1611, the initials only, *W. Sh.*, in the title-page' (Farmer).

194. *Nash.* This reference was added in the second edition. See Arber's reprint of Greene's *Menaphon*, p. 17, or Gregory Smith, *Elizabethan Critical Essays*, i. 307, &c.

'Peele seems to have been taken into the patronage of the Earl of

Northumberland about 1593, to whom he dedicates in that year, "*The Honour of the Garter*, a Poem Gratulatorie—the *Firstling* consecrated to his noble name."—"He was esteemed," says Anthony Wood, "a most noted poet, 1579; but when or where he died, I cannot tell, for *so it is*, and always *hath been*, that most Poets die *poor*, and consequently obscurely, and a hard matter it is to trace them to their graves. *Claruit*, 1599." *Ath. Oxon.*, vol. i, p. 300.—We had lately in a periodical pamphlet, called *The Theatrical Review*, a very *curious* letter, under the name of George Peele, to one Master Henrie Marle, relative to a dispute between Shakespeare and Alleyn, which was compromised by Ben. Jonson.—"I never longed for thy companye more than last night; we were all verie merrie at the Globe, when Ned Alleyn did not scruple to affyrme pleasauntly to thy friende Will, that he had stolen hys speeche about the excellencie of acting in *Hamlet* hys tragedye, from conversaytions manifold, whych had passed between them, and opinions gyven by Alleyn touchyng that subjecte. Shakespeare did not take this talk in good sorte; but Jonson did put an end to the stryfe wyth wittielie saying, thys affaire needeth no contentione; you stole it from Ned no doubte: do not marvel: haue you not seene hym acte tymes out of number?"—This is pretended to be printed from the original MS. dated 1600; which agrees well enough with Wood's *Claruit*: but unluckily Peele was dead at least two years before. "As Anacreon died by the *pot*," says Meres, "so George Peele by the *pox*," *Wit's Treasury*, 1598, p. 286' (Farmer).

Constable in Midsummer Night's Dream. Apparently a mistake for *Much Ado*.

two children. Susannah, Judith, and Hamnet were all born at Stratford. Judith and Hamnet were twins. Cf. p. 21 and note.

195. '*cheers up himself with ends of verse*.' Butler, *Hudibras*, I. iii. 1011.

'Copley's *Wits, Fits, and Fancies* was published in 1595 and twice in 1614. No other editions are known. As the saying of Hannibal Gonzago appears in the editions of 1614 but not in that of 1595, Shakespeare could not have taken it from Copley by 1600, when 2 *Henry IV* was printed. And while it appears in Sir Richard Hawkins's *Voyage into the South Sea. Anno Domini 1593* (p. 13), Hawkins wrote his account late in life and died while it was passing through the press in 1622. We still do not know whether Shakespeare took the saying from a printed source or from hearsay.' (F. P. W.)

Master Page, sit. 2 Henry IV, v. iii. 30.

Heywood. In the 'To the Reader' prefixed to his *Sixt Hundred of Epigrammes* (Spenser Society reprint, 1867, p. 198).

Dekker. Vol. iii, p. 281 (ed. 1873).

Water-poet. See the Spenser Society reprint of the folio of 1630, p. 545.

195. *Rivo, says the Drunkard.* 1 *Henry IV*, II. iv. 124.

196. *What you will.* Act ii, Sc. I (vol. i, p. 224, ed. 1856).

Love's Labour Lost, IV. i. 100. This paragraph was added in the second edition.

Taming of the Shrew, II. i. 73.

Heath. Revisal of Shakespear's Text, p. 159. This quotation was added in the second edition.

Heywood. Epigrammes upon prouerbes, 194 (Spenser Society reprint, p. 158).

197. *Howell*, James (1594–1666), Historiographer, author of the *Epistolae Ho-Elianae*. *Proverbs or old sayed Sawes and Adages in English or the Saxon Tongue* was published together with his *Lexicon Tetraglotton* (1659–60). The allusion to Howell was added in the second edition.

Philpot. John Philipot (1589–1645). See Camden's *Remains concerning Britain*, 1674, 'Much amended, with many rare Antiquities never before Imprinted, by the industry and care of John Philipot, Somerset Herald, and W. D. Gent': 1870 reprint, p. 319.

Grey. Notes on Shakespeare, ii, p. 249.

Romeo. 'It is remarked that "Paris, tho' in one place called *Earl*, is most commonly stiled the *Countie* in this play. Shakespeare seems to have preferred, for some reason or other, the Italian *Conte* to our *Count*:—perhaps he took it from the old English novel, from which he is said to have taken his plot."—He certainly did so: Paris is there first stiled *a young Earle*, and afterward *Counte*, *Countee*, and *County*, according to the unsettled orthography of the time. The word, however, is frequently met with in other writers, particularly in Fairfax', &c. (Farmer).

Painter, vol. ii, 1567, 25th novel. Arthur Broke's verse rendering, founded on Boaistuau's (or Boisteau's) French version of Bandello, appeared in 1562; and it was to Broke, rather than to Painter, that Shakespeare was indebted. See P. A. Daniel's *Originals and Analogues*, Part I (New Shakspere Society, 1875). Also *Narrative and Dramatic Sources of Shakespeare*, ed. G. Bullough, i (1957), p. 274.

Taming of the Shrew. Induction, i. 5.

Hieronymo, iii. 14, 117, 118 (ed. Boas, p. 78); cf. p. 181.

Whalley. Enquiry, p. 48.

Philips—Edward Phillips (1630–96), Milton's nephew. See his *Theatrum Poetarum, or a Compleat Collection of the Poets*, 1675, ii, p. 195. Cf. also Winstanley's *English Poets*, 1687, p. 218.

198. *Heywood*, in the *Apology for Actors*, 1612, alluded to above; see Hawkins's *Origin of the English Drama*, 1773, ii, p. 3, and Boas's *Works of Kyd*, 1901, pp. xiii, civ, and 411. Boas gives Hawkins the credit of discovering the authorship of *The Spanish Tragedy* 'sometime before 1773', but the credit is Farmer's. Hawkins was undoubtedly indebted to Farmer's *Essay*.

198. *Henry the fifth*, Act iii, Sc. 4.

not . . . published by the author. 'Every writer on Shakespeare hath expressed his astonishment that his author was not solicitous to secure his fame by a correct edition of his performances. This matter is not understood. When a poet was connected with a particular playhouse, he constantly sold his works to the *Company*, and it was their interest to keep them from a number of rivals. A favourite piece, as Heywood informs us, only got into print when it was copied *by the ear*, "for a double sale would bring on a suspicion of honestie." Shakespeare therefore himself published nothing in the drama: when he left the stage, his copies remained with his fellow-managers, Heminge and Condell; who at their own retirement, about seven years after the death of the author, gave the world the edition now known by the name of the *first Folio*, and call the previous publications "stolne and surreptitious, maimed and deformed by the frauds and stealths of injurious impostors." But *this* was printed from the playhouse copies; which in a series of years had been frequently altered, thro' convenience, caprice, or ignorance. We have a sufficient instance of the liberties taken by the actors, in an old pamphlet by Nash, called *Lenten Stuffe, with the Prayse of the red Herring*, 4to, 1599, where he assures us that in a play of his, called the *Isle of Dogs*, "*foure acts*, without his consent, or the least guesse of his drift or scope, were supplied by the players."—This, however, was not his first quarrel with them. In the Epistle prefixed to Greene's *Arcadia*, which I have quoted before, Tom hath a lash at some "vaine glorious tragedians," and very plainly at Shakespeare in particular; which will serve for an answer to an observation of Mr. Pope, that had almost been forgotten: "It was thought a praise to Shakespeare that he scarce ever blotted a line. I believe the common opinion of his want of learning proceeded from no better ground. This, too, might be thought a praise by some." But hear Nash, who was far from *praising*: "I leaue all these to the mercy of their *mother-tongue*, that feed on nought but the crums that fall from the *translator's* trencher,—that could scarcely *Latinize* their neck verse if they should haue neede; yet *English Seneca*, read by candle-light, yeelds many good sentences—hee will affoord you whole *Hamlets*, I should say, *handfuls* of tragicall speeches." I cannot determine exactly when this *Epistle* was first published; but, I fancy, it will carry the original *Hamlet* somewhat further back than we have hitherto done; and it may be observed that the oldest copy now extant is said to be "enlarged to almost as much againe as it was." Gabriel Harvey printed at the end of the year 1592 *Foure Letters and certaine Sonnetts, especially touching Robert Greene*: in one of which his *Arcadia* is mentioned. Now Nash's Epistle must have been previous to these, as Gabriel is quoted in it with applause; and the *Foure Letters* were the beginning of a quarrel. Nash replied in *Strange Newes of the intercepting certaine Letters, and a Convoy of Verses, as they were going* privilie *to victuall the Low Countries*, 1593. Harvey rejoined the same year in *Pierce's Supererogation, or a new Praise of the old Asse*; and Nash again, in *Have with you to Saffron Walden, or Gabriel Harvey's Hunt is up; containing a full Answer to the eldest Sonne of the halter-maker*, 1596.—Dr. Lodge calls Nash our *true English Aretine*: and John Taylor, in his *Kicksey Winsey, or a Lerry Come-twang*, even makes an oath "by sweet satyricke Nash his urne." —He died before 1606, as appears from an old comedy called *The Return from Parnassus*' (Farmer). See Gregory Smith, *Elizabethan Critical Essays*, especially i. 424–5; R. B. McKerrow, *Nashe*, v. 34.

198. *Hawkins.* Johnson's Shakespeare, vol. viii, Appendix, note on iv, p. 454. The quotation from Johnson, and the references to Eliot and Du Bartas, were added in the second edition.

Est-il impossible. Henry V, IV. iv. 17.

French Alphabeth of De la Mothe. 'Lond., 1592, 8vo' (Farmer).

Orthoepia of John Eliot. 'Lond., 1593, 4to. Eliot is almost the only *witty* grammarian that I have had the fortune to meet with. In his Epistle prefatory to the *Gentle Doctors of Gaule*, he cries out for persecution, very like Jack in that most poignant of Satires, the *Tale of a Tub*, "I pray you be readie quicklie to cauill at my booke, I beseech you heartily calumniate my doings with speede, I request you humbly controll my method as soone as you may, I earnestly entreat you hisse at my inventions"', &c. (Farmer).

Sejanus. See Jonson's 'To the Readers': 'Lastly, I would inform you that this book, in all numbers, is not the same with that which was acted on the public stage; wherein a second pen had good share: in place of which, I have rather chosen to put weaker, and, no doubt, less pleasing, of mine own, than to defraud so happy a genius of his right by my loathed usurpation'.

Some have thought that the 'second pen' was Chapman's rather than Shakespeare's, but in the absence of the acting version of *Sejanus* conjecture is fruitless. See E. K. Chambers, *Shakespeare*, ii, p. 206.

199. *But what if . . . Capell's Prolusions*, added in the second edition.

Pierce Penilesse, ed. R. B. McKerrow, i, pp. 212–13. Three editions were published in 1592, the Epistle to the Printer being added to the second.

Tarlton, Richard (d. 1588), *Jests, drawn into three parts*, ed. Halliwell (Shakespeare Society, 1844), pp. 24, 25: *Old English Jest Books*, ed. W. C. Hazlitt (1864), pp. 218, 219.

Capell. Cf. pp. 185 and 186. He describes *Edward III* on the title-page of his *Prolusions or Select Pieces of Antient Poetry*, 1760, as 'thought to be writ by Shakespeare'.

the Giant of Rabelais. 'The Gargantua referred to by Laneham, Shakespeare (*As You Like It*, III. ii. 238, and *King Lear*, III. vi. 7, 8) and Taylor was probably the giant of the Folk tale, not of Rabelais. We hear of a pamphlet in English celebrating his exploits as early as 1571 and as late as 1642, yet not a single copy has survived. The first English translation of Rabelais, Urquhart's of Book I, did not appear till 1653.' (F. P. W.)

Laneham, Robert, who appears in Scott's *Kenilworth*. The letter has been reprinted by the Ballad Society (1871), and the New Shakspere Society (1890). Referring to the spelling of the name, Farmer says in a note, 'It is indeed of no importance, but I suspect the former to be right, as I find it corrupted afterward to *Lanam* and *Lanum*'.

Meres. 'This author by a pleasant mistake in some sensible *Conjectures on Shakespeare*, lately printed at Oxford, is quoted by the name of *Maister*. Perhaps the title-page was imperfect; it runs thus: "Palladis Tamia. Wits Treasury. Being the second part of Wits Commonwealth, By *Francis Meres Maister* of Artes of both Universities." I am glad out of gratitude to this man, who hath been of frequent service to me, that I am enabled to perfect Wood's account of him; from the assistance of our *Master's* very accurate list of graduates (which it would do honour to the university to print at the publick expense) and the kind information of a friend from the register of his parish:—He was originally of Pembroke-Hall, B.A. in 1587, and M.A. 1591. About 1602 he became rector of Wing in Rutland; and died there, 1646, in the 81st year of his age' (Farmer). See Gregory Smith's *Elizabethan Critical Essays* or *Shakespeare Allusion Book*, ed. E. K. Chambers, i. 46-49. The reference at the beginning of Farmer's note is to Tyrwhitt's *Observations and Conjectures upon some passages of Shakespeare*, 1766, p. 16.

John Taylor. See note, p. 152. 'I have quoted many pieces of John Taylor, but it was impossible to give their original dates. He may be traced as an author for more than half a century. His works were collected in folio, 1630, but many were printed afterward', &c. (Farmer). The reference to Gargantua will be found on p. 160 of the Spenser Society Reprint of the Folio. Taylor refers to him also in his *Dogge of Warre*, id., p. 364.

200. *Richard the third.* 'Some inquiry hath been made for the first performers of the capital characters in Shakespeare. We learn that Burbage, the *alter Roscius* of Camden, was the original Richard, from a passage in the poems of Bishop Corbet; who introduces his host at Bosworth describing the battle:

> But when he would have said King Richard died,
> And call'd *a horse, a horse*, he *Burbage* cried.

'The play on this subject mentioned by Sir John Harrington in his *Apologie for Poetrie*, 1591, and sometimes mistaken for Shakespeare's, was a Latin one, written by Dr. Legge, and acted at St. John's in our University, some years before 1588, the date of the copy in the Museum. This appears from a better MS. in our library at Emmanuel, with the names of the original performers.

'It is evident from a passage in Camden's *Annals* that there was an old play likewise on the subject of *Richard the Second*; but I know not in what language. Sir Gelley Merrick, who was concerned in the hare-brained business of the Earl of Essex, and was hanged for it with the ingenious Cuffe in 1601, is accused, amongst other things, "quod *exoletam* Tragœdiam de tragica abdicatione Regis Ricardi Secundi in publico theatro coram conjuratis data pecunia agi curasset" ' (Farmer).

Remember whom ye are, &c. *Richard III*, v. iii. 315.

201. *Holingshed.* 'I cannot take my leave of Holingshed without clearing up a difficulty which hath puzzled his biographers. Nicholson and other writers have *supposed* him a *clergyman.* Tanner goes further and tells us that he was educated at Cambridge and actually took the degree of M.A. in 1544.—Yet it appears by his will, printed by Hearne, that at the end of life he was only a *steward*, or a *servant* in some capacity or other, to Thomas Burdett, Esq. of Bromcote, in Warwickshire.—These things Dr. Campbell could not reconcile. The truth is we have no claim to the education of the *Chronicler*: the M.A. in 1544 was not *Raphael*, but one *Ottiwell Holingshed*, who was afterward named by the founder one of the first Fellows of Trinity College' (Farmer).

Hig, hag, hog. Merry Wives, IV. i. 44.

writers of the time. 'Ascham, in the Epistle prefixed to his *Toxophilus*, 1571, observes of them that "Manye Englishe writers, usinge straunge wordes, as *Lattine, Frenche,* and *Italian*, do make all thinges darke and harde" ' &c. (Farmer). *Toxophilus* was first printed in 1545.

all such reading as was never read. See Introduction, p. xliii; *Dunciad*, (Twickenham ed.), i. 166; iv. 250.

Natale solum. 'This alludes to an intended publication of the *Antiquities of the Town of Leicester*. The work was just begun at the press, when the writer was called to the principal tuition of a large college, and was obliged to decline the undertaking. The plates, however, and some of the materials have been long ago put into the hands of a gentleman who is every way qualified to make a proper use of them' (Farmer, omitted in 2nd ed.). This gentleman was John Nichols, the printer, whose *History and Antiquities of the County of Leicester* appeared from 1795 to 1815.

201. *primrose path. Hamlet,* I. iii. 50; cf. *Macbeth,* II. iii. 21.

202. *Age cannot wither. Antony and Cleopatra,* II. ii. 240.

MAURICE MORGANN

208. *Candide,* chapters 9 and 15.

211. *general criticism is uninstructive.* Cf. Joseph Warton, *Adventurer,* No. 116: 'General criticism is on all subjects useless and unentertaining; but it is more than commonly absurd with respect to Shakespeare, who must be accompanied step by step, and scene by scene, in his gradual developments of characters and passions', &c.

217. proof of *impression.* 2nd ed. altered from 'proof Impression'.

225. *Oldcastle.* See Rowe, p. 5, and note.

231. *Barbarian.* See notes on Voltaire, pp. 109, &c.

231, note. *Be thus when thou art dead. Othello,* V. ii. 18.

232. *Love's Labour lost.* In his edition of *L.L.L.* (1768), Capell omitted fifteen lines from Biron's speech in Act iv, Sc. 3 (iv. 1 in his own edition, p. 54). He did not record the omission.

233. *Nothing perishable about him, except that very learning,* &c. Cf. Edward Young, *Conjectures on Original Composition,* 1759, p. 81, and Hurd, Notes on Horace's *Art of Poetry,* line 286 (1757, i, pp. 213–14): 'Our Shakespear was, I think, the first that broke through this bondage of classical superstition. And he owed this felicity, as he did some others, to his want of what is called the advantage of a learned education.'

234. *Macbeth,* I. v. 18, 49; V. v. 13; V. iii. 23.

235. *practicer of arts inhibited. Othello,* I. ii. 78.

237, note. *Shakespeare's magic.* Dryden, Prologue to the *Tempest,* 1667, lines 19, 20.

240. *miching malicho. Hamlet,* III. ii. 147.

242. *but a choleric word. Measure for Measure,* II. ii. 130.

244. *Cadogan,* William (1711–97), a fashionable London doctor, who published in 1771 a *Dissertation on the Gout and on all Chronic Diseases,* in which he held that gout is 'a disease of our own acquiring' and 'the necessary effect of intemperance'.

249, note. *For if the Jew. Merchant of Venice,* IV. i. 280.

251. *Souls made of fire and children of the sun.* Edward Young, *The Revenge,* V. 2.

252. *just where youth ends.* Cf. *Paradise Lost*, xi. 245, 246.

Old, cold, and of intolerable entrails. Merry Wives, v. v. 161.

Mrs. Montague. Two chapters in Mrs. Elizabeth Montagu's *Essay on the Writings and Genius of Shakespear* (1769) deal with the first and second parts of *Henry IV*. She speaks of 'the cowardly and braggart temper of Falstaffe' (p. 103), and says that 'gluttony, corpulency, and cowardice are the peculiarities of Falstaffe's composition' (p. 107).

golden fool. Timon of Athens, iv. iii. 18.

258. *Players . . . the very worst judges of Shakespeare.* Cf. Pope, Preface, p. 48.

266, line 11. *attacked.* The original has *attached*. The reprints of 1820 and 1825 read *attached to*.

282. *He was shaked of a burning quotidian tertian. Henry V*, ii. i. 124, 91; ii. iii. 10.

INDEX